LIFE, LETTERS, AND WRITINGS

OF

CHARLES LAMB

VOL. III.

ADDENDUM

P. 436, aftes the note on "*Birth and Feeling*," add :—

"*Age or length of service.*" Here was a note :—

Mrs. Inchbald seems to have fallen into the common mistake of the character in some otherwise sensible observations on this comedy. "It might be asked," she says, "whether this credulous steward was much deceived in imputing a degraded taste, in the sentiments of love, to his fair lady Olivia, as she actually did fall in love with a domestic, and one who, from his extreme youth, was perhaps a greater reproach to her discretion than had she cast a tender regard upon her old and faithful servant." But where does she gather the fact of his age? Neither Maria nor Fabian ever cast reproach upon him.

Dawsons.Ph.Sc.

From a drawing in the British Museum by G.F.Joseph. A.R.A.
1819.

THE LIFE, LETTERS, AND WRITINGS OF CHARLES LAMB

Edited by
PERCY FITZGERALD

With Portraits

VOLUME III

BOOKS FOR LIBRARIES PRESS
FREEPORT, NEW YORK

First Published 1895
Reprinted 1971

INTERNATIONAL STANDARD BOOK NUMBER:
0-8369-5654-0

LIBRARY OF CONGRESS CATALOG CARD NUMBER:
77-148887

PRINTED IN THE UNITED STATES OF AMERICA

CONTENTS OF VOL. III.

CONTENTS OF VOL. III

LIST OF PORTRAITS

XIV.

MISCELLANEOUS CORRESPONDENCE.

LETTER CCXCVI. [About 1822.]

TO CHARLES LLOYD.

Your lines are not to be understood reading on
one leg. They are sinuous, and to be won with
wrestling. I do assure you in sincerity that nothing you have done has given me greater satisfaction. Your obscurity, where you are dark, which
is seldom, is that of too much meaning, not the
painful obscurity which no toil of the reader can
dissipate; not the dead vacuum and floundering
place in which imagination finds no footing: it is
not the dimness of positive darkness, but of distance;
and he that reads and not discerns must get a better
pair of spectacles. I admire every piece in the
collection. I cannot say the first is best: when I do
so, the last read rises up in judgment. To your
Mother, to your Sister, to Mary dead, they are all
weighty with thought and tender with sentiment.
Your poetry is like no other. Those cursed dryads
and pagan trumperies of modern verse have put me
out of conceit of the very name of poetry. Your
verses are as good and as wholesome as prose, and
I have made a sad blunder if I do not leave you
with an impression that your present is rarely
valued. CHARLES LAMB.

LETTER CCXCVII.]   Dec. 20, 1830.

TO GEORGE DYER.

Dear Dyer,—I should have written before to thank you for your kind letter, written with your own hand. It glads us to see your writing. It will give you pleasure to hear that after so much illness we are in tolerable health and spirits once more. Poor Enfield, that has been so peaceable hitherto, has caught the inflammatory fever; the tokens are upon her; and a great fire was blazing last night in the barns and haystacks of a farmer, about half a mile from us. Where will these things end? There is no doubt of its being the work of some ill-disposed rustic; but how is he to be discovered? They go to work in the dark with strange chemical preparations, unknown to our forefathers. There is not even a dark lantern, to have a chance of detecting these Gux Fauxes. We are past the iron age, and are got into the fiery age, undreamed of by Ovid. You are lucky in Clifford's Inn, where I think you have few ricks or stacks worth the burning. Pray, keep as little corn by you as you can for fear of the worst. It was never good times in England since the poor began to speculate upon their condition. Formerly they jogged on with as little reflection as horses. The whistling ploughman went cheek by jowl with his brother that neighed. Now the biped carries a box of phosphorus in his leather breeches, and in the dead of night the half-illuminated beast steals his magic potion into a cleft in a barn, and half the country is grinning with new fires. Farmer Gray-

stock said something to the touchy rustic, that
he did not relish, and he writes his distaste in
flames. What a power to intoxicate his crude
brains, just muddlingly awake to perceive that something is wrong in the social system,—what a hellish
faculty above gunpowder! Now the rich and poor
are fairly pitted. We shall see who can hang or
burn fastest. It is not always revenge that stimulates
these kindlings. There is a love of exerting mischief. Think of a disrespected clod that was trod
into earth, that was nothing, on a sudden by
damned arts refined into an exterminating angel,
devouring the fruits of the earth and their growers
in a mass of fire ; what a new existence ! What a
temptation above Lucifer's ! Would clod be any
thing but a clod if he could resist it ? Why, here
was a spectacle last night for a whole country, a
bonfire visible to London, alarming her guilty towers,
and shaking the Monument with an ague fit, all
done by a little vial of phosphor in a clown's fob.
How he must grin, and shake his empty noddle in
clouds ! The Vulcanian epicure ! Alas ! can we
ring the bells backward ? Can we unlearn the arts
that pretend to civilize, and then burn the world ?
There is a march of science ; but who shall beat the
drums for its retreat ? Who shall persuade the boor
that phosphor will not ignite ? Seven goodly stacks
of hay, with corn-barns proportionable, lie smoking
ashes and chaff, which man and beast would sputter
out and reject like those apples of asphaltes and
bitumen. The food for the inhabitants of earth will
quickly disappear. Hot rolls may say, " Fuimus
panes, fuit quartern-loaf, et ingens gloria apple-
pasty-orum." That the good old munching system

may last thy time and mine, good un-incendiary
George, is the devout prayer of thine,

To the last crust,   C. LAMB.

LETTER CCXCVIII.]   Feb. 22nd, 1831.

TO THE SAME.

Dear Dyer,—Mr. Rogers, and Mr. Rogers's friends,
are perfectly assured that you never intended any
harm by an innocent couplet, and that in the revivifi-
cation of it by blundering Barker you had no hand
whatever. To imagine that at this time of day
Rogers broods over a fantastic expression of more
than thirty years' standing, would be to suppose him
indulging his " Pleasures of Memory" with a vengeance. You never penned a line which for its own
sake you need, dying, wish to blot. You mistake
your heart if you think you *can* write a lampoon.
Your whips are rods of roses. Your spleen has ever
had for its object vices, not the vicious ; abstract
offences, not the concrete sinner. But you are sensi-
tive, and wince as much at the consciousness of
having committed a compliment, as another man
would at the perpetration of an affront. But do not
lug me into the same soreness of conscience with
yourself. I maintain, and will to the last hour, that
I never writ of you but *con amore;* that if any
allusion was made to your near-sightedness, it was
not for the purpose of mocking an infirmity, but of
connecting it with scholar-like habits : for is it not
erudite and scholarly to be somewhat near of sight
before age naturally brings on the malady? You
could not then plead the *obrepens senectus.* Did I
not moreover make it an apology for a certain *absence,*

which some of our friends may have experienced,
when you have not on a sudden made recognition of
them in a casual street-meeting? And did I not
strengthen your excuse for this slowness of recognition, by further accounting morally for the present
engagement of your mind in worthy objects? Did I
not, in your person, make the handsomest apology
for absent-of-mind people that was ever made? If
these things be not so, I never knew what I wrote, or
meant by my writing, and have been penning libels
all my life without being aware of it. Does it follow
that I should have exprest myself exactly in the
same way of those dear old eyes of yours *now*, now
that Father Time has conspired with a hard task-
master to put a last extinguisher upon them? I
should as soon have insulted the Answerer of
Salmasius when he awoke up from his ended task
and saw no more with mortal vision. But you are
many films removed yet from Milton's calamity. You
write perfectly intelligibly. Marry, the letters are not
all of the same size or tallness ; but that only shows
your proficiency in the *hands*, text, german-hand,
court-hand, sometimes law-hand, and affords variety.
You pen better than you did a twelvemonth ago ; and
if you continue to improve, you bid fair to win the
golden pen which is the prize at your young gentlemen's academy. But you must be aware of Valpy,
and his printing-house, that hazy cave of Trophonius,
out of which it was a mercy that you escaped with a
glimmer. Beware of MSS. and Variæ Lectiones.
Settle the text for once in your mind, and stick to it.
You have some years' good sight in you yet, if you
do not tamper with it. It is not for you (for *us* I
should say) to go poring into Greek contractions, and

star-gazing upon slim Hebrew points. We have yet
the sight

> Of sun, and moon, and star, throughout the year,
> And man and woman.

You have vision enough to discern Mrs.
Dyer from the other comely gentlewoman who lives up at staircase No. 5 ; or, if you should make a blunder in the
twilight, Mrs. Dyer has too much good sense to be
jealous for a mere effect of imperfect optics. But
don't try to write the Lord's Prayer, Creed, and Ten
Commandments in the compass of a half-penny ;
nor run after a midge, or a mote, to catch it ; and
leave off hunting for needles in bundles of hay, for
all these things strain the eyes. The snow is six feet
deep in some parts here. I must put on jack-boots
to get at the Post-Office with this. It is not good
for weak eyes to pore upon snow too much. It lies
in drifts. I wonder what its drift is ; only that it
makes good pancakes, remind Mrs. Dyer. It turns a
pretty green world into a white one. It glares too
much for an innocent colour methinks. I wonder
why you think I dislike gilt edges. They set off a
letter marvellously. Yours, for instance, looks for all
the world like a tablet of curious *hieroglyphics* in a
gold frame. But don't go and lay this to your eyes.
You always wrote hieroglyphically, yet not to come
up to the mystical notations and conjuring characters
of Dr. Parr. You never wrote what I call a schoolmaster's hand, like Mrs. Clarke ; nor a woman's hand,
like Southey ; nor a missal hand, like Porson ; nor
an all-of-the-wrong-side sloping hand, like Miss
Hayes ; nor a dogmatic, Mede-and-Persian, peremptory hand, like Rickman ; but you ever wrote what I
call a Grecian's hand ; what the Grecians write (or

used) at Christ's Hospital; such as Whalley would have admired, and Boyer have applauded, but Smith or Atwood (writing-masters) would have horsed you for. Your boy-of-genius hand and your mercantile hand are various. By your flourishes, I should think you never learned to make eagles or corkscrews, or flourish the governors' names in the writing-school; and by the tenour and cut of your letters, I suspect you were never in it at all. By the length of this scrawl you will think I have a design upon your optics ; but I have writ as large as I could, out of respect to them ; too large, indeed, for beauty. Mine is a sort deputy Grecian's hand ; a little better, and more of a worldly hand, than a Grecian's, but still remote from the mercantile. I don't know how it is, but I keep my rank in fancy still since school-days. I can never forget I was a deputy Grecian ! And writing to you, or to Coleridge, besides affection, I feel a reverential deference as to Grecians still. I keep my soaring way above the Great Erasmians,[1] yet far beneath the other. Alas ! what am I now ? What is a Leadenhall clerk, or India pensioner, to a deputy Grecian ? How art thou fallen, O Lucifer ! Just room for our loves to Mrs. D., &c.   C. LAMB.

---

[1] The third form at Christ's Hospital, is called the *Great Erasmus,* (or, for short, the *Great* Eras,) after Erasmus Smith. The fourth form is called the *Little Erasmus.*—H.

LETTER CCXCIX.]   Dec. 22, 1834.

TO MRS. DYER.

Dear Mrs. Dyer,—I am very uneasy about a *Book*, which I either have lost or left at your house on Thursday. It was the book I went out to fetch from Miss Buffam's while the tripe was frying. It is called "Phillip's Theatrum Poetarum," but it is an English book. I think I left it in the parlour. It is Mr. Carey's book, and I would not lose it for the world. Pray, if you find it, book it at the Swan, Snow Hill, by an Edmonton stage immediately, directed to Mr. Lamb, Church Street, Edmonton, or write to say you cannot find it. I am quite anxious about it. If it is lost, I shall never like tripe again.

    With kindest love to Mr. Dyer and all,

                          Yours truly,

                                C. LAMB.

LETTER CCC.]

TO MR. RICKMAN.

Dear Rickman,—The enclosed letter explains itself. It will save me the danger of a corporal interview with the man-eater, who, if very sharp set, may take a fancy to me, if you will give me a short note, declaratory of probabilities. These from him who hopes to see you once or twice more before he goes hence, to be no more seen : for there is no tipple nor tobacco in the grave, whereunto he hasteneth.

C. LAMB.

16, *Mitre Court Buildings,*
    Inner Temple.

How clearly the Goul writes, and like a gentleman !
April 10*th,* 1802.

LETTER CCCI.]

TO THE SAME.

Dear Rickman,—I enclose you a wonder, a letter from the shades. A dead body wants to return, and be inrolled *inter vivos.* 'Tis a gentle ghost, and in this Galvanic age it may have a chance.

Mary and I are setting out for the Isle of Wight. We make but a short stay, and shall pass the time betwixt that place and Portsmouth, where Fenwick is. I sadly wanted to explore the Peak this Summer; but Mary is against steering without card or compass, and we should be at large in Darbyshire.

We shall be at home this night and to-morrow, if you can come and take a farewell pipe.

I regularly transmitted your Notices to the *Morning Post,* but they have not been duly honoured. The fault lay not in me.

Yours truly,

C. LAMB.

Saturday Morning,
    July 16, 1803.

LETTER CCCII.]   Jan. 25, 1806.

TO THE SAME.

Dear Rickman,—You do not happen to have any place at your disposal which would suit a decayed Literatus ?   I do not much expect that you have, or that you will go much out of the way to serve the object, when you hear it is Fell.   But the case is, by a *mistaking* of his *turn*, as they call it, he is reduced, I am afraid, to extremities, and would be extremely glad of a place in an office.   Now it does sometimes happen, that just as a man wants a place, a place wants him ; and though this is a lottery to which none but G. Burnett would choose to trust his all, there is no harm just to call in at Despair's office for a friend, and see if *his* number is come up, (Burnett's further case I enclose by way of episode.)   Now, if you should happen, or any body you know, to want a *hand*, here is a young man of solid but not brilliant genius, who would turn his hand to the making out of dockets, penning a manifesto, or scoring a tally, not the worse (I hope) for knowing Latin and Greek, and having in youth conversed with the philosophers. But from these follies I believe he is thoroughly awakened, and would bind himself by a terrible oath never to imagine himself an extraordinary genius again.

                Yours, &c.,   C. LAMB.

LETTER CCCIII.]   March, 1806.

TO THE SAME.

Dear Rickman,—I send you some papers about a salt-water soap, for which the inventor is desirous of getting a parliamentary reward, like Dr. Jenner. Whether such a project be feasible, I mainly doubt, taking for granted the equal utility. I should suppose the usual way of paying such projectors is by patent and contracts. The patent, you see, he has got. A contract he is about with the Navy Board. Meantime, the projector is hungry. Will you answer me two questions, and return them with the papers as soon as you can? Imprimis, is there any chance of success in application to Parliament for a reward? Did you ever hear of the invention? You see its benefits and saving to the nation (always the first motive with a true projector) are feelingly set forth: the last paragraph but one of the estimate, in enumerating the shifts poor seamen are put to, even approaches to the pathetic. But, agreeing to all he says, is there the remotest chance of Parliament giving the projector any thing? And *when* should application be made, now, or after a report (if he can get it) from the Navy Board? Secondly, let the infeasibility be as great as you will, you will oblige me by telling me the way of introducing such an application in Parliament, without buying over a majority of members, which is totally out of projector's power. I vouch nothing for the soap myself; for I always wash in *fresh water*, and find it answer tolerably well for all purposes of cleanliness; nor do I know the projector; but a relation of mine has put me on writing to you, for whose parliamentary knowledge he has great veneration.

P.S. The Capt. and Mrs. Burney and Phillips take their chance at cribbage here on Wednesday. Will you and Mrs. R. join the party? Mary desires

her compliments to Mrs. R., and joins in the invita
tion.

Yours truly,

C. LAMB.

LETTER CCCIV.]   [1829.]

TO MR. SERJEANT TALFOURD.

Dear Talfourd,—You could not have told me of a more friendly thing than you have been doing. I am proud of my namesake. I shall take care never to do any dirty action, pick pockets, or anyhow get myself hanged, for fear of reflecting ignominy upon your young Chrisom. I have now a motive to be good. I shall not *omnis moriar;*—my name borne down the black gulf of oblivion.

I shall survive in eleven letters, five more than Cæsar. Possibly I shall come to be knighted, or more ! Sir C. L. Talfourd, Bart. !

Yet hath it an authorish twang with it, which will wear out my name for poetry. Give him a smile from me till I see him. If you do not drop down before, some day in the *week after next* I will come and take one night's lodging with you, if convenient, before you go hence. You shall name it. We are in town to-morrow *speciali gratiâ*, but by no arrangement can get up near you.

Believe us both, with greatest regards, yours and Mrs. Talfourd's.

CHARLES LAMB-PHILO-TALFOURD.

I come as near it as I can.

LETTER CCCV.]   Feb. 1833.

TO THE SAME.

My dear T.,—Now cannot I call him *Serjeant;*
what is there in a coif? Those canvas sleeves pro-
tective from ink,[1] when he was a law-chit—a *Chitty-*
ling, (let the leathern apron be apocryphal,) do more
'specially plead to the Jury Court, of old memory.
The costume (will he agnize it?) was as of a desk-
fellow, or Socius Plutei.   Methought I spied a
brother!

That familiarity is extinct for ever.   Curse me if I
can call him Mr. Serjeant—except, mark me, in *company*.   Honour where honour is due; but should he
ever visit us, (do you think he ever will, Mary?)
what a distinction should I keep up between him and
our less fortunate friend, H. C. R.!   Decent respect
shall always be the Crabb's—but, somehow, short of
reverence.

Well, of my old friends, I have lived to see two
knighted, one made a judge, another in a fair way to
it.   Why am I restive? why stands my sun upon
Gibeon?

Variously, my dear Mrs. Talfourd, [I can be more
familiar with her!]   Mrs. *Serjeant* Talfourd,—my
sister prompts me—(these ladies stand upon ceremonies)—has the congratulable news affected the
members of our small community.   Mary comprehended it at once, and entered into it heartily.   Mrs.
W—— was, as usual, perverse; wouldn't, or couldn't,
understand it.   A Serjeant?   She thought Mr. T.
was in the law.   Didn't know that he ever 'listed.

---

[1] Mr. Lamb always insisted that the costume referred to was worn
when he first gladdened his young friend by a call at Mr. Chitty's
Chambers.   I am afraid it is all apocryphal.—T.

Emma alone truly sympathized. *She* had a silk gown come home that very day, and has precedence before her learned sisters accordingly.

We are going to drink the health of Mr. and Mrs. Serjeant, with all the young serjeantry ; and that is all that I can see that I shall get by the promotion.

Valete, et mementote amici quondam vestri humillimi.   C. L.

LETTER CCCVI.]   Aug. 31st, 1817.

TO MR. BARRON FIELD.

My dear Barron,—The bearer of this letter so far across the seas is Mr. Lawrey, who comes out to you as a missionary, and whom I have been strongly importuned to recommend to you as a most worthy creature by Mr. Fenwick, a very old, honest friend of mine ; of whom, if my memory does not deceive me, you have had some knowledge heretofore as editor of the *Statesman ;* a man of talent, and patriotic. If you can show him any facilities in his arduous undertaking, you will oblige us much. Well, and how does the land of thieves use you? and how do you pass your time, in your extra-judicial intervals ? Going about the streets with a lantern, like Diogenes, looking for an honest man ? You may look long enough, I fancy. Do give me some notion of the manners of the inhabitants where you are. They

don't thieve all day long do they?   No human property could stand such continuous battery.   And
what do they do when they an't stealing?

Have you got a theatre?   What pieces are performed?   Shakspeare's, I suppose ; not so much for
the poetry, as for his having once been in danger of
leaving his country on account of certain " small
deer."

Have you poets among you?   Damn'd plagiarists,
I fancy, if you have any.   I would not trust an idea,
or a pocket-handkerchief of mine, among 'em.   You
are almost competent to answer Lord Bacon's
problem, whether a nation of atheists can subsist
together.   You are practically in one :

> "So thievish 'tis, that the eighth commandment itself
> Scarce seemeth there to be."

Our old honest world goes on with little perceptible
variation.   Of course you have heard of poor
Mitchell's death, and that G. Dyer is one of Lord
Stanhope's residuaries.   I am afraid he has not
touched much of the residue yet.   He is positively
as lean as Cassius.   Barnes is going to Demerara,
or Essequibo, I am not quite certain which.   Alsager
is turned actor.   He came out in genteel comedy at
Cheltenham this season, and has hopes of a London
engagement.

For my own history, I am just in the same spot,
doing the same thing, (videlicet, little or nothing,) as
when you left me ; only I have positive hopes that I
shall be able to conquer that inveterate habit of
smoking which you may remember I indulged in.   I
think of making a beginning this evening, *viz.*
Sunday, 31st Aug., 1817, not Wednesday, 2nd Feb.,
1818, as it will be perhaps when you read this for the

first time. There is the difficulty of writing from one end of the globe (hemispheres I call 'em) to another! Why, half the truths I have sent you in this letter will become lies before they reach you, and some of the lies (which I have mixed for variety's sake, and to exercise your judgment in the finding of them out) may be turned into sad realities before you shall be called upon to detect them. Such are the defects of going by different chronologies. Your "now" is not my "now"; and again, your "then" is not my "then"; but my "now" may be your "then," and vice versa. Whose head is competent to these things?

How does Mrs. Field get on in her geography? Does she know where she is by this time? I am not sure sometimes you are not in another planet; but then I don't like to ask Capt. Burney, or any of those that know any thing about it, for fear of exposing my ignorance.

Our kindest remembrances, however, to Mrs. F., if she will accept of reminiscences from another planet, or at least another hemisphere.   C. L.

LETTER CCCVII.]   [Sept. 22nd, 1822.]

TO THE SAME.

My dear F.,—I scribble hastily at office. Frank wants my letter presently. I and sister are just returned from Paris!! We have eaten frogs. It has been such a treat! You know our monotonous tenor. Frogs are the nicest little delicate things—rabbity-flavoured. Imagine a Lilliputian rabbit! They fricassee them; but in my mind, drest, seethed, plain,

with parsley and butter, would have the decision of
Apicius. Paris is a glorious picturesque old city.
London looks mean and new to it, as the town of
Washington would, seen after it. But they have no
St. Paul's, or Westminster Abbey. The Seine, so
much despised by Cockneys, is exactly the size to run
through a magnificent street; palaces a mile long on
one side, lofty Edinbro' stone (O the glorious anti-
ques!) houses on the other. The Thames disunites
London and Southwark. I had Talma to supper with
me. He has picked up, as I believe, an authentic
portrait of Shakspeare. He paid a broker about 40*l.*
English for it. It is painted on the one half of a pair
of bellows,—a lovely picture, corresponding with the
folio head. The bellows has old carved *wings* round
it, and round the visnomy is inscribed, as near as I
remember, not divided into rhyme—I found out he
rhyme—

> " Whom have we here
> Stuck on the bellows,
> But the Prince of good fellows,
>   Willy Shakspeare?"

At top—

> " O base and coward luck
>   To be here stuck !—Poins."

At bottom—

> " Nay! rather a glorious lot is to him assign'd,
>   Who, like the Almighty, rides upon the *wind.*—Pistol."

This is all in old carved wooden letters. The
countenance smiling, sweet, and intellectual beyond
measure, even as he was immeasurable. It may be
a forgery. They laugh at me and tell me Ireland is
in Paris, and has been putting off a portrait of the

C

Black Prince. How far old wood may be imitated I cannot say. Ireland was not found out by his parchments, but by his poetry. I am confident no painter on either side the Channel could have painted anything near like the face I saw. Again, would such a painter and forger have taken 40*l.* for a thing, if authentic, worth 4000*l.*? Talma is not in the secret, for he had not even found out the rhymes in the first inscription. He is coming over with it, and, my life to Southey's Thalaba, it will gain universal faith.

The letter is wanted, and I am wanted. Imagine the blank filled up with all kind things.

Our joint hearty remembrances to both of you.

Yours, as ever,

C. LAMB.

LETTER CCCVIII.]   [1822.]

TO A BOOKSELLER.

Thank you for the books. I am ashamed to take tithe thus of your press. I am worse to a publisher than the two Universities and the British Museum. A[llan] C[unningham] I will forthwith read. B[arry] C[ornwall] (I can't get out of the A, B, C) I have more than read. Taken altogether, 'tis too lovely; but what delicacies! I like most " King Death ; " glorious 'bove all, "The Lady with the Hundred Rings ; " "The Owl ; " " Epistle to What's his Name" (here may be I'm partial) ; "Sit down, Sad Soul ; " "The Pauper's Jubilee" (but that's old, and yet 'tis never old) ; " The Falcon ; " "Felon's Wife ; " damn " Madame Pasty " (but that is borrowed) ;

Apple-pie is very good,
And so is apple-pasty ;
But ——
O Lord ! 'tis very nasty :

but chiefly the dramatic fragments,—scarce three of which should have escaped my specimens, had an antique name been prefixed. They exceed his first. So much for the nonsense of poetry; now to the serious business of life. Up a court (Blandford Court) in Pall Mall (exactly at the back of Marlborough House), with iron gate in front, and containing two houses, at No. 2, did lately live Leishman, my tailor. He is moved somewhere in the neighbourhood; devil knows where. Pray find him out, and give him the opposite. I am so much better, though my head shakes in writing it, that, after next Sunday, I can well see F. and you. Can you throw B. C. in? Why tarry the wheels of my " Hogarth "?

CHARLES LAMB.

LETTER CCCIX.]

TO A FARMER AND HIS WIFE.

Twelfth Day, '23.

THE pig was above my feeble praise. It was a dear pigmy. There was some contention as to who should have the ears; but, in spite of his obstinacy, (deaf as these little creatures are to advice,) I contrived to get at one of them.

It came in boots too, which I took as a favour. Generally these pretty toes, pretty toes! are missing; but I suppose he wore them to look taller.

He must have been the least of his race. His little foots would have gone into the silver slipper. I take him to have been a Chinese and a female.

If Evelyn could have seen him, he would never have farrowed two such prodigious volumes; seeing how much good can be contained in—how small a compass!

C 2

He crackled delicately.

I left a blank at the top of my letter, not being determined which to address it to : so farmer and farmer's wife will please to divide our thanks. May your granaries be full, and your rats empty, and your chickens plump, and your envious neighbours lean, and your labourers busy, and you as idle and as happy as the day is long !

VIVE L'AGRICULTURE !

How do you make your pigs so little ?
They are vastly engaging at the age :
   I was so myself.
Now I am a disagreeable old hog,
A middle-aged gentleman-and-a-half,
My faculties (thank God !) are not much impaired. [1]

I have my sight, hearing, taste, pretty perfect ; and can read the Lord's Prayer in common type, by the help of a candle, without making many mistakes.

Believe me, that while my faculties last, I shall ever cherish a proper appreciation of your many kindnesses in this way, and that the last lingering relish of past favours upon my dying memory will be the smack of that little ear. It was the left ear, which is lucky. Many happy returns, not of the pig, but of the New Year, to both ! Mary, for her share of the pig and the memoirs, desires to send the same.

Yours truly,

C. LAMB.

---

[1] Thus printed originally. But the passage, as Lamb wrote it, must have run in plain prose shape. The line "I have my sight," &c., continuing the sense of the preceding one.—F.

LETTER CCCX.]

TO LEIGH HUNT.   [1824.]

ILLUSTREZZIMO SIGNOR,—I have obeyed your man-
date to a tittle. I accompany this with a volume;
but what have you done with the first I sent you?
Have you swapped it with some lazzaroni for
macaroni, or pledged it with a gondolierer for a
passage? Peradventuri the Cardinal Gonsalvi took
a fancy to it: his Eminence has done my Nearness
an honour. 'Tis but a step to the Vatican. As you
judge, my works do not enrich the workman; but. I
get vat I can for 'em. They keep dragging me on, a
poor, worn mill-horse, in the eternal round of the
damned magazine; but 'tis they are blind, not I.
Colburn (where I recognize with delight the gay W.
Honeycomb renovated) hath the ascendency. I was
with the Novellos last week. They have a large,
cheap house and garden, with a dainty library
(magnificent) without books; but what will make
you bless yourself, (I am too old for wonder,) something has touched the right organ in Vincentio at last.
He attends a Wesleyan chapel on Kingsland Green.
He at first tried to laugh it off; he only went for the
singing; but the cloven foot—I retract—the lamb's
trotters are at length apparent. Mary Isabella attri-
butes it to a lightness induced by his headaches; but
I think I see in it a less accidental influence. Mr.
Clark is at perfect staggers! the whole fabric of his
infidelity is shaken. He has no one to join him in
his horse-insults and indecent obstreperousnesses

against Christianity; for Holmes (the bonny Holmes) is gone to Salisbury to be organist, and Isabella and the Clark make but a feeble quorum. The children have all neat little clasped pray-books; and I have laid out seven shillings and eight-pence in Watts's Hymns for Christmas presents for them. The eldest girl alone holds out. She has been at Boulogne, skirting upon the vast focus of Atheism, and imported bad principles in patois French. But the strongholds are crumbling. N. appears as yet to have but a confused notion of the Atonement. It makes him giddy, he says, to think much about it; but such giddiness is spiritual sobriety. Well, Byron is gone;[1] and —— is now the best poet in England. Fill up the gap to your fancy. Barry Cornwall has at last carried the pretty A[nne] S[kipper.] They are just in the treacle-moon. Hope it won't clog his wings (gaum, we used to say at school). Mary, my sister, has worn me out with eight weeks' cold and toothache, her average complement in the Winter; and it will not go away. She is otherwise well, and reads novels all day long. She has had an exempt year, a good year; for which, forgetting the minor calamity, she and I are most thankful. Alsager is in a flourishing house, with wife and children about him, in Mecklenburg Square,—almost too fine to visit. Barron Field is come home from Sydney; but as yet I can hear no tidings of a pension. He is plump and friendly; his wife, really a very superior woman. He resumes the bar. I have got acquainted with Mr. Irving, the Scotch preacher, whose fame must have reached you. He is an humble disciple at the foot of

---

[1] He died April 19, 1824.

Gamaliel S. T. C. Judge how his own sectarists must stare, when I tell you he has dedicated a book to S. T. C., acknowledging to have learnt more of the nature of faith, Christianity, and Christian Church, from him than from all the men he ever conversed with! He is a most amiable, sincere, modest man in a room, this Boanerges in the temple. Mrs. Montague told him the dedication would do him no good. " That shall be a reason for doing it," was his answer. Judge, now, whether this man be a quack. Dear H., take this imperfect notelet for a letter: it looks so much the more like conversing on nearer terms. Love to all the Hunts, old friend Thornton,[1] and all.

Yours ever,

C. LAMB.

LETTER CCCXI.]

TO BASIL MONTAGUE.

Winterstow, near Sarum,
July 12th, 1810.

Dear Montague,—I have turned and twisted the MSS. in my head, and can make nothing of them. I knew when I took them that I could not, but I do not like to do an act of ungracious necessity at once; so I am ever committing myself by half engagements,

---

[1] Mr. Leigh Hunt's eldest son,

and total failures. I cannot make any body understand why I can't do such things; it is a defect in
my occiput. I cannot put other people's thoughts
together; I forget every paragraph as fast as I read
it; and my head has received such a shock by an all-
night journey on the top of the coach, that I shall
have enough to do to nurse it into its natural pace
before I go home. I must devote myself to imbecility; I must be gloriously useless while I stay
here. How is Mrs. M.? will she pardon my ineffi-
ciency? The city of Salisbury is full of weeping and
wailing. The bank has stopped payment; and every
body in the town kept money at it, or has got some
of its notes. Some have lost all they had in the
world. It is the next thing to seeing a city with the
plague within its walls. The Wilton people are all
undone; all the manufacturers there kept cash at the
Salisbury bank; and I do suppose it to be the un-
happiest county in England this, where I am making
holiday. We propose setting out for Oxford Tuesday
fortnight, and coming thereby home. But no more
night travelling. My head is sore (understand it of the
inside) with that deduction from my natural rest
which I suffered coming down. Neither Mary nor I
can spare a morsel of our rest: it is incumbent on us
to be misers of it. Travelling is not good for us, we
travel so seldom. If the sun be hell, it is not for the
fire, but for the sempiternal motion of that miserable
body of light. How much more dignified leisure
hath a mussel glued to his unpassable rocky limit,
two inch square! He hears the tide roll over him,
backwards and forwards twice a-day, (as the Salisbury
long coach goes and returns in eight-and-forty hours,)
but knows better than to take an outside night-place

a top on't.   He is the owl of the sea—Minerva's
fish—the fish of wisdom.

Our kindest remembrances to Mrs. M.

Yours truly,   C. Lamb.

Letter CCCXII.]

TO MRS. SHELLEY.

Enfield, July 26, 1827.

Dear Mrs. Shelley,—At the risk of throwing away
some fine thoughts, I must write to say how pleased
we were with your very kind remembering of us (who
have unkindly run away from all our friends) before
you go.   Perhaps you are gone, and then my tropes
are wasted.   If any piece of better fortune has lighted
upon you than you expected, but less than we wish
you, we are rejoiced.   We are here trying to like
solitude, but have scarce enough to justify the experiment.   We get some, however.   The six days are
our Sabbath; the seventh—why, Cockneys will come
for a little fresh air, and so—

But by *your month*, or October at furthest, we hope
to see Islington: I, like a giant refreshed with the
leaving off of wine; and Mary, pining for Mr. Moxon's
books and Mr. Moxon's society.   Then we shall
meet.

I am busy with a farce in two acts; the incidents
tragi-comic.   I can do the dialogue *commey for;* but
the damned plot—I believe I must omit it altogether.
The scenes come after one another like geese, not
marshalling like cranes or a Hyde Park review.   The

story is as simple as G[eorge] D[yer], and the language plain as his spouse. The characters are three women to one man; which is one more than laid hold on him in the " Evangely." I think that prophecy squinted towards my drama.

I want some Howard Paine to sketch a skeleton of artfully succeeding scenes through a whole play, as the courses are arranged in a cookery book : I to find wit, passion, sentiment, character, and the like trifles : to lay in the dead colours,—I'd Titianesque 'em up : to mark the channel in a cheek (smooth or furrowed, yours or mine,) and where tears should course I'd draw the waters down : to say where a joke should come in or a pun be left out : to bring my *personæ* on and off like a Beau Nash; and I'd Frankenstein them there: to bring three together on the stage at once ; they are so shy with me, that I can get no more than two ; and there they stand till it is the time, without being the season, to withdraw them.

I am teaching Emma Latin to qualify her for a superior governess-ship; which we see no prospect of her getting. 'Tis like feeding a child with chopped hay from a spoon. Sisyphus—his labours were as nothing to it.

Actives and passives jostle in her nonsense, till a deponent enters, like Chaos, more to embroil the fray. Her prepositions are suppositions; her conjunctions copulative have no connection in them ; her concords disagree ; her interjections are purely English " Ah !" and " Oh !" with a yawn and a gape in the same tongue; and she herself is a lazy, blockheadly supine. As I say to her, ass *in præsenti* rarely makes a wise man *in futuro*.

But I dare say it was so with you when you began Latin, and a good while after.

Good-by !   Mary's love.

Yours truly,   C. LAMB.

LETTER CCCXIII.]

TO MR. H. C. ROBINSON.

Colebrooke Row, Islington,
Saturday, 20th Jan. 1826.

Dear Robinson,—I called upon you this morning, and found that you were gone to visit a dying friend. I had been upon a like errand.   Poor Norris has been lying dying for now almost a week, such is the penalty we pay for having enjoyed a strong constitution !   Whether he knew me or not, I know not ; or whether he saw me through his poor glazed eyes ; but the group I saw about him I shall not forget. Upon the bed, or about it, were assembled his wife and two daughters, and poor deaf Richard, his son, looking doubly stupified.   There they were, and seemed to have been sitting all the week.   I could only reach out a hand to Mrs. Norris.   Speaking was impossible in that mute chamber.   By this time I hope it is all over with him.   In him I have a loss the world cannot make up.   He was my friend and my father's friend all the life I can remember.   I seem to have made foolish friendships ever since.   Those are friendships which outlive a second generation. Old as I am waxing, in his eyes I was still the child he first knew me.   To the last he called me Charley.

I have none to call me Charley now. He was the
last link that bound me to the Temple. You are but
of yesterday. In him seem to have died the old
plainness of manners and singleness of heart. Letters
he knew nothing of, nor did his reading extend beyond the pages of the *Gentleman's Magazine*. Yet
there was a pride of literature about him from being
amongst books (he was librarian), and from some
scraps of doubtful Latin which he had picked up in
his office of entering students, that gave him very
diverting airs of pedantry. Can I forget the erudite
look with which, when he had been in vain trying to
make out a black-letter text of Chaucer in the Temple
Library, he laid it down and told me that—" in those
old books, Charley, there is sometimes a deal of very
indifferent spelling;" and seemed to console himself
in the reflection! His jokes, for he had his jokes,
are now ended; but they were old trusty perennials,
staples that pleased after *decies repetita*, and were
always as good as new. One song he had, which was
reserved for the night of Christmas Day, which we
always spent in the Temple. It was an old thing,
and spoke of the flat bottoms of our foes, and the
possibility of their coming over in darkness, and
alluded to threats of an invasion many years blown
over; and when he came to the part—

> "We'll still make 'em run, and we'll still make 'em sweat,
> In spite of the Devil and *Brussels Gazette*,"

his eyes would sparkle as with the freshness of an
impending event. And what is the *Brussels Gazette*
now? I cry while I enumerate these trifles. " How
shall we tell them in a stranger's ear?" His poor
good girls will now have to receive their afflicted
mother in an unsuccessful hovel in an obscure village

in Herts, where they have been long struggling to make a school without effect ; and poor deaf Richard, and the more helpless for being so, is thrown on the wide world.

My first motive in writing, and indeed in calling on you, was to ask if you were enough acquainted with any of the Benchers to lay a plain statement before them of the circumstances of the family.   I almost fear not, for you are of another hall.   But if you can oblige me and my poor friend, who is now insensible to any favours, pray exert yourself.   You cannot say too much good of poor Norris and his poor wife.

Yours ever,   CHARLES LAMB.

LETTER CCCXIV.]

TO THE SAME.

Enfield, Feb. 27th, 1829.

Dear R.—Expectation was alert on the receipt of your strange-shaped present, while yet undisclosed from its fusc envelope.   Some said, 'tis a *viol da Gamba*, others pronounced it a fiddle ; I, myself, hoped it a liqueur case, pregnant with *eau-de-vie* and such odd nectar.   When midwifed into daylight, the gossips were at a loss to pronounce upon its species. Most took it for a marrow spoon, an apple scoop, a banker's guinea shovel ; at length its true scope appeared, its drift, to save the back-bone of my sister stooping to scuttles : a philanthropic intent ; borrowed, no doubt, from some of the Colliers.   You save people's backs one way, and break 'em again by loads of obligation.   The spectacles are delicate and Vulcanian.   No lighter texture than their steel did

the cuckoldy blacksmith frame to catch Mrs. Vulcan
and the Captain in.   For ungalled forehead, as
for back unbursten, you have Mary's thanks.   Marry,
for my own peculium of obligation, 'twas supererog-
atory.   A second part of Pamela was enough in
conscience.   Two Pamelas in a house are too much,
without two Mr. B.'s to reward 'em.

Mary, who is handselling her new aerial perspec-
tives upon a pair of old worsted stockings trod out in
Cheshunt lanes, sends her love: I, great good-liking.
Bid us a personal farewell before you see the Vatican.

CHARLES LAMB.

LETTER CCCXV.]

TO THE SAME.

April 10th, 1829.

Dear Robinson,—We are afraid you will slip from
us from England without again seeing us.   It would be
charity to come and see me.   I have these three days
been laid up with strong rheumatic pains, in loins,
back, shoulders.   I shriek sometimes from the violence
of them.   I get scarce any sleep, and the consequence
is, I am restless, and want to change sides as I lie, and
I cannot turn without resting on my hands, and so
turning all my body all at once, like a log with a lever.
While this rainy weather lasts, I have no hope of alle-
viation.   I have tried flannels and embrocation in
vain.   Just at the hip joint the pangs sometimes are
so excruciating, that I cry out.   It is as violent as the
cramp, and far more continuous.   I am ashamed to
whine about these complaints to you, who can ill

enter into them ; but indeed they are sharp. You go about, in rain or fine, at all hours, without discommodity. I envy you your immunity at a time of life not much removed from my own. But you owe your exemption to temperance, which it is too late for me to pursue. I, in my lifetime, have had my good things. Hence my frame is brittle—yours strong as brass. I never knew any ailment you had. You can go out at night in all weathers, sit up all hours. Well, I don't want to moralize; I only wish to say that if you are inclined to a game at double-dumby, I would try and bolster myself in a chair for a rubber or so. My days are tedious, but less so, and less painful than my nights. May you never know the pain and difficulty I have in writing so much! Mary, who is most kind, joins in the wish.

C. LAMB.

Letter CCCXVI.]

TO THE SAME

April 17, 1829.

I do confess to mischief. It was the subtlest diabolical piece of malice heart of man has contrived. I have no more rheumatism than that poker. Never was freer from all pains and aches. Every joint sound, to the tip of the ear from the extremity of the lesser toe. The report of thy torments was blown circuitously here from Bury. I could not resist the jeer. I conceived you writhing when you should just receive my congratulations. How mad you'd be! Well, it is not in my method to inflict pangs. I leave that to Heaven : but in the existing pangs of a friend I have a share. His disquietude crowns my exemption. I imagine you howling, and pace across the room, shooting out my free arms, legs, &c., this way and that way, with an assurance of not kindling a spark of pain from them. I deny that Nature meant us to sympathize with agonies. Those face-contortions, retortions, distortions have the merriness of antics. Nature meant them for farce—not so pleasant to the actor, indeed; but Grimaldi cries when we laugh, and 'tis but one that suffers to make thousands rejoice.

You say that shampooing is ineffectual; but, *per se*, it is good, to show the introvolutions, extravolutions, of which the animal frame is capable—to show what the creature is receptible of, short of dissolution.

You are worst of nights, an't you? You never was rack'd, was you? I should like an authentic map of those feelings.

You seem to have the flying gout. You can scarcely screw a smile out of your face, can you? I sit at immunity and sneer *ad libitum*. 'Tis now the time for you to make good resolutions. I may go on breaking 'em for any thing the worse I find myself. Your doctor seems to keep you on the long cure. Precipitate healings are never good. Don't come while you are so bad; I shan't be able to attend to your throes and the dumby at once. I should like to know how slowly the pain goes off. But don't write, unless the motion will be likely to make your sensibility more exquisite.

Your affectionate and truly healthy friend,

C. LAMB.

Mary thought a letter from me might amuse you in your torment.

LETTER CCCXVII.]

TO J. PAYNE COLLIER.

The Garden of England, Dec. 1c.

Dear J. P. C.,—I know how zealously you feel for our friend S. T. Coleridge; and I know that you and your family attended his lectures four or five years ago. He is in bad health, and worse mind: and unless something is done to lighten his mind he will soon be reduced to his extremities; and even these are not in the best condition. I am sure that you will do for him what you can; but at present he seems in a mood to do for himself. He projects a new course, not of physic, nor of metaphysic, nor a new course of life, but a new course of lectures on Shakespeare and Poetry. There is no man better qualified (always excepting number one); but I am pre-engaged for a series of dissertations on Indian and Indiapendence, to be completed, at the expense of the Company, in' I know not (yet) how many volumes foolscap folio. I am busy getting up my Hindoo mythology; and, for the purpose, I am once more enduring Southey's curse (of "Kehama"). To be serious, Coleridge's state and affairs make me so; and there are particular reasons just now, and have been any time for the last twenty years, why he should succeed. He will do so with a little encouragement. I have not seen him lately; and he does not know that I am writing.

Yours (for Coleridge's sake) in haste,

C. LAMB.

———————

LETTER CCCXVIII.]

TO MR. PATMORE. [1]

Mrs. Leishman's, Chase, Enfield.

Dear P.—Excuse my anxiety, but how is Dash? I should have asked if Mrs. Patmore[2] kept her rules, and was improving; but Dash came uppermost. The order of our thoughts should be the order of our writing. Goes he muzzled, or *aperto ore?* Are his intellects sound, or does he wander a little in *his* conversation? You cannot be too careful to watch the first symptoms of incoherence. The first illogical snarl he makes, to St. Luke's with him! All the dogs here are going mad, if you believe the overseers; but I protest they seem to me very rational and collected. But nothing is so deceitful as mad people, to those who are not used to them. Try him with hot water: if he won't lick it up it is a sign he does not like it. Does his tail wag horizontally, or perpendicularly? That has decided the fate of many dogs in Enfield. Is his general deportment cheerful? I mean when he is pleased—for otherwise there is no judging. You can't be too careful. Has he bit any of the children yet? If he has, have them shot, and keep *him* for curiosity, to see if it was the hydrophobia. They say all our army in India had it at one time; but that was in *Hyder*-Ally's time. Do you get paunch for him? Take care the sheep was sane.

Allusion has been made to this dog in Sir T. Talfourd's Memoir. Mr. Patmore, in his curiously discursive volumes, "My Friends and Acquaintances," has given some details of his intimacy with Lamb. According to Mr. W. C. Hazlitt, he was a Pawnbroker at Dublin, with whom Sheridan had, characteristically, been in the habit of pledging MS. Dramas.—F.

You might pull out his teeth (if he would let you), and then you need not mind if he were as mad as a Bedlamite. It would be rather fun to see his odd ways. It might amuse Mrs. P—— and the children. They'd have more sense than he. He'd be like a fool kept in a family, to keep the household in good humour with their own understanding. You might teach him the mad dance, set to the mad howl. *Madge Owlet* would be nothing to him. " My! how he capers !" [*In the margin is written, " One of the children speaks this.*"] . . . What I scratch out is a German quotation, from Lessing, on the bite of rabid animals ; but I remember you don't read German. But Mrs. P—— may, so I wish I had let it stand. The meaning in English is—" Avoid to approach an animal suspected of madness, as you would avoid fire or a precipice," which I think is a sensible observation. The Germans are certainly profounder than we. If the slightest suspicion arises in your breast that all is not right with him, muzzle him and lead him in a string (common pack-thread will do— he don't care for twist) to Mr. Hood's, his quondam master, and he'll take him in at any time. You may mention your suspicion, or not, as you like, or as you think it may wound or not Mr. H.'s feelings. Hood, I know, will wink at a few follies in Dash, in consideration of his former sense. Besides, Hood is deaf, and if you hinted any thing, ten to one he would not hear you. Besides, you will have discharged your conscience, and laid the child at the right door, as they say.

We are dawdling our time away very idly and pleasantly at a Mrs. Leishman's, Chase, Enfield, where, if you come a-hunting, we can give you cold meat and a tankard.   Her husband is a tailor; but that, you know, does not make her one.   I knew a jailor (which rhymes), but his wife was a fine lady.

Let us hear from you respecting Mrs. P——'s regimen.   I send my love in a —— to Dash.

C. LAMB.

[What follows was written on the *outside* of the letter :—]

Seriously, I wish you would call upon Hood when you are that way.   He's a capital fellow.   I've sent him two poems, one ordered by his wife, and written to order; and 'tis a week since, and I've not heard from him.   I fear something is the matter.

Our kindest remembrance to Mrs. P.

LETTER CCCXIX.]

TO THE SAME.

Dear P.,—I am so poorly.   I have been to a funeral, where I made a pun, to the consternation of the rest of the mourners.   And we had wine.   I can't describe to you the howl which the widow set up at proper intervals.   Dash could, for it was not unlike what he makes.

The letter I sent you was one directed to the care of E. W——, India House, for Mrs. H[azlitt].   *Which* Mrs. H—— I don't yet know; but A—— has taken it to France on speculation.   Really it is embarrassing. There is Mrs. present H., Mrs. late H., and Mrs. John H., and to which of the three Mrs. Wigginses it appertains, I know not.   I wanted to open it, but 'tis transportation.

I am sorry you are plagued about your book. I would strongly recommend you to take for one story Massinger's "Old Law." It is exquisite. I can think of no other.

Dash is frightful this morning. He whines and stands up on his hind legs. He misses Becky, who is gone to town. I took him to Barnet the other day, and he couldn't eat his vittles after it. Pray God his intellectuals be not slipping.

Mary is gone out for some soles. I suppose 'tis no use to ask you to come and partake of 'em ; else there is a steam vessel.

I am doing a tragi-comedy in two acts, and have got on tolerably; but it will be refused, or worse. I never had luck with any thing my name was put to.

O, I am so poorly! I *waked* it at my cousin's the bookbinder, who is now with God ; or, if he is not, 'tis no fault of mine.

We hope the frank wines do not disagree with Mrs P——. By the way, I like her.

Did you ever taste frogs? Get them if you can. They are like little Lilliput rabbits, only a thought nicer.

How sick I am!—not of the world, but of the widow's shrub. She's sworn under £6,ooo, but I think she perjured herself. She howls in E *la*, and I comfort her in B flat. You understand music?

If you hav'n't got Massinger you have nothing to do but go to the first Bibliothèque you can light upon at Boulogne, and ask for it (Gifford's edition); and if they hav'n't got it you can have "Athalie" par Monsieur Racine, and make the best of it. But that "Old Law" is delicious.

"No shrimps!" (that's in answer to Mary's question about how the soles are to be done).

I am uncertain where this wandering letter may reach you. What you mean by Poste Restante, God knows. Do you mean I must pay the postage? So I do, to Dover.

We had a merry passage with the widow at the Commons. She was howling—part howling and part giving directions to the proctor—when crash! down went my sister through a crazy chair, and made the clerks grin, and I grinned, and the widow tittered, and then I knew that she was not inconsolable. Mary was more frightened than hurt.

She'd make a good match for any body (by she, I mean the widow).

> "If he bring but a *relict* away,
> He is happy, nor heard to complain."
>
> SHENSTONE.

Procter has got a wen growing out at the nape of his neck, which his wife wants him to have cut off; but I think it is rather an agreeable excrescence: like his poetry, redundant. Hone has hanged himself for debt. Godwin was taken up for picking pockets. Moxon has fallen in love with Emma, our nut-brown maid. Becky takes to bad courses. Her father was blown up in a steam machine. The coroner found it "insanity." I should not like him to sit on my letter.

Do you observe my direction. Is it Gallic—classical? Do try and get some frogs. You must ask for "grenouilles" (green eels). They don't understand "frogs," though 'tis a common phrase with us.

If you go through Bulloign (Boulogne), inquire if

old Godfrey is living, and how he got home from the crusades. He must be a very old man.

If there is any thing new in politics or literature in France, keep it till I see you again, for I'm in no hurry. Chatty Briant is well I hope.

I think I have no more news; only give both our loves (all three, says Dash,) to Mrs. P——, and bid her get quite well, as I am at present, bating qualms, and the grief incident to losing a valuable relation.

C. L.

Londres, Julie 19, 1827.

LETTER CCCXX.]   Feb. 14, 1834.

TO MISS FRYER.

Dear Miss Fryer, — Your letter found me just returned from keeping my birthday (pretty innocent!) at Dover Street. I see them pretty often. I have since had letters of business to write, or should have replied earlier. In one word, be less uneasy about me; I bear my privations very well; I am not in the depths of desolation, as heretofore. Your admonitions are not lost upon me. Your kindness has sunk into my heart. Have faith in me! It is no new thing for me to be left to my sister. When she is not violent, her rambling chat is better to me than the sense and sanity of this world. Her heart is obscured, not buried; it breaks out occasionally; and one can

discern a strong mind struggling with the billows
that have gone over it.   I could be nowhere happier
than under the same roof with her.   Her memory is
unnaturally strong ; and from ages past, if we may
so call the earliest records of our poor life, she fetches
thousands of names and things that never would
have dawned upon me again, and thousands from the
ten years she lived before me.   What took place from
early girlhood to her coming of age, principally lives
again (every important thing, and every trifle) in her
brain, with the vividness of real presence.   For
twelve hours incessantly she will pour out without
intermission all her past life, forgetting nothing,
pouring out name after name to the Waldens, as a
dream ; sense and nonsense ; truths and errors
huddled together ; a medley between inspiration and
possession.   What things we are !   I know you will
bear with me, talking of these things.   It seems to
ease me, for I have nobody to tell these things to
now.   Emma, I see, has got a harp ! and is learning
to play.   She has framed her three Walton pictures,
and pretty they look.   That is a book you should
read ; such sweet religion in it, next to Woolman's,
though the subject be baits, and hooks, and worms,
and fishes.   She has my copy at present, to do two
more from.

Very, very tired ! I began this epistle, having been
epistolizing all the morning, and very kindly would
I end it, could I find adequate expressions to your
kindness.   We did set our minds on seeing you in
Spring.   One of us will indubitably.   But I am not
skilled in almanack learning to know when Spring
precisely begins and ends.   Pardon my blots ; I am
glad you like your book.   I wish it had been half as

worthy of your acceptance as John Woolman.   But 'tis a good-natured book.

LETTER CCCXXI.]   [No·date.¹

TO THOMAS HOOD.

And what dost thou at the Priory?   *Cucullus non facit Monachum.*   English me that, and challenge old Lignum Janua to make a better.

My old New River has presented no extraordinary novelties lately; but there Hope sits every day, speculating upon traditionary gudgeons.   I think she has taken the fisheries.   I now know the reason why our forefathers were denominated East and West Angles.   Yet is there no lack of spawn; for I wash my hands in fishets that come through the pump every morning thick as motelings,—little things that perish untimely, and never taste the brook.   You do not tell me of those romantic land bays that be as thou goest to Lover's Seat: neither of that little churchling in the midst of a wood (in the opposite direction, nine furlongs from the town), that seems dropped by the Angel that was tired of carrying two packages; marry, with the other he made shift to pick his flight to Loretto.   Inquire out, and see my little Protestant Loretto.   It stands apart from trace of human habitation ; yet hath it pulpit, reading-desk, and trim front of massiest marble, as if Robinson

Crusoe had reared it to soothe himself with old church-going images. I forget its Christian name, and what she-saint was its gossip.

You should also go to No. 13, Standgate Street,—a baker, who has the finest collection of marine monsters in ten sea counties,—sea dragons, polypi, mer-people, most fantastic. You have only to name the old gentleman in black (not the Devil) that lodged with him a week (he'll remember) last July, and he will show courtesy. He is by far the foremost of the savans. His wife is the funniest thwarting little animal! They are decidedly the Lions of green Hastings. Well, I have made an end of my say. My epistolary time is gone by when I could have scribbled as long (I will not say as agreeable) as thine was to both of us. I am dwindled to notes and letterets. But, in good earnest, I shall be most happy to hail thy return to the waters of Old Sir Hugh. There is nothing like inland murmurs, fresh ripples, and our native minnows.

> "He sang in meeds how sweet the brooklets ran,
>   To the rough ocean and red restless sands."

I design to give up smoking; but I have not yet fixed upon the equivalent vice. I must have *quid pro quo;* or *quo pro quid,* as Tom Woodgate would correct me. My service to him.   C. L.

LETTER CCCXXII.] [No date.]

TO THE SAME.

Dear Lamb,—You are an impudent varlet; but I will keep your secret. We dine at Ayrton's on Thursday, and shall try to find Sarah and her two spare beds for that night only. Miss M. and her tragedy may be dished: so may *not* you and your rib. Health attend you.

Yours, T. HOOD, ESQ.[1]

Enfield.

Miss Bridget Hood sends love.

LETTER CCCXXIII.] [No date.]

TO JOSEPH COTTLE.

Dear Sir,—It is so long since I have seen or heard from you, that I fear that you will consider a request I have to make as impertinent. About three years since, when I was in Bristol, I made an effort to see you by calling at Brunswick Square; but you were from home. The request I have to make is, that you would very much oblige me, if you have any small portrait of yourself, by allowing me to have it copied, to accompany a selection of the likenesses of " Living Bards " which a most particular friend of mine is making. If you have no objection, and would oblige

---

[1] One of Lamb's pleasant mystifications, the point of which lay in the anticipated bewilderment of the receiver of the letter, on being greeted by his own signature.—F.

me by transmitting such portrait, I will answer for
taking the greatest care of it, and for its safe return.
I hope you will pardon the liberty.

From an old friend and well-wisher,

CHARLES LAMB.

LETTER CCCXXIV.]   [No date.]
                    TO THE SAME.

Dear Sir,—My friend, whom you have obliged by
the loan of your picture, has had it very nicely copied
(and a very spirited drawing it is; so every one
thinks who has seen it.) The copy is not much
inferior to yours, done by a daughter of Joseph's, R.A.

I accompany the picture with my warm thanks,
both for that, and your better favour, the "Messiah,"
which I assure you I have read through with great
pleasure. The verses have great sweetness, and a
New Testament plainness about them which affected
me very much. I could just wish that in page 63
you had omitted the lines 71 and 72, and had ended
the period with—

> "The willowy brook was there, but that sweet sound—
> When to be heard again on earthly ground?"

Two very sweet lines, and the sense perfect.

And in page 154, line 68,—

> "He spake, 'I come, ordain'd a world to save,
> To be baptized by thee in Jordan's wave.'"

These words are hardly borne out by the story, and
seem scarce accordant with the modesty with which
our Lord came to take his common portion among
the baptismal candidates. They also anticipate the
beauty of John's recognition of the Messiah, and the
subsequent confirmation by the Voice and Dove.

You will excuse the remarks of an old brother bard, whose career, though long since pretty well stopped, was co-eval in its beginning with your own, and who is sorry his lot has been always to be so distant from you. It is not like that C. L. will see Bristol again; but, if J. C. should ever visit London, he will be a most welcome visitor to C. L. My sister joins in cordial remembrances.

Dear sir, yours truly,

CHARLES LAMB.

LETTER CCCXXV.]

TO THE SAME.

London, India House, May 26, 1829.

My dear Sir,—I am quite ashamed of not having acknowledged your kind present earlier; but that unknown something, which was never yet discovered, though so often speculated upon, which stands in the way of lazy folks answering letters, has presented its usual obstacle. It is not forgetfulness nor disrespect nor incivility, but terribly like all these bad things.

I have been in my time a great epistolary scribbler: but the passion, and with it the facility, at length wears out; and it must be pumped up again by the heavy machinery of duty or gratitude, when it should run free. I have read your " Fall of Cambria " with as much pleasure as I did your " Messiah." Your Cambrian poem I shall be tempted to repeat oftenest, as human poems take me in a mood more frequently congenial than divine. The character of Llewellyn pleases me more than any thing else, perhaps; and then some of the lyrical pieces are fine varieties.

It was quite a mistake that I could dislike any thing you should write against Lord Byron; for I have a thorough aversion to his character, and a very moderate admiration of his genius : he is great in so little a way. To be a poet is to be the man, not a petty portion of occasional low passion worked up in a permanent form of humanity. Shakspeare has thrust such rubbishly feelings into a corner,—the dark dusky heart of Don John, in the *Much Ado about Nothing*. The fact is, I have not seen your " Expostulatory Epistle " to him. I was not aware, till your question, that it was out. I shall inquire, and get it forthwith.

Southey is in town, whom I have seen slightly; Wordsworth expected, whom I hope to see much of. I write with accelerated motion; for I have two or three bothering clerks and brokers about me, who always press in proportion as you seem to be doing something that is not business. I could exclaim a little profanely; but I think you do not like swearing.

I conclude, begging you to consider that I feel myself much obliged by your kindness ; and shall be most happy at any and at all times to hear from you.

Dear sir, yours truly,

CHARLES LAMB.

LETTER CCCXXVI.   July 30, 182—
TO J. TAYLOR.

Dear Sir,—You will do me injustice if you do not convey to the writer of the beautiful lines, which 1 now return you, my sense of the extreme kindness which dictated them. Poor Elia (call him *Ellia*) does not pretend to so very clear revelations of a future state of being as Olen seems gifted with. He stumbles about dark mountains at best; but he knows at least how to be thankful for this life, and is too thankful indeed for certain relationships lent him here, not to tremble for a possible resumption of the gift. He is too apt to express himself lightly, and cannot be sorry for the present occasion, as it has called forth a reproof so Christian-like. His *animus* at least (whatever become of it in the female termination) hath always been *cum Christianis.*

Pray make my gratefullest respects to the Poet, (do I flatter myself when I hope it may be M——y ?) and say how happy I should feel myself in an acquaintance with him. I will just mention that in the middle of the second column, where I have affixed a cross, the line

> "One in a skeleton's ribb'd hollow cooped,"

is undoubtedly wrong. Should it not be—

> "A skeleton's rib or ribs?"

or,

> "In a skeleton ribb'd, hollow-coop'd?"

I perfectly remember the plate in Quarles. In the first page exoteric is pronounced exoteric. It should be (if that is the word) exoteric. The false accent may be corrected by omitting the word *old*. Pray, for certain reasons, give me to the 18th *at furthest extremity* for my next.

Poor ELIA, the real, (for I am but a counterfeit,) is dead. The fact is, a person of that name, an Italian, was a fellow clerk of mine at the South Sea House, thirty (not forty) years ago, when the characters I described there existed, but had left it like myself many years; and I having a brother now there, and doubting how he might relish certain descriptions in it, I clapt down the name of Elia to it, which passed off pretty well, for Elia himself added the function of an author to that of a scrivener, like myself.

I went the other day (not having seen him for a year) to laugh over with him at my usurpation of his name, and found him, alas! no more than a name, for he died of consumption eleven months ago, and I knew not of it.

So the name has fairly devolved to me, I think; and 'tis all he has left me.

Dear sir, yours truly,

Messrs. Taylor & Hessey, Fleet Street,   C. LAMB.
for J. Taylor, Esq.

LETTER CCCXXVII.]   Dec. 7, 1822.

TO THE SAME.

Dear Sir,—I should like the enclosed Dedication to be printed, unless you dislike it. I like it. It is in the olden style. But if you object to it, put forth the book as it is; only pray don't let the printer mistake the word *curt* for *curst*.

C. L.

DEDICATION.

TO THE FRIENDLY AND JUDICIOUS READER,

who will take these Papers, as they were meant; not understanding every thing perversely in its absolute and literal sense, but giving fair construction, as to an after-dinner conversation; allowing for the rashness and necessary incompleteness of first thoughts; and not remembering, for the purpose of an after taunt, words spoken peradventure after the fourth glass, the Author wishes (what he would will for himself) plenty of good friends to stand by him, good books to solace him, prosperous events to all his honest undertakings, and a candid interpretation to his most hasty words and actions. The other sort (and he hopes many of them will purchase his book too) he greets with the curt invitation of Timon, "Uncover, dogs, and lap:" or he dismisses them with the confident security of the philosopher,—"you beat but on the case of Elia." On better consideration, pray omit that Dedication. The Essays want no Preface : they are *all Preface.* A Preface is nothing but a talk with the reader; and they do nothing else. Pray omit it.

There will be a sort of Preface in the next Magazine, which may act as an advertisement, but not proper for the volume.

Let ELIA come forth bare as he was born.

C. L.

Messrs. Taylor & Hessey,
  Booksellers, Fleet Street.

N.B. *No* Preface.

LETTER CCCXXVIII.]   8 July, 1831.

TO THE SAME.

Dear Sir,—I am extremely sorry to be obliged to decline the article proposed, particularly as I should have been flattered with a Plate accompanying it. In the first place, Midsummer Day is not a topic I could make any thing of, I am so pure a Cockney, and little read besides in May games and antiquities ; and in the second, I am here at Margate, spoiling my holydays with a Review I have undertaken for a friend, which I shall barely get through before my return, for that sort of work is a hard task to me.

VOL. III.   E

If you will excuse the shortness of my first contribution (and I *know* I can promise nothing more for July) I will endeavour a longer article for *our next*. Will you permit me to say that I think Leigh Hunt would do the Article you propose in a masterly manner, if he has not out-writ himself already upon the subject. I do not return the proof—to save postage—because it is correct, with *one exception*. In the stanza from Wordsworth you have changed *day* into *air* for rhyme's sake. *Day* is the right reading, and *I implore you to restore it*.

The other passage, which you have queried, is to my ear correct. Pray let it stand.

Dear sir, yours truly,

Margate.   C. LAMB.
    J. Taylor, Esq.,

On second consideration I do enclose the proof.

LETTER CCCXXIX.]

TO MR. AINSWORTH.

India House, 9th Dec. 1823.

Dear Sir,—I should have thanked you for your books and compliments sooner, but have been waiting for a revise to be sent, which does not come, though I returned the proof on the receipt of your letter. I have read Warner with great pleasure. What an elaborate piece of alliteration and antithesis! why it must have been a labour far above the most difficult versification. There is a fine simile or picture of Semiramis arming to repel a siege. I do not mean to keep the book, for I suspect you are forming a curious collection, and I do not pretend to any thing of the kind. I have not a black-letter book among mine, old Chaucer excepted, and am not bibliomanist enough to like black-letter. It is painful to read ; therefore I must insist on returning it at opportunity, not from contumacy and reluctance to be obliged, but because it must suit you better than me. The loss of a present *from* should never exceed the gain of a present *to*. I hold this maxim infallible in the accepting line. I read your magazines with satisfaction. I thoroughly agree with you as to " The German Faust," as far as I can do justice to it from an English translation. 'Tis a disagreeable canting tale of seduction, which has nothing to do with the spirit of Faustus — Curiosity. Was the dark secret to be explored to end in the seducing of a weak girl, which might have been accomplished by earthly agency? When Marlow gives *his* Faustus a mistress, he flies him at Helen, flower of Greece, to be sure, and not at Miss Betsy, or Miss Sally Thoughtless.

> ' Cut is the branch that bore the goodly fruit,
> And wither'd is Apollo's laurel tree :
> Faustus is dead."

What a noble natural transition from metaphor to plain speaking ! as if the figurative had flagged in description of such a loss, and was reduced to tell the fact simply.

I must now thank you for your very kind invitation. It is not out of prospect that I may see Manchester some day, and then I will avail myself of your kindness. But holidays are scarce things with me, and the laws of attendance are getting stronger and stronger at Leadenhall. But I shall bear it in

mind. Meantime something may (more probably)
bring you to town, where I shall be happy to see you.
I am always to be found (alas !) at my desk in the
fore part of the day.

I wonder why they do not send the revise. I leave
late at office, and my abode lies out of the way, or I
should have seen about it. If you are impatient,
perhaps a line to the printer, directing him to send
it me, at Accountant's Office, may answer. You
will see by the scrawl that I only snatch a few minutes
from intermitting business.

Your obliged servant,

C. LAMB.

(If I had time I would go over this letter again, and
dot all my *i*'s.)

LETTER CCCXXX.]

TO THE SAME.

I. H., Dec. 29th, 1823.

My dear Sir,—You talk of months at a time, and I
know not what inducements to visit Manchester,
Heaven knows how gratifying! but I have had my
little month of 1823 already. It is all over; and without incurring a disagreeable favour I cannot so much
as get a single holiday till the season returns with
the next year. Even our half-hour's absences from
office are set down in a book! Next year, if I can
spare a day or two of it, I will come to Manchester;
but I have reasons at home against longer absences.

I am so ill just at present, (an illness of my own
procuring last night; who is perfect ?) that nothing
but your very great kindness could make me write.

I will bear in mind the letter to W. W., and you shall have it quite in time, before the 12th.

My aching and confused head warns me to leave off. With a muddled sense of gratefulness, which I shall apprehend more clearly to-morrow, I remain, your friend unseen,   C. L.

Will your occasions or inclination bring you to London ? It will give me great pleasure to show you every thing that Islington can boast, if you know the meaning of that very Cockney sound. We have the New River! I am ashamed of this scrawl; but I beg you to accept it for the present. I am full of qualms.

"A fool at fifty is a fool indeed."

LETTER CCCXXXI.]

[TO A LADY ASKING A SUBSCRIPTION.]

[1828.]

Dear Madam,—I return your list with my name. I should be sorry that any respect should be going on towards Clarkson, and I be left out of the conspiracy. Otherwise I frankly own that to pillarize a man's good feelings in his lifetime is not to my taste. Monuments to goodness, even after death, are equi-vocal. I turn away from Howard's, I scarce know why. Goodness blows no trumpet, nor desires to have it blown. *We should be modest for a modest man*—as he is for himself. The vanities of life—art, poetry, skill military—are subjects for trophies ; not the silent thoughts arising in a good man's mind in lonely places. Was I Clarkson, I should never be able to walk or ride near the spot again. Instead of bread, we are giving him a stone. Instead of the locality recalling the noblest moment of his existence, it is a place at which his friends (that is, himself) blow to the world, "What a good man is he!" I sat down upon a hillock at Forty Hill yesternight,—a fine contemplative evening,—with a thousand good speculations about mankind. How I yearned with cheap benevolence! I shall go and inquire of the stone-cutter, that cuts the tombstones here, what a stone with a short inscription will cost; just to say, "Here C. Lamb loved his brethren of mankind." Every body will come there to love. As I can't well put my own name, I shall put about a subscription :

Mrs. —— . .	£0	5	0
Procter . . .	0	2	6
G. Dyer . . .	0	1	0
Mr. Godwin .	0	0	0
Mrs. Godwin .	0	0	0
Mr. Irving . .	a watch-chain.		
Mr. —— . .	{ the proceeds of —— { first edition.		

$$£0 \quad 8 \quad 6$$

I scribble in haste from here, where we shall be some time. Pray request Mr.—— to advance the guinea for me, which shall faithfully be forthcoming, and pardon me that I don't see the proposal in quite the light that he may. The kindness of his motives, and his power of appreciating the noble passage, I thoroughly agree in.

With most kind regards to him, I conclude,

Dear madam, yours truly,

C. LAMB.

From Mrs. Leishman's, Chase, Enfield.

LETTER CCCXXXII.]

TO REV. E. IRVING.

Dear Sir,—I take advantage from the kindness which I have experienced from you in a slight acquaintance to introduce to you my very respected friend Mr. Hone, who is of opinion that your interference in a point which he will mention to you may prove of essential benefit to him in some present difficulties. I should not take this liberty if I did not feel that you are a person not to be prejudiced by an obnoxious name. All that I know of him obliges me to respect him, and to request your kindness for him, if you can serve him.

With feelings of kindest respect,
I am, dear Sir,
yours truly,
CHAS. LAMB.

Enfield Chase,
3rd April, 1828.

LETTER CCCXXXIII.]

TO WILLIAM AYRTON.

Mr. Westwood's, Chase Side, Enfield.
14th March, 1830.

My dear Ayrton,—Your letter, which was only not so pleasant as your appearance would have been, has

revived some old images,—Phillips,[1] (not the Colonel),
with his few hairs bristling up at the charge of a revoke, which he declares impossible ; the old Captain's
significant nod over the right shoulder (was it not ?) ;[2]
Mrs. B——'s determined questioning of the score,
after the game was absolutely gone to the d—l; the
plain but hospitable cold boiled-beef suppers at side-
board : all which fancies, redolent of middle age and
strengthful spirits, come across us ever and anon in
this vale of deliberate senectitude, ycleped Enfield.

You imagine a deep gulf between you and us; and
there is a pitable hiatus in *kind* between St. James's
Park and this extremity of Middlesex. But the mere
distance in turnpike roads is a trifle. The roof of a
coach swings you down in an hour or two. We have
a sure hot joint on a Sunday; and when had we
better ? I suppose you know that ill health has
obliged us to give up housekeeping ; but we have an
asylum at the very next door, (only twenty-four inches
further from town, which is not material in a country
expedition,) where a *table d'hôte* is kept for us, without trouble on our parts, and we adjourn after dinner,

---

1 Edward Phillips, Esq., Secretary to the Right Hon. Charles Abbott,
Speaker of the House of Commons. The " Colonel " alluded to was
the Lieutenant of Marines who accompanied Capt. Cook in his last
voyage, and who was on shore with that great man when he fell a
victim to his humanity. On the death of his commander, Lieutenant
Phillips, himself wounded, swam off to the boats; but seeing one of
his marines wounded, and struggling in the water to escape the natives
who were pursuing him, he gallantly swam back, protected his man at
the peril of his own life, and both reached their boat in safety. He
afterwards married that accomplished and amiable daughter of Dr.
Burney, whose name so frequently occurs in the Diary and Correspondence of her sister, Madame D'Arblay.—T.

2 Captain (afterwards Admiral) James Burney.—T.

when one of the old world (old friends) drops casually down among us. Come and find us out; and seal our judicious change with your approbation, whenever the whim bites, or the sun prompts. No need of announcement, for we are sure to be at home.

I keep putting off the subject of my answer. In truth I am not in spirits at present to see Mr. Murray on such a business; but pray offer him my acknowledgments, and an assurance that I should like at least one of his propositions, as I have so much additional matter for the SPECIMENS as might make two volumes in all; or ONE, (new edition,) omitting such better-known authors as Beaumont and Fletcher, Jonson, &c.

But we are both in trouble at present. A very dear young friend of ours, who passed her Christmas holidays here, has been taken dangerously ill with a fever, from which she is very precariously recovering, and I expect a summons to fetch her when she is well enough to bear the journey from Bury. It is Emma Isola, with whom we got acquainted at our first visit to your sister at Cambridge, and she has been an occasional inmate with us (and of late years much more frequently) ever since. While she is in this danger, and till she is out of it, and here in a probable way to recovery, I feel that I have no spirits for an engagement of any kind. It has been a terrible shock to us; therefore I beg that you will make my handsomest excuses to Mr. Murray.

Our very kindest loves to Mrs. A. and the younger A's.

Your unforgotten,

C. LAMB.

LETTER CCCXXXIV.]

TO MRS. WILLIAMS.[1]

Enfield, April 2nd, 1830

Dear Madam,—I have great pleasure in letting you
know Miss Isola has suffered very little from fatigue
on her long journey. I am ashamed to say that I
came home rather the more tired of the two; but I
am a very unpractised traveller. We found my sister
very well in health, only a little impatient to see her;
and after a few hysterical tears for gladness, all was
comfortable again. We arrived here from Epping
between five and six.

The incidents of our journey were trifling, but you
bade us tell them. We had then in the coach a
rather talkative gentleman, but very civil all the way;
and took up a servant maid at Stamford going to a
sick mistress. To the latter a participation in the
hospitalities of your nice rusks and sandwiches proved
agreeable, as it did to my companion, who took
merely a sip of the weakest wine and water with
them. The former engaged me in a discourse for
full twenty miles, on the probable advantages of
steam carriages, which, being merely problematical,
I bore my part in with some credit, in spite of my
totally un-engineer-like faculties. But when, somewhere about Stanstead, he put an unfortunate question to me, as to "the probability of its turning out
a good turnip season," and when I, who am still less
of an agriculturist than a steam philosopher, not
knowing a turnip from a potato ground, innocently
made answer, " I believe it depends very much upon
boiled legs of mutton," my unlucky reply set Miss
Isola a laughing to a degree that disturbed her tran-

quillity for the only moment in our journey. I am afraid my credit sank very low with my other fellow-traveller, who had thought he had met with a *well-informed passenger*, which is an accident so desirable in a stage coach. We were rather less communicative, but still friendly, the rest of the way.

How I employed myself between Epping and Enfield, the poor verses in the front of my paper may inform you, which you may please to christen an "Acrostic in a Cross Road," and which I wish were worthier of the lady they refer to; but I trust you will plead my pardon to her on a subject so delicate as a lady's good *name*. Your candour must acknowledge that they are written straight. And now, dear Madam, I have left myself hardly space to express my sense of the friendly reception I found at Fornham. Mr. Williams will tell you that we had the pleasure of a slight meeting with him on the road, where I could almost have told him, but that it seemed ungracious, that such had been your hospitality, that I scarcely missed the good master of the family at Fornham, though heartily I should have rejoiced to have made a little longer acquaintance with him. I will say nothing of our deeper obligations to both of you, because I think we agreed at Fornham that gratitude may be over-exacted on the part of the obliging, and over-expressed on the part of the obliged person.

My sister and Miss Isola join in respects to Mr. Williams and yourself. Miss Isola will have the pleasure of writing to you next week, and we shall hope at your leisure to hear of your own health, &c.

I am, dear Madam, with great respect, your obliged

CHARLES LAMB.

LETTER CCCXXXV.]

TO THE SAME.

Enfield, Good Friday [1830.]

Dear Madam,—I do assure you that your verses gratified me very much, and my sister is quite *proud* of them. For the first time in my life I congratulated myself upon the shortness and meanness of my name. Had it been Schwartzenberg or Esterhazy, it would have put you to some puzzle. I am afraid I shall sicken you of acrostics, but this last was written *to order*. I beg you to have inserted in your county paper something like this advertisement: "To the nobility, gentry, and others, about Bury.—C. Lamb respectfully informs his friends and the public in general, that he is leaving off business in the acrostic line, as he is going into an entirely new line. Rebuses and Charades done as usual, and upon the old terms. Also, Epitaphs to suit the memory of any person deceased."

I thought I had adroitly escaped the rather un-pliable name of "Williams," curtailing your poor daughters to their proper surnames; but it seems you would not let me off so easily. If these trifles amuse you, I am paid. Though really 'tis an operation too much like—"A, apple-pie; B, bit it." To make amends, I request leave to lend you the "Excursion," and to recommend, in particular, the "Churchyard Stories;" in the seventh book, I think. They will strengthen the tone of your mind after its weak diet on acrostics.

Miss Isola is writing, and will tell you that we are going on very comfortably. Her sister is just come. She blames my last verses, as being more written on Mr. Williams than on yourself; but how should I have parted whom a Superior Power has brought together? I beg you will jointly accept of our best respects, and pardon your obsequious if not troublesome correspondent,   C. L.

P.S.—I am the worst folder-up of a letter in the world, except certain Hottentots, in the land of Caffre, who never fold up their letters at all, writing very badly upon skins, &c.

LETTER CCCXXXVI.]

TO MR. ROGERS.

Dec. 1833.

My dear Sir,—Your book, by the unremitting punctuality of your publisher, has reached me thus early. I have not opened it, nor will till to-morrow, when I promise myself a thorough reading of it. The " Pleasures of Memory " was the first school present I made to Mrs. Moxon; it has those nice wood-cuts, and I believe she keeps it still. Believe me, that all the kindness you have shown to the husband of that excellent person seems done unto myself. I have tried my hand at a sonnet in the *Times*; but the turn

I gave it, though I hoped it would not displease you, I thought might not be equally agreeable to your artist. I met that dear old man at poor Henry's, with you, and again at Cary's, and it was sublime to see him sit, deaf, and enjoy all that was going on in mirth with the company. He reposed upon the many graceful, many fantastic images he had created; with them he dined, and took wine. I have ventured at an antagonist copy of verses, in the *Athenæum*, to *him*, in which he is as every thing, and you as nothing. He is no lawyer who cannot take two sides. But I am jealous of the combination of the sister arts. Let them sparkle apart. What injury (short of the theatres) did not Boydell's Shakspeare Gallery do me with Shakspeare? to have Opie's Shakspeare, North-cote's Shakspeare, light-headed Fuseli's Shakspeare, heavy-headed Romney's Shakspeare, wooden-headed West's Shakspeare, (though he did the best in Lear,) deaf-headed Reynolds's Shakspeare, instead of my and every body's Shakspeare; to be tied down to an authentic face of Juliet! to have Imogen's por- trait! to confine the illimitable! I like you and Stothard, (you best,) but " out upon this half-faced fellowship ! " Sir, when I have read the book, I may trouble you, through Moxon, with some faint criti- cisms. It is not the flatteringest compliment, in a letter to an author, to say you have not read his book yet. But the devil of a reader he must be who prances through it in five minutes ; and no longer have I received the parcel. It was a little tantalizing to me to receive a letter from Landor, *Gebir* Landor, from Florence, to say he was just sitting down to read my " Elia," just received : but the letter was to go out before the reading. There are calamities in authorship which only authors know.   I am going to call on Moxon on Monday, if the throng of carriages in Dover Street, on the morn of publication, do not barricade me out.

With many thanks, and most respectful remembrances to your sister,

Yours,   C. LAMB.

Have you seen Coleridge's happy exemplification in English of the Ovidian Elegiac metre ?

> In the Hexameter rises the fountain's silvery current,
> In the Pentameter aye falling in melody down.

My sister is papering up the book,—careful soul !

LETTER CCCXXXVII.]

TO MR. CHILDS.

Monday.   Church Street, Edmonton,
(not Enfield, as you erroneously
direct yours). [Sept. 15, 1834.]

Dear Sir,—The volume which you seem to want is not to be had for love or money.   I with difficulty procured a copy for myself.   Yours is gone to enlighten the tawny Hindoos.   What a supreme felicity to the author (only he is no traveller) on the Ganges or Hydaspes (Indian streams) to meet a smutty Gentoo ready to burst with laughing at the tale of Bo-Bo ! for doubtless it hath been translated into all the dialects of the East.   I grieve the less, that Europe should want it.   I cannot gather from your letter whether you are aware that a second series of the Essays is published by Moxon, in Dover Street, Piccadilly, called " The Last Essays of Elia," and, I am told, is not inferior to the former.   Shall I order a copy for you ? and will you accept it ?   Shall I *lend* you, at the same time, my sole copy of the former volume (Oh! return it) for a month or two?   In return, you shall favour me with the loan of one of those Norfolk-bred grunters that you laud so highly ; I promise not to keep it above a day.   What a funny name Bungay is! I never dreamt of a correspondent thence.[1]   I used to think of it as some Utopian town, or borough in Gotham land.   I now believe in its existence, as part of merry England.

[Here are some lines scratched out.]

The part I have scratched out is the best of the letter. Let me have your commands.

CH. LAMB, *alias* ELIA.

LETTER CCCXXXVIII.]

TO BENJAMIN ROBERT HAYDON.

[No date.]

My dear Haydon,—I will come with pleasure to 22, Lisson Grove, North, at Rosse's, half-way up, right-hand side, if I can find it.

Yours,   C. LAMB.

20, *Russell Court,*
    Covent Garden, East.
        Half-way up, next the corner,
            Left-hand side.

---

[1] Had Lamb never heard of the " Black Dog of Bungay" ?

The twenty-two Letters that follow, have been placed at the Editor's disposal by Mr. Forster. They form a most interesting contribution to the Series, and illustrate Lamb's affectionate nature in a high degree.

---

*LETTER CCCXXXIX.]

TO MRS. COLLIER.

I do not know what news to send you. You will have heard of Alsager's death, and your son John's success in the Lottery. I say he is a wise man if he leaves off while he's well. The weather is wet to weariness; but Mary goes puddling about a-shopping after a gown for the winter. She wants it good and cheap. Now I hold that no good things are cheap, pig-presents always excepted. In this mournful weather I sit moping. Where I now write, in an office dark as Erebus, jammed in between four walls, and writing by candle-light, most melancholy. Never see the light of the sun six hours in the day; and am surprised to find how pretty it shines on Sundays. I wish I were a Caravan driver, or a Penny Postman, to earn my bread in air and sunshine. Such a pedestrian as I am, to be tied by the legs, like a Fauntleroy, without the pleasure of his Exactions! I am interrupted here with an official question, which will take me up till it is time to go to dinner. So with repeated thanks, and both our kindest remembrances to Mr. Collier and yourself, I conclude in haste,

Yours and his sincerely,

C. LAMB.

From my Den in Leadenhall,
November 24.

On further inquiry, Alsager is not dead; but Mrs. A. is brought to bed.

Mrs. Collier,
Smallfield Place,
East Grinstead, Sussex.

---

*LETTER CCCXL.]

TO THE SAME.

Dear Mrs. Collier,—We receive so much pig from your kindness, that I really have not phrase enough to vary successive acknowledgments. I think I shall get a printed form to serve on all occasions. To say it was young, crisp, short, luscious, dainty-toed, is but to say, what all its predecessors have been. It was eaten on Tuesday and Monday, and doubts only exist as to which temperature it eat best at?—hot or cold. I incline to the latter. The petty-feet made a pretty surprising pre-gustation for supper on Saturday night, just as I was loathingly in expectation of bren-cheese. I spell as I speak.

---

*LETTER CCCXLI.]   Chase Side, October, 1827.

TO H. CRABB ROBINSON.

Dear R.,—I am settled for life I hope at Enfield. I have taken the prettiest, compactest house I ever saw, near to Antony Robinson's! but, alas! at the expense of poor Mary, who was taken ill of her old complaint the night before we got into it. So I must suspend the pleasure I expected in the surprise you would have had in coming down, and finding us householders. Farewell, till we can all meet comfortable. Pray apprise Martin Burney. Him I longed to have seen with you; but our house is too small to meet either of you without *her* knowledge.

God bless you.

December 26.

She's well again.

---

*Letter CCCXLII.]

TO CHARLES OLLIER.

Dear O.,—I leave *it entirely to Mr. C*——; but if not too late, I think the Proverbs had better have L signed to them, and reserve *Elia* for Essays *more Eliacal.* May I trouble you to send my Magazine, not to Norris, but H. C. Robinson, Esq., King's Bench Walk, instead.

Yours truly,   C. LAMB.

My friend Hood, a prime genius and hearty fellow, brings this.

Mr. Ollier.

---

*Letter CCCXLIII.]   9 April, 1832.

TO W. S. LANDOR.

Dear Sir,—Pray accept a little volume. 'Tis a legacy from Elia, you'll see. Silver and gold had he none, but such as he had left he you.   I do not know how to thank you for attending to my request about the Album.   I thought you would never remember it.   Are not you proud and thankful, Emma?   Yes;   *very*, *both*.   [Signed.]

EMMA ISOLA.

Many things I had to say to you, which there was not time for.   One, why should I forget? 'tis for Rose Aylmer, which has a charm I cannot explain. I lived upon it for weeks.   Next, I forgot to tell you I knew all your Welsh annoyances, the measureless B.'s[1]   I knew a quarter of a mile of them. Seventeen brothers and sixteen sisters, as they appear to me in memory.   There was one of them that used to fix his long legs on my fender, and tell a tale of a shark every night, endless, immortal. How have I grudged the salt sea ravener not having had his gorge of him !   The shortest of the daughters measured five foot eleven without her shoes.   Well, some day we may confer about them.   But they were tall.   Truly, I have discover'd the longitude.   Sir, if you can spare a moment, I should be happy to hear from you.   That rogue Robinson, detained your verses till I call'd for them.   Don't entrust a bit of prose to the rogue ;   but believe me,

Your obliged,   C. L.

W. S. Landor, Esq.
    From Ch. Lamb.

---

[1] See Mr. Forster's "*Walter Savage Landor*, a Biography." Vol. i. pp. 332 et 384.—F,

*LETTER CCCXLIV.]

TO THE SAME.

I am a little more than half alive. I was more than half dead. The ladies are very agreeable. I flatter myself I am less than disagreeable. Convey this to Mr. Forster; whom with you I shall just be able to see some ten days hence, and believe me,

Ever yours,   C. L.

I take Forster's name to be John; but you know whom I mean, the Pym-praiser, not pimp-raiser.

Mr. Moxon,
64, New Bond Street.
June 1, 1832.

LETTER CCCXLV.]

TO JOHN FORSTER.

(With Acrostics enclosed.)

To M. L. [MARY LOCKE.]

Must I write with pen unwilling,
And describe those graces killing,
Rightly, which I never saw?
Yes—it is the album's law.

Let me then invention strain,
On your excellence grace to feign,
Cold is fiction.   I believe it
Kindly as I did receive it;
Even as I, F.'s tongue did weave it.

To S. L. [SARAH LOCKE.]

Shall I praise a face unseen,
And extol a fancied mien,

Rave on visionary charm,
And from shadows take alarm !
Hatred hates without a cause.

Love may love without applause,
Or, without a reason given,
Charmed be with unknown heaven.
Keep the secret, though, unmocked,
Ever in your bosom Locked.

Am I *right ?*   *Sarah* I distinctly remember; but *Mary* I am not sure ought not to be *Anne.*   It is soon rectified in that case.   *You,* I take to be John.

C. L.

---

*LETTER CCCXLVI.]

TO THE SAME.

There was a talk of Richmond on Sunday ; but we are hampered with an unavoidable engagement that day ; besides that, I wish to show it you when its woods are in full leaf.   Can you have a quiet evening here to-night, or to-morrow night ?

We are certainly at home.

Yours,   C. LAMB.

Friday, 1832.

---

*LETTER CCCXLVII.]   April 24, 1833.

TO THE SAME.

Do come.

I have placed poor Mary at Edmonton.   I shall be very glad to see the Hunch Back[1] and Straight Back,

---

[1] Referring to Knowles' Play of that name.—F.

the first evening they can come. I am very poorly indeed; I have been cruelly thrown out. Come, and don't let me drink too much. I drank more yesterday than I ever did any one day in my life.

---

*LETTER CCCXLVIII.]

TO THE SAME.

Dear Boy,—I send you the original Elias, complete. When I am a little composed, I shall hope to see you and Procter here; may be, may see you first in London.

C. L.

J. Forster, Esq.,
  From C. L. Mr. Walden's,
      Church Street, Edmonton.
May 13th, 1833.

---

*LETTER CCCXLIX.]

TO THE SAME.

Dear F.,—Can you oblige me by sending four Box orders undated, for the Olympic Theatre? I suppose Knowles can get 'em. It is for the Waldens, with whom I live. The sooner the better, that they may not miss the "Wife." I meet you at the Talfourds Saturday week; and if they can't, perhaps you can give me a bed.

Yours, ratherish unwell,

C. LAMB.

Or write immediately to say if you can't get 'em.

*LETTER CCCL.]

TO THE SAME.

If you have lost a little portion of my good will,
it is that you do not come and see me. Arrange
with Procter, when you have done with your moving
accidents.

Yours, Ambulaturus,

C. L.

June 25, 1834.

---

*LETTER CCCLI.]

TO THE SAME.

Swallow your damn'd dinner, and your brandy and
water fast, and come immediately. I want to take
Knowles in to Emma's only female friend for just
five minutes. We are free for the evening. I'll do
a Prologue.

---

*LETTER CCCLII.]

TO THE SAME.

Come down to-morrow or Saturday, be here by two
or half after ; coaches from Snow Hill. I wish you'd
go to Dilke's or let Mockson, and ax him to add this
to what I sent him a few days since, and to continue it the week after. The Plantas, &c., are
capital. Come down with Procter and Dante on
Sunday. I send you the last proof—not of my friendship. I knew you would like the title ; I do

thoroughly. The last Essays of Elia keeps out any notion of its being a second volume.

C. Lamb.

John Foster (or Forrester).

I don't mean at his house, but the Athenæum Office, send it there. Hand shakes.

---

*Letter CCCLIII.]

TO MR. MOXON.

I want to see Forester (not the German Foust) I met with a man at my half-way house, who told me many anecdotes of Kean's younger life. He knew him thoroughly. His name is Wyatt, living near the Bell, Edmonton. Also he referred me to West, a publican opposite St. George's Church, Southwark, who knew him *more* intimately. Is it worth Forster's while to inquire after them ?

E. Moxon, Esq.,
    Edmonton, January 28.

---

*Letter CCCLIV.]

TO THE SAME.

This is my notion. Wait till you are able to throw away a round sum (say £1500) upon a specu-lation, and then don't do it. For all your loving encouragements—till this final damp came in the shape of your letter—thanks; and for books also. Greet the Forsters and Procters—and come singly or conjunctively as soon as you can. Johnson and Fare's sheets have been washed—unless you prefer **Danby's** *last* bed at the Horseshoe. [1]

December, 1832.
   To Mr. Moxon.

PROLOGUE.

Last line alter to—

> A *store* of gratitude is left behind.

Because, as it now stands, if the Author lays his hand upon his heart, and emfattically says—

> I have (so and so) behind,

the audience may think it odd, and, so in fact, it is. Mind, I don't care the 100,000th part of a bad sixpence if Knowles gets a Prologue more to his mind.

       Yours, by old and new ties,

                   C. LAMB.

E. Moxon, Esq.
   1833.

---

*LETTER CCCLV.]

TO THE SAME.

I shall expect Forster and two Moxons on Sunday, and hope for Procter. I am obliged to be in town next Monday. Could we contrive to make a party (paying or not is immaterial) for Miss Kelly's that night; and can you shelter us after the play—I mean Emma and me. I fear I cannot persuade **Mary** to join us.

N.B.—*I can sleep at a public house.* Send an Elia

---

[1] Allusion to a murder which had caused great excitement in his peaceful village.—*Note by Mr. Forster.*—F.

(mind I *insist* on your buying it,) to T. Manning, Esq., at Sir G. Tuthill's, Cavendish Square.   Do write.

E. Moxon.   March 19, 1833.

---

*LETTER CCCLVI.]

TO THE SAME.

Dear M.,—A thousand thanks for your punctualities.   What a cheap book is the last Hogarth you sent me!   I am pleased now that Hunt *diddled* me out of the old one.   Speaking of this, only think of the new farmer with his thirty acres.   There is a portion of land in Lambeth Parish, called Knave's Acre.   I wonder he overlook'd it.   Don't show this to the firm of D—— and Co.   I next want one copy of Leicester's School, and wish you to pay Leishman, Taylor, 2, Blandford Place, Pall Mall, opposite the British Institution, £6 10s., for coat and waistcoat, &c., &c., and I vehemently thirst for the fourth No. of Nichols's Hogarth, to bind one up (the two books) as Hogarth and Supplement.   But as you know the price, don't stay for its appearance; but come as soon as ever you can with your bill of all demands in full, and as I have none but £5 notes, bring with you sufficient change.   Weather is beautiful.   I grieve sadly for Miss Wordsworth.   We are all well again. Emma is with us, and we all shall be glad of a sight of you.   Come on Sunday if you *can*, better if you come before.

Perhaps Rogers would smile at this.   A pest, half chemist, half apothecary in our town who smatters of literature, and is immeasurably unlettered, said to me,

" Pray, sir, may not Hood be reckon'd the Prince of
Wits in the present day ?"   To which I assenting, he
adds "I had always thought that Rogers had been
reckon'd the Prince of Wits, but I suppose that now
Mr. Hood has the better title to that appellation."   To
which I replied, that Mr. R. had wit with much better
qualities, but did not aspire to the principality.   He
had taken all the puns manufactured in John Bull for
our friend, in sad and stupid earnest.   One moro
Album Verses, please.   Adieu.

                                        C. L.

*LETTER CCCLVII.]

TO MR. MOXON.

Dear M.,—Emma has tiezed me to take hei into
the gallery of an opera on Tuesday, and I have
written for orders.   We came up this morning.
Can you house and bed us after the opera ?   Miss M.,
maybe, won't object to sharing half her bed.   And
for *me*, I can sleep on straw, rushes, thorns, Procrustes'
couch I or anywhere.   Do not write if you *can take*
us in.   Write only IF YOU can't.

                                        CH. LAMB.

*LETTER CCCLVIII.]

TO THE SAME.

I wish you would omit " by the Author of Elia"
now, in advertising that damn'd " Devil's Wedding."
I had sneaking hopes you would have dropt in to-day,
'tis my poor birthday.   Don't stay away so.   Give

*F*orster a hint. You are to bring your brother some day—*sisters* in better weather. Pray give me one line to say if you receiv'd and forwarded Emma's pacquet to Miss Adams—and how Dover Street looks. Adieu. Is there no Blackwood this month? What separation will there be between the Friend's preface and THE ESSAYS? Should not " Last Essays, &c., &c.," head them? If 'tis too late, don't mind. I don't care a farthing about it.

Mr. Moxon. February 11, 1833.

---

*LETTER CCCLIX.]

TO H. C. ROBINSON.

For Landor's kindness I have just esteem. I shall tip him a letter when you tell me how to address him. Give Emma's kindest regrets that I could not entice her good friend, your Nephew, here. Our warmest love to the Bury Robinsons. Our all three to H. Crabb.

C. L.

H. C. Robinson, Esq.
2, Plowden's Buildings, Middle Temple.
January, 1833.

---

*LETTER CCCLX.]

TO JAMES KENNEY.

Dear Ken,—I will not see London again without seeing your pleasant Play. In meanwhile, pray send three or four orders to a lady who can't afford to pay, Miss James, No. 1, Grove Road, Lisson Grove, Paddington, a day or two before; and come and see us some evening, with my hitherto uncorrupted and honest bookseller, Moxon.

C. LAMB.

This contribution has a melancholy interest. Mr. Forster was revising these letters when he was seized with his last illness. It will be seen how, when a mere youth, he had won on Charles Lamb, as he was later to win on so many others, who now, like the Editor, bewail the loss of the best and truest of friends, the kindest heart, and most affectionate nature. Only a short time before his death, as he was turning over the originals of these letters, the tears came into his eyes, and his lip trembled as he spoke, of " Poor Charles Lamb !"

Feb. 1, 1876.

LETTER CCCLXI.]

TO———

(A portion of a letter.)

—— Calamy is *good reading;* Mary is always thankful for books in her way. I won't trouble you for any in *my way,* yet having enough to read. Young Hazlitt lives, at least his father does, at 3 or 36 [36 I have it down with the 6 scratch'd out] Bouverie Street, Fleet Street. If not to be found, his mother's address is Mrs. Hazlitt, Mrs. Tomlinson's, Potter's Bar. At one or other he must be heard of. We shall expect you with the full moon. Meantime, our thanks.

C. L.

We go on very quietly, &c.

LETTER CCCLXII.]

TO A PUBLISHER.

Dear Sir,—I beg leave, in the warmest manner, to recommend to your notice, Mr. ———, the bearer of this, if by any chance yourself should want a steady hand in your business, or know of any Publisher that may want such a one. He is at present in the house of Messrs. Longman and Co., where he has been established for more than six years; and has the conduct of one of the four departments of the Country Line. A difference respecting salary, which he expected to be a little raised on his last promotion, makes him wish to try to better himself. I believe him to be a young man of the highest integrity, and a thorough man of business; and should not have taken the liberty of recommending him, if I had not thought him capable of being highly useful.

I am, Sir,

With great respect,

Your obedient Servant,

CHARLES LAMB.

Enfield, Chase Side,
September 25, 1827.

LETTER CCCLXIII.]

TO THOMAS ALLSOP.

Dear Sir,—Many thanks for your offer. I have desired the youth to wait upon you, if you will give him leave, that he may give his own answer to your kind proposal of trying to find something for him.

My sister begs you will accept her thanks with mine. We shall be at home at all times, most happy to see you when you are in town. We are mostly to be found in an evening.

Your obliged,

C. LAMB.

Saturday, November 29, 1819.

LETTER CCCLXIV.]

TO THE SAME.

Dear Sir,—We are most sorry to have missed you twice. We are at home to-night, to-morrow, & Thursday, & should be happy to see you any of these nights. Thanks for the shining bird.

Yours truly,.

C. L.

LETTER CCCLXV.]

TO THE SAME.

Dear Sir,—The hairs of our head are numbered, but those which emanate from your heart defy arithmetic. I would send longer thanks, but your young man is blowing his fingers in the Passage.

Yours gratefully,

C. L.

LETTER CCCLXVI.]

TO THE SAME.

Dear Sir,—Your hare arrived in excellent order

Last night, and I hope will prove the precursor of yourself on Sunday.

Why you should think it necessary to appease us with so many pleasant presents, I know not.

More acknowledgements when we meet; we dine at 3.

Yours truly.

C. LAMB.

Thursday.

———

My dear Sir,—We shall hope to see you to-morrow evening to a rubber. Thanks for your very kind letter, and intentions respecting a bird.

Yours very truly,

C. LAMB.

———

Dear Sir,—We expected you here to-night; but as you have invited us to-morrow evening, we shall dispose of this evening as we intended to have done of to-morrow. We shall be with you by 8, and shall have taken Tea.

Your (not obliging but oblidged)

C. & M. LAMB.

Monday 10th.

———

LETTER CCCLXVII.]

Dear Sir,—I have brought you Rosamund Bp. of Landaff's daughter's novel. We shall have a small party, on Thursday evening, if you will do us the favour to join it.

Yours truly,

C. LAMB.

Tuesday evening, 15 February, 1820.

Dear Sir,—We expect Wordsworth to-morrow evening. Will you look in ?

C. L.

Russell House, Thursday.

Dear Sir,—Wordsworth is with us this Even. Can you come ? We leave Cov. Gard. on Thursday for some time.

C. L.

LETTER CCCLXVIII.]

TO THE SAME.

Dear Sir,—We have arranged to be in the country Saturday & Sunday, having made an engagement to that effect. Pray let us see you on Thursday at Russell House.

With regrets & all proper feelings,

Yours truly,

820

C. L.

Dear Sir,—You shall see us on Thursday, with M.
B., if possible, about 8. We shall have Teaed.

Yours truly,

C. L.

M. B.'s direction is 26, James **Street,** Westminster
—James, not St. James, Street.

LETTER CCCLXIX.]

TO THE SAME.

My Dear Sir,—If you can come next Sunday we
shall be equally glad to see you, but do not trust to
any of Martin's appointments, except on business, in
future. He is notoriously faithless in that point, and
we did wrong not to have warned you. Leg of Lamb,
as before, hot at 4. And the heart of Lamb ever.

Yours truly,

C. L.

30 March, 1821.

LETTER CCCLXX.]

TO THE SAME.

Dear Sir,—Thanks for the Birds and your kindness.
It was but yesterday I was contriving with Talfourd
to meet you ½ way at his chamber. But night
don't do so well at present. I shall want to be home
at Dalston by Eight.

I will pay an afternoon visit to you when you
please. I dine at a chop-house at one always, but I

G 2

can spend an hour with you after that.   Would
Saturday serve?

Yours truly,

C. L.

Ecce iterum:

LDTTER CCCLXXI.]

TO THE SAME.

Dear Sir,—I fear I was obscure. I was plaguily
busy when those tempting birds came. I meant to
say I could not come this evening; but any other, if
I can know a day before, I can come for 2 or 3
afternoon hours, from $\frac{1}{4}$ to four to $\frac{1}{2}$ past six. At
present I cannot command more furlough. I have
nam'd Saturday. I will come, if you don't counter-
mand. I shall have dined. I have been wanting
not not to see you.

C. L.

LETTER CCCLXXII.]

TO THE SAME.

Dear Sir,—I do not know whose fault it is we have
not met so long. We are almost always out of town.
You must come & beat up our quarters there, when
we return from Cambridge. It is not in our power to
accept your invitation. To-day we dine out; and set
out for Cambridge on Saturday morning. Friday of
course will be past in packing, &c., moreover we go
from Dalston. We return from Cam. in 4 weeks,
& will contrive an early meeting. Meantime believe us,

Sincerely yours,

C. L., &c.

Thursday.

LETTER CCCLXXIII.]

TO THE SAME.

Dear Sir,—I hear that you have called in Russell St. I cannot say when I shall be in town. When I am, I must see you; I had hoped to have seen you at Dalston, but my Sister is taken ill, I am afraid will not be able to see any of her friends for a long time.

Believe me, yours truly,

C. LAMB.

India House.

LETTER CCCLXXIV.]

TO THE SAME.

Dear Allsop, — We are going to Dalston on Wednesday. Will you come see the last of us to-morrow night—you and Mrs. Allsop?

Yours truly,

C. LAMB.

Monday Evening.

Dear Allsop,—Your pheasant is glittering, but your company will be more acceptable this evening. Wordsworth is not with us, but the next things to him are.

C. LAMB.

Monday Evening.

LETTER CCCLXXV.]

TO THE SAME.

D. A.,—I expect Procter and Wainwright (Janus W.) this evening: will you come? I suppose it is but a compliment to ask Mrs. Allsop? but it is none to say that we should be glad to see her. Yours Ever. How vexed I am at your Dalston expedition.

C. L.

Tuesday.

LETTER CCCLXXVI.]

TO THE SAME.

My dear A.,—I am going to ask you to do me the greatest favour which a man can do for another. I want to make my will, and to leave my property in trust for my Sister. N.B. I am not therefore going to die.—Would it be unpleasant for you to be named for one? The other two I shall beg the same favour of are Talfourd and Procter. If you feel reluctant, tell me, and it sha'n't abate one jot of my friendly feeling toward you.

Yours ever,

C. LAMB.

E. I. House, 9 Aug. 1823.

LETTER CCCLXXVII.]

TO THE SAME.

Dear Allsop,—I am snugly seated at the cottage. Mary is well, but weak, and comes home on Monday; she will soon be strong enough to see her friends here. In the mean time, will you dine with me at ¼ past four to-morrow? Ayrton and Mr. Burney are coming.

Colebrook Cottage, left hand side, end of Colebrook Row, on the western brink of the New River, a detach'd whitish house.

No answer is required, but come if you can.

C. LAMB.

Saturday, 6 Sep. 1823.

I called on you on Sunday.   Respects to Mrs. A. & boy.

LETTER CCCLXXVIII.]

TO THE SAME.

My dear A.,—Your kindness in accepting my request no words of mine can repay.   It has made you overflow into some romance which I should have check'd at another time.   I hope it may be in the scheme of Providence that my sister may go first (if ever so little a precedence), myself next, and my good Executors survive to remember us with kindness many years.   God bless you.

I will set Procter about the will forthwith.

C. LAMB.

Sep. 10, 1823.

LETTER CCCLXXIX.]

TO THE SAME.

My dear Allsop,—I thank you for thinking of my recreation.   But I am best here—I feel I am ; I have tried town lately, but came back worse.   Here I must wait till my loneliness has its natural cure.   Besides that, though I am not very sanguine, yet I live in hopes of better news from Fulham, and cannot be out

of the way.   'Tis ten weeks to-morrow.—I saw Mary
a week since ; she was in excellent bodily health, but
otherwise far from well.   But a week or so may give
a turn.   Love to Mrs. A. & children, and fair weather
accompany you.

C. L.

Tuesday, 1823.

LETTER CCCLXXX.]

TO THE SAME.

Dear A.,—Your Cheese is the best I ever tasted ;
Mary will tell you so hereafter.   She is at home, but
has disappointed me.   She has gone back rather than
improved.   However, she has sense enough to value
the present ; for she is greatly fond of Stilton.   Yours
is the delicatest, rain-bow-hued, melting piece I ever
flavoured.   Believe me, I took it the more kindly,
following so great a kindness.

Depend upon't, yours shall be one of the first
houses we shall present ourselves at, when we have
got our Bill of Health.

Being both yours and Mrs. Allsop's truly.

1823.   C. L. & M. L.

LETTER CCCLXXXI.]

TO THE SAME.

Dear Sir,—Will Mrs. A. & you dine with us to-
morrow at ¼ past 3 ?   Do not think of troubling yourself to send (if you cannot come), as we shall provide

only a goose (which is in the House), and your not coming will make no difference in our arrangements.

Your obliged,

C. LAMB.

Saturday, 4 October, 1823.

LETTER CCCLXXXII.]

TO THE SAME.

Dear Sir,—Mary has got a cold, and the nights are dreadful; but at the first indication of Spring (alias the first dry weather in November, *early*) it is our intention to surprise you early some evening.

Believe me, most truly yours,

C. L.

The Cottage, Saturday night.

Mary regrets very much Mrs. Allsop's fruitless visit. It made her swear! She was gone to visit Miss Hutchinson, whom she found out.

LETTER CCCLXXXIII.]

TO THE SAME.

Dear Allsop,—Our dinner-hour on Sundays is 4, at which we shall be most happy to see Mrs. A. & yourself—I mean next Sunday, but I also mean any Sunday. Pray come. I am up to my very ears in business, but pray come.

Yours most sincerely,

C. L.

E. I. H., 7th November.

LETTER CCCLXXXIV.]

TO MRS. ALLSOP.

Dear Mrs. A.,—Mary begs me to say how much she regrets we cannot join you to Reigate: our reasons are—1st, I have but one holyday, namely Good Friday, and it is not pleasant to solicit for another, but that might have been got over. 2ndly, Manning is with us, soon to go away, and we should not be easy in leaving him. 3rdly, our school-girl Emma comes to us for a few days on Thursday. 4thly and lastly, Wordsworth is returning home in about a week, and out of respect to them we should not like to absent ourselves just now. In summer I shall have a month, and, if it shall suit, should like to go for a few days of it with you both any where. In the mean time, with many acknowledgements, &c., &c.

> I remain,
> Yours (both) truly,
> C. LAMB.

India House, 13 April.

Remember Sunday's.

LETTER CCCLXXXV.]

TO MR. ALLSOP.

Dear A.,—I am as mad as the devil—but I had engaged myself and Mary to accompany Mrs. Kenny to Kentish-Town to dinner at a common friend's on Friday, before I knew of Mary's engaging you.

Can you and Mrs. A. exchange the day for Sunday, or what other.

Write.

Success to the Gnomes!

C. LAMB.

Tuesday, May 29, 1825.

LETTER CCCLXXXVI.]

TO THE SAME.

Dear Allsop,—We are bent upon coming here to-morrow for a few weeks. Despatch a Porter to me this evening, or by nine to-morrow morning, to say how far it will interfere with your proposed coming down on Saturday. If the house will hold us, we can be together while we stay.

Yours,

C. LAMB.

Enfield, Thursday,

    After a hot walk.

LETTER CCCLXXXVII.]

Dear Allsop,—It is too hot to write. Here we are, having turned you out of your beds, but willing to resign in your favour, or make any shifts with you.

Our best Love's to Mrs. Allsop, from Mrs. Leishman's, this warm Saturday.

Yours truly,

C. LAMB.

This dam'ned afternoon sun ! Thanks for your note, which came in more than good time.

———

We are on a half visit to his [Coleridge's] friend Allsop, at a Mrs. Leishman's, Enfield ; but expect to be at Colebrook Cottage in a week or so.

August 19.

———

LETTER CCCLXXXVIII.]

TO THE SAME.

My Dear Allsop,—Mrs. Leishman gives us hopes of seeing you all on Sunday. We shall provide a bit of beef or something on that day, so you need not market. We are very comfortable here. Our kindest remembrances to Mrs. Allsop and the chits. We lying-in people go out on Saturday, Mrs. L. bids me say, and that you may come that evening and find beds, &c.

Yours truly,

C. LAMB.

Thursday.

———

LETTER CCCLXXXIX.]

TO THE SAME.

Dear A.,—Mary is afraid lest the calico & Handkerchiefs have miscarried which you were to send. Have you sent 'em.

Item a bill with 'em, including the former silks, & balance struck in a Tradesman-like way.

Yours truly,

C. L.

Enfield

LETTER CCCXC.]

TO THE SAME.

My Dear Allsop,—We are exceedingly grieved for your loss. When your note came, my sister went to Pall Mall, to find you, and saw Mrs. L., and was a little comfited to find Mrs. A. had returned to Enfield before the distressful event. I am very feeble. Can scarce move a pen; got home from Enfield on the Friday. And on Monday following was laid up with a most violent nervous fever—second this summer; have had Leeches to my Temples; have not had, nor can get, a night's sleep. So you will excuse more from

Yours truly,

C. LAMB.

Islington, 9 Sep.

Our most kind remembrances to poor Mrs. Allsop. A line to say how you both are will be most acceptable.

LETTER CCCXCI.]

TO THE SAME.

My Dear Allsop,—Come not near this unfortunate

roof vet a while. My disease is clearly but slowly going. Field is an excellent attendant. But Mary's anxieties have overturned her. She has her old Miss James with her, without whom I should not feel a support in the world. We keep in separate apart-ments, & must weather it. Let me know all of your healths. Kindest love to Mrs. Allsopp.

C. LAMB.

Saturday, Sep., 1825.

Can you call at Mrs. Burney, 26, James Street, and tell her, & that I can see no one here in this state. If Martin return, if well enough, I will meet him some where; don't let him come.

LETTER CCCXCII.]

TO THE SAME.

Dear Allsop,—Your kindness pursues us every where. That 8l. 4. 6. is a substantial proof, I think; I never should have ask'd for it. Pray keep it, when you get it, till we see each other. I have plenty of current cash; thank you over and over for your offer.

We came down on Monday with Miss James. The 1st night I lay broad awake like an owl till 8 o'clock, then got a poor doze. Have had something like sleep and a forgetting last night. We go on tolerably in this deserted house. It is melancholy, but I could not have gone into a quite strange one.

Newspapers come to you here. Pray stop them. Shall I send what have come?

Give mine and Mary's kindest love to Mrs. Allsop, with every good wish to Elizabeth and Rob. This house is not what it was.   May we all meet chearful some day soon.

Yours gratefully and sincerely,

C. LAMB.

How long a letter have I written with my own hand.

Jane says she has sent a cradle yesterday morning; she does for us very well.

Wednesday, Sept., 25.

LETTER CCCXCIII.]   Oct. 5, 1825.

TO THE SAME.

Dear A.,—Have received your drafts. We will talk that over Sunday morning. I am strongish, but have not good nights, & cannot settle my inside.

Farewell till Sunday.

I have no possible use for the 1st draft, so shall keep them as above.

Yours truly,

C. L.

Wednesday.

I only trouble you now because, if the drafts had miscarried, any one might have cash'd 'em. Remember at home.

Ludlow is charming.

LETTER CCCXCIV.

TO THE SAME.

My Dear Allsop,—Thanks for the Birds. Your announcement puzzles me sadly, as nothing came.

I send you back a word in your letter which I can positively make nothing [of], and therefore return to you as useless. It means to refer to the birds, but gives me no information. They are [on], the fire, however.

My Sister's illness is the most obstinate she ever had. It will not go away, and I am afraid Miss James will not be able to stay above a day or two longer. I am desperate to think of it sometimes.

'Tis eleven weeks !

The day is sad as my prospects.

With kindest love to Mrs. A. and the Children.

Yours,

C. L.

No Atlas this week. Poor Hone's good boy Alfred has fractured his skull ; another son is returned " dead " from the Navy Office ; & his Book is going to be given up, not having answered. What a world of troubles this is !

LETTER CCCXCV.]

TO THE SAME.

Dear Allsop.—My injunctions about not calling here had solely reference to your being unwell, &c. at home. I am most glad to see you on my own account. I dine at 3 on either Sunday ; come then, or earlier or later ; only before dinner I generally walk. Your dining here will be quite convenient. I of course have a Joint that day. I owe you for Newspapers, Cobbetts, pheasants, what not ?

Yours Most Obliged,

C. L.

P.S. I am so well (except Rheumatism, which

forbids my being out on evenings) that I forgot to mention my health in the above.   Mary is very poorly yet.   Love to Mrs. Allsop.

LETTER CCCXCVI.]   [December 5, 1825.]

TO THE SAME.

Dear A.,—You will be glad to hear we are at home to Visitors ; not too many or noisy.   Some fine day shortly Mary will surprise Mrs. Allsop.   The weather is not seasonable for formal engagements.

Yours most ever,
C. LAMB.

Saturday.

LETTER CCCXCVII.]

Dear Allsop,—Mary will take her chance of an early lunch or dinner with you on Thursday :   She can't come on Wednesday.   If I can, I will fetch her home.   But I am near killed with Christmasing ; and, if incompetent, your kindness will excuse me.   I can scarce set foot to ground for a cramp that I took me last night.

Yours,
C. LAMB.

Tuesday.

LETTER CCCXCVIII.]

TO THE SAME.

Dear Allsop,—I acknowledge with thanks the receipt of a draft on Messrs. Wms. for 8l. 11. 3.

which I haste to cash in the present alarming state
of the money market.   Hurst and Robinson gone.   I
have imagined a Chorus of ill-used Authors singing
on the Occasion :

What should we when Booksellers break?
We should rejoice.

Da capo.

We regret exceedingly Mrs. Allsopp's being unwell.
Mary or both will come and see her soon.   The frost
is cruel, and we have both colds.   I take Pills again,
which battle with your Wine ; and Victory hovers
doubtful.   By the by, tho' not disinclined to presents,
I remember our bargain to take a dozen at sale price,
and must demur.

With once again thanks and best loves to Mrs. A.
Turn over—Yours,

C. LAMB.

Colebrook Cottage, Islington, 7 Jan., 1825.

LETTER CCCXCIX.]   Jan. 25, 1827.

TO THE SAME.

My Dear Allsop,—I cannot forbear thanking you
for your kind interference with Taylor, whom I do
not expect to see in haste at Islington.

It is hardly weather to ask a dog up here, but I
need hardly say how happy we shall be to see you.   I
cannot be out of evenings till John Frost be routed.
We came home from Newman St. the other night
late, and I was crampt all night.

Loves to Mrs. Allsop.

Yours truly,

C. L.

Letter CCCC.]

My Dear Allsop,—I have writ to say to you that I
hope to have a comfortable X-mas-day with Mary,
and I cannot bring myself to go from home at present.
Your kind offer, and the kind consent of the young
Lady to come, we feel as we should do; pray accept
all of you our kindest thanks: at present I think a
Visitor (good and excellent as we remember her to be)
might a little put us out of our way. Emma is with
us, and our small house just holds us, without
obliging Mary to sleep with Becky, &c.

We are going on extremely comfortable, and shall
soon be in capacity of seeing our friends. Much weakness is left still. With thanks and old remembrances,
Yours,

C. L.

Dec. 20, 1827.

Letter CCCCI.]

TO THE SAME.

Dear Allsop,—I have been very poorly and nervous
lately; but on recovering sleep, &c., I do not write or
make engagements for particular days: but I need
not say how pleasant your dropping in any Sunday
morning would be. Perhaps Jameson would accompany you. Pray beg him to keep an accurate record
of the warning I sent him to old Pau., for I dread lest
he should at the 12 months' end deny the warning.
The house is his daughter's, but we took it through
him, and have paid the rent to his receipts for his

H 2

daughter's. Consult J. if he thinks the warning sufficient. I am very nervous, or have been, about the house; lost my sleep, & expected to be ill; but slumbered gloriously last night, golden slumbers. I shall not relapse ; you fright me with your inserted slips in the most welcome Atlas. They begin to charge double for it, and call it two sheets. How can I confute them by opening it, when a note of yours might slip out, and we get in a hobble? When you write, write real letters. Mary's best love and mine to Mrs. A.

Yours Ever,

C. LAMB.

Jan. 2, 1828.

LETTER CCCCII.]

TO THE SAME.

Dear A.,—I am better. Mary quite well. We expected to see you before. I can't write long letters. So a friendly love to you all.

Yours ever,

C. L.

Enfield.

This Sunshine is healing.

LETTER CCCCIII.

TO THE SAME.

Dear Allsop.,—Old Star is setting. Take him & cut him into Little Stars. Nevertheless, the extinction of the greater light is not by the lesser light (Stella, or Mrs. Star) apprehended so nigh, but that she will be thankful if you can let young Scintillation (Master Star) twinkle down by the coach on Sunday to catch the last glimmer of the decaying parental light.   No news is good news, so we conclude Mrs. A. and little A. are doing well.   Our kindest loves.

C. L.

LETTER CCCCIV.]

TO THE SAME.

At midsummer, or soon after (I will let you know the previous day), I will take a day with you in the purlieus of my old haunts.   No offence has been taken, any more than meant.   My house is full at present, but empty of its chief pride.   She is dead to me for many months.   But when I see you, then I will say, Come and see me.   With undiminished friendship to you both,

Your faithful, but queer,

C. L.

How you frighted me!   Never write again, ' Coleridge is dead,' at the end of a line, and tamely come in with, ' to his friends ' at the beginning of another.   Love is quicker, and fear from love, than the transition ocular from line to line.

LETTER CCCCV.]

TO THE SAME.

Dear Allsop,—I will find out your Bijoux some day.   At present, I am sorry to say, we have neither of us very good spirits; and I cannot look to any pleasant expeditions.

You speak of your trial as a known thing, but I am quite in the dark about it; but wish you a safe issue most heartily.

Our loves to Mrs. Allsop and children.

C. L.

1829.

LETTER CCCCVI.]

TO THE SAME.

My Dear Allsop,[1]—I think it will be impossible for us to come to Highgate in the time you propose. We have friends coming to-morrow, who may stay the week; and we are in a bustle about Emma's leaving us—so we will put off the hope of seeing Mrs. Allsop till we come to Town, after Emma's going, which is in a fortnight and a half, when we mean to spend a time in Town, but shall be happy to see you on Sunday, or any day.

In haste.   Hope our little Porter does.

Yours ever,

C. L.

July, 1833.

---

[1] This friendly correspondent of Lamb's still lives, and has interested himself in the present edition.—F

LETTER CCCCVII.]

East-India House, August 19, 1824.

TO THE REV. H. F. CARY.

Dear Sir,—I shall have much pleasure in dining with you on Wednesday next, with much shame that I have not noticed your kind present of the *Birds*,[1] which I found very chirping and whimsical.   I believe at the time I was daily thinking of paying you a visit, and put it off—till I should come.   Somehow it slipt, and [I] must crave your pardon.

Yours truly,

C. LAMB.

LETTER CCCCVIII.]

Colebrooke Row, Islington,
1st Feb., 1826.

TO MR. HUDSON.

Sir,—I was requested by Mr. Godwin to enquire about a nurse that you want for a lady who requires constraint.   The one I know does not go out now; but at Whitmore House, Mr. Warburton's, Hoxton, (to which she belongs), I dare say you may be very properly provided.   The terms are eight-and-twenty shillings a week, with her board; she finding her beer and washing: which is less expensive than for a female patient to be taken into a house of that description with any tolerable accommodation.

I am, Sir,

Your humble Servant,

C. LAMB.

[Indorsed:]
Mr. Hudson, Legacy Office, Somerset House.†

---

[1] Mr. Cary's version of the *Birds* of Aristophanes.

LETTER CCCCIX.]   March, 1827.

TO BENJAMIN HAYDON.

Dear Raffaele Haydon,—Did the maid tell you I came to see your picture, not on Sunday but the day before? I think the face and bearing of the Bucephalus tamer very noble, his flesh too effeminate or painty. The skin of the female's back kneeling is much more carnous. I had small time to pick out praise or blame, for two lord-like Bucks came in, upon whose strictures my presence seemed to impose restraint; I plebeian'd off therefore.

I think I have hit on a subject for you, but can't swear it was never executed—I never heard of its being—" Chaucer beating a Franciscan Friar in Fleet Street." Think of the old dresses, houses, &c. " It seemeth that both these learned men (Gower and Chaucer) were of the Inner Temple; for not many years since Master Buckley did see a record in the same house where Geoffry Chaucer was fined two shillings for beating a Franciscan Friar in Fleet Street."

Yours in haste (salt fish waiting),

C. LAMB.

LETTER CCCCX.]   August, 1828.

TO THE SAME.

Dear Haydon,—I have been tardy in telling you that your Chairing the Member gave me great pleasure— 'tis true broad Hogarthian fun, the High Sheriff capital. Considering, too, that you had the materials imposed upon you, and that you did not select them from the rude world as H. did, I hope to see many more such from your hand. If the former picture went beyond this I have had a loss, and the King a bargain. I longed to rub the back of my hand across the hearty canvas that two senses might be gratified. Perhaps the subject is a little discordantly placed opposite to another act of Chairing, where the huzzas were Hosannahs ! but I was pleased to see so many of my old acquaintances brought together notwithstanding.

Believe me, yours truly,

C. LAMB.

LETTER CCCCXI.]

TO MR. GILMAN.

Dear Sir,—You dine so late on Friday, it will be impossible for us to go home by the eight o'clock stage. Will you oblige us by securing us beds at some house, from which a stage goes to the Bank in the morning?   I would write to Coleridge, but cannot think of troubling a dying man with such a request.

Yours truly,

C. LAMB.

If the beds in the town are all engaged in consequence of Mr. Mathews's appearance, a Hackney coach will serve.

Wednesy, May 21.

We shall neither of us come much before the time.

LETTER CCCCXII.]   [April 9, 1810.]

TO JOHN MATHEW GUTCH.

Dear Gutch,—I did not see your brother, who brought me Wither; but he understood, he said, you were daily expecting to come to town: this has prevented my writing. The books have pleased me excessively: I should think you could not have made a better selection. I never saw *Philarete* before—judge of my pleasure. I could not forbear scribbling certain critiques in pencil on the blank leaves. Shall I send them, or may I expect to see you in town? Some of them are remarks on the character of Wither and of his writings. Do you mean to have any thing of that kind? What I have said on *Philarete* is poor, but I think some of the rest not so bad: perhaps I have exceeded my commission in scrawling over the copies; but my delight therein must excuse me, and pencil-marks will rub out. Where is the Life? Write, for I am quite in the dark.

                    Yours, with many thanks,
                                        C. LAMB.

Perhaps I could digest the few critiques prefixed to the Satires, Shepherds Hunting, &c., into a short abstract of Wither's character and works, at the end of his Life. But, may be, you don't want any thing, and have said all you wish in the Life.

LETTER CCCCXIII.   Indifferent Wednesday, 1821.

TO LEIGH HUNT.

Dear Hunt,—There was a sort of side-talk at Mr.

Novello's about our spending *Good Friday* at Hampstead ; but my sister has got so bad a cold, and we both want rest so much, that you shall excuse our putting off the visit some time longer.   Perhaps, after all, you know nothing of it.

Believe me,

Yours truly,

C. Lamb.

[1825.]

Letter CCCCXIV.]

TO THE SAME.

Dear H.,—I am here almost in the eleventh week of the longest illness my sister ever had, and no symptoms of amendment.   Some had begun, but relapsed with a change of nurse.   If she ever gets well, you will like my house, and I shall be happy to show you Enfield country.

As to my head, it is perfectly at your or any one's service ; either Myers' or Hazlitt's,—which last (done fifteen or twenty years since) White, of the Accountant's Office, India House, has ; he lives in Kentish Town—I forget where ; but is to be found in Leadenhall daily.   Take your choice.   I should be proud to hang up as an alehouse-sign even ; or, rather, I care not about my head or any thing, but how we are to get well again, for I am tired out.

God bless you and yours from the worst calamity.

Yours truly,

C. L.

Kindest remembrances to Mrs. Hunt.   H.'s is in a queer dress.   M.'s would be preferable *ad populum.*

LETTER CCCCXV.]

TO MESSRS. OLLIER.

Dear Sir, (whichever opens it),—I am going off to Birmingh^m. I find my books, whatever faculty of selling they may have (I wish they had more for {$\frac{your}{my}$} sake), are admirably adapted for giving away. You have been bounteous. Six more, and I shall have satisfied all just claims. Am I taking too great a liberty in begging you to send 4 as follows, and reserve 2 for me when I come home ? That will make 31. Thirty-one times 12 is 372 shillings— eighteen pounds twelve shillings ! ! ! But here are my friends, to whom, if you *could* transmit them, as I shall be away a month, you will greatly

Oblige the obliged,

C. LAMB.

Mr. Ayrton, James Street, Buckingham Gate ;

Mr. Alsager, Suffolk Street East, Southwark, by Horsemonger Lane ;

And in one parcel,

directed to R. Southey, Esq., Keswick, Cumberland :

One for R. S. ;

And one for W^m. Wordsworth, Esq.

If you will be kind enough simply to write " From the Author " in all 4, you will still further, &c.

Either Longman or Murray is in the frequent habit of sending books to Southey, and will take charge of the parcel. It will be as well to write in at the beginning thus :

" R. Southey, Esq. From the Author."

" W. Wordsworth, Esq. From the Author."

Then, if I can find the remaining 2 left for me at

Russell S^t when I return, rather than encroach any more on the heap, I will engage to make no more new friends *ad infinitum*, yourselves being the last.

Yours truly,

C. L.

I think Southey will give us a lift in that damn'd *Quarterly*. I meditate an attack upon that Cobbler Gifford, which shall appear immediately after any favorable mention which S. may make in the *Quarterly*. It can't, in decent *gratitude, appear before*.

18th June, 1818.

LETTER CCCCXVI.]   [No Date.

TO C. OLLIER.

Dear O.,—We lamented your absence last night. The grouse were piquant : the bucks incomparable. You must come in to cold mutton and oysters some evening. Name your evening; though I have qualms at the distance. Do you never leave early ? My head is very queerish, and indisposed for much company; but we will get Hood, that half Hogarth, to meet you. The scrap I send should come in AFTER the " Rising with the Lark."

Yours truly,

Colburn, I take it, pays postages.

LETTER CCCCXVII.]   [January 27, 1824.]

TO THE SAME.

¹ Dear Ollier,—Many thanks from both of us for *Inesilla*. I wished myself younger, that I might

have more enjoyed the terror of that desolate city, and the damned palace. I think it as fine as any thing in its way, and wish you joy of success, &c.

With better weather, I shall hope to see you at Islington.

Meantime, believe me,

Yours truly,

C. LAMB.

Scribbled midst official flurry.

LETTER CCCCXVIII.]   [No Date.]

Dear Ollier—I send you two more proverbs, which will be the last of this batch, unless I send you one more by the post on THURSDAY; none will come after that day; so do not leave any open room in that case. Hood sups with me to-night. Can you come and eat grouse? 'Tis not often I offer at delicacies

Yours most kindly,

C. LAMB.

Tuesday.

Colebrook Cottage, Colebrook Row.

LETTER CCCCXIX.]   [Aug. 9, 1872.]

TO SIR JOHN STODDART.

Dear Knight—Old Acquaintance,—'Tis with a violence to the *pure imagination* (*vide* the " Excursion " *passim*) that I can bring myself to believe I am writing to Dr. Stoddart once again, at Malta. But the deductions of severe reason warrant the proceed-

ing. I write from Enfield, where we are seriously
weighing the advantages of dulness over the over-
excitement of too much company, but have not yet
come to a conclusion. What is the news? for we
see no paper here; perhaps you can send us an old
one from Malta. Only, I heard a butcher in the
market-place whisper something about a change of
ministry. I don't know who's in or out, or care, only
as it might affect *you*. For domestic doings, I have
only to tell, with extreme regret, that poor Elisa
Fenwick (that was)—Mrs. Rutherford—is dead; and
that we have received a most heart-broken letter from
her mother—left with four grandchildren, orphans of
a living scoundrel lurking about the pothouses of
Little Russell Street, London : they and she—God
help 'em !—at New York. I have just received
Godwin's third volume of the *Republic*, which only
reaches to the commencement of the Protectorate. I
think he means to spin it out to his life's thread.
Have you seen Fearn's *Anti Tooke?* I am no judge
of such things—you are ; but I think it very clever
indeed. If I knew your bookseller, I'd order it for
you at a venture: 'tis two octavos, Longman and
Co. Or do you read now? Tell it not in the
Admiralty Court, but my head aches *hesterno vino*. I
can scarce pump up words, much less ideas, con-
gruous to be sent so far. But your son must have
this by to-night's post. . . . Manning is gone to
Rome, Naples, &c., probably to touch at Sicily, Malta,
Guernsey, &c. ; but I don't know the map. Hazlitt
is resident at Paris, whence he pours his lampoons
in safety at his friends in England. He has his boy
with him. I am teaching Emma Latin. By the
time you can answer this, she will be qualified to

instruct young ladies: she is a capital English reader: and S. T. C. acknowledges that a part of a passage in Milton she read better than he, and part he read best, her part being the shorter. But, seriously, if Lady St——— (oblivious pen, that was about to write *Mrs.!*) could hear of such a young person wanted (she smatters of French, some Italian, music of course), we'd send our loves by her. My congratulations and assurances of old esteem.

C. L.

LETTER CCCCXX.]   [April 25, 1825.]

TO VINCENT NOVELLO.

Dear Novello,—My sister's cold is as obstinate as an old Handelian, whom a modern amateur is trying to convert to Mozart-ism. As company must, and always does, injure it, Emma and 1 propose to come to you in the evening of to-morrow, *instead of meeting here.* An early bread-and-cheese supper at half-past eight will oblige us. Loves to the bearer of many children.

C. LAMB.

Tuesday. Colebrook.

I sign with a black seal, that you may [begin] to think her cold has killed Mary; which will be an agreeable unsurprise when you read the note.

V. Novello, Esq., Green, Shacklewell.

LETTER CCCCXXI.]   [No Date.]

TO THE SAME.

Dear Fugueist, or bear'st thou rather Contra-
puntist ?—We expect you four (as many as the table
will hold without squeezing at Mrs. Westwood's *Table
d' Hôte* on Thursday.   You will find the *White House*
shut up, and us moved under the wing of the *Phœnix*
which gives us friendly refuge.   Beds for guests,
we have none, but cleanly accomodings at the *Crown
and Horse-shoe.*

Yours harmonically,   C. L.

Vincentio (what, ho !) Novello, a Squire,
      66, Great Queen Street, Lincoln's-Inn Fields.

LETTER CCCCXXII.]   [No date.]

TO THE SAME.

Dear N.,—Pray write immediately, to say, " The
book has come safe."   I am curious not so much for
the autographs as for that bit of the hair-brush.   I
enclose a cinder, which belonged to *Shield* when he
was poor, and lit his own fires.   Any memorial of a
great musical genius, I know, is acceptable ; and
Shield has his merits, though Clementi, in my opinion,
is far above him in the *sostenuto.*

Mr. Westwood desires his compliments, and begs to
present you with a nail that came out of Jomelli's
coffin, who is buried at Naples.

LETTER CCCCXXIII.]   Tuesday, 29.

TO ROBERT HAYDON.[1]

Dear H.,—I have written a very respectful letter to Sir W. S. Godwin did not write, because he leaves all to his Committee, as I will explain to you. If this rascally weather holds you will see but one of us on that day.

Yours, with many thanks,

CHARLES LAMB.

LETTER CCCCXXIV.]   India House, 9th Oct., 1822.

TO THE SAME.

Dear Haydon,—Poor Godwin has been turned out of his home and business in Skinner Street, and if he does not pay two years' arrears of rent, he will have the whole stock, furniture, &c., of his new house (in the Strand) seized when term begins. We are trying to raise a subscription for him. My object in writing this is simply to ask you if this is a kind of case which would be likely to interest Mrs. Coutts in his behalf, and *who* in your opinion is the best person to speak with her on his behalf. Without the aid of from £300 to £400, by that time, early in November he must be ruined. You are the only person I can think

---

[1] Messrs. Chatto and Windus, of Piccadilly, have allowed the following letters, from the recently published Life of Haydon, edited by the Painter's Son, to be included in the series. They have also permitted the use of the letters to Sir John Stoddart and other correspondents, given in Mr. W. C. Hazlitt's Memoir.—F.

Dawsons.Ph.Sc.

Wm. Godwin.

From the engraving by G. Dawe after Northcote.

of, of her acquaintance, and can, perhaps, if not yourself, recommend the person most likely to influence her. Shelley had engaged to clear him of all demands and he has since turned out to be deeply insolvent.

Yours truly,

C. LAMB.

Is Sir Walter to be applied to and by what channel?

LETTER CCCCXXV.]   April 1827.]

TO HIS ESTEEMED FRIEND, AND EXCELLENT MUSICIAN, V. N., ESQ.

Dear Sir,—I conjure you, in the name of all the Sylvan Deities, and of the Muses, whom you honour, and they reciprocally love and honour you, rescue this old and passionate *Ditty*—the very flower of an old, forgotten *Pastoral*, which, had it been in all parts equal, the *Faithful Shepherdess* of Fletcher had been but a second name in this sort of Writing—rescue it from the profane hands of every Common Composer ; and in one of your tranquillest moods, when you have most leisure from those sad thoughts which sometimes unworthily beset you—yet a mood in itself not unallied to the better sort of melancholy— laying by, for once, the lofty Organ, with which you shake the Temples, attune, as to the Pipe of Paris himself, to some milder and love-according instrument, this pretty Courtship between Paris and his (then-not-as-yet-forsaken) Œnone.   Oblige me, and all more knowing Judges of Music and of Poesy, by the adaptation of fit musical numbers, which it only

I 2

wants, to be the rarest Love Dialogue in our Language.

Your Implore

C. L.

LETTER CCCCXXVI.]   Friday [May 14, 1830].

TO THE SAME.

Dear Novello,—Mary hopes you have not forgot you are to spend a day with us on Wednesday. That it may be a long one, cannot you secure places now for Mrs. Novello, yourself, and the Clarkes? We have just table-room for four. Five make my good landlady fidgetty; six, to begin to fret; seven, to approximate to fever-point. But, seriously, we shall prefer four to two or three. We shall have from half-past ten to six, when the coach goes off to scent the country. And pray write *now*, to say you do so come, for dear Mrs. Westwood else will be on the tenters of incertitude.

C. L.

Vincent Novello, Esq.,
    66, Great Queen Street, Lincoln's-Inn Fields.

LETTER CCCCXXVII.]

TO THE SAME.[1]

Dear N.,—You will not expect us to-morrow, I am sure, while these damn'd North-Easters continue. We must wait the Zephyrs' pleasures. By the bye, I

---

[1] From the Originals in the British Museum.—F.

was at Highgate on Wednesday, the only one of the party.

Yours truly,

C. LAMB.

Summer, as my friend Coleridge waggishly writes, has set in with its usual severity.

Kind remembces. to Mrs. Novello, &c.

May 9, 1826.

LETTER CCCCXXVIII.]

Tuesday, [September 18, 1827.]

TO THOMAS HOOD.

Dear Hood,—If I have any thing in my head, I will send it to Mr. Watts. Strictly speaking, he should have had my album-verses, but a very intimate friend importun'd me for the trifles, and I believe I forgot Mr. Watts, or lost sight at the time of his similar *souvenir*. Jamieson conveyed the farce from me to Mrs. C. Kemble; *he* will not be in town before the 27th. Give our kind loves to all at Highgate, and tell them that we have finally torn ourselves outright away from Colebrooke, where I had *no* health, and are about to domiciliate for good at Enfield, where I have experienced *good*.

> "Lord, what good hours do we keep!
> How quietly we sleep!"

See the rest in the *Complete Angler*.

We have got our books into our new house. I am a dray-horse, if [I] was not asham'd of the undigested, dirty lumber, as I toppled 'em out of the cart, and blest Becky that came with 'em for her having an

unstuff'd brain with such rubbish. We shall get in
by Michael's Mass. 'Twas with some pain we were
evuls'd from Colebrook. You may find some of our
flesh sticking to the door-posts. To change habitations
is to die to them; and in my time I have died seven
deaths. But I don't know whether every such change
does not bring with it a rejuvenescence. 'Tis an
enterprise; and shoves back the sense of death's
approximating, which, tho' not terrible to me, is at
all times particularly distasteful. My house-deaths
have generally been periodical, recurring after seven
years; but this last is premature by half that time.
Cut off in the flower of Colebrook! The Middletonian
stream, and all its echoes, mourn. Even minnows
dwindle. *A parvis fiunt minimi!* I fear to invite
Mrs. Hood to our new mansion, lest she envy it, and
hate us. But when we are fairly in, I hope she will
come and try it. I heard she and you were made
uncomfortable by some unworthy-to-be-cared-for
attacks, and have tried to set up a feeble counter-
action thro' the *Table Book* of last Saturday. Has it
not reach'd you, that you are silent about it? Our
new domicile is no manor-house; but new, and
externally not inviting, but furnish'd within with
every convenience: capital new locks to every door,
capital grates in every room ; with nothing to pay for
incoming; and the rent 10*l.* less than the Islington
one. It was built, a few years since, at 1100*l.*
expence, they tell me—and I perfectly believe it.
And I get it for 35*l.*, exclusive of moderate taxes.
We think ourselves most lucky.

It is not our intention to abandon Regent Street,
and West-End perambulations (monastic and terrible
thought !), but occasionally to breathe the fresher air

of the metropolis.   We shall put up a bedroom or
two (all we want) for occasional ex-rustication, where
we shall visit—not be visited.   Plays, too, we'll see—
perhaps our own; Urbani Sylvani and Sylvan Ur-
banuses in turn ; courtiers for a sport, then philosopher ; old, homely tell-truths and learn-truths in the
virtuous shades of Enfield, liars again and mocking
gibers in the coffee-houses and resorts of London.
What can a mortal desire more for his bi-parted
nature ?

O, the curds-and-cream you shall eat with us here !

O, the turtle-soup and lobster-salads we shall
devour with you there !

O, the old books we shall peruse here !

O, the new nonsense we shall trifle over there !

O, Sir T. Browne, here !

O, Mr. Hood and Mr. Jerdan, there !
Thine,

C. (URBANUS) L. (SYLVANUS)—(ELIA ambo)——
Inclos'd are verses which Emma sat down to write
(her first) on the eve after your departure.   Of course,
they are only for Mrs. H.'s perusal.   They will shew,
at least, that one of our party is not willing to cut
old friends.   What to call 'em I don't know.   Blank
verse they are not, because of the rhymes ; rhymes
they are not, because of the blank verse ; heroics they
are not, because they are lyric ; lyric they are not,
because of the heroic measure.   They must be call'd
Emmaics.

The Hoods, 2, Robert Street, Adelphi, London.

LETTER CCCCXXIX.]   [No Date.]

TO GEORGE DYER.

Dear Dyer,—My very good friend, and Charles Clarke's father-in-law, Vincent Novello, wishes to shake hands with you. Make him play you a tune. He is a damn'd fine musician, and, what is better, a good man and true. He will tell you how glad we should be to have Mrs. Dyer and you here for a few days. Our young friend, Miss Isola, has been here holiday-making, but leaves us to-morrow.

Yours ever,

CH. LAMB.

Enfield.

Emma's love to Mr. and Mrs. Dyer.

George Dyer, Esq., Clifford's Inn.

LETTER CCCCXXX.]   May 21, 1830.

TO MR. HONE.

Dear Hone,—I thought you would be pleased to see this letter. Pray if you have time call on Novello, No. 66, Great Queen St. I am anxious to learn whether he received his album I sent on Friday by our nine o'clock morning stage. If not, beg him inquire at the *Old Bell*, Holborn.

CHARLES LAMB.

Southey will see in the *Times* all we proposed omitting is omitted.

LETTER CCCCXXXI.]   [1827.]

TO THE SAME.

Dear Hone,—By the verses in yesterday's *Table Book*, sign'd *, I judge you are going on better ; but *I want to be resolv'd.* Alsop promised to call on you, and let me know, but has not. Pray attend to this ; and send me the number before the present (pages 225 to 256), which my newsman has neglect'd. Your book improves every week. I have written here a thing in 2 acts, and sent it to Cov^t Gard.

Yours,

C. LAMB.

Sunday, 2d Sept.

———————

LETTER CCCCXXXII.]   [Edmonton, 1833.]

TO MR. TUFF.

D^r S^r,—I learn that Covent Garden, from its thin houses every night, is likely to be shut up after Saturday ; so that no time is to be lost in using the orders.

Yours,

C. LAMB.

———————

LETTER CCCCXXXIII.]   October 4, 1827.

TO BARRON FIELD, ESQ.

I am not in humour to return a fit reply to your pleasant letter. We are fairly housed at Enfield, and an angel shall not persuade me to wicked London again. We have now six Sabbath-days in a week for—*none !* The change has worked on my sisters' mind to make her ill; and I must wait a tedious time before we can hope to enjoy this place in unison. Enjoy it, when she recovers, I know we shall. I see no shadow, but in her illness, for repenting the step ! For Mathews—I know my own utter unfitness for such a task. I am no hand at describing costumes, a great requisite in an account of mannered pictures. I have not the slightest acquaintance with pictorial language even. An imitator of me, or rather pretender to be *me*, in his "Rejected Articles," has made me minutely describe the dresses of the poissardes at Calais !—I could as soon resolve Euclid. I have no eye for forms and fashions. I substitute analysis, and get rid of the phenomenon by slurring in for it its impression. I am sure you must have observed this defect, or peculiarity, in my writings ; else the delight would be incalculable in doing such a thing for Mathews, whom I greatly like — and Mrs. Mathews, whom I almost greatlier like. What a feast 'twould be to be sitting at the pictures painting 'em into words ; but I could almost as soon make words into pictures. I speak this deliberately, and not out of modesty. I pretty well know what I can't do.

My sister's verses are homely, but just what they should be ; I send them, not for the poetry, but the good sense and good will of them. I was beginning to transcribe ; but Emma is sadly jealous of its getting into more hands, and I won't spoil it in her eyes by divulging it. Come to Enfield, and *read it.* As my poor cousin, the bookbinder, now with God, told me most sentimentally, that having purchased a picture of fish at a dead man's sale, his heart ached to see how the widow grieved to part with it, being her dear husband's favourite ; and he almost apologised for his generosity by saying he could not help telling the widow she was " welcome to come and look at it "—*e.g.* at *his house*—" as often as she pleased." There was the germ of generosity in an uneducated mind.   He had just *reading* enough from the backs of books for the " nec sinit esse feros ;" had he read inside, the same impulse would have lead him to give back the two-guinea thing—with a request to see it, now and then, at *her* house.   We are parroted into delicacy.—Thus you have a tale for a Sonnet.

Adieu ! with (imagine both) our loves.

C. L.

LETTER CCCCXXXIV.]

TO MR. DILKE.

May I now claim of you the benefit of the loan of some books ? *Do not fear sending too many.* But do not, if it be irksome to yourself, such as shall make you say, ' Damn it, here's Lamb's box come again.' *Dogs' leaves ensured.* Any light stuff; no natural history, or useful learning, such as Pyramids, Catacombs, Giraffes, Adventures in South Africa, &c.

P.S.—Novels for the last two years, or further back ; nonsense of any period.

Letter CCCCXXXV.]

TO THE PRINTER OF THE ATHENÆUM.

I have read the enclosed five-and-forty times over. I have submitted it to my Edmonton friends. At last (O! Argus penetration!) I have discovered a dash that might be dispensed with. Pray don't trouble yourself with such useless courtesies. I can well trust your editor when I don't use queer phrases which *prove themselves wrong* by creating a distrust in the sober compositor.

Letter CCCCXXXVI.]   Enfield, November 9, 1828.

TO LAMAN BLANCHARD.

Sir,—I beg to return my acknowledgments for the present of your elegant volume, which I should have esteemed, without the bribe of the name prefixed to it. I have been much pleased with it throughout, but am most taken with the peculiar delicacy of some of the sonnets. I shall put them up among my poetical treasures.

Your obliged Servant,

C. Lamb.

Letter CCCCXXXVII.]

FRAGMENT OF A LETTER TO HIS SISTER.[1]

...Then you must walk all along the borough side of

---

[1] This fragment is curious, as being the only letter of Lamb's to his sister that has been preserved. The truth is, they were never apart, except on one occasion, connected with her malady, such as the present was.—F.

the Seine, facing the Tuileries.   There is a mile and
a half of print shops and Bookstalls.   If the latter
were but English !   Then there is a place where the
Paris people put all the dead people, and bring them
flowers and dolls, and gingerbread nuts, and sonnets,
and such trifles ; and that is all, I think worth seeing
as sights, except that the streets and shops of Paris
are themselves the best sight."

---

*The Editor has been unable to include in the Collec-
tion certain letters protected by copyright.   He has
thought it advisable, therefore, to point out where such
letters may be found.*

*Mrs. Cowden Clarke contributed to the " Gentleman's
Magazine " for December, 1873, seven letters ; five
addressed to C. Cowden Clarke, and two to V. Novello.
They were written during the course of the years
1828-29-30.   Some of them are delightfully gay, and
full of characteristic little touches.   Almost unique
might be considered the musical letter, dated Nov. 6,
1829, with a mock, " Serenata for two Voices," on Mr.
Clarke's marriage ; the others are almost equally good.*

*Allusion was made in the Preface to some letters
in the possession of the Wordsworth Family.   Mr.
William Wordsworth, Junior, the poet's grandson,
writes in reference to the subject :—" There are certain
passages in the letters published by Talfourd, which
were withheld from publication by my Grandfather
the Poet's express wish; and one or two complete
letters also remain unpublished.   The unpublished
portions are principally of a private character, relating
to domestic incidents, and were evidently withheld*

on that ground alone: one or two passages, and
perhaps, one or two letters, were perhaps kept back
for other reasons."

There are also some letters of Lamb's to be found
in the recently published Memoirs of Godwin—which
Mr. Kegan Paul, the author, would have allowed the
Editor to use, had this edition appeared a little later.

———————

SUPPLEMENTAL LETTERS.

_The following reached the Editor too late for insertion
in their proper place in the Correspondence. It should
be added, that all the Letters in the Collection marked
with a star have never before been published._

FRAGMENTS OF LETTERS TO MR. HONE.

Who is your compositor?   I cannot praise
enough the beauty and accuracy of the Garrick
play Types.   That of Zelidaura, &c., 2 or 3 numbers
back was really a poser.   He must be no ordinary
person who got through it (so quaint) without a slip.
Not one in a 1000 would have done it. . . Moxon
is a little fretful that you have extracted a bit
(only) from his friend Coles' book about Harvey and
Weston Favell.   C. is gaping for it, and has sent M.
a very curious old man's will for your book, which
M. only keeps till you gratify him by a timely notice.
Any thing about the meditation among your Tombs?
A digressive P.S. of the great house of Longman,
Shortman and Co. . . I send you a trifle.   You have
seen my lines, I suppose, in the "London?" I
cannot tell you how much I like St. Chad's Well.—
P.S.—Why did you not stay or come again yester-
day? . . Mercy!   What a dose you have sent me of
Burney—a perfect opening draught!

Oct. 24, 1825.

* TO THE SAME.

Dear H.—Come to our house and not come in. I
am quite vex't.—Yours, C.L. . . There is in Blackwood this month an article MOST AFFECTING indeed,
called *Le Revenant,* and would do more towards
abolishing capital punishments than 40,000 Romillies
or Montagues. I beg you to read it and see if you
can extract any of it—the trial scene in particular.

* TO A FRIEND.

My dear Boy.—Scamper off with this to Dilke and
get it in for to-morrow; then we shall have two
things in in the first week.

YOUR LAUREAT.

* TO MR. ALLSOP.

My dear friend,—I went to Highgate this day. I
gave to S. T. C. your letter which he immediately
answered, and to which Mrs. G. insisted upon adding
her own. They seem to me *all* exceedingly to partake in your troubles. Pray get over your reluctance
to paying him a visit, see and talk with him. Hear
what he has to say, connected closely with his own
expectations, as to your desire. Something, I believe,
is doing for him. But hear him himself, look him
and your affairs in the face. Older men than you
have surmounted worse difficulties. I should have
written strait to you from Highgate, but we have had a

source of troubles this last week or two, and yours added to it, have broke my spirits. I could hardly drag to and from Highgate. If you don't like to go, better appoint him *your*, *my* house, or any where, but meet him. I am sure there is great reason you should not shun him, for I found him thinking on your perplexities and wanting to see you.

Mary's and my best love to Mrs. Allsop,

Yours ever,

C. LAMB.

Feb. 2nd, 1827

---

* TO THE SAME.

Dear A.,—Don't come yet. The house is so small. Mary hears every person and every knock. She is very bad yet, but I hope ere long to have you here. Thanks for the paper. N.B., none came last week.

God bless you, and love to Mrs. A.,

C. L.

1827. Enfield.

---

* TO THE SAME.

My dear Sir,—I have to thank you for a fine hare, and, unless I am mistaken, for *two*. The first I received a week since, the account given with it was that it came from Mr. Alfourd. I have no friend of that name, but two who come near to it, *Mr. Talfourd*. So my gratitude must be divided between you, till I know the true sender. We are, and shall be, some time, I fear, at Dalston, a distance which does not improve hares by the circuitous route of Covent Garden, though for the sweetness of *this last* I will answer. We dress it to-day. I suppose you know my sister has been and is ill. I do not see much hopes, though there is a glimmer of her speedy recovery. When we are all well, I hope to come among our town friends, and shall have great pleasure in welcoming you from Beresford Hall. Yours and old Mr. Walton's, and Honest Mr. Cotton's,

Piscatorum Amicus,

C. L.

India House,
  19th Oct., '21,

---

* TO MR. HONE.

I send the scrap,—is it worth postage? My friends are fairly surprised that you should set me down so unequivocally for an ass, as you have done. (P. 10—58.)

"HERE HE IS,
What follows
THE ASS."

Call you that friendship? Mercy! what a dose you have sent me of Burney! A perfect opening[1] draught!

Oct. 25th, 1825.

---

[1] A pun is here intended.—C. L.

TO H. C. ROBINSON.

Chase Side, Oct. 1, 1827.

Dear R.,—I am settled for life, I hope, at Enfield. I have taken the prettiest, compactest house I ever saw, near to Antony Robinson's; but alas! at the expense of my poor Mary, who was taken ill of the old complaint the night before we got into it. So I must suspend the pleasure I expected in the surprise you would have had, in coming down and finding us householders.

Farewell! till we can all meet comfortable. Pray apprise Martin Burney. Him I have longed to have seen with you; but our house is too small to meet either of you without *her* knowledge.

God bless you !
C. LAMB.

TO THE SAME.

1810.

Dear R.,—My brother, whom you have met at my rooms (a plump, good-looking man of seven-and-forty) has written a book about humanity, which I transmit to you herewith. Wilson, the publisher, has put it into his head that you can get it reviewed for him. I daresay it is not in the scope of your Review; but if you could put it in any likely train, he would rejoice. For alas! our boasted humanity partakes of vanity. As it is, he teazes me to death with choosing to suppose that I could get it into all the Reviews at a moment's notice. *I!!* who have been set up as a mark for them to throw at, and would willingly consign them all to Megæra's snaky locks.

But here's the book, and don't show it to Mrs. Collier; for I remember she makes excellent *eel* soup, and the leading points of the book are directed against that very process.

Yours truly,

C. LAMB.

TO JOHN CLARE.

" *India House,* 31st Aug. 1822.

DEAR CLARE,—I thank you heartily for your present. I am an inveterate old Londoner, but while I am among your choice collections I seem to be native to them and free of the country. The quantity of your observation has astonished me. What have most pleased me have been " Recollections after a Ramble," and those " Grongar Hill " kind of pieces in eight-syllable lines, my favourite measure, such as " Cowper Hill " and " Solitude." In some of your story-telling ballads the provincial phrases sometimes startle me. I think you are too profuse with them. In poetry, *slang* of every kind is to be avoided. There is a rustic Cockneyism as little pleasing as ours of London. Transplant Arcadia to Helpstone. The true rustic style, the Arcadian English, I think is to be found in Shenstone. Would his " Schoolmistress," the prettiest of poems, have been better if he had used quite the Goody's own language ? Now and then a home rusticism is fresh and startling, but where nothing is gained in expression it is out of tenor. It may make folks smile and stare, but the ungenial coalition of barbarous with refined phrases will prevent you in the end from being so generally tasted as you deserve to be.   Excuse my freedom, and take the same liberty with my *puns*.

I send you two little volumes of my spare hours. They are of all sorts.   There's a Methodist hymn for Sundays, and a farce for Saturday night.   Pray give them a place on your shelf, and accept a little volume of which I have duplicate, that I may return in equal number to your welcome present.

I think I am indebted to you for a sonnet in the " London " for August.

Since I saw you I have been in France and have eaten frogs.   The nicest little rabbity things you ever tasted.   Do look about for them.   Make Mrs. Clare pick off the hind quarters ; boil them plain with parsley and butter.   The fore quarters are not so good.   She may let them hop off by themselves.

Yours sincerely,
CHAS. LAMB.

TO MR. C. CHAMBERS.

1 *Sept.* 1817.

With regard to a John Dory, which you desire to be particularly informed about,—I honour the fish, but it is rather on account of Quin, who patronised it, and whose taste (of a *dead* man) I had as lieve go by as any body's, Apicius and Heliogabalus excepted—this latter started nightingales' brains and peacocks' tongues as a garnish.   Else, in *itself*, and trusting to my own poor single judgment, it hath not that moist, mellow, oleaginous, gliding, smooth descent from the tongue to the palate, thence to the stomach, etc., as your Brighton turbot hath, which I take to be the most friendly and familiar flavour of any that swims—most genial and at home to the palate.

Nor has it, on the other hand, that fine falling-off flakiness, that obsequious peeling off (as it were like a sea onion) which endears your cod's-head and shoulders to some appetites, that manly firmness, combined with a sort of womanish coming-in-pieces, which the same cod's-head and shoulders hath—where the *whole* is easily separable, pliant to a knife or spoon, but each *individual flake* presents a pleasing resistance to the opposed tooth—you understand me; these delicate subjects are necessarily obscure.

But it has a third flavour of its own, totally distinct from cod or turbot, which it must be owned may to some not injudicious palates render it acceptable; but to my unpractised tooth it presented rather a crude river-fish-flavour, like your pike or carp, and perhaps, like them, should have been tamed and corrected by some laborious and well-chosen sauce. Still I always suspect a fish which requires so much of artificial settings-off. Your choicest relishes (like native loveliness) need not the foreign aid of ornament, but are, when unadorned (that is, with nothing but a little plain anchovy and a squeeze of lemon)—are then adorned the most. However, I shall go to Brighton again, next summer, and shall have an opportunity of correcting my judgment, if it is not sufficiently informed. I can only say that when Nature was pleased to make the John Dory so notoriously deficient in outward graces (as, to be sure, he is the very rhinoceros of fishes, the ugliest dog that swims, except perhaps the sea satyr, which I never saw, but which they say is terrible)—when she formed him with so few external advantages, she might have bestowed a more elaborate finish on his parts internal, and have given him a relish, a sapor, to recommend him, as she made Pope a poet to make up for making him crooked.

I am sorry to find that you have got a knack of saying things which are not true to show your wit. If I had no wit, but what I must show at the expense of my virtue or my modesty, I had as lieve be as stupid as . . . at the tea warehouse. Depend upon it, my dear Chambers, that an ounce of integrity at our death-bed will stand us in more avail than all the wit of Congreve or . . . For instance, you tell me a fine story about Truss, and his playing at Leamington, which I know to be false, because I have advice from Derby that he was whipt through the town on that very day you say he appeared in some character or other for robbing an old woman at church of a seal ring. And Dr. Parr has been two months dead. So it won't do to scatter these random stories about among people that know anything. Besides, your forte is not invention. It is *judgment*, particularly shown in your choice of dishes. We seem in that instance born under one star. I like you for liking hare. I esteem you for disrelishing minced veal. Liking is too cold a word : I love you for your noble attachment to the fat, unctuous juices of deer's flesh and the green unspeakable of turtle. I honour you for your endeavours to esteem and approve of my favourite, which I ventured to recommend to you as substitute for hare, bullock's heart, and I am not offended that you cannot taste it with *my* palate. A true son of

Epicurus should reserve one taste peculiar to himself. For a long time I kept the secret about the exceeding deliciousness of the marrow of boiled knuckle of veal, till my tongue weakly run out in its praises, and now it is prostitute and common.   But I have made one discovery which I will not impart till my dying scene is over—perhaps it will be my last mouthful in this world : delicious thought, enough to sweeten (or rather make savoury) the hour of death.   It is a little square bit about this _____ size, in or near the knuckle- bone of a fried joint of . . . fat I can't call it, nor . lean neither alto- gether, it is that beautiful compound _____ which Nature must have made in Paradise, Park Venison, before she separated the two substances, the dry and the oleagi- nous, to punish sinful mankind : Adam ate them entire and inseparable, and this little taste of Eden in the knuckle-bone of a fried . . . seems the only relique of a Paradisaical state.   When I die, an exact description of its topography shall be left in a cupboard with a key, inscribed on which these words, 'C. Lamb, dying, imparts this to C. Chambers, as the only worthy deposi- tory of such a secret.'   You 'll drop a tear. . . .

TO MR. OLLIER.

(MR. COLBURN, NEW BURLINGTON STREET.)

January 1826.

Dear O.,—I send you eight more jests, with the terms which my friend asks, which you will be so kind as to get an answer to from Mr. Colburn, that I may tell him whether to go on with them. You will see his short note to me at the end, and tear it off. It is not for me to judge, but, considering the scarceness of the materials, what he asks is, I think, mighty reasonable. *Do not let him be even known as a friend of mine.* You see what he says about five going in first as a taste, but these will make thirteen in all. Tell me by what time he need send more; I suppose not for some time (if you do not bring them out this month).

Keep a place for me till the middle of the month, for I cannot hit on anything yet. I mean nothing by my crotchets but extreme difficulty in writing. But I will go on as long as I can.

C. LAMB.

ELIA.

ESSAYS WHICH HAVE APPEARED UNDER THAT SIGNA-
TURE IN THE "LONDON MAGAZINE."

ELIA.

ESSAYS WHICH HAVE APPEARED UNDER THAT SIGNA-
TURE IN THE " LONDON MAGAZINE."

THE SOUTH SEA HOUSE.

READER, in thy passage from the Bank—where thou
hast been receiving thy half-yearly dividends (supposing thou art a lean annuitant like myself)—to the
Flower Pot, to secure a place for Dalston, or Shacklewell, or some other thy suburban retreat northerly,—
didst thou never observe a melancholy-looking, handsome, brick and stone edifice, to the left—where
Threadneedle Street abuts upon Bishopsgate? I dare
say thou hast often admired its magnificent portals
ever gaping wide, and disclosing to view a grave court,
with cloisters and pillars, with a few or no traces of

goers-in or comers-out,—a desolation something like
Balclutha's.[1]

This was once a house of trade,—a centre of busy
interests.   The throng of merchants was here—the
quick pulse of gain—and here some forms of business
are still kept up, though the soul be long since fled.
Here are still to be seen stately porticos, imposing
staircases, offices roomy as the state apartments in
palaces—deserted, or thinly peopled with a few
straggling clerks ; the still more sacred interiors of
court and committee-rooms, with venerable faces of
beadles, door-keepers—directors seated in form on
solemn days (to proclaim a dead dividend) at long
worm-eaten tables, that have been mahogany, with
tarnished gilt-leather coverings, supporting massy
silver inkstands long since dry ;—the oaken wainscots
hung with pictures of deceased governors and sub-
governors, of Queen Anne, and the first two monarchs
of the Brunswick dynasty ; huge charts, which subsequent discoveries have antiquated ; dusty maps of
Mexico, dim as dreams, and soundings of the Bay
of Panama ; the long passages hung with buckets,
appended in idle rows to walls whose substance
might defy any, short of the last, conflagration ;
with vast ranges of cellarage under all, where dollars
and pieces-of-eight once lay, an " unsunned heap,"
for Mammon to have solaced his solitary heart
withal,—long since dissipated, or scattered into air at
the blast of the breaking of that famous BUBBLE.——

Such is the SOUTH SEA HOUSE.   At least, such it
was forty years ago, when I knew it,—a magnificent

---

[1] I passed by the walls of Balclutha, and they were desolate.—
OSSIAN.

relic ! What alterations may have been made in it
since, I have had no opportunities of verifying. Time,
I take for granted, has not freshened it. No wind
has resuscitated the face of the sleeping waters. A
thicker crust by this time stagnates upon it. The
moths, that were then battening upon its obsolete
ledgers and day-books, have rested from their depredations, but other light generations have succeeded,
making fine fretwork among their single and double
entries. Layers of dust have accumulated (a super-
fœtation of dirt !) upon the old layers, that seldom
used to be disturbed, save by some curious finger,
now and then, inquisitive to explore the mode of book-
keeping in Queen Anne's reign ; or, with less
hallowed curiosity, seeking to unveil some of the
mysteries of that tremendous HOAX, the extent of
which the petty peculators of our day look back upon
with the same expression of incredulous admiration
and hopeless ambition of rivalry as would become
the puny face of modern conspiracy contemplating the
Titan size of Vaux's superhuman plot.

Peace to the manes of the BUBBLE ! Silence and
destitution are upon thy walls, proud house, for a
memorial !

Situated as thou art in the very heart of stirring
and living commerce,—amid the fret and fever of
speculation,—with the Bank, and the 'Change, and
the India House about thee, in the hey-day of present
prosperity, with their important faces, as it were, insulting thee, their *poor neighbour out of business*—to
the idle and merely contemplative,—to such as me,
old House, there is a charm in thy quiet,—a cessation
—a coolness from business—an indolence almost
cloisteral—which is delightful. With what reverence

have I paced thy great bare rooms and courts at
eventide ! They spoke of the past : the shade of some
dead accountant, with visionary pen in ear, would flit
by me, stiff as in life.   Living accounts and account-
ants puzzle me.   I have no skill in figuring.   But
thy great dead tomes, which scarce three degenerate
clerks of the present day could lift from their enshrin-
ing shelves—with their old fantastic flourishes and
decorative rubric interlacings—their sums in triple
columniations, set down with formal superfluity of
ciphers—with pious sentences at the beginning,
without which our religious ancestors never ventured
to open a book of business or bill of lading—the
costly vellum covers of some of them almost persuad-
ing us that we are got into some *better library*,—are
very agreeable and edifying spectacles. I can look upon
these defunct dragons with complacency.   Thy heavy
odd-shaped ivory-handled pen-knives (our ancestors
had every thing on a larger scale than we have hearts
for) are as good as any thing from Herculaneum.
The pounce-boxes of our days have gone retrograde.

The very clerks which I remember in the South
Sea House—I speak of forty years back—had an air
very different from those in the public offices that I
have had to do with since.   They partook of the
genius of the place.

They were mostly (for the establishment did not
admit of superfluous salaries) bachelors ; generally
(for they had not much to do) persons of a curious
and speculative turn of mind ; old-fashioned, for a
reason mentioned before.   Humourists, for they were
of all descriptions ; and not having been brought
together in early life, (which has a tendency to
assimilate the members of corporate bodies to each

other,) but, for the most part, placed in this house in ripe or middle age, they necessarily carried into it their separate habits and oddities, unqualified, if I may so speak, as into a common stock. Hence they formed a sort of Noah's ark: odd fishes; a lay-monastery; domestic retainers in a great house, kept more for show than use; yet pleasant fellows, full of chat; and not a few among them had arrived at considerable proficiency on the German flute.

The cashier at that time was one Evans, a Cambro-Briton. He had something of the choleric complexion of his countrymen stamped on his visage, but was a worthy sensible man at bottom. He wore his hair, to the last, powdered and frizzed out, in the fashion which I remember to have seen in caricatures of what were termed, in my young days, *Maccaronies*. He was the last of that race of beaux. Melancholy as a gib-cat over his counter all the forenoon, I think I see him, making up his cash (as they call it) with tremulous fingers, as if he feared every one about him was a defaulter; in his hypochondry ready to imagine himself one; haunted, at least, with the idea of the possibility of his becoming one; his tristful visage clearing up a little over his roast neck of veal at Anderton's at two, (where his picture still hangs, taken a little before his death by desire of the master of the coffee-house, which he had frequented for the last five-and-twenty years,) but not attaining the meridian of its animation till evening brought on the hour of tea and visiting. The simultaneous sound of his well-known rap at the door with the stroke of the clock announcing six was a topic of never-failing mirth in the families with this dear old bachelor gladdened with his presence. Then was his *forte*, his glorified hour! How would he chirp and expand over a muffin! How would he dilate into secret history! His countryman, Pennant himself, in particular, could not be more eloquent than he in relation to old and new London—the site of old theatres, churches, streets gone to decay—where Rosamond's Pond stood—the Mulberry Gardens—and the Conduit in Cheap—with many a pleasant anecdote, derived from paternal tradition, of those grotesque figures which Hogarth has immortalized in his picture of *Noon*,—the worthy descendants of those heroic confessors, who, flying to this country from the wrath of Louis the Fourteenth and his dragoons, kept alive the flame of pure religion in the sheltering obscurities of Hog Lane and the vicinity of the Seven Dials!

Deputy, under Evans, was Thomas Tame. He had the air and stoop of a nobleman. You would have taken him for one, had you met him in one of the passages leading to Westminster Hall. By stoop, I mean that gentle bending of the body forwards, which, in great men, must be supposed to be the effect of an habitual condescending attention to the applications of their inferiors. While he held you in converse, you felt strained to the height in the colloquy. The conference over, you were at leisure to smile at the comparative insignificance of the pretensions which had just awed you. His intellect was of the shallowest order. It did not reach to a saw or a proverb. His mind was in its original state of white paper. A sucking babe might have posed him. What was it then? Was he rich? Alas, no! Thomas Tame was very poor. Both he and his wife looked outwardly gentlefolks, when I fear all was not well at

all times within. She had a neat meagre person, which
it was evident she had not sinned in over-pampering;
but in its veins was noble blood. She traced her
descent, by some labyrinth of relationship, which I
never thoroughly understood,—much less can explain
with any heraldic certainty at this time of day,—to
the illustrious but unfortunate house of Derwent-
water. This was the secret of Thomas's stoop.
This was the thought—the sentiment—the bright
solitary star of your lives,—ye mild and happy pair,
—which cheered you in the night of intellect, and in
the obscurity of your station! This was to you
instead of riches, instead of rank, instead of glittering
attainments; and it was worth them all together.
You insulted none with it; but, while you wore it as
a piece of defensive armour only, no insult likewise
could reach you through it. *Decus et solamen.*

Of quite another stamp was the then accountant,
John Tipp. He neither pretended to high blood, nor,
in good truth, cared one fig about the matter. He
thought an accountant the greatest character in the
world, and himself the greatest accountant in it.
Yet John was not without his hobby. The fiddle
relieved his vacant hours. He sang, certainly, with
other notes than to the Orphean lyre. He did,
indeed, scream and scrape most abominably. His fine
suite of official rooms in Threadneedle Street, which,
without any thing very substantial appended to them,
were enough to enlarge a man's notions of himself
that lived in them, (I know not who is the occupier
of them now,) resounded fortnightly to the notes of
a concert of " sweet breasts," as our ancestors would
have called them, culled from the club-rooms and
orchestras, chorus singers, first and second violon-

cellos, double-basses, and clarionets, who ate his cold
mutton, and drank his punch, and praised his ear.
He sate like Lord Midas among them. But at the
desk Tipp was quite another sort of creature. Thence
all ideas that were purely ornamental were banished.
You could not speak of any thing romantic without
rebuke. Politics were excluded. A newspaper was
thought too refined and abstracted. The whole duty
of man consisted in writing off dividend warrants.
The striking of the annual balance in the Company's
books (which, perhaps, differed from the balance of
last year in the sum of £25 1s. 6d.) occupied his
days and nights for a month previous. Not that Tipp
was blind to the deadness of *things* (as they call
them in the City) in his beloved house, or did not
sigh for a return of the old stirring days when South
Sea hopes were young—(he was indeed equal to the
wielding of any, the most intricate accounts of the
most flourishing Company in these or those days :)—
but to a genuine accountant the difference of proceeds
is as nothing. The fractional farthing is as dear to
his heart as the thousands which stand before it.
He is the true actor, who, whether his part be a prince
or a peasant, must act it with like intensity. With
Tipp, form was every thing. His life was formal.
His actions seemed ruled with a ruler. His pen
was not less erring than his heart. He made the
best executor in the world; he was plagued with
incessant executorships accordingly, which excited his
spleen and soothed his vanity in equal ratios. He
would swear (for Tipp swore) at the little orphans,
whose rights he would guard with a tenacity like the
grasp of the dying hand, that commended their
interests to his protection. With all this there was

about him a sort of timidity—(his few enemies used to give it a worse name)—a something which, in reverence to the dead, we will place, if you please, a little on this side of the heroic. Nature certainly had been pleased to endow John Tipp with a sufficient measure of the principle of self-preservation. There is a cowardice which we do not despise, because it has nothing base or treacherous in its elements; it betrays itself, not you: it is mere temperament; the absence of the romantic and the enterprising; it sees a lion in the way, and will not, with Fortinbras, " greatly find quarrel in a straw," when some supposed honour is at stake. Tipp never mounted the box of a stage coach in his life; or leaned against the rails of a balcony; or walked upon the ridge of a parapet; or looked down a precipice; or let off a gun; or went upon a water party; or would willingly let you go, if he could have helped it: neither was it recorded of him, that for lucre, or for intimidation, he ever forsook friend or principle.

Whom next shall we summon from the dusty dead, in whom common qualities become uncommon? Can I forget thee, Henry Mann, the wit, the polished man of letters, the *author*, of the South Sea House? who never enteredst thy office in a morning, or quittedst it in mid-day—(what didst *thou* in an office?)— without some quirk that left a sting! Thy gibes and thy jokes are now extinct, or survive but in two forgotten volumes, which I had the good fortune to rescue from a stall in Barbican, not three days ago, and found thee terse, fresh, epigrammatic, as alive. Thy wit is a little gone by in these fastidious days; the topics are staled by the " new-born gauds " of the time :—but great thou used to be in Public Ledgers, and in Chronicles, upon Chatham, and Shelburne, and Rockingham, and Howe, and Burgoyne, and Clinton, and the war which ended in the tearing from Great Britain her rebellious colonies,—and Keppel, and Wilkes, and Sawbridge, and Bull, and Dunning, and Pratt, and Richmond,—and such small politics.

A little less facetious, and a great deal more obstreperous, was fine rattling, rattle-headed Plumer. He was descended,—not in a right line, reader, (for his lineal pretensions, like his personal, favoured a little of the sinister bend,) from the Plumers of Hertfordshire.   So tradition gave him out; and certain family features not a little sanctioned the opinion.   Certainly old Walter Plumer (his reputed author) had been a rake in his days, and visited much in Italy, and had seen the world.   He was uncle, bachelor-uncle to the fine old Whig still living, who has represented the county in so many successive Parliaments, and has a fine old mansion near Ware. Walter flourished in George the Second's days, and was the same who was summoned before the House of Commons about a business of franks, with the old Duchess of Marlborough.   You may read of it in Johnson's Life of Cave.   Cave came off cleverly in that business.   It is certain our Plumer did nothing to discountenance the rumour.   He rather seemed pleased whenever it was, with all gentleness, insinuated.   But, besides his family pretensions, Plumer was an engaging fellow, and sang gloriously.

Not so sweetly sang Plumer as thou sangest, mild, child-like pastoral M ——; a flute's breathing less divinely whispering than thy Arcadian melodies, when, in tones worthy of Arden, thou didst chant that song sung by Amiens to the banished Duke, which proclaims the winter wind more lenient than for a man to be ungrateful. Thy sire was old surly M ——, the unapproachable churchwarden of Bishopsgate. He knew not what he did, when he begat thee, like Spring, gentle offspring of blustering Winter:—only unfortunate in thy ending, which should have been mild, conciliatory, swan-like.

Much remains to sing. Many fantastic shapes rise up, but they must be mine in private. Already I have fooled the reader to the top of his bent; else could I omit that strange creature Woollett, who existed in trying the question, and *bought litigations ?* —and still stranger, inimitable, solemn Hepworth, from whose gravity Newton might have deduced the law of gravitation. How profoundly would he nib a pen! With what deliberation would he wet a wafer!

But it is time to close; night's wheels are rattling fast over me; it is proper to have done with this solemn mockery.

Reader, what if I have been playing with thee all this while? Peradventure the very *names* which I have summoned up before thee are fantastic—insubstantial—like Henry Pimpernel, and old John Naps of Greece.

Be satisfied that something answering to them has had a being. Their importance is from the past.

OXFORD IN THE VACATION.

CASTING a preparatory glance at the bottom of this article—as the wary connoisseur in prints, with cursory eye, (which, while it reads, seems as though it read not,) never fails to consult the *quis sculpsit* in the corner, before he pronounces some rare piece to be a Vivares or a Woollet—methinks I hear you exclaim, reader, *Who is Elia ?*

Because in my last I tried to divert thee with some half-forgotten humours of some old clerks defunct, in an old house of business, long since gone to decay, doubtless you have already set me down in your mind as one of the self-same college, a votary of the desk, a notched and cropt scrivener, one that sucks his sustenance, as certain sick people are said to do, through a quill.

Well, I do agnize something of the sort. I confess that it is my humour, my fancy, in the fore part of the day, when the mind of your man of letters requires some relaxation, (and none better than such as at first sight seems most abhorrent from his beloved studies,) to while away some good hours of my time in the contemplation of indigos, cottons, raw silks, piece-goods,

flowered o1 otherwise. In the first place * * * *
and then it sends you home with such increased
appetite to your books * * * not to say, that
your outside sheets and waste wrappers of foolscap
do receive into them, most kindly and naturally, the
impression of sonnets, epigrams, *essays*—so that the
very parings of a counting-house are, in some sort,
the settings up of an author. The enfranchised
quill, that has plodded all the morning among the
cart-rucks of figures and ciphers, frisks and curvets
so at its ease over the flowery carpet ground of a
midnight dissertation. It feels its promotion. * * *
So that you see, upon the whole, the literary dignity
of *Elia* is very little, if at all, compromised in the
condescension.

Not that, in my anxious detail of the many com-
modities incidental to the life of a public office, I
would be thought blind to certain flaws, which a
cunning carper might be able to pick in this Joseph's
vest. And here I must have leave, in the fulness of
my soul, to regret the abolition, and doing-away-with
altogether, of those consolatory interstices and
sprinklings of freedom, through the four seasons—the
red-letter days, now become, to all intents and purposes,
dead-letter days. There was Paul, and Stephen, and
Barnabas, " Andrew, and John, men famous in old
times," we were used to keep all their days holy as long
back as I was at school at Christ's. I remember
their effigies, by the same token, in the old Basket
Prayer Book. There hung Peter in his uneasy
posture, holy Bartlemy in the troublesome act of
flaying, after the famous Marsyas by Spagnoletti. I
honoured them all, and could almost have wept the
defalcation of Iscariot,—so much did we love to keep

holy memories sacred :—only methought I a little
grudged at the coalition of the *better Jude* with
Simon—clubbing (as it were) their sanctities together,
to make up one poor gaudy day between them—as an
economy unworthy of the dispensation.

These were bright visitations in a scholar's and a
clerk's life—" far off their coming shone." I was as
good as an almanack in those days. I could hav
told you such a saint's day falls out next week, or the
week after. Peradventure the Epiphany, by some
periodical infelicity, would, once in six years, merge
in a Sabbath. Now am I little better than one of
the profane. Let me not be thought to arraign the
wisdom of my civil superiors, who have judged the
further observation of these holy tides to be papistical,
superstitious. Only in a custom of such long standing, methinks if their Holinesses the Bishops had, in
decency, been first sounded,—but I am wading out of
my depths. I am not the man to decide the limits of
civil and ecclesiastical authority; I am plain Elia—
no Selden, nor Archbishop Usher—though at present
in the thick of their books, here in the heart of learning, under the shadow of the mighty Bodley.

I can here play the gentleman, enact the student.
To such a one as myself, who has been defrauded in
his young years of the sweet food of academic institution, nowhere is so pleasant, to while away a few
idle weeks at, as one or other of the Universities. Their
vacation, too, at this time of the year, falls in so pat
with *ours*. Here I can take my walks unmolested,
and fancy myself of what degree or standing I please.
I seem admitted *ad eundem*. I fetch up past opportunities. I can rise at the chapel bell, and dream
that it rings for *me*. In moods of humility I can be

a Sizar, or a Servitor.   When the peacock vein rises
I strut a Gentleman Commoner.   In graver moments
I proceed Master of Arts.   Indeed I do not think I
am much unlike that respectable character.   I have
seen your dim-eyed vergers, and bed-makers in spectacles, drop a bow or a curtsy as I pass, wisely mistaking me for something of the sort.   I go about in black,
which favours the notion.   Only in Christ Church
reverend quadrangle I can be content to pass for
nothing short of a Seraphic Doctor.

The walks at these times are so much one's own—
the tall trees of Christ's, the groves of Magdalen!
The halls deserted, and with open doors inviting one
to slip in unperceived, and pay a devoir to some
Founder, or noble or royal Benefactress, (that should
have been ours,) whose portrait seems to smile upon
their over-looked beadsman, and to adopt me for their
own.   Then, to take a peep in by the way at the
butteries and sculleries, redolent of antique hospitality:
the immense caves of kitchens, kitchen fireplaces,
cordial recesses; ovens whose first pies were baked
four centuries ago; and spits which have cooked for
Chaucer!   Not the meanest minister among the
dishes but is hallowed to me through his imagination,
and the Cook goes forth a Manciple.

Antiquity! thou wondrous charm, what art thou?
that, being nothing, art every thing!   When thou
wert, thou wert not antiquity—then thou wert nothing,
but hadst a remoter *antiquity*, as thou calledst it, to
look back to with blind veneration; thou thyself
being to thyself flat, jejune, *modern!*   What mystery
lurks in this retroversion?   or what half Januses[1] are

---

[1] Januses of one face.—SIR THOMAS BROWNE.

we, that cannot look forward with the same idolatry with which we for ever revert! The mighty future is as nothing, being every thing : the past is every thing, being nothing!

What were thy *dark ages?* Surely the sun rose as bright then as now, and man got him to his work in the morning. Why is it we can never hear mention of them without an accompanying feeling, as though a palpable obscure had dimmed the face of things, and that our ancestors wandered to and fro groping!

Above all thy rarities, old Oxenford, what do most arride and solace me are thy repositories of mouldering learning, thy shelves.

What a place to be in is an old library! It seems as though all the souls of all the writers, that have bequeathed their labours to these Bodleians, were reposing here, as in some dormitory, or middle state. I do not want to handle, to profane the leaves, their winding-sheets. I could as soon dislodge a shade. I seem to inhale learning, walking amid their foliage ; and the odour of their old moth-scented coverings is fragrant as the first bloom of those sciential apples which grew amid the happy orchard.

Still less have I curiosity to disturb the elder repose of MSS. Those *variæ lectiones,* so tempting to the more erudite palates, do but disturb and unsettle my faith. I am no Herculanean raker. The credit of the three witnesses might have slept unimpeached for me. I leave these curiosities to Porson, and to G. D.—whom, by the way, I found busy as a moth over some rotten archive, rummaged out of some seldom explored press, in a nook at Oriel. With long poring, he is grown almost into a book. He stood as passive as one by the side of the old shelves. I longed to new coat him in russia, and assign him his place. He might have mustered for a tall Scapula.

D. is assiduous in his visits to these seats of learning. No inconsiderable portion of his moderate fortune, I apprehend, is consumed in journeys between them and Clifford's Inn, where, like a dove on the asp's nest, he has long taken up his unconscious abode, amid an incongruous assembly of attorneys, attorneys' clerk, apparitors, promoters, vermin of the law, among whom he sits "in calm and sinless peace." The fangs of the law pierce him not ; the winds of litigation blow over his humble chambers ; the hard sheriff's officer moves his hat as he passes ; legal nor illegal discourtesy touches him ; none thinks of offering violence or injustice to him ; you would as soon "strike an abstract idea."

D[yer] has been engaged, he tells me, through a course of laborious years, in an investigation into all curious matter connected with the two Universities ; and has lately lit upon a MS. collection of charters relative to C[ambridge],[1] by which he hopes to settle some disputed points, particularly that long controversy between them as to priority of foundation. The ardour with which he engages in these liberal pursuits, I am afraid, has not met with all the encouragement it deserved, either here or at C[ambridge]. Your caputs and heads of colleges care less than any body else about these questions.—Contented to suck the milky fountains of their Alma Maters, without inquiring into the venerable gentlewomen's years,

---

[1] Dyer published The History of the University and Colleges of Cambridge in 2 vols. royal 8vo., 1814. The work here alluded to is, *The Privileges of the University of Cambridge.*—H.

they rather hold such curiosities to be impertinent—
unreverend. They have their good glebe lands *in
manu*, and care not much to rake into the title-deeds.
I gather at least so much from other sources, for D.
is not a man to complain.

D. started like an unbroke heifer when I interrupted him. *A priori* it was not very probable that
we should have met in Oriel. But D. would have
done the same, had I accosted him on the sudden in
his own walks in Clifford's Inn, or in the Temple. In
addition to a provoking short-sightedness (the effect
of late studies and watchings at the midnight oil) D.
is the most absent of men. He made a call the other
morning at our friend M.'s in Bedford Square ;[1] and,
finding nobody at home, was ushered into the hall,
where, asking for pen and ink, with great exactitude
of purpose he enters me his name in the book—which
ordinarily lies about in such places, to record the
failures of the untimely or unfortunate visitor—and
takes his leave with many ceremonies and professions
of regret. Some two or three hours after, his walking
destinies returned him into the same neighbourhood
again, and again the quiet image of the fire-side circle
at M.'s—Mrs. M. presiding at it like a Queen Lar,
with pretty A. S.[2] at her side—striking irresistibly on
his fancy, he makes another call, (forgetting that they
were " certainly not to return from the country before
that day week,") and disappointed a second time,
inquires for pen and paper as before ; again the book
is brought, and in the line just above that in which
he is about to print his second name (his re-script)—

[1] Mr. Basil Montagu's.—H.
[2] Miss A. Skipper, now Mrs. Procter.—H.

his first name (scarce dry) looks out upon him like another Sosia, or as if a man should suddenly encounter his own duplicate !—The effect may be conceived. D. made many a good resolution against any such lapses in future. I hope he will not keep them too rigorously.

For with G.D., to be absent from the body is sometimes (not to speak it profanely) to be present with the Lord. At the very time when, personally encountering thee, he passes on with no recognition—or, being stopped, starts like a thing surprised,—at that moment, reader, he is on Mount Tabor,—or Parnassus—or co-sphered with Plato—or, with Harrington, framing " immortal commonwealths" —devising some plan of amelioration to thy country, or thy species,—peradventure meditating some individual kindness or courtesy, to be done to *thee thyself*, the returning consciousness of which made him to start so guiltily at thy obtruded personal presence.

D. is delightful anywhere, but he is at the best in such places as these. He cares not much for Bath. He is out of his element at Buxton, at Scarborough, or Harrowgate. The Cam and the Isis are to him " better than all the waters of Damascus." On the Muses' hill he is happy, and good, as one of the Shepherds on the Delectable Mountains ; and when he goes about with you to show you the halls and colleges, you think you have with you the Interpreter at the House Beautiful.

L 2

CHRIST'S HOSPITAL FIVE-AND-THIRTY YEARS AGO.

In Mr. Lamb's "Works," published a year or two since, I find a magnificent eulogy on my old school,[1] such as it was, or now appears to him to have been, between the years 1782 and 1789. It happens very oddly that my own standing at Christ's was nearly corresponding with his; and, with all gratitude to him for his enthusiasm for the cloisters, I think he has contrived to bring together whatever can be said in praise of them, dropping all the other side of the argument most ingeniously.

I remember L. at school, and can well recollect that he had some peculiar advantages, which I and others of his schoolfellows had not. His friends lived in town, and were near at hand; and he had the privilege of going to see them almost as often as he wished, through some invidious distinction, which was denied to us. The present worthy sub-treasurer to the Inner Temple can explain how that happened. He had his tea and hot rolls in a morning, while we were battening upon our quarter of a penny loaf—our *crug*—moistened with attenuated small beer, in wooden piggins, smacking of the pitched leathern jack it was poured from. Our Monday's milk porritch, blue and tasteless, and the pease soup of Saturday, coarse and choking, were enriched for him with a slice of " extra-

---

[1] Recollections of Christ's Hospital.

ordinary bread and butter," from the hot loaf of the Temple. The Wednesday's mess of millet, somewhat less repugnant—(we had three banyan to four meat days in the week)—was endeared to his palate with a lump of double-refined, and a smack of ginger (to make it go down the more glibly) or the fragrant cinnamon. In lieu of our *halfpickled* Sundays, or *quite fresh* boiled beef on Thursdays, (strong as *caro equina*,) with detestable marigolds floating in the pail to poison the broth—our scanty mutton scrags on Fridays—and rather more savoury, but grudging, portions of the same flesh, rotten-roasted or rare, on the Tuesdays, (the only dish which excited our appetites and disappointed our stomachs in almost equal proportion,)—he had his hot plate of roast veal, or the more tempting griskin, (exotics unknown to our palates,) cooked in the paternal kitchen, (a great thing,) and brought him daily by his maid or aunt ! I remember the good old relative (in whom love forbade pride) squatting down upon some odd stone in a by-nook of the cloisters, disclosing the viands (of higher regale than those cates which the ravens ministered to the Tishbite) and the contending passions of L. at the unfolding. There was love for the bringer ; shame for the thing brought, and the manner of its bringing ; sympathy for those who were too many to share in it ; and, at top of all, hunger, (eldest, strongest of the appetites !) predominant, breaking down the stony fences of shame, and awkwardness, and a troubling over-consciousness.

I was a poor friendless boy. My parents, and those who should care for me, were far away. Those few acquaintances of theirs, which they could reckon upon being kind to me in the great city, after a little forced notice which they had the grace to take of me on my first arrival in town, soon grew tired of my holiday visits. They seemed to them to recur too often, though I thought them few enough ; and, one after another, they all failed me, and I felt myself alone among six hundred playmates.

O the cruelty of separating a poor lad from his early homestead ! The yearnings which I used to have towards it in those unfledged years ! How, in my dreams, would my native town (far in the West) come back, with its church, and trees, and faces ! How I would wake weeping, and in the anguish of my heart exclaim upon sweet Calne, in Wiltshire !

To this late hour of my life I trace impressions left by the recollection of those friendless holidays. The long warm days of Summer never return but they bring with them a gloom from the haunting memory of those *whole-day leaves*, when by some strange arrangement we were turned out for the live-long day, upon our own hands, whether we had friends to go to or none. I remember those bathing excursions to the New River, which L. recalls with such relish, better, I think, than he can ; for he was a home-seeking lad, and did not much care for such water pastimes. How merrily we would sally forth into the fields; and strip under the first warmth of the sun ; and wanton like young dace in the streams ; getting us appetites for noon, which those of us that were penniless (our scanty morning crust long since exhausted) had not the means of allaying—while the cattle, and the birds, and the fishes were at feed about us, and we had nothing to satisfy our cravings —the very beauty of the day, and the exercise of the pastime, and the sense of liberty, setting a keener edge upon them! How faint and languid, finally, we would return towards night-fall, to our desired morsel, half-rejoicing, half-reluctant, that the hours of our uneasy liberty had expired!

It was worse in the days of Winter, to go prowling about the streets objectless—shivering at cold windows of print-shops, to extract a little amusement; or haply, as a last resort in the hopes of a little novelty, to pay a fifty-times repeated visit (where our individual faces should be as well known to the warden as those of his own charges) to the Lions in the Tower; to whose levee, by courtesy immemorial, we had a prescriptive title to admission.

L.'s governor (so we called the patron who presented us to the foundation) lived in a manner under his paternal roof. Any complaint which he had to make was sure of being attended to. This was understood at Christ's, and was an effectual screen to him against the severity of masters, or worse tyranny of the monitors. The oppressions of these young brutes are heart-sickening to call to recollection. I have been called out of my bed, and *waked for the purpose*, in the coldest Winter nights—and this not once, but night after night—in my shirt, to receive the discipline of a leathern thong, with eleven other sufferers, because it pleased my callow overseer, when there has been any talking heard after we were gone to bed, to make the last six beds in the dormitory, where the youngest children of us slept, answerable for an offence they neither dared to commit nor had the power to hinder. The same execrable tyranny drove the younger part of us from the fires, when our feet were perishing with snow; and, under the cruelest penalties, forbade the indulgence of a drink of water when we lay in sleepless Summer nights fevered with the season and the day's sports.

There was one H——, who, I learned, in after days was seen expiating some maturer offence in the hulks. (Do I flatter myself in fancying that this might be the planter of that name who suffered—at Nevis, I think, or St. Kitts,—some few years since! My friend Tobin was the benevolent instrument of bringing him to the gallows.) This petty Nero actually branded a boy who had offended him with a red-hot iron; and nearly starved forty of us with exacting contributions, to the one half of our bread, to pamper a young ass, which, incredible as it may seem, with the connivance of the nurse's daughter (a young flame of his) he had contrived to smuggle in, and keep upon the leads of the *ward*, as they called our dormitories.   This game went on for better than a week, till the foolish beast, not able to fare well but he must cry roast meat—happier than Caligula's minion, could he have kept his own counsel—but foolisher, alas, than any of his species in the fables !— waxing fat, and kicking, in the fulness of bread, one unlucky minute would needs proclaim his good fortune to the world below; and, laying out his simple throat, blew such a ram's-horn blast, as (toppling down the walls of his own Jericho) set concealment any longer at defiance.   The client was dismissed, with certain attentions, to Smithfield ; but I never understood that the patron underwent any censure on the occasion.   This was in the stewardship of L.'s admired Perry.

Under the same *facile* administration, can L. have forgotten the cool impunity with which the nurses used to carry away openly, in open platters,

for their own tables, one out of two of every hot
joint, which the careful matron had been seeing scru-
pulously weighed out for our dinners ?   These things
were daily practised in that magnificent apartment
which L. (grown connoisseur since, we presume,)
praises so highly for the grand paintings "by Verrio
and others" with which it is " hung round and
adorned." But the sight of sleek, well-fed blue-coat
boys in pictures was, at that time, I believe, little
consolatory to him, or us, the living ones, who saw
the better part of our provisions carried away before
our faces by harpies, and ourselves reduced (with
the Trojan in the hall of Dido)

> To feed our mind with idle portraiture.

L. has recorded the repugnance of the school to
gags, or the fat of fresh beef boiled, and sets it down
to some superstition. But these unctuous morsels
are never grateful to young palates, (children are universally fat-haters,) and in strong, coarse, boiled
meats, *unsalted*, are detestable. A *gag-eater* in our
time was equivalent to a *goule*, and held in equal de-
testation. —— suffered under the imputation :

> ————'Twas said
> He ate strange flesh.

He was observed, after dinner, carefully to gather
up the remnants left at his table, (not many nor very
choice fragments, you may credit me,)—and, in an
especial manner, these disreputable morsels he
would convey away and secretly stow in the settle
that stood at his bed side. None saw when he ate
them. It was rumoured that he privately devoured
them in the night. He was watched, but no traces
of such midnight practices were discoverable. Some

reported that on leave-days he had been seen to carry
out of the bounds a large blue check handkerchief
full of something. This then must be the accursed
thing. Conjecture next was at work to imagine how
he could dispose of it. Some said he sold it to the
beggars. This belief generally prevailed. He went
about moping. None spake to him. No one would
play with him. He was excommunicated; put out
of the pale of the school. He was too powerful a
boy to be beaten, but he underwent every mode of
that negative punishment which is more grievous
than many stripes. Still he persevered. At length
he was observed by two of his schoolfellows, who
were determined to get at the secret, and had traced
him one leave-day for the purpose, to enter a large
worn-out building, such as there exist specimens of in
Chancery Lane, which are let out to various scales of
pauperism, with open door and a common staircase.
After him they silently slunk in, and followed by
stealth up four flights, and saw him tap at a poor
wicket, which was opened by an aged woman, meanly
clad. Suspicion was now ripened into certainty.
The informers had secured their victim. They had
him in their toils. Accusation was formally preferred, and retribution most signal was looked for.
Mr. Hathaway, the then steward, (for this happened a
little after my time,) with that patient sagacity which
tempered all his conduct, determined to investigate
the matter before he proceeded to sentence. The
result was that the supposed mendicants, the re-
ceivers or purchasers of the mysterious scraps, turned
out to be the parents of ——, an honest couple come
to decay, whom this seasonable supply had, in all
probability, saved from mendicancy; and that this

young stork, at the expense of his own good name, had all this while been only feeding the old birds! The governors on this occasion, much to their honour, voted a present relief to the family of ——, and presented him with a silver medal. The lesson which the steward read upon RASH JUDGMENT, on the occasion of publicly delivering the medal to ——, I believe would not be lost on his auditory. I had left school then ; but I well remember ——. He was a tall, shambling youth, with a cast in his eye, not at all calculated to conciliate hostile prejudices. I have since seen him carrying a baker's basket. I think I heard he did not do quite so well by himself as he had done by the old folks.

I was a hypochondriac lad ; and the sight of a boy in fetters, upon the day of my first putting on the blue clothes, was not exactly fitted to assuage the natural terrors of initiation. I was of tender years, barely turned of seven ; and had only read of such things in books, or seen them but in dreams. I was told he had *run away*. This was the punishment for the first offence. As a novice I was soon after taken to see the dungeons. These were little, square, Bedlam cells, where a boy could just lie at his length upon straw and a blanket,— a mattress, I think, was afterwards substituted,—with a peep of light, let in askance, from a prison-orifice at top, barely enough to read by. Here the poor boy was locked in by himself all day, without sight of any but the porter who brought him his bread and water, (who *might not speak to him*,) or of the beadle, who came twice a week to call him out to receive his periodical chastisement, which was almost welcome, because it separated him for a brief interval from solitude :—and here he

was shut up by himself *of nights* out of the reach of
any sound, to suffer whatever horrors the weak nerves
and superstition incident to his time of life might
subject him to.[1] This was the penalty for the second
offence. Wouldst thou like, reader, to see what became of him in the next degree ?

The culprit who had been a third time an offender,
and whose expulsion was at this time deemed irreversible, was brought forth as at some solemn *auto da fè*,
arrayed in uncouth and most appalling attire—all
trace of his late "watchet weeds" carefully effaced, he
was exposed in a jacket resembling those which London
lamplighters formerly delighted in, with a cap of the
same. The effect of this divestiture was such as the
ingenious devisers of it could have anticipated. With
his pale and frighted features, it was as if some of
those disfigurements in Dante had seized upon him.
In this disguisement he was brought into the hall,
(*L.'s favourite state-room,*) where awaited him the
whole number of his school-fellows, whose joint
lessons and sports he was thenceforth to share no
more ; the awful presence of the steward, to be seen
for the last time ; of the executioner beadle, clad in
his state robe for the occasion ; and of two faces
more, of direr import, because never but in these extremities visible. These were governors ; two of whom
by choice, or charter, were always accustomed to
officiate at these *Ultima Supplicia;* not to mitigate

---

[1] One or two instances of lunacy, or attempted suicide, accordingly,
at length convinced the governors of the impolicy of this part of the
sentence, and the midnight torture to the spirits was dispensed with.—
This fancy of dungeons for children was a sprout of Howard's brain;
for which (saving the reverence due to Holy Paul) methinks I could
willingly spit upon his statue.

(so at least we understood it), but to enforce the
uttermost stripe.   Old Bamber Gascoigne and Peter
Aubert, I remember, were colleagues on one occasion, when the beadle turning rather pale, a glass
of brandy was ordered to prepare him for the mysteries.   The scourging was, after the old Roman
fashion, long and stately.   The lictor accompanied
the criminal quite round the hall. We were generally
too faint with attending to the previous disgusting
circumstances to make accurate report with our
eyes of the degree of corporal suffering inflicted.
Report, of course, gave out the back knotty and
livid.   After scourging he was made over, in his
San Benito, to his friends, if he had any, (but commonly such poor runagates were friendless,) or to his
parish officer, who, to enhance the effect of the scene,
had his station allotted to him on the outside of the
hall gate.

These solemn pageantries were not played off so
often as to spoil the general mirth of the community.
We had plenty of exercise and recreation *after* school
hours ; and, for myself, I must confess that I was
never happier than *in* them.   The Upper and the
Lower Grammar Schools were held in the same
room; and an imaginary line only divided their
bounds.   Their character was as different as that of
the inhabitants on the two sides of the Pyrenees.
The Rev. James Boyer was the Upper Master; but
the Rev. Matthew Field presided over that portion of
the apartment of which I had the good fortune to be
a member. We lived a life as careless as birds. We
talked and did just what we pleased, and nobody
molested us. We carried an accidence, or a grammar,
for form ; but, for any trouble it gave us, we might

take two years in getting through the verbs deponent, and another two in forgetting all that we had learned about them. There was now and then the formality of saying a lesson; but if you had not learned it, a brush across the shoulders (just enough to disturb a fly) was the sole remonstrance. Field never used the rod; and in truth he wielded the cane with no great good will, holding it "like a dancer." It looked in his hands rather like an emblem than an instrument of authority; and an emblem, too, which he was ashamed of. He was a good easy man, that did not care to ruffle his own peace, nor perhaps set any great consideration upon the value of juvenile time. He came among us now and then, but often stayed away whole days from us; and when he came it made no difference to us : he had his private room to retire to, the short time he stayed, to be out of the sound of our noise. Our mirth and uproar went on. Without being beholden to "insolent Greece or haughty Rome," we had classics of our own, that passed current among us,—" Peter Wilkins ; " "the Adventures of the Hon. Captain Robert Boyle ; " "the Fortunate Blue Coat Boy ; " and the like. Or we cultivated a turn for mechanic and scientific operations ; making little sun-dials of paper ; or weaving those ingenious parentheses called *cat-cradles ;* or making dry peas to dance upon the end of a tin pipe ; or studying the art military over the laudable game "French and English," and a hundred other such devices to pass away the time—mixing the useful with the agreeable —as would have made the souls of Rousseau and John Locke chuckle to have seen us.

Matthew Field belonged to that class of modest divines who affect to mix in equal proportion the *gentleman,* the *scholar,* and the *Christian ;* but, I know not how, the first ingredient is generally found to be the predominating dose in the composition. He was engaged in gay parties, or with his courtly bow at some episcopal levee, when he should have been attending upon us. He had for many years the classical charge of a hundred children, during the four or five first years of their education ; and his very highest form seldom proceeded further than two or three of the introductory fables of Phædrus. How things were suffered to go on thus, I cannot guess. Boyer, who was the proper person to have remedied these abuses, always affected, perhaps felt, a delicacy in interfering in a province not strictly his own. I have not been without my suspicions that he was not altogether displeased at the contrast we presented to his end of the school. We were a sort of Helots to his young Spartans. He would sometimes, with ironic deference, send to borrow a rod of the Under Master, and then, with Sardonic grin, observe to one of his upper boys, "how neat and fresh the twigs looked." While his pale students were battering their brains over Xenophon and Plato, with a silence as deep as that enjoyed by the Samite, we were enjoying ourselves at our ease in our little Goshen. We saw a little into the secrets of his discipline, and the pro- spect did but the more reconcile us to our lot. His thunders rolled innocuous for us : his storms came near, but never touched us : contrary to Gideon's miracle, while all around were drenched, our fleece was dry.[1] His boys turned out the better scholars ; we, I suspect, have the advantage in temper. His

---

[1] Cowley.

pupils cannot speak of him without something of terror allaying their gratitude ; the remembrance of Field comes back with all the soothing images of indolence, and summer slumbers, and work like play, and innocent idleness, and Elysian exemptions, and life itself a " playing holiday."

Though sufficiently removed from the jurisdiction of Boyer, we were near enough (as I have said) to understand a little of his system. We occasionally heard sounds of the *Ululantes*, and caught glances of Tartarus. B. was a rabid pedant. His English style was cramped to barbarism. His Easter anthems (for his duty obliged him to those periodical flights) were grating as scrannel pipes.[1] He would laugh, ay and heartily ; but then it must be at Flaccus's quibble about *Rex*, or at the *tristis severitas in vultu*, or *inspicere in patinas*, of Terence ;—thin jests, which at their first broaching could hardly have had *vis* enough to move a Roman muscle. He had two wigs, both pedantic, but of different omen. The one serene, smiling, fresh powdered, betokening a mild day. The other an old, discoloured, unkempt, angry caxon, denoting frequent and bloody execution. Woe to the school when he made his morning appearance in his *passy*, or *passionate wig*. No comet expounded surer. J—— B—— had a heavy hand. I have known

---

[1] In this and every thing B. was the antipodes of his coadjutor. While the former was digging his brains for crude anthems, worth a pig-nut, F. would be recreating his gentlemanly fancy in the more flowery walks of the Muses. A little dramatic effusion of his, under the name of Vertumnus and Pomona, is not yet forgotten by the chroniclers of that sort of literature. It was accepted by Garrick, but the town did not give it their sanction.—B. used to say of it, in a way of half-compliment, half-irony, that it was *too classical for repre- sentation*.

him double his knotty fist at a poor trembling child
(the maternal milk hardly dry upon its lips) with a
" Sirrah, do you presume to set your wits at me?"
Nothing was more common than to see him make a
headlong entry into the school-room, from his inner
recess, or library, and, with turbulent eye, singling
out a lad, roar out, "Od's my life, sirrah," (his
favourite adjuration,) " I have a great mind to whip
you ; " then, with as sudden a retracting impulse,
fling back into his lair ; and, after a cooling lapse of
some minutes, (during which all but the culprit had
totally forgotten the context,) drive headlong out
again, piecing out his imperfect sense, as if it had
been some Devil's Litany, with the expletory yell—
"*and I* WILL *too.*"—In his gentler moods, when the
rabidus furor was assuaged, he had resort to an ingenious method, peculiar, from what I have heard, to
himself, of whipping the boy and reading the Debates
at the same time ; a paragraph, and a lash between ;
which in those times, when parliamentary oratory
was most at a height and flourishing in these realms,
was not calculated to impress the patient with a
veneration for the diffuser graces of rhetoric.

Once, and but once, the uplifted rod was known to
fall ineffectual from his hand, when droll squinting
W—— having been caught putting the inside of the
master's desk to a use for which the architect had
clearly not designed it, to justify himself, with great
simplicity averred, that *he did not know that the thing
had been forewarned.* This exquisite irrecognition of
any law antecedent to the *oral* or *declaratory*, struck
so irresistibly upon the fancy of all who heard it
(the pedagogue himself not accepted)—that remis·
sion was unavoidable.

L. has given credit to B.'s great merits as an instructor. Coleridge, in his literary life, has pronounced a more intelligible and ample encomium on them. The author of the *Country Spectator* doubts not to compare him with the ablest teachers of antiquity. Perhaps we cannot dismiss him better than with the pious ejaculation of C.—when he heard that his old master was on his death-bed : " Poor J. B !— may all his faults be forgiven : and may he be wafted to bliss by little cherub boys all head and wings, with no *bottoms* to reproach his sublunary infirmities."

Under him were many good and sound scholars bred.—First Grecian of my time was Lancelot Pepys Stevens, kindest of boys and men, since Co-grammar-master (and inseparable companion) with Dr. T——e. What an edifying spectacle did this brace of friends present to those who remembered the anti-socialities of their predecessors! You never met the one by chance in the street without a wonder, which was quickly dissipated by the almost immediate sub-appearance of the other. Generally arm-in-arm, these kindly coadjutors lightened for each other the toilsome duties of their profession ; and when, in advanced age, one found it convenient to retire, the other was not long in discovering that it suited him to lay down the fasces also. Oh, it is pleasant, as it is rare, to find the same arm linked in yours at forty, which at thirteen helped it to turn over the *Cicero De Amicitiâ*, or some tale of Antique Friendship, which the young heart even then was burning to anticipate !—Co-Grecian with S. was Th——, who has since executed with ability various diplomatic functions at the Northern Courts. Th—— was a tall, dark, saturnine youth, sparing of speech, with raven locks. Thomas

Fanshaw Middleton followed him (now Bishop of Calcutta), a scholar and a gentleman in his teens. He has the reputation of an excellent critic; and is author (besides the *Country Spectator*) of a *Treatise on the Greek Article*, against Sharpe. M. is said to bear his mitre high in India, where the *regni novitas* (I dare say) sufficiently justifies the bearing. A humility quite as primitive as that of Jewel or Hooker might not be exactly fitted to impress the minds of those Anglo-Asiatic diocesans with a reverence for home institutions and the church which those fathers watered. The manners of M. at school, though firm, were mild and unassuming. Next to M. (if not senior to him) was Richards, author of the *Aboriginal Britons*, the most spirited of the Oxford Prize Poems; a pale, studious Grecian. Then followed poor S———, ill-fated M———? of these the Muse is silent.

> Finding some of Edward's race
> Unhappy, pass their annals by.

Come back into memory, like as thou wert in the dayspring of thy fancies, with hope like a fiery column before thee—the dark pillar not yet turned—Samuel Taylor Coleridge—Logician, Metaphysician, Bard! How have I seen the casual passer through the cloisters stand still, intranced with admiration (while he weighed the disproportion between the *speech* and the *garb* of the young Mirandula) to hear thee unfold, in thy deep and sweet intonations, the mysteries of Jamblichus, or Plotinus, (for even in those years thou waxedst not pale at such philosophic draughts,) or reciting Homer in his Greek, or Pindar, —while the walls of the old Grey Friars re-echoed to the accents of the *inspired charity-boy!* Many were the " wit-combats " (to dally awhile with the words of old Fuller) between him and C. V. Le G—— " which two I behold like a Spanish great galleon and an English man-of-war. Master Coleridge, like the former, was built far higher in learning, solid, but slow in his performances. C. V. L., with the English man-of-war, lesser in bulk, but lighter in sailing, could turn with all tides, tack about, and take advantage of all winds, by the quickness of his wit and invention."

Nor shalt thou, their compeer, be quickly forgotten, Allen, with the cordial smile and still more cordial laugh with which thou wert wont to make the old Cloisters shake, in thy cognition of some poignant jest of theirs ; or the anticipation of some more material, and peradventure practical one, of thine own. Extinct are those smiles, with that beautiful countenance, with which, (for thou wert the *Nireus formosus* of the school,) in the days of thy maturer waggery, thou didst disarm the wrath of infuriated town-damsel, who, incensed by provoking pinch, turning tigeress-like round, suddenly converted by thy angel-look, exchanged the half-formed terrible "*bl*——," for a gentler greeting—"*bless thy handsome face !*"

Next follow two, who ought to be now alive, and the friends of Elia — the junior Le G—— and F—— ; who impelled, the former by a roving temper, the latter by too quick a sense of neglect— ill capable of enduring the slights poor Sizars are sometimes subject to in our seats of learning—exchanged their Alma Mater for the camp ; perishing, one by climate, and one on the plains of Salamanca :— Le G——, sanguine, volatile, sweet-natured ; F——, dogged, faithful, anticipative of insult, warm-hearted, with something of the old Roman height about him.

Fine, frank-hearted F——, the present Master of Hertford, with Marmaduke T——, mildest of Missionaries—and both my good friends still—close the catalogue of Grecians in my time.

THE TWO RACES OF MEN.

THE human species, according to the best theory I can form of it, is composed of two distinct races, *the men who borrow, and the men who lend*. To these two original diversities may be reduced all those impertinent classifications of Gothic and Celtic tribes, white men, black men, red men. All the dwellers upon earth, "Parthians, and Medes, and Elamites," flock hither, and do naturally fall in with one or other of these primary distinctions. The infinite superiority of the former, which I choose to designate as the *great race*, is discernible in their figure, port, and a certain instinctive sovereignty. The latter are born degraded. " He shall serve his brethren." There is something in the air of one of this cast, lean and suspicious ; contrasting with the open, trusting, generous manners of the other.

Observe who have been the greatest borrowers of all ages—Alcibiades—Falstaff—Sir Richard Steele— our late incomparable Brinsley,—what a family like- ness in all four !

What a careless, even deportment hath your borrower! what rosy gills! what a beautiful reliance on
Providence doth he manifest,—taking no more
thought than lilies! What contempt for money,—
accounting it (yours and mine especially) no better
than dross! What a liberal confounding of those
pedantic distinctions of *meum* and *tuum!* or rather,
what a noble simplification of language, (beyond
Tooke,) resolving these supposed opposites into
one clear, intelligible pronoun adjective! What
near approaches doth he make to the primitive *community*,—to the extent of one half of the principle at
least.

He is the true taxer who " calleth all the world up
to be taxed ; " and the distance is as vast between
him and *one of us*, as subsisted between the Augustan
Majesty and the poorest obolary Jew that paid his
tribute-pittance at Jerusalem !—His exactions, too,
have such a cheerful, voluntary air !—so far removed
from your sour parochial or state-gatherers,—those
ink-horn varlets, who carry their want of welcome in
their faces! He cometh to you with a smile, and
troubleth you with no receipt; confining himself to
no set season. Every day is his Candlemas, or his
Feast of Holy Michael. He applieth the *lene tor-
mentum* of a pleasant look to your purse,—which to
that gentle warmth expands her silken leaves, as
naturally as the cloak of the traveller, for which sun
and wind contended. He is the true Propontic which
never ebbeth,—the sea which taketh handsomely at
each man's hand. In vain the victim, whom he de-
lighteth to honour, struggles with destiny; he is in
the net. Lend therefore cheerfully, O man ordained
to lend, that thou lose not in the end, with thy

worldly penny, the reversion promised. Combine
not preposterously in thine own person the penalties
of Lazarus and of Dives ;—but when thou seest the
proper authority coming, meet it smilingly, as it were
half-way. Come, a handsome sacrifice! See how
light *he* makes of it! Strain not courtesies with a
noble enemy.

Reflections like the foregoing were forced upon
my mind by the death of my old friend, Ralph
Bigod, Esq., who parted this life on Wednesday
evening; dying, as he had lived, without much
trouble. He boasted himself a descendant from
mighty ancestors of that name, who heretofore held
ducal dignities in this realm. In his actions and
sentiments he belied not the stock to which he pretended. Early in life he found himself invested with
ample revenues ; which, with that noble disinterest-
edness which I have noticed as inherent in men of
the *great race,* he took almost immediate measures
entirely to dissipate and bring to nothing : for there
is something revolting in the idea of a king holding a
private purse; and the thoughts of Bigod were all
regal. Thus furnished by the very act of disfurnish-
ment,—getting rid of the cumbersome luggage of
riches, more apt (as one sings)

> To slacken virtue, and abate her edge,
> Than prompt her to do aught may merit praise.

he set forth, like some Alexander, upon his great
enterprise, " borrowing and to borrow !"

In his periegesis, or triumphant progress throughout this island, it has been calculated that he laid a
tythe part of the inhabitants under contribution. I
reject this estimate as greatly exaggerated; but
having had the honour of accompanying my friend

divers times in his perambulations about this vast
city, I own I was greatly struck at first with the prodigious number of faces we met who claimed a sort
of respectful acquaintance with us. He was one day
so obliging as to explain the phenomenon. It seems
these were his tributaries; feeders of his exchequer;
gentlemen, his good friends, (as he was pleased to
express himself,) to whom he had occasionally been
beholden for a loan. Their multitudes did no way
disconcert him. He rather took a pride in numbering
them; and, with Comus, seemed pleased to be
" stocked with so fair a herd."

With such sources, it was a wonder he contrived
to keep his treasury always empty. He did it by
force of an aphorism, which he had often in his mouth,
that " money kept longer than three days stinks."
So he made use of it while it was fresh. A good
part he drank away (for he was an excellent toss-
pot); some he gave away, the rest he threw away,
literally tossing and hurling it violently from him—
as boys do burrs, or as if it had been infectious—into
ponds, or ditches, or deep holes, inscrutable cavities
of the earth ;—or he would bury it (where he would
never seek it again) by a river's side under some
bank, which (he would facetiously observe) paid no
interest; but out away from him it must go peremptorily, as Hagar's offspring into the wilderness, while
it was sweet. He never missed it. The streams
were perennial which fed his fisc. When new supplies became necessary, the first person that had the
felicity to fall in with him, friend or stranger, was
sure to contribute to the deficiency; for Bigod had
an *undeniable* way with him. He had a cheerful, open
exterior, a quick jovial eye, **a** bald forehead, just

touched with grey (*cana fides*). He anticipated no excuse, and found none. And, waiving for a while my theory as to the *great race*, I would put it to the most untheorising reader, who may at times have disposable coin in his pocket, whether it is not more repugnant to the kindliness of his nature to refuse such a one as I am describing, than to say *no* to a poor petitionary rogue (your bastard borrower) who, by his mumping visnomy, tells you that he expects nothing better; and, therefore, whose preconceived notions and expectations you do in reality so much less shock in the refusal.

When I think of this man,—his fiery glow of heart, his swell of feeling,—how magnificent, how *ideal* he was; how great at the midnight hour; and when I compare with him the companions with whom I have associated since, I grudge the saving of a few idle ducats, and think that I am fallen into the society of *lenders* and *little* men.

To one like Elia whose treasures are rather cased in leather covers than closed in iron coffers, there is a class of alienators more formidable than that which I have touched upon; I mean your *borrowers of books* —those mutilators of collections, spoilers of the symmetry of shelves, and creators of odd volumes. There is Comberbatch, matchless in his depredations!

That foul gap in the bottom shelf facing you, like a great eye-tooth knocked out—(you are now with me in my little back study in Bloomsbury, reader!—with the huge Switzer-like tomes on each side (like the Guildhall giants, in their reformed posture, guardant of nothing) once held the tallest of my folios, *Opera Bonaventuræ*, choice and massive divinity, to which its

two supporters (school divinity also, but of a lesser
calibre,—Bellarmine, and Holy Thomas) showed but
as dwarfs,—itself an Ascapart!—*that* Comberbatch
abstracted upon the faith of a theory he holds,
which is more easy, I confess, for me to suffer
by than to refute, namely, that "the title to property in a book (my Bonaventure, for instance,) is
in exact ratio to the claimant's powers of understanding and appreciating the same." Should he
go on acting upon this theory, which of our shelves
is safe?

The slight vacuum in the left-hand case—two
shelves from the ceiling—scarcely distinguishable but
by the quick eye of a loser—was whilom the commodious resting-place of Brown on Urn Burial. C.
will hardly allege that he knows more about that
treatise than I do, who introduced it to him, and was
indeed the first (of the moderns) to discover its
beauties; but so have I known a foolish lover to
praise his mistress in the presence of a rival more
qualified to carry her off than himself. Just below,
Dodsley's dramas want their fourth volume, where
Vittoria Corombona is! The remainder nine are as
distasteful as Priam's refuse sons when the Fates
borrowed Hector. Here stood the *Anatomy of Melancholy*, in sober state. There loitered the *Complete
Angler;* quiet as in life, by some stream side. In
yonder nook, John Buncle, a widower-volume, with
"eyes closed," mourns his ravished mate.

One justice I must do my friend, that if he sometimes, like the sea, sweeps away a treasure, at another
time, sea-like, he throws up as rich an equivalent to
match it. I have a small under-collection of this
nature, (my friend's gatherings in his various calls,)

picked up, he has forgotten at what odd places, and deposited with as little memory at mine. I take in these orphans, the twice-deserted. These proselytes of the gate are welcome as the true Hebrews. There they stand in conjunction; natives and naturalized. The latter seem as little disposed to inquire out their true lineage as I am.—I charge no warehouse-room for these deodands, nor shall ever put myself to the ungentlemanly trouble of advertising a sale of them to pay expenses.

To lose a volume to C. carries some sense and meaning in it. You are sure that he will make one hearty meal on your viands, if he can give no account of the platter after it. But what moved thee, way-ward, spiteful K——, to be so importunate to carry off with thee, in spite of tears and adjurations to thee to forbear, the Letters of that princely woman, the thrice noble Margaret Newcastle ?—knowing at the time, and knowing that I knew also, thou most assuredly wouldst never turn over one leaf of the illustrious folio :—what but the mere spirit of contra-diction, and childish love of getting the better of thy friend ?—Then (worst cut of all !) to transport it with thee to the Gallican land—

> Unworthy land to harbour such a sweetness,
> A virtue in which all ennobling thoughts dwelt,
> Pure thoughts, kind thoughts, high thoughts, her sex's wonder!

hadst thou not thy play-books, and books of jests and fancies, about thee, to keep thee merry, even as thou keepest all companies with thy quips and mirth-ful tales ? Child of the Green-room, it was unkindly done of thee. Thy wife, too, that part-French, better-part English woman !—that *she* could fix upon no other treatise to bear away, in kindly token of remem-

bering us, than the works of Fulke Greville, Lord
Brook,—of which no Frenchman, nor woman of
France, Italy, or England, was ever by nature constituted to comprehend a tittle!—*Was there not Zim-
merman on Solitude ?*

Reader, if haply thou art blest with a moderate
collection, be shy of showing it ; or if thy heart over-
floweth to lend them, lend thy books ; but let it be to
such a one as S. T. C. : he will return them (generally
anticipating the time appointed) with usury, enriched with annotations tripling their value.   I have
had experience.   Many are these precious MSS. of
his—(in *matter* oftentimes, and almost in *quantity* not
unfrequently, vying with the originals) in no very
clerkly hand—legible in my Daniel ; in old Burton ;
in Sir Thomas Browne; and those abstruser cogita-
tions of the Greville,—now, alas, wandering in Pagan
lands !   I counsel thee, shut not thy heart nor thy
library against S. T. C.

NEW YEAR'S EVE.

EVERY man hath two birthdays: two days, at least, in every year, which set him upon revolving the lapse of time, as it affects his mortal duration. The one is that which in an especial manner he termeth *his*. In the gradual desuetude of old observances, this custom of solemnizing our proper birthday hath nearly passed away, or is left to children, who reflect nothing at all about the matter, nor understand any thing in it beyond cake and orange. But the birth of a New Year is of an interest too wide to be pretermitted by king or cobbler. No one ever regarded the first of January with indifference. It is that from which all date their time, and count upon what is left. It is the nativity of our common Adam.

Of all sound of all bells—(bells, the music nighest bordering upon heaven)—most solemn and touching is the peal which rings out the Old Year. I never hear it without a gathering-up of my mind to a concentration of all the images that have been diffused over the past twelvemonth; all I have done or suffered, performed or neglected, in that regretted time. I begin to know its worth, as when a person dies. It takes a personal colour; nor was it a poetical flight in a contemporary when he exclaimed—

I saw the skirts of the departing Year.

It is no more than what in sober sadness every one

of us seems to be conscious of, in that awful leave
taking. I am sure I felt it, and all felt it with me,
last night ; though some of my companions affected
rather to manifest an exhilaration at the birth of the
coming year, than any very tender regrets for the decease of its predecessor. But I am none of those
who—

Welcome the coming, speed the parting guest.

I am naturally, beforehand, shy of novelties,—new
books, new faces, new years,—from some mental
twist which makes it difficult in me to face the prospective. I have almost ceased to hope ; and am
sanguine only in the prospects of other (former) years.
I plunge into foregone visions and conclusions. I
encounter pell-mell with past disappointments. I am
armour-proof against old discouragements. I forgive,
or overcome in fancy, old adversaries. I play over
again *for love*, as the gamesters phrase it, games for
which I once paid so dear. I would scarce now have
any of those untoward accidents and events of my life
reversed. I would no more alter them than the incidents of some well-contrived novel. Methinks it is
better that I should have pined away seven of my
goldenest years, when I was thrall to the fair hair
and fairer eyes of Alice W————n, than that so
passionate a love-adventure should be lost. It was
better that our family should have missed that legacy,
which old Dorrell cheated us of, than that I should
have at this moment two thousand pounds *in banco*,
and be without the idea of that specious old rogue.

In a degree beneath manhood, it is my infirmity to
look back upon those early days. Do I advance a
paradox, when I say, that, skipping over the interven-

tion of forty years, a man may have leave to love *himself*, without the imputation of self-love ?

If I know aught of myself, no one whose mind is introspective—and mine is painfully so—can have a less respect for his present identity than I have for the man Elia. I know him to be light, and vain, and humoursome; a notorious * * *; addicted to * * * *: averse from counsel, neither taking it nor offering it ;—* * * besides ; a stammering buffoon ; what you will ; lay it on, and spare not : I subscribe to it all, and much more than thou canst be willing to lay at his door : but for the child Elia, that "other me," there, in the back-ground, I must take leave to cherish the remembrance of that young master,—with as little reference, I protest, to this stupid changeling of five-and-forty as if it had been a child of some other house, and not of my parents. I can cry over its patient small-pox at five, and rougher medicaments. I can lay its poor fevered head upon the sick pillow at Christ's, and wake with it in surprise at the gentle posture of maternal tenderness hanging over it, that unknown had watched its sleep. I know how it shrank from any the least colour of falsehood. God help thee, Elia, how art thou changed !—Thou art sophisticated.—I know how honest, how courageous (for a weakling) it was,—how religious, how imaginative, how hopeful ! From what have I not fallen, if the child I remember was indeed myself, and not some dissembling guardian, presenting a false identity, to give the rule to my unpractised steps, and regulate the tone of my moral being !

That I am fond of indulging beyond a hope of sympathy, in such retrospection, may be the symptom of some sickly idiosyncrasy. Or is it owing to another cause : simply, that being without wife or family, I have not learned to project myself enough out of myself; and having no offspring of my own to dally with, I turn back upon memory, and adopt my own early idea as my heir and favourite ? If these speculations seem fantastical to thee, reader, (a busy man perchance,) if I tread out of the way of thy sympathy, and am singularly conceited only, I retire, impenetrable to ridicule, under the phantom cloud of Elia.

The elders, with whom I was brought up, were of a character not likely to let slip the sacred observance of any old institution ; and the ringing out of the Old Year was kept by them with circumstances of peculiar ceremony. In those days the sound of those midnight chimes, though it seemed to raise hilarity in all around me, never failed to bring a train of pensive imagery into my fancy. Yet I then scarce conceived what it meant, or thought of it as a reckoning that concerned me. Not childhood alone, but the young man till thirty, never feels practically that he is mortal. He knows it indeed, and, if need were, he could preach a homily on the fragility of life ; but he brings it not home to himself, any more than in a hot June we can appropriate to our imagination the freezing days of December. But now (shall I confess a truth ?) I feel these audits but too powerfully. I begin to count the probabilities of my duration, and to grudge at the expenditure of moments and shortest periods, like misers' farthings. In proportion as the years both lessen and shorten, I set more count upon their periods, and would fain lay my ineffectual finger upon the spoke of the great wheel. I am not content to pass away " like a weaver's shuttle." Those metaphors solace me not, nor sweeten the unpalatable draught of mortality. I care not to be carried with the tide that smoothly bears human life to eternity ; and reluct at the inevitable course of destiny. I am in love with this green earth,—the face of town and country,—the unspeakable rural solitudes, and the sweet security of streets. I would set up my taber- nacle here. I am content to stand still at the age to which I am arrived,—I and my friends,—to be no younger, no richer, no handsomer. I do not want to be weaned by age ; or drop, like mellow fruit, as they say, into the grave. Any alteration, on this earth of mine, in diet or in lodging, puzzles and discomposes me. My household gods plant a terrible fixed foot, and are not rooted up without blood. They do not willingly seek Lavinian shores. A new state of being staggers me.

Sun, and sky, and breeze, and solitary walks, and Summer holidays, and the greenness of fields, and the delicious juices of meats and fishes, and society, and the cheerful glass, and candle-light, and fireside con- versations, and innocent vanities, and jests, and *irony itself*,—do these things go out with life ?

Can a ghost laugh, or shake his gaunt sides, when you are pleasant with him ?

And you, my midnight darlings, my Folios ! must I part with the intense delight of having you (huge armfuls) in my embraces ? Must knowledge come to me, if it come at all, by some awkward experiment of intuition, and no longer by this familiar process of reading ?

Shall I enjoy friendships there, wanting the smiling indications which point me to them here,—the recog- nisable face,—the " sweet assurance of a look ? "

In Winter this intolerable disinclination to dying—
to give it its mildest name—does more especially
haunt and beset me. In a genial August noon,
beneath a sweltering sky, death is almost problematic.
At those times do such poor snakes as myself enjoy
an immortality. Then we expand and burgeon.
Then we are as strong again, as valiant again, as wise
again, and a great deal taller. The blast that nips
and shrinks me, puts me in thoughts of death. All
things allied to the insubstantial wait upon that
master feeling,—cold, numbness, dreams, perplexity,
moonlight itself, with its shadowy and spectral appearances,—that cold ghost of the sun, or Phœbus's sickly
sister, like that innutritious one denounced in the
Canticles :—I am none of her minions ; I hold with
the Persian.

Whatsoever thwarts, or puts me out of my way,
brings death into my mind. All partial evils, like
humours, run into that capital plague-sore. I have
heard some profess an indifference to life. Such hail
the end of their existence as a port of refuge; and
speak of the grave as of some soft arms, in which
they may slumber as on a pillow. Some have wooed
Death ; but out upon thee, I say, thou foul, ugly
phantom ! I detest, abhor, execrate, and (with Friar
John) give thee to six score thousand devils, as in no
instance to be excused or tolerated, but shunned as
an universal viper,—to be branded, proscribed, and
spoken evil of ! In no way can I be brought to digest
thee, thou thin, melancholy *Privation*, or more frightful and confounding *Positive !*

Those antidotes, prescribed against the fear of
thee, are altogether frigid and insulting, like thyself.
For what satisfaction hath a man, that he shall " lie

down with kings and emperors in death," who in his lifetime never greatly coveted the society of such bed-fellows ?—or, forsooth, that " so shall the fairest face appear?"—why, to comfort me, must A ice W———n be a goblin? More than all, I conceive disgust at those impertinent and misbecoming familiarities inscribed upon your ordtnary tombstones. Every deadman must take upon himself to be lecturing me with his odious truism, that " Such as he now is I must shortly be." Not so shortly, friend, perhaps, as thou imaginest. In the mean time I am alive. I move about. I am worth twenty of thee. Know thy betters! Thy New Years' days are past. I survive, a jolly candidate for 1821. Another cup of wine !—and while that turncoat bell, that just now mournfully chanted the obsequies of 1820 departed, with changed notes lustily rings in a successor, let us attune to its peal the song made on a like occasion, by hearty, cheerful Mr. Cotton :—

THE NEW YEAR.

Hark ! the cock crows ! and yon bright star
Tells us, the day himself's not far.
And see where, breaking from the night,
He gilds the western hills with light !
With him old Janus doth appear,
Peeping into the future year,
With such a look as seems to say
The prospect is not good that way.
Thus do we rise ill sights to see,
And 'gainst ourselves do prophesy ;
When the prophetic fear of things
A more tormenting mischief brings,
More full of soul-tormenting gall
Than direst mischiefs can befall.
But stay ! but stay ! methinks my sigh
Better inform'd by clearer light.

Discerns sereneness in that brow,
That all contracted seem'd but now.
His revers'd face may show distaste,
And frown upon the ills are past;
But that which this way looks is clear
And smiles upon the New-born Year.
He looks too from a place so high,
The year lies open to his eye;
And all the moments open are
To the exact discoverer.
Yet more and more he smiles upon
The happy revolution.
Why should we then suspect or fear
The influences of a year,
So smiles upon us the first morn,
And speaks us good so soon as born?
Plague on't! the last was ill enough,
This cannot but make better proof;
Or, at the worst, as we brush'd through
The last, why so we may this too;
And then the next in reason shou'd
Be superexcellently good:
For the worst ills (we daily see)
Have no more perpetuity
Than the best fortunes that do fall;
Which also bring us wherewithal
Longer their being to support,
Than those do of the other sort:
And who has one good year in three,
And yet repines at destiny,
Appears ungrateful in the case,
And merits not the good he has.
Then let us welcome the New Guest
With lusty brimmers of the best;
Mirth always should Good Fortune meet,
And renders e'en Disaster sweet:
And though the Princess turn her back,
Let us but line ourselves with sack,
We better shall by far hold out,
Till the next Year she face about.

How say you, reader—do not these verses smack of the rough magnanimity of the old English vein? Do they not fortify like a cordial; enlarging the heart, and productive of sweet blood, and generous spirits, in the concoction? Where be those puling fears of death, just now expressed or affected?— Passed like a cloud—absorbed in the purging sunlight of clear poetry—clean washed away by a wave of genuine Helicon, your only Spa for these hypochon- dries. And now another cup of the generous! and a merry New Year, and many of them to you all, my masters!

MRS. BATTLE'S OPINIONS ON WHIST.

"A CLEAR fire, a clean hearth, and the rigour of the game." This was the celebrated *wish* of old Sarah Battle, (now with God,) who, next to her devotions, loved a good game at whist. She was none of your lukewarm gamesters, your half-and-half players, who have no objection to take a hand, if you want one to make up a rubber; who affirm that they have no pleasure in winning; that they like to win one game and lose another; that they can while away an hour very agreeably at a card-table, but are indifferent whether they play or no; and will desire an adversary who has slipped a wrong card to take it up and play

another.   These insufferable triflers are the curse of
a table. One of these flies will spoil a whole pot. Of
such it may be said that they do not play at cards,
but only play at playing at them.

Sarah Battle was none of that breed. She detested
them, as I do, from her heart and soul, and would
not, save upon a striking emergency, willingly seat
herself at the same table with them. She loved a
thorough-paced partner, a determined enemy. She
took, and gave, no concessions.   She hated favours.
She never made a revoke, nor ever passed it over in
her adversary without exacting the utmost forfeiture.
She fought a good fight: cut and thrust. She held
not her good sword (her cards) " like a dancer."   She
sat bolt upright; and neither showed you her cards,
nor desired to see yours.   All people have their blind
side—their superstitions; and I have heard her declare,
under the rose, that hearts was her favourite suit.

I never in my life—and I knew Sarah Battle many
of the best years of it—saw her take out her snuff-
box when it was her turn to play ; or snuff a candle
in the middle of a game ; or ring for a servant till
it was fairly over. She never introduced, or connived
at, miscellaneous conversation during its process. As
she emphatically observed, cards were cards ; and if
ever I saw unmingled distate in her fine last-century
countenance, it was at the airs of a young gentleman
of a literary turn, who had been with difficulty persuaded to take a hand ; and who, in his excess of
candour, declared that he thought there was no
harm in unbending the mind now and then, after
serious studies, in recreations of that kind! She could
not bear to have her noble occupation, to which she
wound up her faculties, considered in that light.   It

was her business, her duty, the thing she came into the world to do,—and she did it. She unbent her mind afterwards over a book.

Pope was her favourite author: his *Rape of the Lock* her favourite work. She once did me the favour to play over with me (with the cards) his celebrated game of Ombre in that poem; and to explain to me how far it agreed with, and in what points it would be found to differ from, tradrille. Her illustrations were apposite and poignant; and I had the pleasure of sending the substance of them to Mr. Bowles; but I suppose they came too late to be inserted among his ingenious notes upon that author.

Quadrille, she has often told me, was her first love; but Whist had engaged her maturer esteem. The former, she said, was showy and specious, and likely to allure young persons. The uncertainty and quick shifting of partners—a thing which the constancy of Whist abhors; the dazzling supremacy and regal investiture of Spadille—absurd, as she justly observed, in the pure aristocracy of Whist, where his crown and garter give him no proper power above his brother-nobility of the Aces;—the giddy vanity, so taking to the inexperienced, of playing alone; above all, the overpowering attractions of a *Sans Prendre Vole*,—to the triumph of which there is certainly nothing parallel or approaching in the contingencies of Whist;—all these, she would say, make Quadrille a game of captivation to the young and enthusiastic. But Whist was the *solider* game: that was her word. It was a long meal; not, like Quadrille, a feast of snatches. One or two rubbers might co-extend in duration with an evening. They gave time to form rooted friendships, to cultivate steady enmities. She despised the chance-started, capricious, and even fluctuating alliances of the other. The skirmishes of Quadrille, she would say, reminded her of the petty ephemeral embroilments of the little Italian States, depicted by Machiavel : perpetually changing postures and connections; bitter foes today, sugared darlings to-morrow ; kissing and scratching in a breath : but the wars of whist were comparable to the long, steady, deep-rooted, rational, antipathies of the great French and English nations.

A grave simplicity was what she chiefly admired in her favourite game. There was nothing silly in it, like the nob in Cribbage,—nothing superfluous. No *flushes*, (the most irrational of all pleas that a reasonable being can set up,) that any one should claim four by virtue of holding cards of the same mark and colour, without reference to the playing of the game, or the individual worth or pretentions of the cards themselves ! She held this to be a solecism; as pitiful an ambition at cards as alliteration is in authorship. She despised superficiality, and looked deeper than the colours of things. Suits were soldiers, she would say, and must have an uniformity of array to distinguish them : but what should we say to a foolish squire, who should claim a merit from dressing up his tenantry in red jackets, that never were to be marshalled, never to take the field ? She even wished that whist were more simple than it is ; and, in mind, would have stripped it of some appendages, which, in a state of human frailty, may be venially, and even commendably, allowed of. She saw no reason for the deciding of the trump by the turn of the card. Why not one suit always trumps ? Why two colours, when the mark of the suits would have sufficiently distinguished them without it?

" But the eye, my dear Madam, is agreeably refreshed with the variety. Man is not a creature of pure reason : he must have his senses delightfully appealed to. We see it in Roman Catholic countries, where the music and the paintings draw in many to worship, whom your Quaker spirit of unsensualizing would have kept out. You yourself have a pretty collection of paintings ; but confess to me, whether, walking in your gallery at Sandham, among those clear Vandykes, or among the Paul Potters in the ante-room, you ever felt your bosom glow with an elegant delight, at all comparable to *that* you have it in you power to experience most evenings over a well-arranged assortment of the Court cards ?—the pretty antic habits, like heralds in a procession—the gay triumph-assuring scarlets—the contrasting deadly-killing sables—the ' hoary majesty of spades '—Pam in all his glory !

" All these might be dispensed with ; and with their naked names upon the drab pasteboard, the game might go on very well, pictureless. But the *beauty* of cards would be extinguished for ever. Stripped of all that is imaginative in them, they must degenerate into mere gambling. Imagine a dull deal board, or drum-head, to spread them on, instead of that nice verdant carpet, (next to Nature's,) fittest arena for those courtly combatants to play their gallant jousts and turneys in !—Exchange those delicately-turned ivory markers—(work of Chinese artist, unconscious of their symbol,—or as profanely slighting their true application as the arrantest Ephesian journeyman that turned out those little shrines for **the**

goddess)—exchange them for little bits of leather
(our ancestors' money) or chalk and a slate ! "—

The old lady with a smile confessed the soundness
of my logic ; and to her approbation of my arguments
on her favourite topic that evening I have always
fancied myself indebted for the legacy of a curious
cribbage-board, made of the finest Sienna marble,
which her maternal uncle (old Walter Plumer, whom
I have elsewhere celebrated) brought with him from
Florence :—this, and a trifle of five hundred pounds,
came to me at her death.

The former bequest (which I do not least value) I
have kept with religious care ; though she herself, to
confess a truth, was never greatly taken with Cribbage.
It was an essentially vulgar game, I have heard her
say, disputing with her uncle, who was very partial to
it.   She could never heartily bring her mouth to pronounce "*Go* " or "*That's a go.*" She called it an
ungrammatical game. The pegging teased her. I
once knew her to forfeit a rubber (a five-dollar stake)
because she would not take advantage of the turn-up
knave, which would have given it her, but which she
must have claimed by the disgraceful tenure of declaring "*two for his heels.*" There is something
extremely genteel in this sort of self-denial. Sarah
Battle was a gentlewoman born.

Piquet she held the best game at the cards for two
persons, though she would ridicule the pedantry of
the terms—such as pique—repique—the capot: they
savoured (she thought) of affectation. But games
for two, or even three, she never greatly cared for.
She loved the quadrate, or square. She would argue
thus :—Cards are warfare: the ends are gain, with
glory. But cards are war, in disguise of a sport :

when single adversaries encounter, the ends proposed are too palpable. By themselves, it is too close a fight ; with spectators, it is not much bettered. No looker-on can be interested, except for a bet, and then it is a mere affair of money; he cares not for your luck *sympathetically*, or for your play. Three are still worse ; a mere naked war of every man against every man, as in Cribbage, without league or alliance ; or a rotation of petty and contradictory interests, a succession of heartless leagues, and not much more hearty infractions of them, as in tradrille. But in square games (*she meant Whist*) all that is possible to be attained in card-playing is accomplished. There are the incentives of profit with honour, common to every species, though the *latter* can be but very imperfectly enjoyed in those other games, where the spectator is only feebly a participator. But the parties in Whist are spectators and principals too. They are a theatre to themselves, and a looker-on is not wanted. He is rather worse than nothing, and an impertinence. Whist abhors neutrality, or interests beyond its sphere. You glory in some surprising stroke of skill or fortune, not because a cold—or even an interested— bystander witnesses it, but because your *partner* sympathizes in the contingency. You win for two. You triumph for two. Two are exalted. Two again are mortified ; which divides their disgrace, as the conjunction doubles (by taking off the invidiousness) your glories. Two losing to two are better reconciled than one to one in that close butchery. The hostile feeling is weakened by multiplying the channels. War becomes a civil game. By such reasonings as these the old lady was accustomed to defend her favourite pastime.

No inducement could ever prevail upon her to play at any game, where chance entered into the composition, *for nothing*. Chance, she would argue, (and here again, admire the subtlety of her conclusion,) chance is nothing, but where something else depends upon it. It is obvious that cannot be *glory*. What rational cause of exultation could it give to a man to turn up size ace a hundred times together by himself? or before spectators, where no stake was depending? Make a lottery of a hundred thousand tickets with but one fortunate number, and what possible principle of our nature, except stupid wonderment, could it gratify to gain that number as many times successively, without a prize? Therefore she disliked the mixture of chance in backgammon, where it was not played for money. She called it foolish, and those people idiots who were taken with a lucky hit under such circumstances. Games of pure skill were as little to her fancy. Played for a stake, they were a mere system of over-reaching. Played for glory, they were a mere setting of one man's wit—his memory, or combination-faculty rather—against another's; like a mock-engagement at a review, bloodless and profitless. She could not conceive a *game* wanting the spritely infusion of chance, the handsome excuses of good fortune. Two people playing at chess in a corner of a room, while Whist was stirring in the centre, would inspire her with insufferable horror and ennui. Those well-cut similitudes of castles and knights, the *imagery* of the board, she would argue, (and I think in this case justly,) were entirely misplaced and senseless. Those hard-head contests can in no instance ally with the fancy. They reject form and colour. A pencil and dry slate (she used to say) were the proper arena for such combatants.

To those puny objectors against cards, as nurturing the bad passions, she would retort, that man is a gaming animal. He must be always trying to get the better in something or other; that this passion can scarcely be more safely expended than upon a game at cards; that cards are a temporary illusion; in truth, a mere drama; for we do but *play* at being mightily concerned, where a few idle shillings are at stake; yet, during the illusion, we *are* as mightily concerned as those whose stake is crowns and king-doms. They are a sort of dream-fighting; much ado; great battling, and little bloodshed; mighty means for disproportioned ends, quite as diverting, and a great deal more innoxious, than many of those more serious *games* of life, which men play, without esteeming them to be such.

With great deference to the old lady's judgment in these matters, I think I have experienced some moments in my life when playing at cards *for nothing* has even been agreeable. When I am in sickness, or not in the best spirits, I sometimes call for the cards, and play a game at piquet *for love* with my cousin Bridget,—Bridget Elia.

I grant there is something sneaking in it; but with a tooth-ache, or a sprained ankle, when you are sub-dued and humble, you are glad to put up with an inferior spring of action.

There is such a thing in nature, I am convinced, as *sick Whist*.

I grant it is not the highest style of man. I de-precate the manes of Sarah Battle: she lives not, alas, to whom I should apologize !

At such times, those *terms* which my old friend objected to come in as something admissible. I love to get a tierce or a quatorze, though they mean nothing. I am subdued to an inferior interest. Those shadows of winning amuse me.

That last game I had with my sweet cousin (I capoted her :—dare I tell thee, how foolish I am ?) I wished it might have lasted for ever, though we gained nothing, and lost nothing, though it was a mere shade of play : I would be content to go on in that idle folly for ever. The pipkin should be ever boiling, that was to prepare the gentle lenitive to my foot, which Bridget was doomed to apply after the game was over : and, as I do not much relish appliances, there it should ever bubble. Bridget and I should be ever playing.

A CHAPTER ON EARS.

I HAVE no ear.—

Mistake me not, reader ; nor imagine that I am by nature destitute of those exterior twin appendages, hanging ornaments, and (architecturally speaking) handsome volutes to the human capital. Better my mother had never borne me. I am, I think, rather delicately than copiously provided with those conduits; and I feel no disposition to envy the mule for his

plenty, or the mole for her exactness, in those ingenious labyrinthine inlets—those indispensable side-
intelligencers.

Neither have I incurred, or done any thing to incur,
with Defoe, that hideous disfigurement, which con-
strained him to draw upon assurance—to feel " quite
unabashed," and at ease upon that article. I was
never, I thank my stars, in the pillory; nor, if I read
them aright, is it within the compass of my destiny
that I ever should be.

When therefore I say that I have no ear, you will
understand me to mean—*for music*. To say that this
heart never melted at the concord of sweet sounds,
would be a foul self-libel. " *Water parted from the
Sea*" never fails to move it strangely. So does " *In
Infancy*." But they were used to be sung at her
harpsichord (the old-fashioned instrument in vogue in
those days) by a gentlewoman—the gentlest, sure,
that ever merited the appellation—the sweetest. Why
should I hesitate to name Mrs. S———, once the
blooming Fanny Weatheral of the Temple—who had
power to thrill the soul of Elia, small imp as he was,
even in his long coats; and to make him glow,
tremble, and blush with a passion, that not faintly in-
dicated the day-spring of that absorbing sentiment
which was afterwards destined to overwhelm and
subdue his nature quite for Alice W———n.

I even think that *sentimentally* I am disposed to
harmony; but *organically* I am incapable of a tune.
I have been practising " *God save the King*" all my
life: whistling and humming it over to myself in
solitary corners; and am not yet arrived, they tell
me, within many quavers of it. Yet hath the loyalty
of Elia never been impeached.

I am not without suspicion that I have an unde-
veloped faculty of music within me. For thrumming,
in my wild way, on my friend A.'s piano, the other
morning, while he was engaged in an adjoining
parlour,—on his return he was pleased to say *he
thought it could not be the maid!* On his first
surprise at hearing the keys touched in somewhat an
airy and masterful way, not dreaming of me, his suspicions had lighted on *Jenny*. But a grace, snatched
from a superior refinement, soon convinced him that
some being—technically perhaps deficient, but higher
informed from a principle common to all the fine
arts—had swayed the keys to a mood which Jenny,
with all her (less cultivated) enthusiasm, could never
have elicited from them. I mention this as a proof of
my friend's penetration, and not with any view of
disparaging Jenny.

Scientifically I could never be made to understand
(yet have I taken some pains) what a note in music
is ; or how one note should differ from another.
Much less in voices can I distinguish a soprano from
a tenor.   Only sometimes the thorough-bass I contrive to guess at, from its being supereminently harsh
and disagreeable.   I tremble, however, for my mis-
application of the simplest terms of *that* which I
disclaim.   While I profess my ignorance, I scarce
know what to *say* I am ignorant of.   I hate, perhaps,
by misnomers. *Sostenuto* and *adagio* stand in the like
relation of obscurity to me ; and *Sol, Fa, Mi, Re,* is
as conjuring as *Baralipton*.

It is hard to stand alone in an age like this, (constituted to the quick and critical perception of all
harmonious combinations, I verily believe, beyond all
preceding ages, since Jubal stumbled upon the gamut,)

to remain, as it were, singly unimpressible to the magic influences of an art which is said to have such an especial stroke at soothing, elevating, and refining the passions. Yet, rather than break the candid current of my confessions, I must avow to you, that I have received a great deal more pain than pleasure from this so cried-up faculty.

I am constitutionally susceptible of noises. A carpenter's hammer, in a warm Summer noon, will fret me into more than Midsummer madness. But those unconnected, unset sounds are nothing to the measured malice of music. The ear is passive to those single strokes ; willingly enduring stripes while it hath no task to con. To music it cannot be passive. It will strive—mine at least will—spite of its inaptitude, to thrid the maze ; like an unskilled eye painfully poring upon hieroglyphics. I have sat through an Italian Opera, till, for sheer pain, and inexplicable anguish, I have rushed out into the noisiest places of the crowded streets, to solace myself with sounds which I was not obliged to follow, and get rid of the distracting torment of endless, fruitless, barren attention ! I take refuge in the unpretending assemblage of honest common-life sounds ; and the purgatory of the Enraged Musician becomes my paradise.

I have sat at an Oratorio (that profanation of the purposes of the cheerful play-house) watching the faces of the auditory in the pit (what a contrast to Hogarth's Laughing Audience!) immoveable, or affecting some faint emotion—till (as some have said that our occupations in the next world will be but a shadow of what delighted us in this) I have imagined myself in some cold Theatre in Hades, where some of the *forms* of the earthly ones should be kept up, with none of the *enjoyment* ; or like that

——Party in a parlour
All silent and all DAMN'D.

Above all, those insufferable concertos, and pieces of music, as they are called, do plague and embitter my apprehension. Words are something: but to be exposed to an endless battery of mere sounds; to be long a dying; to lie stretched upon a rack of roses; to keep up languor by unintermitted effort; to pile honey upon sugar, and sugar upon honey, to an interminable tedious sweetness; to fill up sound with feeling, and strain ideas to keep pace with it; to gaze on empty frames, and be forced to make the pictures for yourself; to read a book, *all stops*, and be obliged to supply the verbal matter; to invent extempore tragedies to answer to the vague gestures of an inexplicable rambling mime ;—these are faint shadows of what I have undergone from a series of the ablest-executed pieces of this empty *instrumental music*.

I deny not that in the opening of a concert I have experienced something vastly lulling and agreeable : afterwards followeth the languor and the oppression. Like that disappointing book in Patmos, or like the comings on of melancholy, described by Burton, doth Music make her first insinuating approaches :—"Most pleasant it is to such as are melancholy given to walk alone in some solitary grove, betwixt wood and water, by some brook side, and to meditate upon some delightsome and pleasant subject, which shall affect him most, *amabilis insania*, and *mentis gratissimus error;* a most incomparable delight to build castles in the air, to go smiling to themselves, acting an infinite variety of parts, which they suppose, and strongly imagine, they act, or that they see done. So delightsome these toys at first, they could spend whole days and nights without sleep, even whole years in such contemplations and fantastical meditations, which are like so many dreams, and will hardly be drawn from them—winding and unwinding themselves as so many clocks, and still pleasing their humours, until at the last the SCENE TURNS UPON A SUDDEN, and they being now habitated to such meditations and solitary places, can endure no company, can think of nothing but harsh and distasteful subjects. Fear, sorrow, suspicion, *subrusticus pudor*, discontent, cares, and weariness of life, surprise them on a sudden, and they can think of nothing else. Continually suspecting, no sooner are their eyes open, but this infernal plague of melancholy seizeth on them, and terrifies their souls, representing some dismal object to their minds ; which now, by no means, no labour, no persuasions, they can avoid, they cannot be rid of, they cannot resist."

Something like this "SCENE TURNING" I have experienced at the evening parties at the house of my good Catholic friend *Nov*——; who, by the aid of a capital organ, himself the most finished of players, converts his drawing-room into a chapel, his week days into Sundays, and these latter into minor heavens.[1]

When my friend commences upon one of those solemn anthems, which peradventure struck upon my heedless ear, rambling in the side aisles of

---

[1] I have been there, and still would go ;
'Tis like a little heaven below.—DR. WATTS.

the dim Abbey, some five-and-thirty years since,
waking a new sense, and putting a soul of old religion into my young apprehension—(whether it be
that in which the Psalmist, weary of the persecutions of bad men, wisheth to himself dove's wings—
or *that other*, which, with a like measure of sobriety
and pathos, inquireth by what means the young man
shall best cleanse his mind)—a holy calm pervadeth
me. I am for the time

> —rapt above earth,
> And possess joys not promised at my birth.

But when this master of the spell, not content to
have laid a soul prostrate, goes on in his power to
inflict more bliss than lies in her capacity to receive,
impatient to overcome her "earthly" with his
"heavenly," still pouring in, for protracted hours,
fresh waves and fresh from the sea of sound, or from
that inexhausted *German* ocean, above which in
triumphant progress, dolphin-seated, ride those Arions
Haydn and *Mozart*, with their attendant Tritons,
Bach, Beethoven, and a countless tribe, whom to
attempt to reckon up would but plunge me again in
the deeps; I stagger under the weight of harmony,
reeling to and fro at my wit's end; clouds as of
frankincense oppress me—priests, altars, censers,
dazzle before me—the genius of *his* religion hath
me in her toils—a shadowy triple tiara invests the
brow of my friend, late so naked, so ingenuous—he
is Pope,—and by him sits, like as in the anomaly of
dreams, a she-Pope too,—tri-coroneted like himself!
I am converted, and yet a Protestant; at once *malleus
hereticorum*, and myself grand heresiarch : or three
heresies centre in my person. I am Marcion, Ebion,

and Cerinthus—Gog and Magog—what not? till the coming in of the friendly supper-tray dissipates the fragment, and a draught of true Lutheran beer (in which chiefly my friend shows himself no bigot) at once reconciles me to the rationalities of a purer faith; and restores to me the genuine unterrifying aspects of my pleasant-countenanced host and hostess.

ALL FOOLS' DAY.

THE compliments of the season to my worthy masters, and a merry first of April to us all!

Many happy returns of this day to you—and you, and *you*, Sir,—nay, never frown, man, nor put a long face upon the matter. Do not we know one another? what need of ceremony among friends? We have all a good touch of *that same*—you understand me—a speck of the motley. Beshrew the man who on such a day as this, the *general festival*, should affect to stand aloof. I am none of those sneakers. I am free of the corporation, and care not who knows it. He that meets me in the forest to-day shall meet no wise-acre, I can tell him. *Stultus sum.* Translate me that, and take the meaning of it to yourself for your pains. What! man, we have four quarters of the globe on our side, at the least computation.

Fill us a cup of that sparkling gooseberry—we will drink no wise, melancholy, politic port on this day—and let us troll the catch of Amiens—*duc ad me—duc ad me*—how goes it?

Here shall he see
Gross fools as he

Now would I give a trifle to know historically and authentically, who was the greatest fool that ever lived. I would certainly give him a bumper. Marry, of the present breed, I think I could without much difficulty name you the party.

Remove your cap a little further, if you please : it hides my bauble. And now each man bestride his hobby, and dust away his bells to what tune he pleases. I will give you, for my part,

> ————The crazy old church clock,
> And the bewilder'd chimes.

Good master Empedocles, you are welcome. It is long since you went a salamander-gathering down Ætna : worse than samphire-picking by some odds. 'Tis a mercy your worship did not singe your mustachios.

Ha! Cleombrotus! and what salads in faith did you light upon at the bottom of the Mediterranean? You were founder, I take it, of the disinterested sect of the Calenturists.

Gebir, my old free-mason, and prince of plasterers at Babel, bring in your trowel, most Ancient Grand! You have claim to a seat here at my right hand, as patron of the stammerers. You left your work, if I remember Herodotus correctly, at eight hundred million toises, or thereabout, above the level of the sea. Bless us, what a long bell you must have pulled, to call your top workmen to their nuncheon on the low grounds of Shinar! Or did you send up your garlic and onions by a rocket? I am a rogue if I am not ashamed to show you our Monument on Fish Street Hill, after your altitudes. Yet we think it somewhat.

What, the magnanimous Alexander in tears! Cry, baby; put its fingers in its eye it shall have another globe, round as an orange, pretty moppet!

Mister Adams——'odso, I honour your coat—pray do us the favour to read to us that sermon, which you lent to Mistress Slipslop, (the twenty and second in your portmanteau there,) on Female Incontinence —the same—it will come in most irrelevantly and impertinently seasonable to the time of the day.

Good master Raymund Lully, you look wise. Pray correct that error.

Duns, spare your definitions. I must fine you a bumper, or a paradox. We will have nothing said or done syllogistically this day. Remove those logical forms, waiter, that no gentleman break the tender shins of his apprehension stumbling across them.

Master Stephen, you are late. Ha! Cokes, is it you? Aguecheek, my dear knight, let me pay my devoir to you. Master Shallow, your worship's poor servant to command. Master Silence, I will use few words with you. Slender, it shall go hard if I edge not you in somewhere. You six will engross all the poor wit of the company to-day. I know it, I know it.

Ha! honest R——, my fine old Librarian of Ludgate,[1] time out of mind, art thou here again? Bless thy doublet, it is not over-new, threadbare as thy stories: what dost thou flitting about the world at this rate? Thy customers are extinct, defunct, bed-rid, have ceased to read long ago. Thou goest still among them, seeing if, peradventure, thou canst

---

[1] The London Library.—H.

hawk a volume or two.   Good Granville S——, thy
last patron, is flown.

> King Pandion, he is dead,
> All thy friends are lapt in lead.

Nevertheless, noble R——, come in, and take your
seat here, between Armado and Quisada ; for in true
courtesy, in gravity, in fantastic smiling to thyself,
in courteous smiling upon others, in the goodly orna-
ture of well-apparelled speech, and the commendation of wise sentences, thou art nothing inferior to
those accomplished Dons of Spain.   The spirit of
chivalry forsake me for ever when I forget thy singing
the song of Macheath, which declares that he might
be *happy with either*, situated between those two
ancient spinsters—when I forget the inimitable formal
love which thou didst make, turning now to the one and
now to the other, with that Malvolian smile—as if
Cervantes, not Gay, had written it for his hero ; and
as if thousands of periods must revolve before the
Mirror of Courtesy could have given his invidious
preference between a pair of so goodly-propertied and
meritorious-equal damsels.   *   *   *   *

To descend from these altitudes, and not to protract
our Fools' Banquet beyond its appropriate day, (for I
fear the second of April is not many hours distant,) in
sober verity I will confess a truth to thee, reader : I
love a *Fool*—as naturally as if I were of kith and
kin to him.   When a child, with child-like apprehensions, that dived not below the surface of the matter,
I read those *Parables*.   Not guessing at the involved
wisdom, I had more yearnings towards that simple
architect that built his house upon the sand than I
entertained for his more cautious neighbour.   I
grudged at the hard censure pronounced upon the

quiet soul that kept his talent; and (prizing their simplicity beyond the more provident, and, to my apprehension, somewhat *unfeminine* wariness of their competitors) I felt a kindliness, that almost amounted to a *tendre*, for those fjve thoughtless virgins. I have never since made acquaintance that lasted, or a friendship that answered, with any that had not some tincture of the absurd in their characters. I venerate an honest obliquity of understanding. The more laughable blunders a man shall commit in your company, the more tests he giveth you that he will not betray or overreach you. I love the safety which a palpable hallucination warrants; the security which a word out of season ratifies. And take my word for this, reader, (and say a fool told it you, if you please,) that he who hath not a dram of folly in his mixture hath pounds of much worse matter in his composition. It is observed, that "the foolisher the fowl or fish,—woodcocks,—dotterels—cods'-heads, &c.,—the finer the flesh thereof;" and what are commonly the world's received fools but such whereof the world is not worthy? and what have been some of the kindliest patterns of our species but so many darlings of absurdity, minions of the goddess, and her white boys? Reader, if you wrest my words beyond their fair construction, it is not I, but you, that are the *April Fool.*

A QUAKERS' MEETING.

Still-born Silence!—thou that art
Flood-gate of the deeper heart,
Offspring of a heavenly kind,
Frost o' the mouth, and thaw o' the mind,
Secrecy's confidant, and he
Who makes religion mystery,
Admiration's speaking'st tongue,—
Leave, thy desert shades among,
Reverend hermits' hallow'd cells,
Where retired devotion dwells ;
With thy enthusiasms come,
Seize our tongues, and strike us dumb ![1]

READER, would'st thou know what true peace and quiet mean; would'st thou find a refuge from the noises and clamours of the multitude; would'st thou enjoy at once solitude and society; would'st thou possess the depth of thine own spirit in stillness, without being shut out from the consolatory faces of thy species; would'st thou be alone and yet accompanied; solitary, yet not desolate; singular, yet not without some to keep thee in countenance; a unit in aggregate; a simple in composite: come with me into a Quakers' Meeting.

Dost thou love silence deep as that " before the winds were made? " go not out into the wilderness, descend not into the profundities of the earth; shut

---

[1] From " Poems of all Sorts," by Richard Fleckno, 1653.

not up thy casements ; nor pour wax into the little
cells of thy ears, with little-faith'd self-mistrusting
Ulysses.   Retire with me into a Quakers' Meeting.

For a man to refrain even from good words, and
to hold his peace, it is commendable; but for a multitude it is great mastery.

What is the stillness of the desert compared with
this place ? what the uncommunicating muteness of
fishes? Here the goddess reigns and revels. "Boreas,
and Cesias, and Argestes loud," do not with their in-
terconfounding uproars more augment the brawl—
nor the waves of the blown Baltic with their clubbed
sounds—than their opposite (Silence her sacred self)
is multiplied and rendered more intense by numbers,
and by sympathy.   She too hath her deeps, that call
unto deeps.   Negation itself hath a positive more
and less ; and closed eyes would seem to obscure the
great obscurity of midnight.

There are wounds which an imperfect solitude cannot heal.   By " imperfect " I mean that which a man
enjoyeth by himself.   The perfect is that which he
can sometimes attain in crowds, but nowhere so absolutely as in a Quakers' Meeting.   Those first
hermits did certainly understand this principle, when
they retired into Egyptian solitudes, not singly but in
shoals, to enjoy one another's want of conversation.
The Carthusian is bound to his brethren by his agreeing spirit of incommunicativeness.   On secular
occasions, what so pleasant as to be reading a book
through a long Winter evening, with a friend sitting
by—say, a wife—he, or she, too, (if that be probable,)
reading another, without interruption, or oral communication ?—can there be no sympathy without the
gabble of words ? Away with this inhuman, shy,

single, shade-and-cavern-haunting solitariness! Give
me, Master Zimmermann, a sympathetic solitude.

To pace alone in the cloisters or side-aisles of some
cathedral, time-stricken;

> Or under hanging mountains,
> Or by the fall of fountains;

is but a vulgar luxury compared with that which those
enjoy who come together for the purposes of more
complete, abstracted solitude.   This is the loneliness
"to be felt."   The Abbey Church of Westminster
hath nothing so solemn, so spirit-soothing, as the
naked walls and benches of a Quakers' Meeting.
Here are no tombs, no inscriptions,

> ———— Sands, ignoble things,
> Dropt from the ruin'd sides of kings—

but here is something which throws Antiquity herself
into the foreground—SILENCE—eldest of things—
language of old Night—primitive Discourser—to
which the insolent decays of mouldering grandeur
have but arrived by a violent, and, as we may say,
unnatural progression.

> How reverend is the view of these hush'd heads,
> Looking tranquillity!

Nothing-plotting, nought-caballing, unmischievous
synod! convocation without intrigue! parliament
without debate! what a lesson dost thou read to
council, and to consistory!   If my pen treat of you
lightly, (as haply it will wander,) yet my spirit hath
gravely felt the wisdom of your custom, when sitting
among you in deepest peace, which some out-welling
tears would rather confirm than disturb, I have re-
verted to the times of your beginnings, and the

sowings of the seed by Fox and Dewesbury. I have witnessed that which brought before my eyes your heroic tranquillity, inflexible to the rude jests and serious violences of the insolent soldiery, republican or royalist, sent to molest you—for ye sat betwixt the fires of two persecutions, the outcast and off-scouring of Church and Presbytery. I have seen the reeling sea-ruffian, who had wandered into your receptacle with the avowed intention of disturbing your quiet, from the very spirit of the place receive in a moment a new heart, and presently sit among ye as a lamb amidst lambs. And I remember Penn before his accusers, and Fox in the bail dock, where he was lifted up in spirit, as he tells us, and "the Judge and the Jury became as dead men under his feet."

Reader, if you are not acquainted with it, I would recommend to you, above all Church narratives, to read *Sewell's History of the Quakers*. It is in folio, and is the abstract of the journals of Fox and the primitive Friends. It is far more edifying and affecting than any thing you will read of Wesley and his colleagues. Here is nothing to stagger you, nothing to make you mistrust, no suspicion of alloy, no drop or dreg of the worldly or ambitious spirit. You will here read the true story of that much-injured, ridiculed man (who perhaps hath been a by-word in your mouth)—James Nayler : what dreadful sufferings, with what patience, he endured, even to the boring through of his tongue with red-hot irons, without a murmur ; and with what strength of mind, when the delusion he had fallen into, which they stigmatized as blasphemy, had given way to clearer thoughts, he could renounce his error, in a strain of the beauti-fullest humility, yet keep his first grounds, and be a

Quaker still!—so different from the practice of your common converts from enthusiasm, who, when they apostatize, *apostatize all*, and think they can never get far enough from the society of their former errors, even to the renunciation of some saving truths, with which they had been mingled, not implicated.

Get the writings of John Woolman[1] by heart; and love the early Quakers.

How far the followers of these good men in our days have kept to the primitive spirit, or in what proportion they have substituted formality for it, the Judge of Spirits can alone determine. I have seen faces in their assemblies upon which the dove sate visibly brooding. Others, again, I have watched, when my thoughts should have been better engaged, in which I could possibly detect nothing but a blank inanity. But quiet was in all, and the disposition to unanimity, and the absence of the fierce controversial workings. If the spiritual pretensions of the Quakers have abated, at least they make few pretences. Hypocrites they certainly are not, in their preaching. It is seldom, indeed, that you shall see one get up amongst them to hold forth. Only now and then a trembling, female, generally *ancient*, voice is heard, (you cannot guess from what part of the meeting it proceeds,) with a low buzzing, musical sound, laying out a few words which " she thought might suit the condition of some present," with a quaking diffidence, which leaves no possibility of supposing that any thing of female vanity was mixed up, where the tones were so full of tenderness, and a restraining modesty.

---

[1] The works of Woolman, the Quaker, were printed, with his Journal, in 1794.—H.

The men, from what I have observed, speak sel-domer.

Once only, and it was some years ago, I witnessed a sample of the old Foxian orgasm. It was a man of giant stature, who, as Wordsworth phrases it, might have danced " from head to foot equipt in iron mail." His frame was of iron, too. But *he* was malleable. I saw him shake all over with the spirit—I dare not say of delusion. The strivings of the outer man were unutterable : he seemed not to speak, but to be spoken from. I saw the strong man bowed down, and his knees to fail—his joints all seemed loosening. It was a figure to set off against Paul preaching. The words uttered were few, and sound : he was evidently resisting his will ; keeping down his own word-wisdom with more mighty effort than the world's orators strain for theirs. " He had been a WIT in his youth," he told us, with expressions of a sober remorse. And it was not till long after the impression had begun to wear away that I was enabled, with something like a smile, to recall the striking incongruity of the confes-sion—understanding the term in its worldly accepta-tion—with the frame and physiognomy of the person before me. His brow would have scared away the Levities—the Jocos Risus-que—faster than the Loves fled the face of Dis at Enna. By *wit*, even in his youth, I will be sworn he understood something far within the limits of an allowable liberty.

More frequently the Meeting is broken up without a word having been spoken. But the mind has been fed. You go away with a sermon not made with hands. You have been in the milder caverns of Tro-phonius ; or as in some den, where that fiercest and savagest of all wild creatures, the TONGUE, that unruly member, has strangely lain tied up and captive. You have bathed with stillness. O, when the spirit is sore fretted, even tired to sickness of the janglings and nonsense-noises of the world, what a balm and a solace it is to go and seat yourself for a quiet half hour upon some undisputed corner of a bench, among the gentle Quakers !

Their garb and stillness conjoined, present a uniformity, tranquil and herd-like—as in the pasture—" forty feeding like one."

The very garments of a Quaker seem incapable of receiving a soil ; and cleanliness in them to be something more than the absence of its contrary. Every Quakeress is a lily ; and when they come up in bands to their Whitsun conferences, whitening the easterly streets of the metropolis, from all parts of the United Kingdom, they show like troops of the Shining Ones.

THE OLD AND THE NEW SCHOOLMASTER.

My reading has been lamentably desultory and immethodical. Odd, out of the way, old English plays and treatises have supplied me with most of my notions and ways of feeling. In every thing that relates to *science* I am a whole Encyclopædia behind the rest of the world. I should have scarcely cut a figure among the franklins, or country gentlemen, in King John's days. I know less geography than a school-boy of six weeks' standing. To me a map of old Ortelius is as authentic as Arrowsmith. I do not know whereabout Africa merges into Asia; whether Ethiopia lie in one or other of those great divisions; nor can form the remotest conjecture of the position of New South Wales, or Van Diemen's Land. Yet do I hold a correspondence with a very dear friend in the first-named of these two Terræ Incognitæ. I have no astronomy. I do not know where to look for the Bear, or Charles's Wain; the place of any star; or the name of any of them at sight. I guess at Venus only by her brightness; and if the sun on some portentous morn were to make his first appearance in the West, I verily believe, that while all the world were gasping in apprehension about me, I alone should stand unterrified, from sheer incuriosity and want of observation. Of history and chronology I possess some vague points, such as one cannot help picking up in the course of miscellaneous

study ; but I never deliberately sat down to a chronicle,
even of my own country.   I have most dim apprehensions of the four great monarchies ; and sometimes
the Assyrian, sometimes the Persian, floats as *first* in
my fancy.   I make the widest conjectures concerning
Egypt, and her shepherd kings.   My friend M————,
with great painstaking, got me to think I understood
the first proposition in Euclid, but gave me over in
despair at the second.   I am entirely unacquainted
with the modern languages ; and, like a better man
than myself, have " small Latin and less Greek."   I
am a stranger to the shapes and texture of the commonest trees, herbs, flowers—not from the circumstance of my being town-born, for I should have
brought the same inobservant spirit into the world
with me had I first seen it " on Devon's leafy shores,"
—and am no less at a loss among purely town
objects, tools, engines, mechanic processes.   Not that
I affect ignorance ; but my head has not many man-
sions, nor spacious ; and I have been obliged to fill it
with such cabinet curiosities as it can hold without
aching.   I sometimes wonder how I have passed my
probation with so little discredit in the world as I
have done, upon so meagre a stock.   But the fact is,
a man may do very well with a very little knowledge,
and scarce be found out, in mixed company ; every
body is so much more ready to produce his own, than
to call for a display of your acquisitions.   But in a
tête-à-tête there is no shuffling.   The truth will out.
There is nothing which I dread so much as being left
alone for a quarter of an hour with a sensible, well-
informed man, that does not know me.   I lately got
into a dilemma of this sort.

In one of my daily jaunts between Bishopsgate and

Shacklewell, the coach stopped to take up a staid-looking gentleman, about the wrong side of thirty, who was giving his parting directions, (while the steps were adjusting,) in a tone of mild authority, to a tall youth, who seemed to be neither his clerk, his son, nor his servant, but something partaking of all three. The youth was dismissed, and we drove on. As we were the sole passengers, he naturally enough addressed his conversation to me ; and we discussed the merits of the fare, the civility and punctuality of the driver ; the circumstance of an opposition coach having been lately set up, with the probabilities of its success ; (to all of which I was enabled to return pretty satisfactory answers, having been drilled into this kind of etiquette by some years' daily practice of riding to and fro in the stage aforesaid ;) when he suddenly alarmed me by a startling question, whether I had seen the show of prize cattle that morning in Smithfield ?   Now, as I had not seen it, and do not greatly care for such sort of exhibitions, I was obliged to return a cold negative.   He seemed a little mortified, as well as astonished, at my declaration, as (it appeared) he was just come fresh from the sight, and doubtless had hoped to compare notes on the subject. However, he assured me that I had lost a fine treat, as it far exceeded the show of last year.   We were now approaching Norton Folgate, when the sight of some shop goods *ticketed* freshened him up into a dissertation upon the cheapness of cottons this Spring. I was now a little in heart, as the nature of my morning avocations had brought me into some sort of familiarity with the raw material ; and I was surprised to find how eloquent I was becoming on the state of the India market—when, presently, he dashed my incipient vanity to the earth at once, by inquiring whether I had ever made any calculation as to the value of the rental of all the retail shops in London. Had he asked of me what songs the Syrens sang, or what name Achilles assumed when he hid himself among women, I might, with Sir Thomas Browne, have hazarded a " wide solution."[1] My companion saw my embarrassment, and, the almshouses beyond Shoreditch just coming in view, with great good-nature and dexterity he shifted his conversation to the subject of public charities ; which led to the comparative merits of provision for the poor in past and present times, with observations on the old monastic institutions and charitable orders ; but finding me rather dimly impressed with some glimmering notions from old poetic associations than strongly fortified with any speculations reduceable to calculation on the subject, he gave the matter up ; and the country beginning to open more and more upon us as we approached the turnpike at Kingsland, (the destined termination of his journey,) he put a home-thrust upon me, in the most unfortunate position he could have chosen, by advancing some queries relative to the North Pole Expedition.   While I was muttering out something about the Panorama of those strange regions, (which I had actually seen,) by way of parrying the question, the coach stopping relieved me from any further apprehensions.   My companion getting out, left me in the comfortable possession of my ignorance ; and I heard him, as he went off, putting questions to an outside passenger, who had alighted with him, regarding an epidemic disorder that had

----

[1] Urn Burial.

been rife about Dalston, and which my friend assured him had gone through five or six schools in that neighbourhood. The truth now flashed upon me that my companion was a schoolmaster, and that the youth whom he had parted from at our first acquaintance must have been one of the bigger boys, or the usher. He was evidently a kind-hearted man, who did not seem so much desirous of provoking discussion by the questions which he put, as of obtaining information at any rate. It did not appear that he took any interest either in such kind of inquiries, for their own sake, but that he was in some way bound to seek for knowledge. A greenish-coloured coat, which he had on, forbade me to surmise that he was a clergyman. The adventure gave birth to some reflections on the difference between persons of his profession in past and present times.

Rest to the souls of those fine old Pedagogues,— the breed, long since extinct, of the Lilys, and the Linacres,—who believing that all learning was contained in the languages which they taught, and despising every other acquirement as superficial and useless, came to their task as to a sport! Passing from infancy to age, they dreamed away all their days as in a grammar-school. Revolving in a perpetual cycle of declensions, conjugations, syntaxes, and prosodies; renewing constantly the occupations which had charmed their studious childhood; rehearsing continually the part of the past; life must have slipped from them at last like one day. They were always in their first garden, reaping harvests of their golden time, among their *Flori* and their *Spici-legia;* in Arcadia still, but kings; the ferule of their sway not much harsher, but of like dignity with that mild

sceptre attributed to King Basileus; the Greek and
Latin, their stately Pamela and their Philoclea; with
the occasional duncery of some untoward tyro, serving for a refreshing interlude of a Mopsa, or a clown
Damœtas!

With what a savour doth the Preface to Colet's, or
(as it is sometimes called) Paul's Accidence, set forth!
" To exhort every man to the learning of grammar,
that intendeth to attain the understanding of the
tongues, wherein is contained a great treasury of
wisdom and knowledge, it would seem but vain and
lost labour; for so much as it is known that nothing
can surely be ended whose beginning is either feeble
or faulty, and no building be perfect where the foundation
and groundwork is ready to fall, and unable to uphold
the burden of the frame." How well doth this stately
preamble (comparable to those which Milton com-
mendeth as "having been the usage to prefix to some
solemn law, then first promulgated by Solon or Ly-
curgus") correspond with and illustrate that pious
zeal for conformity, expressed in a succeeding clause,
which would fence about grammar rules with the
severity of faith articles!—" As for the diversity of
grammars, it is well profitably taken away by the
king majesties wisdom, who foreseeing the inconveni-
ence, and favourably providing the remedie, caused
one kind of grammar by sundry learned men to be
diligently drawn, and so to be set out, only everywhere to be taught for the use of learners, and for the
hurt in changing of schoolmaisters." What a *gusto*
in that which follows!—" wherein it is profitable that
he [the pupil] can orderly decline his noun and his
verb." *His* noun!

The fine dream is fading away fast; and the least

concern of a teacher in the present day is to inculcate grammar rules.

The modern schoolmaster is expected to know a little of every thing, because his pupil is required not to be entirely ignorant of any thing. He must be superficially, if I may so say, omniscient. He is to know something of pneumatics; of chemistry; of whatever is curious or proper to excite the attention of the youthful mind; an insight into mechanics is desirable, with a touch of statistics; the quality of soils, &c., botany, the constitution of his country, *cum multis aliis*. You may get a notion of some part of his expected duties by consulting the famous Tractate on Education, addressed to Mr. Hartlib.

All these things—these, or the desire of them—he is expected to instil, not by set lessons from professors, which he may charge in the bill, but at school intervals, as he walks the streets, or saunters through green fields (those natural instructors) with his pupils. The least part of what is expected from him is to be done in school hours. He must insinuate knowledge at the *mollia tempora fandi*. He must seize every occasion—the season of the year—the time of the day—a passing cloud—a rainbow—a waggon of hay —a regiment of soldiers going by—to inculcate some thing useful. He can receive no pleasure from a casual glimpse of Nature, but must catch at it as an object of instruction. He must interpret beauty into the picturesque. He cannot relish a beggar-man, or a gipsy, for thinking of the suitable improvement. Nothing comes to him not spoiled by the sophisticating medium of moral uses. The Universe—that Great Book, as it has been called—is to him, indeed, to all intents and purposes, a book out of which he is

doomed to read tedious homilies to distasting school-
boys. Vacations themselves are none to him; he is
only rather worse off than before; for commonly he has
some intrusive upper boy fastened upon him at such
times; some cadet of a great family; some neglected
lump of nobility, or gentry; that he must drag after
him to the play, to the Panorama, to Mr. Bartley's
Orrery, to the Panopticon, or into the country, to a
friend's house, or his favourite watering-place. Wherever he goes this uneasy shadow attends him. A boy
is at his board, and in his path, and in all his move-
ments. He is boy-rid, sick of perpetual boy.

Boys are capital fellows in their own way, among
their mates; but they are unwholesome companions
for grown people. The restraint is felt no less on
the one side than on the other. Even a child, that
" plaything for an hour," tires *always*. The noises of
children, playing their own fancies—as I now hearken
to them, by fits, sporting on the green before my
window, while I am engaged in these grave speculations at my neat suburban retreat at Shacklewell, by
distance made more sweet—inexpressibly take from
the labour of my task. It is like writing to music.
They seem to modulate my periods. They ought at
least to do so; for in the voice of that tender age
there is a kind of poetry, far unlike the harsh prose-
accents of man's conversation. I should but spoil
their sport and diminish my own sympathy for them
by mingling in their pastime.

I would not be domesticated all my days with a
person of very superior capacity to my own;—not, if
I know myself at all, from any considerations of
jealousy or self-comparison, (for the occasional com-
munion with such minds has constituted the fortune

and felicity of my life,) but the habit of too constant intercourse with spirits above you, instead of raising you, keeps you down. Too frequent doses of original thinking from others restrain what lesser portion of that faculty you may possess of your own. You get entangled in another man's mind, even as you lose yourself in another man's grounds. You are walking with a tall varlet, whose strides out-pace yours to lassitude. The constant operation of such potent agency would reduce me, I am convined, to imbecility. You may derive thoughts from others : your way of thinking, the mould in which your thoughts are cast, must be your own. Intellect may be imparted, but not each man's intellectual frame.

As little as I should wish to be always thus dragged upwards, as little (or rather still less) is it desirable to be stunted downwards by your associates. The trumpet does not more stun you by its loudness than a whisper teases you by its provoking inaudibility.

Why are we never quite at our ease in the presence of a schoolmaster ?—because we are conscious that he is not quite at his ease in ours. He is awkward, and out of place, in the society of his equals. He comes like Gulliver from among his little people, and he cannot fit the stature of his understanding to yours. He cannot meet you on the square. He wants a point given him, like an indifferent whist player. He is so used to teaching, that he wants to be teaching *you*. One of these professors, upon my complaining that these little sketches of mine were any thing but methodical, and that I was unable to make them otherwise, kindly offered to instruct me in the method by which young gentlemen in *his* seminary were taught to compose English themes. The jests of a

schoolmaster are coarse, or thin. They do not *tell*
out of school. He is under the restraint of a formal
or didactive hypocrisy in company, as a clergyman is
under a moral one. He can no more let his intellect
loose in society than the other can his inclinations.
He is forlorn among his coevals ; his juniors cannot
be his friends.

"I take blame to myself," said a sensible man of
this profession, writing to a friend respecting a youth
who had quitted his school abruptly, "that your
nephew was not more attached to me. But persons
in my situation are more to be pitied than can well be
imagined. We are surrounded by young, and conse-
quently ardently affectionate hearts, but *we* can never
hope to share an atom of their affections. The
relation of master and scholar forbids this. *How
pleasing this must be to you ! how I envy your feelings !* my friends will sometimes say to me, when
they see young men whom I have educated return
after some years' absence from school, their eyes
shining with pleasure, while they shake hands with
their old master, bringing a present of game to me, or
a toy to my wife, and thanking me in the warmest
terms for my care of their education. A holiday is
begged for the boys ; the house is a scene of happiness ; I, only, am sad at heart. This fine-spirited
and warm-hearted youth, who fancies he repays his
master with gratitude for the care of his boyish years,—
this young man, in the eight long years I watched
over him with a parent's anxiety, never could repay
me with one look of genuine feeling. He was proud
when I praised, he was submissive when I reproved
him ; but he did never *love* me ; and what he now
mistakes for gratitude and kindness for me, is but the

pleasant sensation which all persons feel at revisiting
the scenes of their boyish hopes and fears, and seeing
on equal terms the man they were accustomed to
look up to with reverence.   My wife too," this interesting correspondent goes on to say, " my once darling
Anna, is the wife of a schoolmaster.   When I married
her (knowing that the wife of a schoolmaster ought to
be a busy notable creature, and fearing that my gentle
Anna would ill supply the loss of my dear bustling
mother, just then dead, who never sat still, was in
every part of the house in a moment, and whom I was
obliged sometimes to threaten to fasten down in a
chair, to save her from fatiguing herself to death,) I
expressed my fears that I was bringing her into a way
of life unsuitable to her ; and she, who loved me
tenderly, promised for my sake to exert herself to perform the duties of her new situation.   She promised,
and she has kept her word.   What wonders will not
woman's love perform ?—My house is managed with
a propriety and decorum unknown in other schools ;
my boys are well fed, look healthy, and have every
proper accommodation ; and all this performed with
a careful economy, that never descends to meanness.
But I have lost my gentle *helpless* Anna !   When we
sit down to enjoy an hour of repose, after the fatigue
of the day, I am compelled to listen to what have
been her useful (and they are really useful) employ-
ments through the day, and what she proposes for
her to-morrow's task.   Her heart and her features are
changed by the duties of her situation.   To the boys,
she never appears other than the *master's wife*, and
she looks up to me as the *boys' master ;* to whom all
show of love and affection would be highly improper,
and unbecoming the dignity of her situation and mine.

Yet *this* my gratitude forbids me to hint to her.   For
my sake she submitted to be this altered creature ; and
can I reproach her for it ? "—For the communication
of this letter I am indebted to my cousin Bridget.

IMPERFECT SYMPATHIES.

I am of a constitution so general, that it consorts and sympathizeth
with all things. I have no antipathy, or rather idiosyncrasy in any
thing.   Those natural repugnancies do not touch me ; nor do I behold
with prejudice the French, Italian, Spaniard, or Dutch.—*Religio
Medici.*

THAT the author of the Religio Medici, mounted upon
the airy stilts of abstraction, conversant about notional
and conjectural essences, in whose categories of
Being the possible took the upper hand of the actual,
should have overlooked the impertinent individualities
of such poor concretions as mankind, is not much to
be admired.   It is rather to be wondered at, that in
the genus of animals he should have condescended
to distinguish that species at all.   For myself,—earth-
bound and fettered to the scene of my activities,—

Standing on earth, not rapt above the sky,

I confess that I do feel the differences of mankind,
national or individual, to an unhealthy excess.   I can
look with no indifferent eye upon things or persons.
Whatever is, is to me a matter of taste or distaste ;
or when once it becomes indifferent, it begins to
be disrelishing.   I am, in plainer words, a bundle of
prejudices—made up of likings and dislikings—the
veriest thrall to sympathies, apathies, antipathies.
In a certain sense, I hope it may be said of me that I

am a lover of my species. I can feel for all indifferently, but I cannot feel towards all equally. The
more purely English word that expresses sympathy,
will better explain my meaning. I can be a friend to
a worthy man, who upon another account cannot be
my mate or *fellow*. I cannot *like* all people alike.[1]

I have been trying all my life to like Scotchmen,
and am obliged to desist from the experiment in
despair. They cannot like me ; and in truth, I never
knew one of that nation who attempted to do it.
There is something more plain and ingenuous in their
mode of proceeding. We know one another at first
sight. There is an order of imperfect intellects
(under which mine must be content to rank) which in
its constitution is essentially anti-Caledonian. The
owners of the sort of faculties I allude to have
minds rather suggestive than comprehensive. They

---

[1] I would be understood as confining myself to the subject of *imperfect sympathies*. To nations or classes of men there can be no
direct antipathy. There may be individuals born and constellated so
opposite to another individual nature, that the same sphere cannot hold
them. I have met with my moral antipodes, and can believe the story
of two persons meeting (who never saw one another before in their
lives) and instantly fighting.

　　　　　——We by proof find there should be
'Twixt man and man such an antipathy,
That though he can show no just reason why
For any former wrong or injury,
Can neither find a blemish in his fame,
Nor aught in face or feature justly blame,
Can challenge or accuse him of no evil,
Yet notwithstanding hates him as a devil.

The lines are from old Heywood's "Hierarchie of Angels," and he
subjoins a curious story in confirmation, of a Spaniard who attempted
to assassinate a King Ferdinand of Spain, and being put to the rack
could give no other reason for the deed but an inveterate antipathy
which he had taken to the first sight of the King.

　　　　　——The cause which to that act compell'd him
Was, he ne'er loved him since he first beheld him.

have no pretences to much clearness or precision in
their ideas, or in their manner of expressing them.
Their intellectual wardrobe (to confess fairly) has few
whole pieces in it.   They are content with fragments
and scattered pieces of Truth.   She presents no full
front to them—a feature or side-face at the most.
Hints and glimpses, germs and crude essays at a
system, is the utmost they pretend to.   They beat up
a little game peradventure, and leave it to knottier
heads, more robust constitutions, to run it down.
The light that lights them is not steady and polar,
but mutable and shifting : waxing, and again waning.
Their conversation is accordingly.   They will throw
out a random word in or out of season, and be content
to let it pass for what it is worth.   They cannot speak
always as if they were upon their oath, but must be
understood, speaking or writing, with some abate-
ment.   They seldom wait to mature a proposition,
but e'en bring it to market in the green ear.   They
delight to impart their defective discoveries as they
arise, without waiting for their full development.
They are no systematizers, and would but err more
by attempting it.   Their minds, as I said before, are
suggestive merely.   The brain of a true Caledonian
(if I am not mistaken) is constituted upon quite a
different plan.   His Minerva is born in panoply.
You are never admitted to see his ideas in their
growth—if indeed they do grow, and are not rather
put together upon principles of clock-work.   You
never catch his mind in an undress.   He never hints
or suggests any thing, but unlades his stock of ideas
in perfect order and completeness.   He brings his
total wealth into company, and gravely unpacks it.
His riches are always about him.   He never stoops

to catch a glittering something in your presence to
share it with you, before he quite knows whether it be
true touch or not.   You cannot cry *halves* to any
thing that he finds.   He does not find, but bring.
You never witness his first apprehension of a thing.
His understanding is always at its meridian : you
never see the first dawn, the early streaks.   He has
no falterings of self-suspicion.   Surmises, guesses,
misgivings,   half-intuitions,   semi-consciousnesses,
partial illuminations, dim instincts, embryo conceptions, have no place in his brain or vocabulary.   The
twilight of dubiety never falls upon him.   Is he ortho-
dox—he has no doubts.   Is he an infidel—he has
none either.   Between the affirmative and the negative there is no border-land with him.   You cannot
hover with him upon the confines of truth, or wander
in the maze of a probable argument.   He always
keeps the path.   You cannot make excursions with
him, for he sets you right.   His taste never fluc-
tuates.   His morality never abates.   He cannot compromise, or understand middle actions.   There can
be but a right and a wrong.   His conversation is as a
book.   His affirmations have the sanctity of an oath.
You must speak upon the square with him.   He stops
a metaphor like a suspected person in an enemy's
country.   " A healthy book ! "—said one of his
countrymen to me, who had ventured to give that
appellation to John Buncle,—" Did I catch rightly
what you said ? I have heard of a man in health, and
of a healthy state of body, but I do not see how that
epithet can be properly applied to a book."   Above
all, you must beware of indirect expressions before a
Caledonian.   Clap an extinguisher upon your irony
if you are unhappily blest with a vein of it.   Remem-

ber you are upon your oath. I have a print of a graceful female after Leonardo da Vinci, which I was showing off to Mr. * * * After he had examined it minutely, I ventured to ask him how he liked MY BEAUTY, (a foolish name it goes by among my friends,) when he very gravely assured me that " he had considerable respect for my character and talents," (so he was pleased to say,) " but had not given himself much thought about the degree of my personal pretensions." The misconception staggered me, but did not seem much to disconcert him. Persons of this nation are particularly fond of affirming a truth, which nobody doubts. They do not so properly affirm as annunciate it. They do indeed appear to have such a love of truth (as if, like virtue, it were valuable for itself) that all truth becomes equally valuable, whether the proposition that contains it be new or old, disputed, or such as is impossible to become a subject of disputation. I was present not long since at a party of North Britons, where a son of Burns was expected, and happened to drop a silly expression (in my South British way,) that I wished it were the father instead of the son—when four of them started up at once to inform me that " that was impossible, because he was dead." An impracticable wish, it seems, was more than they could conceive. Swift has hit off this part of their character, namely their love of truth, in his biting way, but with an illiberality that necessarily confines the passage to the margin.¹ The tedious-

---

¹ There are some people who think they sufficiently acquit themselves, and entertain their company, with relating facts of no consequence, not at all out of the road of such common incidents as happen every day ; and this I have observed more frequently among the Scots

ness of these people is certainly provoking. I wonder if they ever tire one another!—In my early life I had a passionate fondness for the poetry of Burns. I have sometimes foolishly hoped to ingratiate myself with his countrymen by expressing it. But I have always found that a true Scot resents your admiration of his compatriot, even more than he would your contempt of him. The latter he imputes to your " imperfect acquaintance with many of the words which he uses;" and the same objection makes it a presumption in you to suppose that you can admire him. Thomson they seem to have forgotten. Smollett they have neither forgotten nor forgiven, for his delineation of Rory and his companion, upon their first introduction to our metropolis. Speak of Smollett as a great genius, and they will retort upon you Hume's History compared with *his* Continuation of it. What if the historian had continued Humphrey Clinker?

I have, in the abstract, no disrespect for Jews. They are a piece of stubborn antiquity, compared with which Stonehenge is in its nonage. They date beyond the pyramids. But I should not care to be in habits of familiar intercourse with any of that nation. I confess that I have not the nerves to enter their synagogues. Old prejudices cling about me. I cannot shake off the story of Hugh of Lincoln. Centuries of injury, contempt, and hate, on the one side,—of cloaked revenge, dissimulation, and hate, on the other, between our and their fathers, must and

than any other nation, who are very careful not to omit the minutest circumstances of time or place: which kind of discourse, if it were not a little relieved by the uncouth terms and phrases, as well as accent and gesture, peculiar to that country, would be hardly tolerable.—*Hints towards an Essay on Conversation.*

ought to affect the blood of the children. I cannot believe it can run clear and kindly yet ; or that a few fine words, such as candour, liberality, the light of a nineteenth century, can close up the breaches of so deadly a disunion. A Hebrew is nowhere congenial to me. He is least distasteful on 'Change, for the mercantile spirit levels all distinctions, as all are beauties in the dark. I boldly confess that I do not relish the approximation of Jew and Christian, which has become so fashionable. The reciprocal endearments have, to me, something hypocritical and un· natural in them. I do not like to see the Church and Synagogue kissing and congeeing in awkward postures of an affected civility. If *they* are converted, why do they not come over to us altogether ? Why keep up a form of separation, when the life of it is fled ? If they can sit with us at table, why do they keck at our cookery ? I do not understand these half convertites. Jews christianizing—Christians judaizing—puzzle me. I like fish or flesh. A moderate Jew is a more confounding piece of anomaly than a wet Quaker. The spirit of the synagogue is essentially *separative*. B—— would have been more in keeping if he had abided by the faith of his forefathers. There is a fine scorn in his face, which nature meant to be of Christians. The Hebrew spirit is strong in him, in spite of his proselytism. He cannot conquer the Shibboleth. How it breaks out, when he sings, " The Children of Israel passed through the Red Sea !" The auditors, for the moment, are as Egyptians to him, and he rides over our necks in triumph. There is no mistaking him. B—— has a strong expression of sense in his countenance, and it is confirmed by his singing. The foundation of his vocal excellence is sense. He sings with understanding, as Kemble delivered dialogue. He would sing the Commandments, and give an appropriate character to each prohibition. His nation, in general, have not over-sensible countenances. How should they ?—but you seldom see a silly expression among them. Gain, and the pursuit of gain, sharpen a man's visage. I never heard of an idiot being born among them. Some admire the Jewish female physiognomy. I admire it, but with trembling. Jael had those full, dark, inscrutable eyes.

In the Negro countenance you will often meet with strong traits of benignity. I have felt yearnings of tenderness towards some of these faces—or rather masks—that have looked out kindly upon one in casual encounters in the streets and highways. I love what Fuller beautifully calls these—" images of God cut in ebony." But I should not like to associate with them, to share my meals and my good-nights with them—because they are black.

I love Quaker ways and Quaker worship. I venerate the Quaker principles. It does me good for the rest of the day when I meet any of their people in my path. When I am ruffled or disturbed by any occurrence, the sight or quiet voice of a Quaker acts upon me as a ventilator, lightening the air, and taking off a load from the bosom. But I cannot like the Quakers (as Desdemona would say) " to live with them." I am all over sophisticated—with humours, fancies, craving hourly sympathy. I must have books, pictures, theatres, chit-chat, scandal, jokes, ambiguities, and a thousand whim-whams, which their simpler taste can do without. I should starve at their primitive banquet. My appetites are too high

for the salads which (according to Evelyn) Eve
dressed for the angel, my gusto too excited

To sit a guest with Daniel at his pulse.

The indirect answers which Quakers are often
found to return to a question put to them may be
explained, I think, without the vulgar assumption that
they are more given to evasion and equivocating than
other people.   They naturally look to their words
more carefully, and are more cautious of committing
themselves.   They have a peculiar character to keep
up on this head.   They stand in a manner upon their
veracity.   A Quaker is by law exempted from taking
an oath.   The custom of resorting to an oath in
extreme cases, sanctified as it is by all religious
antiquity, is apt (it must be confessed) to introduce
into the laxer sort of minds the notion of two kinds
of truth—the one applicable to the solemn affairs of
justice, and the other to the common proceedings of
daily intercourse.   As truth bound upon the conscience by an oath can be but truth, so in the common
affirmations of the shop and the market-place a
latitude is expected and conceded upon questions
wanting this solemn covenant.   Some thing less than
truth satisfies.   It is common to hear a person say,
" You do not expect me to speak as if I were upon
my oath."   Hence a great deal of incorrectness and
inadvertency, short of falsehood, creeps into ordinary
conversation ; and a kind of secondary or laic-truth
is tolerated, where clergy-truth—oath-truth, by the
nature of the circumstances, is not required.   A
Quaker knows none of this distinction.   His simple
affirmation being received, upon the most sacred occasions, without any further test, stamps a value upon

the words which he is to use upon the most indifferent topics of life.   He looks to them, naturally, with
more severity.   You can have of him no more than
his word.   He knows, if he is caught tripping in a
casual expression, he forfeits, for himself at least, his
claim to the invidious exemption.   He knows that his
syllables are weighed ; and how far a consciousness
of this particular watchfulness, exerted against a
person, has a tendency to produce indirect answers,
and a diverting of the question by honest means,
might be illustrated, and the practice justified, by a
more sacred example than is proper to be adduced
upon this occasion.   The admirable presence of mind,
which is notorious in Quakers upon all contingencies,
might be traced to this imposed self-watchfulness—
if it did not seem rather an humble and secular scion
of that old stock of religious constancy, which never
bent or faltered, in the Primitive Friends, or gave
way to the winds of persecution, to the violence of
judge or accuser, under trials and racking examina-
tions. " You will never be the wiser if I sit here
answering your questions till midnight," said one of
those upright Justicers to Penn, who had been putting
law-cases with a puzzling subtlety.   " Thereafter as
the answers may be," retorted the Quaker.   The
astonishing composure of this people is sometimes
ludicrously displayed in lighter instances.   I was
travelling in a stage-coach with three male Quakers,
buttoned up in the straitest non-conformity of their
sect.   We stopped to bait at Andover, where a meal,
partly tea apparatus, partly supper, was set before us.
My friends confined themselves to the tea-table.   I in
my way took supper.   When the landlady brought in
the bill, the eldest of my companions discovered that

she had charged for both meals.   This was resisted.
Mine hostess was very clamorous and positive.   Some
mild arguments were used on the part of the Quakers,
for which the heated mind of the good lady seemed
by no means a fit recipient.   The guard came in with
his usual peremptory notice.   The Quakers pulled out
their money and formally tendered it—so much for
tea.   I, in humble imitation, tendering mine for the
supper which I had taken.   She would not relax in
her demand.   So they all three quietly put up their
silver, as did myself, and marched out of the room,
the eldest and gravest going first, with myself closing
up the rear, who thought I could not do better than
follow the example of such grave and warrantable
personages.   We got in.   The steps went up.   The
coach drove off.   The murmurs of mine hostess, not
very indistinctly or ambiguously pronounced, became
after a time inaudible ; and now my conscience, which
the whimsical scene had for a while suspended,
beginning to give some twitches, I waited, in the
hope that some justification would be offered by these
serious persons for the seeming injustice of their conduct.   To my great surprise not a syllable was
dropped on the subject.   They sat as mute as at a
meeting.   At length the eldest of them broke silence,
by inquiring of his next neighbour, " Hast thee heard
how indigos go at the India House ?" and the question operated as a soporific on my moral feeling as far
as Exeter.

WITCHES, AND OTHER NIGHT FEARS.

WE are too hasty when we set down our ancestors in the gross for fools, for the monstrous inconsistencies (as they seem to us) involved in their Creed of Witchcraft. In the relations of this visible world we find them to have been as rational and shrewd to detect an historic anomaly as ourselves. But when once the invisible world was supposed to be opened, and the lawless agency of bad spirits assumed, what measures of probability, of decency, of fitness, or proportion—of that which distinguishes the likely from the palpable absurd—could they have to guide them in the rejection or admission of any particular testimony ?—That maidens pined away, wasting inwardly as their waxen images consumed before a fire—that corn was lodged, and cattle lamed—that whirlwinds uptore in diabolic revelry the oaks of the forest—or that spits and kettles only danced a fearful innocent vagary about some rustic's kitchen when no wind was stirring—were all equally probable where no law of agency was understood. That the Prince of the Powers of Darkness, passing by the flower and pomp of the earth, should lay preposterous siege to

the weak fantasy of indigent eld—has neither likeli-
hood nor unlikelihood *à priori* to us, who have no
measure to guess at his policy, or standard to estimate
what rate those anile souls may fetch in the Devil's
market. Nor, when the wicked are expressly sym-
bolized by a goat, was it to be wondered at so much,
that *he* should come sometimes in that body, and
assert his metaphor. That the intercourse was
opened at all between both worlds was perhaps the
mistake ; but that once assumed, I see no reason for
disbelieving one attested story of this nature more
than another on the score of absurdity. There is no
law to judge of the lawless, or canon by which a
dream may be criticized.

I have sometimes thought that I could not have
existed in the days of received witchcraft ; that I
could not have slept in a village where one of those
reputed hags dwelt. Our ancestors were bolder, or
more obtuse. Amidst the universal belief that these
wretches were in league with the Author of all Evil,
holding hell tributary to their muttering, no simple
Justice of the Peace seems to have scrupled issuing,
or silly Headborough serving, a warrant upon them—
as if they should subpœna Satan !—Prospero in his
boat, with his books and wand about him, suffers
himself to be conveyed away at the mercy of his
enemies to an unknown island. He might have
raised a storm or two, we think, on the passage. His
acquiescence is in exact analogy to the non-resistance
of witches to the constituted Powers. What stops
the Fiend in Spenser from tearing Guyon to pieces—
or who had made it a condition of his prey that Guyon
must take assay of the glorious bait—we have no
guess. We do not know the laws of that country.

From my childhood I was extremely inquisitive
about witches and witch stories.   My maid, and more
legendary aunt, supplied me with good store.   But I
shall mention the accident which directed my curiosity
originally into this channel.   In my father's book
closet the History of the Bible, by Stackhouse, occupied a distinguished station.   The pictures with
which it abounds—one of the ark, in particular, and
another of Solomon's Temple, delineated with all the
fidelity of ocular admeasurement, as if the artist had
been upon the spot—attracted my childish attention.
There was a picture, too, of the Witch raising up
Samuel, which I wish that I had never seen.   We
shall come to that hereafter.   Stackhouse is in two
huge tomes ; and there was a pleasure in removing
folios of that magnitude, which, with infinite strain-
ing, was as much as I could manage, from the situation which they occupied upon an upper shelf.   I have
not met with the work from that time to this ; but I
remember it consisted of Old Testament stories,
orderly set down, with the *objection* appended to each
story, and the *solution* of the objection regularly
tacked to that.   The *objection* was a summary of
whatever difficulties had been opposed to the credibility of the history, by the shrewdness of ancient or
modern infidelity, drawn up with an almost compli-
mentary excess of candour.   The *solution* was brief,
modest, and satisfactory.   The bane and antidote
were both before you.   To doubts so put, and so
quashed, there seemed to be an end for ever.   The
Dragon lay dead, for the foot of the veriest babe to
trample on.   But—like as was rather feared than
realized from that slain Monster in Spenser—from the
womb of those crushed Errors young Dragonets would

creep, exceeding the prowess of so tender a Saint
George as myself to vanquish. The habit of expecting objections to every passage set me upon starting
more objections, for the glory of finding a solution of
my own for them. I became staggered and perplexed,
a sceptic in long coats. The pretty Bible stories
which I had read, or heard read in church, lost their
purity and sincerity of impression, and were turned
into so many historic or chronologic theses to be
defended against whatever impugners. I was not to
disbelieve them, but—the next thing to that—I was to
be quite sure that some one or other would or had
disbelieved them. Next to making a child an infidel
is the letting him know that there are infidels at all.
Credulity is the man's weakness, but the child's
strength. O, how ugly sound Scriptural doubts from
the mouth of a babe and a suckling!—I should have
lost myself in these mazes, and have pined away, I
think, with such unfit sustenance as these husks
afforded but for a fortunate piece of ill-fortune which
about this time befell me. Turning over the
picture of the Ark with too much haste, I unhappily
made a breach in its ingenious fabric—driving my
inconsiderate fingers right through the two larger
quadrupeds—the Elephant and the Camel—that stare
(as well they might) out of the two last windows next
the steerage in that unique piece of naval architecture.
Stackhouse was henceforth locked up, and became an
interdicted treasure. With the book, the *objections*
and *solutions* gradually cleared out of my head, and
have seldom returned since in any force to trouble
me. But there was one impression which I had
imbibed from Stackhouse which no lock or bar could
shut out, and which was destined to try my childish

nerves rather more seriously.   That detestable
picture !

I was dreadfully alive to nervous terrors.   The
night-time, solitude, and the dark, were my hell.
The sufferings I endured in this nature would justify
the expression.   I never laid my head on my pillow,
I suppose, from the fourth to the seventh or eighth
year of my life—so far as memory serves in things
so long ago—without an assurance, which realised its
own prophecy, of seeing some frightful spectre.   Be
old Stackhouse then acquitted in part, if I say, that to
his picture of the Witch raising up Samuel, (O that
old man covered with a mantle !) I owe, not my midnight terrors, the hell of my infancy, but the shape
and manner of their visitation.   It was he who
dressed up for me a hag that nightly sate upon my
pillow—a sure bed-fellow, when my aunt or my maid
was far from me.   All day long, while the book was
permitted me, I dreamed waking over his delineation,
and at night (if I may use so bold an expression)
awoke into sleep, and found the vision true.   I durst
not, even in the day light, once enter the chamber
where I slept, without my face turned to the window,
aversely from the bed where my witch-ridden pillow
was.   Parents do not know what they do when they
leave tender babes alone to go to sleep in the dark.
The feeling about for a friendly arm, the hoping for a
familiar voice, when they wake screaming, and find
none to soothe them, what a terrible shaking it is to
their poor nerves !   Keeping them up till midnight,
through candle light and the unwholesome hours,
as they are called,—would, I am satisfied, in a medical
point of view, prove the better caution.   That detestable picture, as I have said, gave the fashion to my

dreams—if dreams they were—for the scene of them
was invariably the room in which I lay. Had I never
met with the picture, the fears would have come self-
pictured in some shape or other—

> Headless bear, black man, or ape—

but, as it was, my imaginations took that form. It is
not book, or picture, or the stories of foolish servants,
which create these terrors in children. They can at
most but give them a direction. Dear little T———
H———, who of all children has been brought up
with the most scrupulous exclusion of every taint of
superstition—who was never allowed to hear of goblin
or apparition, or scarcely to be told of bad men, or to
read or hear of any distressing story—finds all this
world of fear, from which he has been so rigidly
excluded *ab extra*, in his own " thick-coming fancies;"
and from his little midnight pillow, this nurse-child of
optimism will start at shapes, unborrowed of tradition,
in sweats to which the reveries of the cell-damned
murderer are tranquillity.

Gorgons, and Hydras, and Chimæras dire—stories
of Celæno and the Harpies—may reproduce themselves in the brain of superstition ; but they were
there before. They are transcripts, types,—the
archetypes are in us, and eternal. How else should
the recital of that, which we know in a waking sense
to be false, come to affect us at all ?—or

> ———Names, whose sense we see not,
> Fray us with things that be not ?

Is it that we naturally conceive terror from such
objects considered, in their capacity of being able to
inflict upon us bodily injury? O, least of all ! These
terrors are of older standing. They date beyond

body--or, without the body, they would have been the same. All the cruel, tormenting, defined devils in Dante—tearing, mangling, choking, stifling, scorching demons—are they one half so fearful to the spirit of a man as the simple idea of a spirit unembodied following him—

> Like one that on a lonesome road
> Doth walk in fear and dread,
> And having once turn'd round, walks on
> And turns no more his head ;
> Because he knows a frightful fiend
> Doth close behind him tread [1]

That the kind of fear here treated of is purely spiritual—that it is strong in proportion as it is objectless upon earth—that it predominates in the period of sinless infancy—are difficulties, the solution of which might afford some probable insight into our antemundane condition, and a peep at least into the shadowland of pre-existence.

My night fancies have long ceased to be afflictive. I confess an occasional nightmare ; but I do not, as in early youth, keep a stud of them. Fiendish faces, with the extinguished taper, will come and look at me ; but I know them for mockeries, even while I cannot elude their presence, and I fight and grapple with them. For the credit of my imagination, I am almost ashamed to say how tame and prosaic my dreams are grown. They are never romantic, seldom even rural. They are of architecture and of buildings—cities abroad, which I have never seen and hardly have hope to see. I have traversed, for the seeming length of a natural day, Rome, Amsterdam, Paris, Lisbon — their churches, palaces, squares,

---

[1] Mr. Coleridge's *Ancient Mariner.*

market-places, shops, suburbs, ruins, with an inex·
pressible sense of delight—a map-like distinctness of
trace—and a day-ligth vividness of vision that was all
but being awake.   I have formerly travelled among the
Westmoreland fells—my highest Alps—but they were
objects too mighty for the grasp of my dreaming
recognition ; and I have again and again awoke with
ineffectual struggles of the "inner eye," to make out
a shape in any way whatever of Helvellyn.   Methought I was in that country, but the mountains
were gone.   The poverty of my dreams mortifies me.
There is Coleridge, at his will can conjure up icy
domes, and pleasure-houses for Kubla Khan, and
Abyssinian maids, and songs of Abara, and caverns,

Where Alph, the sacred river, runs,

to solace his night solitudes—when I cannot muster
a fiddle.   Barry Cornwall has his Tritons and his
Nereids gamboling before him in nocturnal visions,
and proclaiming sons born to Neptune—when my
stretch of imaginative activity can hardly in the night
season raise up the ghost of a fish-wife.   To set my
failures in somewhat a mortifying light—it was after
reading the noble "Dream" of this poet, that my
fancy ran strong upon these marine spectra ; and the
poor plastic power, such as it is, within me set to
work to humour my folly in a sort of dream that very
night.   Methought I was upon the ocean billows at
some sea nuptials, riding and mounted high, with the
customary train sounding their conchs, before me, (I
myself you may be sure the *leading god,*) and jollily
we went cantering over the main, till just where Ino
Leucothea should have greeted me (I think it was Ino)
with a white embrace, the billows gradually subsiding,
fell from a sea roughness to a sea calm, and thence to

a river motion, and that river (as happens in the familiarization of dreams) was no other than the gentle Thames, which landed me in the wafture of a placid wave or two, safe and inglorious, somewhere at the foot of Lambeth Palace.

The degree of the soul's creativeness in sleep might furnish no whimsical criterion of the quantum of poetical faculty resident in the same soul waking. An old gentleman, a friend of mine, and a humourist, used to carry this notion so far, that when he saw any stripling of his acquaintance ambitious of becoming a poet, his first question would be—" Young man, what sort of dreams have you ?" I have so much faith in my old friend's theory, that when I feel that idle vein returning upon me, I presently subside into my proper element of prose, remembering those eluding nereids, and that inauspicious inland landing.

VALENTINE'S DAY.

HAIL to thy returning festival, old Bishop Valentine! Great is thy name in the Rubric, thou venerable Arch-flamen of Hymen! Immortal Go-between, who and what manner of person art thou? Art thou but a *name*, typifying the restless principle which impels poor humans to seek perfection in union? or wert thou indeed a mortal prelate, with thy tippet and thy rochet, thy apron on, and decent lawn sleeves? Mysterious personage! like unto thee, assuredly, there is no other mitred father in the Calendar; not Jerome, nor Ambrose, nor Cyril; nor the consigner of undipt infants to eternal torments, Austin, whom all mothers hate; nor he who hated all mothers, Origen; nor Bishop Bull, nor Archbishop Parker, nor Whitgift. Thou comest attended with thousands and ten thousands of little Loves, and the air is

Brush'd with the hiss of rustling wings.

Singing Cupids are thy choristers and thy precentors; and instead of the crosier, the mystical arrow is borne before thee.

In other words, this is the day on which those charming little missives, ycleped Valentines, cross and intercross each other at every street and turning. The weary and all forspent twopenny postman sinks beneath a load of delicate embarrassments, not his own. It is scarcely credible to what an extent this ephemeral courtship is carried on in this loving town, to the great enrichment of porters, and detriment of knockers and bell-wires. In these little visual interpretations no emblem is so common as the *heart*,—that little three-cornered exponent of all our hopes and fears,—the bestuck and bleeding heart ; it is twisted and tortured into more allegories and affectations than an opera-hat. What authority we have in history or mythology for placing the headquarters and metropolis of God Cupid in this anatomical seat rather than in any other, is not very .clear ; but we have got it, and it will serve as well as any other. Else we might easily imagine, upon some other system which might have prevailed for any thing which our pathology knows to the contrary, a lover addressing his mistress, in perfect simplicity of feeling, " Madam, my *liver* and fortune are entirely at your disposal ;" or putting a delicate question, " Amanda, have you a *midriff* to bestow ?" But custom has settled these things, and awarded the seat of sentiment to the aforesaid triangle, while its less fortunate neighbours wait at animal and anatomical distance.

Not many sounds in life, and I include all urban and all rural sounds, exceed in interest a *knock at the door*. It " gives a very echo to the throne where hope is seated." But its issues seldom answer to this oracle within. It is so seldom that just the person we want to see comes. But of all the clamorous visitations the welcomest in expectation is the sound that ushers in, or seems to usher in, a Valentine. As the raven himself was hoarse that announced the fatal entrance of Duncan, so the knock of the postman on this day is light, airy, confident, and befitting one that bringeth good tidings. It is less mechanical than on

other days ; you will say, " That is not the post, I am
sure." Visions of Love, of Cupids, of Hymens !—
delightful eternal common-places, which "having
been will always be ;" which no school-boy nor school-
man can write away ; having your irreversible throne
in the fancy and affections—what are your transports,
when the happy maiden, opening with careful finger,
careful not to break the emblematic seal, bursts upon
the sight of some well-designed allegory, some type,
some youthful fancy, not without verses—

> Lovers all,
> A madrigal,

or some such device, not over-abundant in sense—
young Love disclaims it,—and not quite silly—something between wind and water, a chorus where the
sheep might almost join the shepherd, as they did, or
as I apprehend they did, in Arcadia.

All Valentines are not foolish ; and I shall not
easily forget thine, my kind friend, (if I may have
leave to call you so,) E——— B———. E.B.
lived opposite a young maiden whom he had often
seen, unseen, from his parlour window in C——e
Street. She was all joyousness and innocence, and
just of an age to enjoy receiving a Valentine, and just
of a temper to bear the disappointment of missing one
with good-humour. E.B. is an artist of no common
powers ; in the fancy parts of designing, perhaps
inferior to none ; his name is known at the bottom of
many a well-executed vignette in the way of his profession, but no further ; for E. B. is modest, and the
world meets nobody half way. E. B. meditated how
he could repay this young maiden for many a favour
which she had done him unknown ; for when a kindly
face greets us, though but passing by, and never

knows us again, nor we it, we should feel it as an obligation : and E. B. did. This good artist set himself at work to please the damsel. It was just before Valentine's Day three years since. He wrought, unseen and unsuspected, a wondrous work. We need not say it was on the finest gilt paper, with borders ; full, not of common hearts and heartless allegory, but all the prettiest stories of love from Ovid, and older poets than Ovid, (for E. B. is a scholar.) There was Pyramus and Thisbe, and be sure Dido was not forgot, nor Hero and Leander, and swans more than sang in Cayster, with mottos and fanciful devices, such as beseemed,—a work, in short, of magic. Iris dipt the woof. This on Valentine's Eve he commended to the all-swallowing indiscriminate orifice—(O ignoble trust !)—of the common post ; but the humble medium did its duty ; and from his watchful stand, the next morning, he saw the cheerful messenger knock, and by and by the precious charge delivered. He saw, unseen, the happy girl unfold the Valentine, dance about, clap her hands, as one after one the pretty emblems unfolded themselves. She danced about, not with light love, or foolish expectations, for she had no lover ; or, if she had, none she knew that could have created those bright images which delighted her. It was more like some fairy present ; a God-send, as our familiarly pious ancestors termed a benefit received where the benefactor was unknown. It would do her no harm. It would do her good for ever after. It is good to love the unknown. I only give this as a specimen of E. B. and his modest way of doing a concealed kindness.

Good morrow to my Valentine, sings poor Ophelia ; and no better wish, but with better auspices, we wish to all faithful lovers, who are not too wise to despise old legends, but are content to rank themselves humble diocesans of old Bishop Valentine and his true Church.

MY RELATIONS.

I AM arrived at that point of life at which a man may acccunt it a blessing, as it is a singularity, if he have either of his parents surviving. I have not that felicity—and sometimes think feelingly of a passage in Browne's Christian Morals, where he speaks of a man that hath lived sixty or seventy years in the world. "In such a compass of time," he says, "a man may have a close apprehension what it is to be forgotten, when he hath lived to find none who could remember his father, or scarcely the friends of his youth, and may sensibly see with what a face in no long time OBLIVION will look upon himself."

I had an aunt, a dear and good one. She was **one** whom single blessedness had soured to the world. She often used to say that I was the only thing in it which she loved ; and when she thought I was quitting it, she grieved over me with a mother's tears. A partiality quite so exclusive my reason cannot altogether approve. She was from morning till night poring over good books and devotional exercises. Her favourite volumes were Thomas à Kempis, in Stanhope's translation, and a Roman Catholic Prayer

Book, with the *matins* and *complines* regularly set down,—terms which I was at that time too young to understand. She persisted in reading them, although admonished daily concerning their Papistical tendency, and went to church every Sabbath, as a good Protestant should do. These were the only books she studied ; though I think at one period of her life she told me she had read with great satisfaction the "Adventures of an Unfortunate Young Nobleman." Finding the door of the chapel in Essex Street open one day—it was in the infancy of that heresy—she went in, liked the sermon and the manner of worship, and frequented it at intervals for some time after. She came not for doctrinal points, and never missed them. With some little asperities in her constitution, which I have above hinted at, she was a steadfast, friendly being, and a fine *old Christian*. She was a woman of strong sense and a shrewd mind ; extraordinary at a *repartee*—one of the few occasions of her breaking silence ; else she did not much value wit. The only secular employment I remember to have seen her engaged in was the splitting of French beans, and dropping them into a china basin of fair water. The odour of those tender vegetables to this day comes back upon my sense, redolent of soothing recollections. Certainly it is the most delicate of culinary operations.

Male aunts, as somebody calls them, I had none to remember. By the uncle's side I may be said to have been born an orphan. Brother, or sister, I never had any, to know them. A sister, I think, that should have been Elizabeth, died in both our infancies. What a comfort, or what a care, may I not have missed in her ! But I have cousins sprinkled about in Hertfordshire, besides *two*, with whom I have been all my life in habits of the closest intimacy, and whom I may term cousins *par excellence*. These are James and Bridget Elia. They are older than myself by twelve, and ten, years ; and neither of them seems disposed, in matters of advice and guidance, to waive any of the prerogatives which primogeniture confers. May they continue still in the same mind ; and when they shall be seventy-five and seventy-three years old, (I cannot spare them sooner,) persist in treating me in my grand climacteric precisely as a stripling or younger brother !

James is an inexplicable cousin. Nature hath her unities, which not every critic can penetrate : or, if we feel, we cannot explain them. The pen of Yorick, and of none since his, could have drawn J. E. entire —those fine Shandian lights and shades which make up his story. I must limp after in my poor antithetical manner, as the Fates have given me grace and talent. J. E. then (to the eye of a common observer at least) seemeth made up of contradictory principles. The genuine child of impulse, the frigid philosopher of prudence, the phlegm of my cousin's doctrine is invariably at war with his temperament, which is high sanguine. With always some fire-new project in his brain, J. E. is the systematic opponent of innovation, and crier down of every thing that has not stood the test of age and experiment. With a hundred fine notions chasing one another hourly in his fancy, he is startled at the least approach to the romantic in others : and, determined by his own sense in every thing, commends *you* to the guidance of common sense on all occasions. With a touch of the eccentric in all which he does or says, he is only anxious that

you should not commit yourself by doing any thing
absurd or singular. On my once letting slip at table
that I was not fond of a certain popular dish, he
begged me at any rate not to *say* so, for the world
would think me mad. He disguises a passionate
fondness for works of high art, (whereof he hath
amassed a choice collection,) under the pretext of
buying only to sell again, that his enthusiasm may
give no encouragement to yours. Yet, if it were so,
why does that piece of tender, pastoral Domenichino
hang still by his wall ? Is the ball of his sight much
more dear to him ?—or what picture-dealer can talk
like him ?

Whereas mankind in general are observed to warp
their speculative conclusions to the bent of their
individual humours, *his* theories are sure to be in
diametrical opposition to his constitution. He is
courageous as Charles of Sweden, upon instinct ;
chary of his person upon principle, as a travelling
Quaker. He has been preaching up to me, all my
life, the doctrine of bowing to the great,—the necessity of forms and manner to a man's getting on in
the world. He himself never aims at either, that I
can discover,—and has a spirit that would stand
upright in the presence of the Cham of Tartary. It
is pleasant to hear him discourse of patience—
extolling it as the truest wisdom—and to see him
during the last seven minutes that his dinner is
getting ready. Nature never ran up in her haste a
more restless piece of workmanship than when she
moulded this impetuous cousin ; and Art never turned
out a more elaborate orator than he can display himself to be upon this favourite topic of the advantages
of quiet and contentedness, in the state, whatever it be

that we are placed in. He is triumphant on this
theme when he has you safe in one of those short
stages that ply for the western road, in a very obstruct-
ing manner, at the foot of John Murray's street—
where you get in when it is empty, and are expected
to wait till the vehicle hath completed her just freight
—a trying three-quarters of an hour to some people.
He wonders at your fidgetiness— " where could we
be better than we are, *thus sitting, thus consulting ?*"—
" prefers, for his part, a state of rest to locomotion,"—
with an eye all the while upon the coachman,—till at
length, waxing out of all patience, at *your want of it*,
he breaks out into a pathetic remonstrance at the
fellow for detaining us so long over the time which
he had professed, and declares peremptorily that
" the gentleman in the coach is determined to get out
if he does not drive on that instant."

Very quick at inventing an argument, or detecting
a sophistry, he is incapable of attending *you* in any
chain of arguing.   Indeed he makes wild work with
logic ; and seems to jump at most admirable conclusions by some process not at all akin to it.   Conso-
nantly enough to this, he hath been heard to deny,
upon certain occasions, that there exists such a
faculty at all in man as *reason ;* and wondereth how
man came first to have a conceit of it,—enforcing his
negation with all the might of *reasoning* he is master
of.   He has some speculative notions against laughter,
and will maintain that laughing is not natural to *him*,
when peradventure the next moment his lungs shall
crow like Chanticleer.   He says some of the best
things in the world, and declareth that wit is his
aversion.   It was he who said, upon seeing the Eton
boys at play in their grounds, " *What a pity to think*

that these fine ingenuous lads in a few years will all be changed into frivolous Members of Parliament !"

His youth was fiery, glowing, tempestuous; and in age he discovereth no symptom of cooling. This is that which I admire in him. I hate people who meet Time half-way. I am for no compromise with that inevitable spoiler. While he lives, J. E. will take his swing. It does me good, as I walk towards the street of my daily avocation, on some fine May morning, to meet him marching in a quite opposite direction, with a jolly handsome presence, and shining sanguine face, that indicates some purchase in his eye,—a Claude, or a Hobbima; for much of his enviable leisure is consumed at Christie's and Phillips's, or where not, to pick up pictures and such gauds. On these occasions he mostly stoppeth me, to read a short lecture on the advantage a person like me possesses above himself, in having his time occupied with business which he *must* do; assureth me that he often feels it hang heavy on his hands; wishes he had fewer holidays; and goes off—Westward Ho!—chanting a tune, to Pall Mall, perfectly convinced that he has convinced me, while I proceed in my opposite direction tuneless.

It is pleasant, again, to see this Professor of Indifference doing the honours of his new purchase, when he has fairly housed it. You must view it in every light, till *he* has found the best; placing it at this distance, and at that, but always suiting the focus of your sight to his own. You must spy at it through your fingers, to catch the aerial perspective, though you assure him that to you the landscape shows much more agreeable without that artifice. Woe be to the luckless wight who does not only not respond to his rapture, but who should drop an unseasonable intimation of preferring one of his anterior bargains to the present! The last is always his best hit—his "Cynthia of the minute."—Alas, how many a mild Madonna have I known to *come in!*—a Raphael!— keep its ascendancy a few brief moons—then, after certain intermedial degradations, from the front draw- ing-room to the back gallery, thence to the dark parlour,—adopted in turn by each of the Carracci, under successive lowering ascriptions of filiation, mildly breaking its fall—consigned to the oblivious lumber-room, *go out* at last a Lucca Giordano, or plain Carlo Maratti!—which things when I beheld— musing upon the chances and mutabilities of fate below, hath made me to reflect upon the altered con- dition of great personages, or that woeful Queen of Richard the Second—

> ————set forth in pomp,
> She came adorned hither like sweet May,
> Sent back like Hollowmass or shortest day.

With great love for *you*, J. E. hath but a limited sympathy with what you feel or do. He lives in a world of his own, and makes slender guesses at what passes in your mind. He never pierces the marrow of your habits. He will tell an old-established play- goer, that Mr. Such-a-one, of So-and-so, (naming one of the theatres,) is a very lively comedian—as a piece of news! He advertised me but the other day of some pleasant green lanes which he had found out for me, *knowing me to be a great walker,* in my own immediate vicinity—who have haunted the identical spot any time these twenty years! He has not much respect for that class of feelings which goes by the name of sentimental. He applies the definition of real evil to bodily sufferings exclusively, and rejecteth

all others as imaginary. He is affected by the sight,
or the bare supposition, of a creature in pain, to a
degree which I have never witnessed out of womankind. A constitutional acuteness to this class of sufferings may in part account for this. The animal
tribe in particular he taketh under his especial protection. A broken-winded or spur-galled horse is sure
to find an advocate in him. An over-loaded ass is
his client for ever. He is the apostle to the brute
kind; the never-failing friend of those who have none
to care for them. The contemplation of a lobster
boiled or eels skinned *alive* will wring him so, that
" all for pity he could die." It will take the savour
from his palate and the rest from his pillow for days
and nights. With the intense feeling of Thomas
Clarkson, he wanted only the steadiness of pursuit
and unity of purpose of that " true yoke-fellow with
Time," to have effected as much for the *Animal* as *he*
hath done for the *Negro Creation.* But my uncon-
trollable cousin is but imperfectly formed for purposes
which demand co-operation. He cannot wait. His
amelioration plans must be ripened in a day. For
this reason he has cut but an equivocal figure in
benevolent societies, and combinations for the allevia-
tion of human sufferings. His zeal constantly makes
him to outrun, and put out, his coadjutors. He thinks
of relieving,—while they think of debating. He was
black-balled out of a society for the Relief of *   *
*   *   *   * because the fervour of his humanity
toiled beyond the formal apprehension and creeping
processes of his associates. I shall always consider
this distinction as a patent of nobility in the Elia family.

Do I mention these seeming inconsistencies to
smile at, or upbraid, my unique cousin? Marry,

heaven, and all good manners, and the understanding
that should be between kinsfolk, forbid ! With all the
strangenesses of this *strangest of the Elias*, I would
not have him in one jot or tittle other than he is;
neither would I barter or exchange my wild kinsman
for the most exact, regular, and every way consistent
kinsman breathing.

In my next, reader, I may perhaps give you some
account of my cousin Bridget—if you are not already
surfeited with cousins—and take you by the hand, if
you are willing to go with us, on an excursion which
we made a summer or two since, in search of *more
cousins*—

Through the green plains of pleasant Hertfordshire.

MACKERY END, IN HERTFORDSHIRE.

BRIDGET ELIA has been my housekeeper for many a
long year. I have obligations to Bridget, extending
beyond the period of memory. We house together,
old bachelor and maid, in a sort of double singleness;
with such tolerable comfort, upon the whole, that I,
for one, find in myself no sort of disposition to go out
upon the mountains, with the rash king's offspring,
to bewail my celibacy. We agree pretty well in our
tastes and habits—yet so, as "with a difference."
We are generally in harmony, with occasional bicker-
ings—as it should be among near relations. Our
sympathies are rather understood than expressed;

and once, upon my dissembling a tone in my voice more kind than ordinary, my cousin burst into tears, and complained that I was altered. We are both great readers in different directions. While I am hanging over (for the thousandth time) some passage in old Burton, or one of his strange contemporaries, she is abstracted in some modern tale, or adventure, whereof our common reading-table is daily fed with assiduously fresh supplies. Narrative teases me. I have little concern in the progress of events. She must have a story—well, ill, or indifferently told—so there be life stirring in it, and plenty of good or evil incidents. The fluctuations of fortune in fiction, and almost in real life, have ceased to interest, or operate but dully upon me. Out-of-the-way humours and opinions—heads with some diverting twist in them—the oddities of authorship, please me most. My cousin has a native disrelish of any thing that sounds odd or bizarre. Nothing goes down with her that is quaint, irregular, or out of the road of common sympathy. She "holds Nature more clever." I can pardon her blindness to the beautiful obliquities of the Religio Medici ; but she must apologize to me for certain disrespectful insinuations, which she has been pleased to throw out latterly, touching the intellectuals of a dear favourite of mine, of the last century but one—the thrice noble, chaste, and virtuous, but again somewhat fantastical, and original-brained, generous Margaret Newcastle.

It has been the lot of my cousin, oftener perhaps than I could have wished, to have had for her associates and mine free-thinkers, leaders and disciples of novel philosophies and systems ; but she neither wrangles with nor accepts their opinions. That which was good and venerable to her when a child retains its authority over her mind still. She never juggles or plays tricks with her understanding.

We are both of us inclined to be a little too positive; and I have observed the result of our disputes to be almost uniformly this—that in matters of fact, dates and circumstances, it turns out that I was in the right, and my cousin in the wrong. But where we have differed upon moral points, upon something proper to be done, or let alone, whatever heat of opposition or steadiness of conviction I set out with, I am sure always in the long run to be brought over to her way of thinking.

I must touch upon the foibles of my kinswoman with a gentle hand, for Bridget does not like to be told of her faults. She hath an awkward trick (to say no worse of it) of reading in company: at which times she will answer *yes* or *no* to a question without fully understanding its purport, which is provoking, and derogatory in the highest degree to the dignity of the putter of the said question. Her presence of mind is equal to the most pressing trials of life, but will sometimes desert her upon trifling occasions. When the purpose requires it, and is a thing of moment, she can speak to it greatly; but in matters which are not stuff of the conscience, she hath been known sometimes to let slip a word less seasonably.

Her education in youth was not much attended to; and she happily missed all that train of female garniture which passeth by the name of accomplishments. She was tumbled early, by accident or design, into a spacious closet of good old English reading, without much selection or prohibition, and broused at will upon that fair and wholesome pasturage. Had I twenty girls, they should be brought up exactly in this fashion. I know not whether their chance in wedlock might not be diminished by it; but I can answer for it, that it makes (if the worst come to the worst) most incomparable old maids.

In a season of distress she is the truest comforter; but in the teasing accidents and minor perplexities, which do not call out the *will* to meet them, she sometimes maketh matters worse by an excess of participation. If she does not always divide your trouble, upon the pleasanter occasions of life she is sure always to treble your satisfaction. She is excellent to be at a play with, or upon a visit; but best when she goes a journey with you.

We made an excursion together a few summers since into Hertfordshire, to beat up the quarters of some of our less-known relations in that fine corn country.

The oldest thing I remember is Mackery End; or Mackarel End, as it is spelt, perhaps more properly, in some old maps of Hertfordshire; a farm-house, delightfully situated within a gentle walk from Wheat-hampstead. I can just remember having been there, on a visit to a great-aunt, when I was a child, under the care of Bridget, who, as I have said, is older than myself by some ten years. I wish that I could throw into a heap the remainder of our joint existences, that we might share them in equal division. But that is impossible. The house was at that time in the occupation of a substantial yeoman, who had married my grandmother's sister. His name was Gladman. My grandmother was a Bruton, married to a Field. The Gladmans and the Brutons are still flourishing

in that part of the county, but the Fields are almost
extinct.   More than forty years had elapsed since the
visit I speak of; and for the greater portion of that
period we had lost sight of the other two branches also.
Who or what sort of persons inherited Mackery End
—kindred or strange folk—we were afraid almost to
conjecture, but determined some day to explore.

By somewhat a circuitous route, taking the noble
park at Luton in our way from St. Albans, we arrived
at the spot of our anxious curiosity about noon.   The
sight of the old farm-house, though every trace of it
was effaced from my recollection, affected me with a
pleasure which I had not experienced for many a
year.   For though *I* had forgotten it, *we* had never
forgotten being there together, and we had been
talking about Mackery End all our lives, till memory
on my part became mocked with a phantom of itself,
and I thought I knew the aspect of the place, which
when present, O how unlike it was to *that* which I
had conjured up so many times instead of it !

Still the air breathed balmily about it ; the season
was in the " heart of June," and I could say with the
poet,

> But thou, that didst appear so fair
> To fond imagination,
> Dost rival in the light of day
> Her delicate creation.

Bridget's was more a waking bliss than mine, for
she easily remembered her old acquaintance again—
some altered features, of course a little grudged at.
At first, indeed, she was ready to disbelieve for joy ;
but the scene soon re-confirmed itself in her affections,
and she traversed every out-post of the old mansion,
—to the wood-house, the orchard, the place where

the pigeon-house had stood (house and birds were alike flown)—with a breathless impatience of recognition, which was more pardonable perhaps than decorous at the age of fifty odd. But Bridget in some things is behind her years.

The only thing left was to get into the house; and that was a difficulty which to me singly would have been insurmountable; for I am terribly shy in making myself known to strangers and out-of-date kinsfolk. Love, stronger than scruple, winged my cousin in without me ; but she soon returned with a creature that might have sat to a sculptor for the image of Welcome. It was the youngest of the Gladmans, who, by marriage with a Bruton, had become mistress of the old mansion. A comely brood are the Brutons. Six of them, females, were noted as the handsomest young women in the county. But this adopted Bruton, in my mind, was better than they all—more comely. She was born too late to have remembered me. She just recollected in early life to have had her cousin Bridget once pointed out to her, climbing a stile. But the name of kindred and of cousinship was enough. Those slender ties, that prove slight as gossamer in the rending atmosphere of a metropolis, bind faster, as we found it, in hearty, homely, loving Hertford-shire. In five minutes we were as thoroughly acquainted as if we had been born and bred up together ; were familiar, even to the calling each other by our Christian names. So Christians should call one another. To have seen Bridget and her—it was like the meeting of the two scriptural cousins ! There was a grace and dignity, an amplitude of form and stature, answering to her mind, in this farmer's wife, which would have shined in a palace—or so we thought it. We were made welcome by husband and wife equally—we, and our friend that was with us. I had almost forgotten him; but B—— F—— will not so soon forget that meeting, if peradventure he shall read this on the far distant shores where the kangaroo haunts. The fatted calf was made ready, or rather was already so, as if in anticipation of our coming; and, after an appropriate glass of native wine, never let me forget with what honest pride this hospitable cousin made us proceed to Wheathampstead, to introduce us (as some new-found rarity) to her mother and sister Gladmans, who did indeed know something more of us at a time when she almost knew nothing. With what corresponding kindness we were received by them also—how Bridget's memory, exalted by the occasion, warmed into a thousand half-obliterated recollections of things and persons, to my utter astonishment and her own—and to the astoundment of B. F., who sat by, almost the only thing that was not a cousin there,—old effaced images of more than half-forgotten names and circumstances still crowding back upon her, as words written in lemon come out upon exposure to a friendly warmth,—when I forget all this, then may my country cousins forget me, and Bridget no more remember, that in the days of weakling infancy I was her tender charge—as I have been her care in foolish manhood since—in those pretty pastoral walks, long ago, about Mackery End, in Hertfordshire.

MY FIRST PLAY.

———

AT the north end of Cross Court there yet stands a portal, of some architectural pretensions, though reduced to humble use, serving at present for an entrance to a printing-office. This old doorway, if you are young, reader, you may not know was the identical pit-entrance to old Drury—Garrick's Drury—all of it that is left. I never pass it without shaking some forty years from off my shoulders, recurring to the evening when I passed through it to see *my first play*. The afternoon had been wet, and the condition of our going (the elder folks and myself) was, that the rain should cease. With what a beating heart did I watch from the window the puddles, from the stillness of which I was taught to prognosticate the desired cessation! I seem to remember the last spurt, and the glee with which I ran to announce it.

We went with orders, which my godfather F. had sent us. He kept the oil shop (now Davies's) at the corner of Featherstone Buildings, in Holborn. F. was a tall, grave person, lofty in speech, and had pretensions above his rank. He associated in those days with John Palmer, the comedian, whose gait and bearing he seemed to copy; if John (which is quite as likely) did not rather borrow somewhat of his manner from my godfather. He was also known to, and visited by, Sheridan. It was to his house in Holborn that young Brinsley brought his first wife on her

S 2

elopement with him from a boarding-school at Bath
—the beautiful Maria Linley.   My parents were
present (over a quadrille table) when he arrived in
the evening with his harmonious charge.   From
either of these connections it may be inferred that
my godfather could command an order for the then
Drury Lane theatre at pleasure ; and indeed a pretty
liberal issue of those cheap billets, in Brinsley's easy
autograph, I have heard him say was the sole re-
muneration which he had received for many years'
nightly illumination of the orchestra and various
avenues of that theatre ; and he was content it should
be so.   The honour of Sheridan's familiarity, or
supposed familiarity, was better to my godfather than
money.

F. was the most gentlemanly of oilmen ; grandilo-
quent, yet courteous.   His delivery of the commonest
matters of fact was Ciceronian.   He had two Latin
words almost constantly in his mouth, (how odd
sounds Latin from an oilman's lips !) which my better
knowledge since has enabled me to correct.   In strict
pronunciation they should have been sounded *vice
versâ ;* but in those young years they impressed me
with more awe than they would now do, read aright
from Seneca or Varro—in his own peculiar pronunciation, monosyllabically elaborated, or Anglicised, into
something like *verse verse.*   By an imposing manner,
and the help of these distorted syllables, he climbed
(but that was little) to the highest parochial honours
which St. Andrew's has to bestow.

He is dead : and thus much I thought due to his
memory, both for my first orders, (little wondrous
talismans !—slight keys, and insignificant to outward
sight, but opening to me more than Arabian para-

dises !) and moreover that by his testamentary beneficence I came into possession of the only landed
property which I could ever call my own, situated
near the road-way village of pleasant Puckeridge, in
Hertfordshire. When I journeyed down to take
possession, and planted foot on my own ground, the
stately habits of the donor descended upon me, and
I strode (shall I confess the vanity?) with larger
paces over my allotment of three-quarters of an acre,
with its commodious mansion in the midst, with the
feeling of an English freeholder that all betwixt sky
and centre was my own. The estate has passed into
more prudent hands, and nothing but an agrarian can
restore it.

In those days were pit orders.—Beshrew the uncomfortable manager who abolished them — with one of
these we went. I remember the waiting at the door
—not that which is left—but between that and an
inner door in shelter.—O when shall I be such an
expectant again !—with the cry of nonpareils, an indispensable play-house accompaniment in those days.
As near as I can recollect, the fashionable pronunciation of the theatrical fruiteresses then was, " Chase
some oranges, chase some numparels, chase a bill of
the play ;"—chase *pro* chuse. But when we got in,
and I beheld the green curtain that veiled a heaven to
my imagination, which was soon to be disclosed—the
breathless anticipations I endured ! I had seen something like it in the plate prefixed to *Troilus and
Cressida*, in Rowe's Shakspeare—the tent-scene with
Diomede—and a sight of that plate can always bring
back in a measure the feeling of that evening. The
boxes at that time, full of well-dressed women of
quality, projected over the pit; and the pilasters

reaching down were adorned with a glistering substance (I know not what) under glass, (as it seemed,)
resembling—a homely fancy—but I judged it to be
sugar-candy; yet, to my raised imagination, divested
of its homelier qualities, it appeared a glorified candy!
The orchestra lights at length arose, those "fair
Auroras!" Once the bell sounded. It was to ring
out yet once again; and, incapable of the anticipation,
I reposed my shut eyes in a sort of resignation upon
the maternal lap. It rang the second time. The
curtain drew up, (I was not past six years old,) and
the play was *Artaxerxes !*

I had dabbled a little in the *Universal History*—the
ancient part of it—and here was the court of Persia.
It was being admitted to a sight of the past. I took
no proper interest in the action going on, for I understood not its import; but I heard the word Darius,
and I was in the midst of Daniel. All feeling was
absorbed in vision. Gorgeous vests, gardens, palaces,
princesses, passed before me. I knew not players.
I was in Persepolis for the time, and the burning idol
of their devotion almost converted me into a worship-
per. I was awe-struck, and believed those significa-
tions to be something more than elemental fires. It
was all enchantment and a dream. No such pleasure
has since visited me but in dreams. Harlequin's
invasion followed; where, I remember, the trans-
formation of the magistrates into reverend beldams
seemed to me a piece of grave historic justice, and
the tailor carrying his own head to be as sober a
verity as the legend of St. Denys.

The next play to which I was taken was the *Lady
of the Manor;* of which, with the exception of some
scenery, very faint traces are left in my memory. It

was followed by a pantomime, called *Lun's Ghost*—a satiric touch, I apprehend, upon Rich, not long since dead—but to my apprehension (too sincere for satire) Lun was as remote a piece of antiquity as Lud—the father of a line of Harlequins — transmitting his dagger of lath (the wooden sceptre) through countless ages. I saw the primeval Motley come from his silent tomb in a ghastly vest of white patchwork, like the apparition of a dead rainbow. So Harlequins (thought I) look when they are dead.

My third play followed in quick succession. It was the *Way of the World*. I think I must have sat at it as grave as a judge ; for I remember the hysteric affectations of good Lady Wishfort affected me like some solemn tragic passion. *Robinson Crusoe* followed ; in which Crusoe, man Friday, and the parrot were as good and authentic as in the story. The clownery and pantaloonery of these pantomimes have clean passed out of my head. I believe I no more laughed at them than at the same age I should have been disposed to laugh at the grotesque Gothic heads (seeming to me then replete with devout meaning) that gape and grin in stone around the inside of the old Round Church (my church) of the Templars.

I saw these plays in the season 1781-2, when I was from six to seven years old. After the intervention of six or seven other years (for at school all playgoing was inhibited) I again entered the doors of a theatre. That old Artaxerxes evening had never done ringing in my fancy. I expected the same feelings to come again with the same occasion. But we differ from ourselves less at sixty and sixteen, than the latter does from six. In that interval what had I not lost ! At the first period I knew nothing, understood nothing, discriminated nothing.   I felt all, loved all, wondered all—

Was nourish'd, I could not tell how—

I had left the temple a devotee, and was returned a rationalist.   The same things were there materially; but the emblem, the reference, was gone !   The green curtain was no longer a veil, drawn between two worlds, the unfolding of which was to bring back past ages to present a " royal ghost,"—but a certain quantity of green baize, which was to separate the audience for a given time from certain of their fellow-men who were to come forward and pretend those parts.   The lights —the orchestra lights—came up a clumsy machinery. The first ring and the second ring was now but a trick of the prompter's bell—which had been, like the note of the cuckoo, a phantom of a voice, no hand seen or guessed at which ministered to its warning. The actors were men and women painted.   I thought the fault was in them ; but it was in myself, and the alteration which those many centuries—of six short twelvemonths—had wrought in me.   Perhaps it was fortunate for me that the play of the evening was but an indifferent comedy, as it gave me time to drop some unreasonable expectations, which might have inter-fered with the genuine emotions with which I was soon after enabled to enter upon the first appearance to me of Mrs. Siddons in *Isabella*.   Comparison and retrospection soon yielded to the present attraction of the scene ; and the theatre became to me, upon a new stock, the most delightful of recreations.

MODERN GALLANTRY.

In comparing modern with ancient manners, we are pleased to compliment ourselves upon the point of gallantry; a certain obsequiousness, or deferential respect, which we are supposed to pay to females, as females.

I shall believe that this principle actuates our conduct when I can forget that in the nineteenth century of the era from which we date our civility we are but just beginning to leave off the very frequent practice of whipping females in public, in common with the coarsest male offenders.

I shall believe it to be influential when I can shut my eyes to the fact that in England women are still occasionally—hanged.

I shall believe in it when actresses are no longer subject to be hissed off a stage by gentlemen.

I shall believe in it when Dorimant hands a fish-wife across the kennel; or assists the apple-woman to pick up her wandering fruit, which some unlucky dray has just dissipated.

I shall believe in it when the Dorimants in humbler life, who would be thought in their way notable adepts in this refinement, shall act upon it in places where they are not known, or think themselves not observed; when I shall see the traveller for some rich tradesman part with his admired box-coat, to spread it over the defenceless shoulders of the poor woman who is passing to her parish on the roof of the same stage coach with him, drenched in the rain ; when I shall no longer see a woman standing up in the pit of a London theatre till she is sick and faint with the exertion, with men about her, seated at their ease, and jeering at her distress ; till one, that seems to have more manners or conscience than the rest, significantly declares " she should be welcome to his seat if she were a little younger and handsomer." Place this dapper warehouseman, or that rider, in a circle of his own female acquaintance, and you shall confess you have not seen a politer-bred man in Lothbury.

Lastly, I shall begin to believe that there is some such principle influencing our conduct when more than one half of the drudgery and coarse servitude of the world shall cease to be performed by women.

Until that day comes I shall never believe this boasted point to be any thing more than a conventional fiction ; a pageant got up between the sexes, in a certain rank, and at a certain time of life, in which both find their account equally.

I shall be even disposed to rank it among the salutary fictions of life when in polite circles I shall see the same attentions paid to age as to youth, to homely features as to handsome, to coarse complexions as to clear,—to the woman, as she is a woman, not as she is a beauty, a fortune, or a title.

I shall believe it to be something more than a name when a well-dressed gentleman in a well-dressed company can advert to the topic of *female old age* without exciting, and intending to excite, a sneer ; when the phrases " antiquated virginity," and such a one has " overstood her market," pronounced in good

company, shall raise immediate offence in man or
woman that shall hear them spoken.

Joseph Paice,[1] of Bread Street Hill, merchant, and
one of the Directors of the South Sea Company—the
same to whom Edwards, the Shakspeare commentator, has addressed a fine sonnet—was the only
pattern of consistent gallantry I have met with. He
took me under his shelter at an early age, and
bestowed some pains upon me. I owe to his precepts
and example whatever there is of the man of
business (and that is not much) in my composition.
It was not his fault that I did not profit more.
Though bred a Presbyterian, and brought up a merchant, he was the finest gentleman of his time. He
had not *one* system of attention to females in the
drawing-room, and *another* in the shop, or at the stall.
I do not mean that he made no distinction ; but he
never lost sight of sex, or overlooked it in the casualties of a disadvantageous situation. I have seen him
stand bareheaded—smile if you please—to a poor
servant girl, while she has been inquiring of him the
way to some street—in such a posture of unforced
civility as neither to embarrass her in the acceptance
nor himself in the offer of it. He was no dangler, in
the common acceptation of the word, after women :
but he reverenced and upheld, in every form in which
it came before him, *womanhood*. I have seen him
—nay, smile not,—tenderly escorting a market woman,
whom he had encountered in a shower, exalting his
umbrella over her poor basket of fruit, that it might
receive no damage, with as much carefulness as if she

---

[1] This gentleman was no fictitious character, as Lamb assured one of
his correspondents.—H.

had been a Countess. To the reverend form of Female Eld he would yield the wall (though it were to an ancient beggar woman) with more ceremony than we can afford to show our grandams. He was the Preux Chevalier of Age; the Sir Calidore, or Sir Tristan, to those who have no Calidores or Tristans to defend them. The roses, that had long faded thence, still bloomed for him in those withered and yellow cheeks.

He was never married, but in his youth he paid his addresses to the beautiful Susan Winstanley,—old Winstanley's daughter, of Clapton,—who dying in the early days of their courtship, confirmed in him the resolution of perpetual bachelorship. It was during their short courtship, he told me, that he had been one day treating his mistress to a profusion of civil speeches, the common gallantries, (to which kind of thing she had hitherto manifested no repugnance,) but in this instance with no effect. He could not obtain from her a decent acknowledgment in return. She rather seemed to resent his compliments. He could not set it down to caprice, for the lady had always shown herself above that littleness. When he ventured on the following day, finding her a little better humoured, to expostulate with her on her coldness of yesterday, she confessed, with her usual frankness, that she had no sort of dislike to his attentions; that she could even endure some high-flown compliments; that a young woman placed in her situation had a right to expect all sort of civil things said to her; that she hoped she could digest a dose of adulation, short of insincerity, with as little injury to her humility as most young women; but that—a little before he had commenced his compliments—she had overheard him by accident, in rather rough language, rating a young woman, who had not brought home his cravats quite to the appointed time, and she thought to herself, " As I am Miss Susan Winstanley, and a young lady,—a reputed beauty, and known to be a fortune,—I can have my choice of the finest speeches from the mouth of this very fine gentleman who is courting me ; but if I had been poor Mary Such-a-one, (*naming the milliner,*) and had failed of bringing home the cravats to the appointed hour, though perhaps I had sat up half the night to forward them, what sort of compliments should I have received then ?   And my woman's pride came to my assistance ; and I thought that if it were only to do *me* honour, a female, like myself, might have received handsomer usage : and I was determined not to accept any fine speeches, to the compromise of that sex, the belonging to which was after all my strongest claim and title to them."

I think the lady discovered both generosity, and a just way of thinking, in this rebuke which she gave her lover; and I have sometimes imagined that the uncommon strain of courtesy which through life regulated the actions and behaviour of my friend towards all of womankind indiscriminately, owed its happy origin to this seasonable lesson from the lips of his lamented mistress.

I wish the whole female world would entertain the same notion of these things that Miss Winstanley showed.   Then we should see something of the spirit of consistent gallantry ; and no longer witness the anomaly of the same man,—a pattern of true politeness to a wife ; of cold contempt, or rudeness, to a sister ; the idolater of his female mistress, the dis-

parager and despiser of his no less female aunt, or
unfortunate—still female—maiden cousin.   Just so
much respect as a woman derogates from her own
sex, in whatever condition placed—her handmaid, or
dependant—she deserves to have diminished from
herself on that score ; and probably will feel the
diminution, when youth, and beauty, and advantages
not inseparable from sex, shall lose of their attraction.
What a woman should demand of a man in courtship,
or after it, is first—respect for her as she is a
woman ; and next to that, to be respected by him
above all other women.   But let her stand upon her
female character as upon a foundation ; and let the
attentions incident to individual preference be so
many pretty additaments and ornaments—as many
and as fanciful as you please—to that main structure.   Let her first lesson be---with sweet Susan
Winstanley—to *reverence her sex.*

THE OLD BENCHERS OF THE INNER
TEMPLE.

I was born, and passed the first seven years of my
life, in the Temple.   Its church, its halls, its gardens,
its fountain, its river, I had almost said,—for in those
young years, what was this king of rivers to me but a
stream that watered our pleasant places ?—these are
of my oldest recollections.   I repeat, to this day, no
verses to myself more frequently, or with kindlier

emotion, than those of Spenser, where he speaks of this spot :—

> " There when they came, whereas those bricky towers,
> The which on Themmes brode aged back doth ride,
> Where now the studious lawyers have their bowers,
> There whylome wont the Templer knights to bide,
> Till they decay'd through pride."

Indeed it is the most elegant spot in the metropolis. What a transition for a countryman visiting London for the first time—the passing from the crowded Strand or Fleet Street, by unexpected avenues, into its magnificent ample squares, its classic green recesses ! What a cheerful, liberal look hath that portion of it which from three sides overlooks the greater garden,—that goodly pile

> " Of building strong, albeit of Paper hight,"

confronting with massy contrast the lighter, older, more fantastically shrouded one, named of Harcourt, with the cheerful Crown Office Row, (place of my kindly engendure,) right opposite the stately stream, which washes the garden-foot with her yet scarcely trade-polluted waters, and seems but just weaned from her Twickenham Naiades ! A man would give something to have been born in such places. What a collegiate aspect has that fine Elizabethan hall, where the fountain plays, which I have made to rise and fall (how many times !) to the astonishment of the young urchins, my contemporaries, who, not being able to guess at its recondite machinery, were almost tempted to hail the wondrous work as magic ! What an antique air had the now almost effaced sundials, with their moral inscriptions, seeming coevals with that Time which they measured, and to take their

revelations of its flight immediately from heaven,
holding correspondence with the fountain of light !
How would the dark line steal imperceptibly on,
watched by the eye of childhood, eager to detect its
movement, never catched, nice as an evanescent
cloud, or the first arrests of sleep !

> " Ah ! yet doth beauty, like a dial hand,
> Steal from his figure, and no pace perceived ! "

What a dead thing is a clock, with its ponderous
embowelments of lead and brass, its pert or solemn
dulness of communication, compared with the simple,
altar-like structure, and heart-language of the old dial !
It stood as the garden-god of Christian gardens. Why
is it almost everywhere banished ?   If its business
use be superseded by more elaborate inventions, its
moral uses, its beauty, might have pleaded for its con-
tinuance.   It spoke of moderate labours, of pleasures
not protracted after sunset, of temperance, and good
hours.   It was the primitive clock, the horologe of
the first world.   Adam could scarce have missed it in
Paradise.   It was the measure appropriate for sweet
plants and flowers to spring by, for the birds to appor-
tion their silver warblings by, for flocks to pasture and
be led to fold by. The shepherd " carved it out
quaintly in the sun ; " and, turning philosopher by the
very occupation, provided it with mottoes more touching than tombstones.   It was a pretty device of the
gardener, recorded by Marvell, who, in the days of
artificial gardening, made a dial out of herbs and
flowers.   I must quote his verses a little higher up,
for they are full, as all his serious poetry was, of a
witty delicacy. They will not come in awkwardly, I

hope, in a talk of fountains and sundials. He is speaking of sweet garden scenes :—

> " What wondrous life is this I lead !
> Ripe apples drop about my head.
> The luscious clusters of the vine
> Upon my mouth do crush their wine.
> The nectarine, and curious peach,
> Into my hands themselves do reach.
> Stumbling on melons, as I pass,
> Insnared with flowers, I fall on grass.
> Meanwhile the mind from pleasure less
> Withdraws into its happiness:
> The mind, that ocean, where each kind
> Does straight its own resemblance find ;
> Yet it creates, transcending these,
> Far other worlds and other seas ;
> Annihilating all that's made
> To a green thought in a green shade
> Here at the fountain's sliding foot,
> Or at some fruit-tree's mossy root,
> Casting the body's vest aside,
> My soul into the boughs does glide ;
> There, like a bird, it sits and sings,
> Then wets and claps its silver wings,
> And, till prepared for longer flight,
> Waves in its plumes the various light.
> How well the skilful gardener drew,
> Of flowers and herbs, this dial new !
> Where, from above, the milder sun
> Does through a fragrant zodiac run :
> And, as it works, the industrious bee
> Computes its time as well as we.
> How could such sweet and wholesome hours
> Be reckon'd but with herbs and flowers ?" [1]

The artificial fountains of the metropolis are, in like manner, fast vanishing. Most of them are dried up or bricked over. Yet, where one is left, as in that

---

[1] From a copy of verses entitled " The Garden."

little green nook behind the South Sea House, what a freshness it gives to the dreary pile ! Four little winged marble boys used to play their virgin fancies, spouting out ever fresh streams from their innocent wanton lips in the square of Lincoln's Inn, when I was no bigger than they were figured. They are gone, and the spring is choked up. The fashion, they tell me, is gone by, and these things are esteemed childish. Why not, then, gratify children, by letting them stand ? Lawyers, I suppose, were children once. They are awakening images to them at least. Why must every thing smack of man and mannish ? Is the world all grown up ? Is childhood dead ? Or is there not in the bosoms of the wisest and the best some of the child's heart left, to respond to its earliest enchantments ? The figures were grotesque. Are the stiff-wigged living figures, that still flitter and chatter about that area, less Gothic in appearance ? or is the splutter of their hot rhetoric one half so refreshing and innocent as the little cool playful streams which those exploded cherubs uttered ?

They have lately gothicized the entrance to the Inner Temple Hall, and the library front ; to assimilate them, I suppose, to the body of the hall, which they do not at all resemble. What is become of the winged horse that stood over the former ? a stately arms ! And who has removed those frescoes of the Virtues, which Italianized the end of the Paper Buildings ?—my first hint of allegory ! They must account to me for these things, which I miss so greatly.

The terrace is indeed left, which we used to call the parade ; but the traces are passed away of the footsteps which made its pavement awful ! It is become common and profane. The old benchers had it almost sacred to themselves, in the forepart of the day at least. They might not be sided or jostled. Their air and dress asserted the parade. You left wide spaces betwixt you when you passed them. We walk on even terms with their successors. The roguish eye of J——ll, ever ready to be delivered of a jest, almost invites a stranger to vie a repartee with it. But what insolent familiar durst have mated Thomas Coventry ? whose person was a quadrate, his step massy and elephantine, his face square as the lion's, his gait peremptory and path-keeping, indivertible from his way as a moving column, the scarecrow of his inferiors, the brow-beater of equals and superiors, who made a solitude of children wherever he came, for they fled his insufferable presence, as they would have shunned an Elisha bear. His growl was as thunder in their ears, whether he spake to them in mirth or in rebuke ; his invitatory notes being indeed, of all, the most repulsive and horrid. Clouds of snuff, aggravating the natural terrors of his speech, broke from each majestic nostril, darkening the air. He took it, not by pinches, but a palmful at once,—diving for it under the mighty flaps of his old-fashioned waistcoat pocket ; his waistcoat red and angry, his coat dark rappee, tinctured by dye original, and by adjuncts, with buttons of obsolete gold. And so he paced the terrace.

By his side a milder form was sometimes to be seen,—the pensive gentility of Samuel Salt. They were coevals, and had nothing but that and their benchership in common. In politics Salt was a Whig, and Coventry a staunch Tory. Many a sarcastic growl did the latter cast out (for Coventry had a rough spinous humour) at the political confederates of his associate, which rebounded from the gentle

T 2

bosom of the latter like cannon balls from wool. You could not ruffle Samuel Salt.

S. had the reputation of being a very clever man, and of excellent discernment in the chamber practice of the law. I suspect his knowledge did not amount to much. When a case of difficult disposition of money, testamentary or otherwise, came before him, he ordinarily handed it over, with a few instructions, to his man Lovel, who was a quick little fellow, and would despatch it out of hand by the light of natural understanding, of which he had an uncommon share. It was incredible what repute for talents S. enjoyed by the mere trick of gravity. He was a shy man; a child might pose him in a minute; indolent and pro-crastinating to the last degree. Yet men would give him credit for vast application, in spite of himself. He was not to be trusted with himself with impunity. He never dressed for a dinner party but he forgot his sword (they wore swords then) or some other neces-sary part of his equipage. Lovel had his eye upon him on all these occasions, and ordinarily gave him his cue. If there was any thing which he could speak unseasonably, he was sure to do it. He was to dine at a relative's of the unfortunate Miss Blandy on the day of her execution; and L., who had a wary fore-sight of his probable hallucinations, before he set out schooled him, with great anxiety, not in any possible manner to allude to her story that day. S. promised faithfully to observe the injunction. He had not been seated in the parlour, where the company was expect-ing the dinner summons, four minutes, when, a pause in the conversation ensuing, he got up, looked out of window, and pulling down his ruffles—an ordinary motion with him—observed, " it was a gloomy day," and added, "Miss Blandy must be hanged by this time, I suppose." Instances of this sort were perpetual. Yet S. was thought by some of the greatest men of his time a fit person to be consulted, not alone in matters pertaining to the law, but in the ordinary niceties and embarrassments of conduct,—from force of manner entirely. He never laughed. He had the same good fortune among the female world,—was a known toast with the ladies, and one or two are said to have died for love of him:—I suppose because he never trifled or talked gallantry with them, or paid them indeed hardly common attentions. He had a fine face and person, but wanted, methought, the spirit that should have shown them off with advantage to the women. His eyes lacked lustre.—Not so, thought Susan P——, who, at the advanced age of sixty, was seen in the cold evening time, unaccompanied, wetting the pavement of B—— Row with tears that fell in drops which might be heard, because her friend had died that day,—he whom she had pursued with a hopeless passion for the last forty years; a passion which years could not extinguish or abate; nor the long-resolved yet gently-enforced puttings-off of un-relenting bachelorhood dissuade from its cherished purpose. Mild Susan P——, thou hast now thy friend in heaven!

Thomas Coventry was a cadet of the noble family of that name. He passed his youth in contracted circumstances, which gave him early those parsimonious habits which in after-life never forsook him; so that with one windfall or another, about the time I knew him, he was master of four or five hundred thousand pounds; nor did he look or walk worth a moidore less. He lived in a gloomy house opposite

the pump in Serjeants' Inn, Fleet Street. J., the
counsel, is doing self-imposed penance in it, for what
reason I divine not, at this day. C. had an agreeable
seat at North Cray, where he seldom spent above a
day or two at a time in the Summer; but preferred,
during the hot months, standing at his window in
this damp, close, well-like mansion, to watch, as he
said, "the maids drawing water all day long." I
suspect he had his within-door reasons for the preference. *Hic currus et arma fuêre*. He might think his
treasures more safe. His house had the aspect of a
strong box. C. was a close hunks—a hoarder rather
than a miser—or, if a miser, none of the mad Elwes
breed, who have brought discredit upon a character
which cannot exist without certain admirable points
of steadiness and unity of purpose. One may hate
a true miser, but cannot, I suspect, so easily despise
him. By taking care of the pence he is often enabled
to part with the pounds upon a scale that leaves us
careless generous fellows halting at an immeasurable
distance behind. C. gave away 30,000*l.* at once in
his life-time to a blind charity. His house-keeping
was severely looked after, but he kept the table of a
gentleman. He would know who came in and who
went out of his house, but his kitchen chimney was
never suffered to freeze.

Salt was his opposite in this, as in all—never knew
what he was worth in the world; and having but a
competency for his rank, which his indolent habits
were little calculated to improve, might have suffered
severely if he had not had honest people about him.
Lovel took care of every thing. He was at once his
clerk, his good servant, his dresser, his friend, his
"flapper," his guide, stopwatch, auditor, treasurer.

He did nothing without consulting Lovel, nor failed
in any thing without expecting and fearing his ad-
monishing. He put himself almost too much in his
hands, had they not been the purest in the world.
He resigned his title almost to respect as a master,
if L. could ever have forgotten for a moment that he
was a servant.

I knew this Lovel. He was a man of an incorrigi-
ble and losing honesty; a good fellow withal, and
" would strike." In the cause of the oppressed he
never considered inequalities, or calculated the number
of his opponents. He once wrested a sword out of
the hand of a man of quality that had drawn upon
him, and pommelled him severely with the hilt of it.
The swordsman had offered insult to a female; an
occasion upon which no odds against him could have
prevented the interference of Lovel. He would stand
next day bareheaded to the same person modestly to
excuse his interference ; for L. never forgot rank
where something better was not concerned. L. was the
liveliest little fellow breathing, had a face as gay as
Garrick's, whom he was said greatly to resemble, (I
have a portrait of him which confirms it,) possessed
a fine turn for humorous poetry—next to Swift and
Prior—moulded heads in clay or plaster of Paris to
admiration, by the dint of natural genius merely;
turned cribbage-boards, and such small cabinet toys,
to perfection ; took a hand at quadrille or bowls with
equal facility ; made punch better than any man of
his degree in England ; had the merriest quips and
conceits ; and was altogether as brimful of rogueries
and inventions as you could desire. He was a brother
of the angle, moreover, and just such a free, hearty,
honest companion, as Mr. Izaak Walton would have

chosen to go a-fishing with. I saw him in his old
age and the decay of his faculties, palsy-smitten, in
the last sad stage of human weakness,—" a remnant
most forlorn of what he was,"—yet even then his eye
would light up upon the mention of his favourite
Garrick.   He was greatest, he would say, in Bayes—
" was upon the stage nearly throughout the whole
performance, and as busy as a bee."   At intervals,
too, he would speak of his former life, and how he
came up a little boy from Lincoln, to go to service ;
and how his mother cried at parting with him ; and
how he returned, after some few years' absence, in his
smart new livery, to see her, and she blessed herself
at the change, and could hardly be brought to believe
that it was " her own bairn."   And then, the excitement subsiding, he would weep, till I have wished
that sad second-childhood might have a mother still
to lay its head upon her lap.   But the common mother
of us all in no long time after received him gently into
hers.

   With Coventry, and with Salt, in their walks upon
the terrace, most commonly Peter Pierson would join
to make up a third.   They did not walk linked arm-
in-arm in those days,—" as now our stout triumvirs
sweep the streets,"—but generally with both hands
folded behind them for state, or with one at least behind, the other carrying a cane.   P. was a benevolent,
but not a prepossessing man.   He had that in his
face which you could not term unhappiness ; it rather
implied an incapacity of being happy.   His cheeks
were colourless, even to whiteness.   His look was
uninviting, resembling (but without his sourness) that
of our great philanthropist.   I know that he *did* good
acts, but I never could make out what he *was*.   Con-

temporary with these, but subordinate, was Daines Barrington,—another oddity. He walked burly and square—in imitation, I think, of Coventry—howbeit he attained not to the dignity of his prototype. Nevertheless he did pretty well, upon the strength of being a tolerable antiquary, and having a brother a bishop. When the account of his year's treasurership came to be audited the following singular charge was unanimously disallowed by the bench: " Item, disbursed Mr. Allen, the gardener, twenty shillings for stuff to poison the sparrows, by my orders." Next to him was old Barton—a jolly negation, who took upon him the ordering of the bills of fare for the parliament chamber, where the benchers dine—answering to the combination rooms at college—much to the easement of his less epicurean brethren. I know nothing more of him.—Then Read, and Twopeny : Read, good-humoured and personable; Twopeny, good-humoured, but thin, and felicitous in jests upon his own figure. If T. was thin, Wharry was attenuated and fleeting. Many must remember him (for he was rather of later date) and his singular gait, which was performed by three steps and a jump regularly succeeding. The steps were little efforts, like that of a child beginning to walk; the jump comparatively vigorous, as a foot to an inch. Where he learned this figure, or what occasioned it, I could never discover. It was neither graceful in itself, nor seemed to answer the purpose any better than common walking. The extreme tenuity of his frame, I suspect, set him upon it. It was a trial of poising. Twopeny would often rally him upon his leanness, and hail him as Brother Lusty; but W. had no relish of a joke. His features were spiteful. I have heard that he would pinch his

cat's ears extremely when any thing had offended
him. Jackson (the omniscient Jackson he was called)
was of this period. He had the reputation of possessing more multifarious knowledge than any man
of his time. He was the Friar Bacon of the less
literate portion of the Temple. I remember a pleasant passage of the cook applying to him, with much
formality of apology, for instructions how to write
down *edge* bone of beef in his bill of commons. He
was supposed to know, if any man in the world did.
He decided the orthography to be as I have given it,
fortifying his authority with such anatomical reasons
as dismissed the manciple (for the time) learned and
happy. Some do spell it yet, perversely, *aitch* bone,
from a fanciful resemblance between its shape and
that of the aspirate so denominated. I had almost
forgotten Mingay with the iron hand; but he was
somewhat later. He had lost his right hand by some
accident, and supplied it with a grappling-hook, which
he wielded with a tolerable adroitness. I detected the
substitute before I was old enough to reason whether it
were artificial or not. I remember the astonishment
it raised in me. He was a blustering, loud-talking
person; and I reconciled the phenomenon to my
ideas as an emblem of power, somewhat like the
horns in the forehead of Michael Angelo's Moses.
Baron Maseres, who walks (or did till very lately) in
the costume of the reign of George the Second, closes
my imperfect recollections of the old benchers of the
Inner Temple.

Fastastic forms, whither are ye fled ? Or, if the
like of you exist, why exist they no more for me ?
Ye inexplicable, half-understood appearances, why
comes in reason to tear away the preternatural mist,

bright or gloomy, that enshrouded you ? Why make ye so sorry a figure in my relation, who made up to me—to my childish eyes—the mythology of the Temple ? In those days I saw Gods, as "old men covered with a mantle," walking upon the earth. Let the dreams of classic idolatry perish,—extinct be the fairies and fairy trumpery of legendary fabling,—in the heart of childhood there will for ever spring up a well of innocent or wholesome superstition ; the seeds of exaggeration will be busy there, and vital,—from every-day forms educing the unknown and the uncommon. In that little Goshen there will be light when the grown world flounders about in the darkness of sense and materiality. While childhood, and while dreams, reducing childhood, shall be left, imagination shall not have spread her holy wings totally to fly the earth.

————

P.S.—I have done injustice to the soft shade of Samuel Salt. See what it is to trust to imperfect memory, and the erring notices of childhood ! Yet I protest I always thought that he had been a bachelor ! This gentleman, R—— N—— informs me, married young, and losing his lady in childbed, within the first year of their union, fell into a deep melancholy ; from the effects of which, probably, he never thoroughly recovered. In what a new light does this place his rejection (O call it by a gentler name !) of mild Susan P——, unravelling into beauty certain peculiarities of this very shy and retiring character ! Henceforth let no one receive the narratives of Elia for true records ! They are, in truth,

284 THE ESSAYS OF ELIA.

but shadows of fact—verisimilitudes, not verities—
or sitting but upon the remote edges and outskirts of
history.   He is no such honest chronicler as R. N.,
and would have done better perhaps to have consulted
that gentleman before he sent these incondite reminiscences to press.   But the worthy sub-treasurer,
who respects his old and his new masters, would but
have been puzzled at the indecorous liberties of Elia.
The good man wots not, peradventure, of the licence
which *Magazines* have arrived at in this plain-speak-
ing age, or hardly dreams of their existence beyond
the *Gentleman's*, his furthest monthly excursions
in this nature having been long confined to the holy
ground of honest *Urban's* obituary.   May it be long
before his own name shall help to swell those columns
of unenvied flattery !—Meantime, O ye New Benchers
of the Inner Temple, cherish him kindly, for he is
himself the kindliest of human creatures.   Should
infirmities overtake him, (he is yet in green and vigorous senility,) make allowances for them, remembering
that " ye yourselves are old."   So may the Winged
Horse, your ancient badge and cognisance, still
flourish ! so may future Hookers and Seldens illustrate your church and chambers ! so may the sparrows,
in default of more melodious quiristers, unpoisoned
hop about your walks ; so may the fresh-coloured and
cleanly nursery-maid, who, by leave, airs her playful
charge in your stately gardens, drop her prettiest
blushing courtesy as ye pass, reductive of juvenes-
cent emotion ! so may the younkers of this generation
eye you, pacing your stately terrace, with the same
superstitious veneration with which the child Elia
gazed on the Old Worthies that solemnised the parade
before ye !

GRACE BEFORE MEAT.

———

THE custom of saying grace at meals had probably
its origin in the early times of the world, and the
hunter-state of man, when dinners were precarious
things, and a full meal was something more than a
common blessing; when a belly-full was a wind-fall,
and looked like a special providence. In the shouts
and triumphal songs with which, after a season of
sharp abstinence, a lucky booty of deer's or goat's
flesh would naturally be ushered home, existed perhaps the germ of the modern grace. It is not otherwise easy to be understood why the blessing of food,
the act of eating, should have had a particular expression of thanksgiving annexed to it, distinct from that
implied and silent gratitude with which we are expected to enter upon the enjoyment of the many
other various gifts and good things of existence.

I own that I am disposed to say grace upon twenty
other occasions in the course of the day besides my
dinner. I want a form for setting out upon a pleasant
walk, for a moonlight ramble, for a friendly meeting,
or a solved problem. Why have we none for books,
those spiritual repasts?—a grace before Milton; a
grace before Shakspeare; a devotional exercise proper

to be said before reading the Fairy Queen? But the received ritual having prescribed these forms to the solitary ceremony of manducation, I shall confine my observations to the experience which I have had of the grace, properly so called; commending my new scheme for extension to a niche in the grand philosophical, poetical, and perchance in part heretical, liturgy, now compiling by my friend Homo Humanus, for the use of a certain snug congregation of Utopian Rabelæsian Christians, no matter where assembled.

The form, then, of the benediction before eating has its beauty at a poor man's table, or at the simple and unprovocative repast of children. It is here that the grace becomes exceedingly graceful. The indigent man, who hardly knows whether he shall have a meal the next day or not, sits down to his fare with a present sense of the blessing, which can be but feebly acted by the rich, into whose minds the conception of wanting a dinner could never, but by some extreme theory, have entered. The proper end of food—the animal sustenance—is barely contemplated by them. The poor man's bread is his daily bread, literally his bread for the day. Their courses are perennial.

Again: the plainest diet seems the fittest to be preceded by the grace. That which is least stimulative to appetite leaves the mind most free for foreign considerations. A man may feel thankful, heartily thankful, over a dish of plain mutton with turnips, and have leisure to reflect upon the ordinance and institution of eating; when he shall confess a perturbation of mind, inconsistent with the purposes of the grace, at the presence of venison or turtle. When

I have sate (a *rarus hospes*) at rich men's tables, with the savoury soup and messes steaming up the nostrils, and moistening the lips of the guests with desire and a distracted choice, I have felt the introduction of that ceremony to be unseasonable. With the ravenous orgasm upon you, it seems impertinent to interpose a religious sentiment. It is a confusion of purpose to mutter out praises from a mouth that waters. The heats of epicurism put out the gentle flame of devotion. The incense which rises round is pagan, and the belly-god intercepts it for his own. The very excess of the provision beyond the needs takes away all sense of proportion between the end and means. The giver is veiled by his gifts. You are startled at the injustice of returning thanks—for what?—for having too much, while so many starve. It is to praise the gods amiss.

I have observed this awkwardness felt, scarce consciously perhaps, by the good man who says the grace. I have seen it in clergymen and others—a sort of shame—a sense of the co-presence of circumstances which unhallow the blessing. After a devotional tone put on for a few seconds, how rapidly the speaker will fall into his common voice! helping himself or his neighbour, as if to get rid of some uneasy sensation of hypocrisy. Not that the good man was a hypocrite, or was not most conscientious in the discharge of the duty; but he felt in his inmost mind the incompatibility of the scene and the viands before him with the exercise of a calm and rational gratitude.

I hear somebody exclaim,—Would you have Christians sit down at table, like hogs to their troughs, without remembering the Giver? No: I would have

them sit down as Christians, remembering the Giver
and less like hogs. Or if their appetites must run
riot, and they must pamper themselves with delicacies
for which East and West are ransacked, I would have
them postpone their benediction to a fitter season,
when appetite is laid; when the " still small voice "
can be heard, and the reason of the grace returns
with temperate diet and restricted dishes. Gluttony
and surfeiting are no proper occasions for thanksgiving. When Jeshurun waxed fat, we read that he
kicked. Virgil knew the harpy nature better, when
he put into the mouth of Celæno any thing but a
blessing. We may be gratefully sensible of the
deliciousness of some kinds of food beyond others,
though that is a meaner and inferior gratitude : but
the proper object of the grace is sustenance, not
relishes ; daily bread, not delicacies ; the means of
life, and not the means of pampering the carcass.
With what frame or composure, I wonder, can a City
chaplain pronounce his benediction at some great
Hall feast, when he knows that his last concluding
pious word (and that, in all probability, the sacred
name which he preaches) is but the signal for so
many impatient harpies to commence their foul
orgies, with as little sense of true thankfulness (which
is temperance) as those Virgilian fowl ! It is well if
the good man himself does not feel his devotions a
little clouded, those foggy sensuous steams mingling
with and polluting the pure altar sacrifice.

The severest satire upon full tables and surfeits is
the banquet which Satan, in *Paradise Regained*,
provides for a temptation in the wilderness :

> A table richly spread, in regal mode,
> With dishes piled, and meats of noblest sort

> And savour; beasts of chase, or fowl of game,
> In pastry built, or from the spit, or boil'd,
> Gris-amber-steam'd ; all fish, from sea or shore,
> Freshet or purling brook, for which was drain'd
> Pontus, and Lucrine bay, and Afric coast.

The Tempter, I warrant you, thought these cates
would go down without the recommendatory preface
of a benediction.   They are like to be short graces
where the Devil plays the host.   I am afraid the poet
wants his usual decorum in this place.   Was he
thinking of the old Roman luxury, or of a gaudy day
at Cambridge ?   This was a temptation fitter for a
Heliogabalus.   The whole banquet is too civic and
culinary, and the accompaniments altogether a profanation of that deep, abstracted, holy scene.   The
mighty artillery of sauces, which the cook-fiend con-
jures up, is out of proportion to the simple wants and
plain hunger of the guest.   He that disturbed him in
his dreams, from his dreams might have been taught
better.   To the temperate fantasies of the famished
Son of God, what sort of feasts presented themselves ?
—He dreamed indeed,

> ——— As appetite is wont to dream,
> Of meats and drinks, Nature's refreshment sweet.

But what meats ?—

> Him thought, he by the brook of Cherith stood,
> And saw the ravens with their horny beaks
> Food to Elijah bringing, even and morn;
> Though ravenous, taught to abstain from what they brought:
> He saw the prophet also, how he fled
> Into the desert, and how there he slept
> Under a juniper; then how, awaked,
> He found his supper on the coals prepared,
> And by the angel was bid rise and eat,

And eat the second time after repose,
The strength whereof sufficed him forty days:
Sometimes that with Elijah he partook,
Or as a guest with Daniel at his pulse.

Nothing in Milton is finelier fancied than these temperate dreams of the divine Hungerer. To which of these two visionary banquets, think you, would the introduction of what is called the grace have been the most fitting and pertinent?

Theoretically I am no enemy to graces; but practically I own that (before meat especially) they seem to involve something awkward and unseasonable. Our appetites, of one or other kind, are excellent spurs to our reason, which might otherwise but feebly set about the great ends of preserving and continuing the species. They are fit blessings to be contemplated at a distance with a becoming gratitude; but the moment of appetite (the judicious reader will apprehend me) is, perhaps, the least fit season for that exercise. The Quakers, who go about their business of every description with more calmness than we, have more title to the use of these benedictory prefaces. I have always admired their silent grace, and the more because I have observed their applications to the meat and drink following to be less passionate and sensual than ours. They are neither gluttons nor wine-bibbers as a people. They eat, as a horse bolts his chopped hay, with indifference, calmness, and cleanly circumstances. They neither grease nor slop themselves. When I see a citizen in his bib and tucker, I cannot imagine it a surplice.

I am no Quaker at my food. I confess I am not indifferent to the kinds of it. Those unctuous morsels

of deer's flesh were not made to be received with
dispassionate services.   I hate a man who swallows
it, affecting not to know what he is eating.   I suspect
his taste in higher matters.   I shrink instinctively
from one who professes to like minced veal.   There
is a physiognomical character in the tastes for food.
C—— holds that a man cannot have a pure mind
who refuses apple dumplings.   I am not certain but
he is right.   With the decay of my first innocence, I
confess a less and less relish daily for those innocuous
cates.   The whole vegetable tribe have lost their gust
with me.   Only I stick to asparagus, which still
seems to inspire gentle thoughts.   I am impatient
and querulous under culinary disappointments, as to
come home at the dinner hour, for instance, expecting
some savoury mess, and to find one quite tasteless
and sapidless.   Butter ill melted—that commonest
of kitchen failures—puts me beside my tenor.   The
author of the *Rambler* used to make inarticulate
animal noises over a favourite food.   Was this the
music quite proper to be preceded by the grace ? or
would the pious man have done better to postpone
his devotions to a season when the blessing might
be contemplated with less perturbation ?   I quarrel
with no man's tastes, nor would set my thin face
against those excellent things, in their way, jollity
and feasting.   But as these exercises, however laudable, have little in them of grace or gracefulness, a
man should be sure, before he ventures so to grace
them, that while he is pretending his devotions other-
where, he is not secretly kissing his hand to some
great fish—his Dagon—with a special consecration
of no ark but the fat tureen before him.   Graces are the
sweet preluding strains to the banquets of angels and

children ; to the roots and severer repasts of the Char-
treuse ; to the slender, but not slenderly acknowledged, refection of the poor and humble man : but at the
heaped-up boards of the pampered and the luxurious
they become of dissonant mood, less timed and tuned
to the occasion, methinks, than the noise of those
better befitting organs would be which children hear
tales of at Hog's Norton. We sit too long at our
meals, or are too curious in the study of them, or too
disordered in our application to them, or engross too
great a portion of those good things (which should be
common) to our share, to be able with any grace to
say grace. To be thankful for what we grasp exceeding our proportion, is to add hypocrisy to injustice.
A lurking sense of this truth is what makes the performance of this duty so cold and spiritless a service
at most tables. In houses where the grace is as
indispensable as the napkin, who has not seen that
never-settled question arise, as to *who shall say it?*
while the good man of the house and the visitor
clergyman, or some other guest belike of next
authority, from years or gravity, shall be bandying
about the office between them as a matter of compliment, each of them not unwilling to shift the
awkward burthen of an equivocal duty from his own
shoulders !

I once drank tea in company with two Methodist
divines of different persuasions, whom it was my
fortune to introduce to each other for the first time
that evening. Before the first cup was handed round,
one of these reverend gentlemen put it to the other,
with all due solemnity, whether he chose to *say any
thing*. It seems it is the custom with some sectaries
to put up a short prayer before this meal also. His

reverend brother did not at first quite apprehend him ;
but, upon an explanation, with little less importance
he made answer that it was not a custom known in his
Church : in which courteous evasion the other
acquiescing for good manners' sake, or in compliance
with a weak brother, the supplementary or tea-grace
was waived altogether. With what spirit might not
Lucian have painted two priests, of *his* religion, playing into each other's hands the compliment of per-
forming or omitting a sacrifice,—the hungry god
meantime, doubtful of his incense, with expectant
nostrils hovering over the two flamens, and (as between two stools) going away in the end without his
supper !

A short form upon these occasions is felt to want
reverence ; a long one, I am afraid, cannot escape the
charge of impertinence. I do not quite approve of
the epigrammatic conciseness with which that equivocal wag (but my pleasant school-fellow) C. V. L.,
when importuned for a grace, used to inquire, first
slyly leering down the table, " Is there no clergyman
here ?"—significantly adding, " Thank G—." Nor
do I think our old form at school quite pertinent,
where we were used to preface our bald bread-and-
cheese suppers with a preamble, connecting with that
humble blessing a recognition of benefits the most
awful and overwhelming to the imagination which
religion has to offer. *Non tunc illis erat locus.* I remember we were put to it to reconcile the phrase
" good creatures," upon which the blessing rested,
with the fare set before us, wilfully understanding
that expression in a low and animal sense,—till
some one recalled a legend, which told how, in the
golden days of Christ's, the young Hospitallers

were wont to have smoking joints of meat upon their nightly boards, till some pious benefactor, commiserating the decencies rather than the palates of the children, commuted our flesh for garments, and gave us (*horresco referens !*) trousers instead of mutton.

DREAM CHILDREN ; A REVERIE.

CHILDREN love to listen to stories about their elders, when *they* were children ; to stretch their imagination to the conception of a traditionary great-uncle or grandame whom they never saw.   It was in this spirit that my little ones crept about me the other evening to hear about their great-grandmother Field, who lived in a great house in Norfolk, (a hundred times bigger than that in which they and papa lived,) which had been the scene (so at least it was generally believed in that part of the country) of the tragic incidents which they had lately become familiar with from the ballad of the Children in the Wood.   Certain it is that the whole story of the children and their uncle was to be seen fairly carved out in wood upon the chimney-piece of the great hall, the whole story down to the Robin Redbreasts ; till a foolish rich person pulled it down to set up a marble one of

modern invention in its stead, with no story upon it.
Here Alice put out one of her dear mother's looks,
too tender to be called upbraiding. Then I went on
to say how religious and how good their great-grandmother Field was, how beloved and respected by every
body, though she was not indeed the mistress of this
great house, but had only the charge of it (and yet in
some respects she might be said to be the mistress of
it too) committed to her by the owner, who preferred
living in a newer and more fashionable mansion which
he had purchased somewhere in the adjoining county ;
but still she lived in it in a manner as if it had been
her own, and kept up the dignity of the great house in
a sort while she lived, which afterwards came to
decay, and was nearly pulled down, and all its old
ornaments stripped and carried away to the owner's
other house, where they were set up, and looked as
awkward as if some one were to carry away the old
tombs they had seen lately at the Abbey, and stick
them up in Lady C.'s tawdry gilt drawing-room.
Here John smiled, as much as to say, " that would be
foolish indeed."   And then I told how, when she
came to die, her funeral was attended by a concourse
of all the poor, and some of the gentry too, of the
neighbourhood for many miles round, to show their
respect for her memory, because she had been such a
good and religious woman ; so good indeed that she
knew all the Psaltery by heart, ay, and a great part of
the Testament besides.   Here little Alice spread her
hands.   Then I told what a tall, upright, graceful
person their great-grandmother Field once was ; and
how in her youth she was esteemed the best dancer,
(here Alice's little right foot played an involuntary
movement, till, upon my looking grave, it desisted,)

the best dancer, I was saying, in the county, till a
cruel disease, called a cancer, came, and bowed her
down with pain ; but it could never bend her good
spirits, or make them stoop, but they were still
upright, because she was so good and religious.
Then I told how she was used to sleep by herself in a
lone chamber of the great lone house ; and how she
believed that an apparition of two infants was to be
seen at midnight gliding up and down the great staircase near where she slept, but she said "those
innocents would do her no harm ;" and how frightened
I used to be, though in those days I had my maid to
sleep with me, because I was never half so good or
religious as she ; and yet I never saw the infants.
Here John expanded all his eyebrows and tried to look
courageous.   Then I told how good she was to all her
grandchildren, having us to the great house in the
holidays, where I in particular used to spend many
hours by myself, in gazing upon the old busts of the
twelve Cæsars, that had been Emperors of Rome, till
the old marble heads would seem to live again, or I to
be turned into marble with them ; how I never could
be tired with roaming about that huge mansion, with
its vast empty rooms, with their worn-out hangings,
fluttering tapestry, and carved oaken panels, with
the gilding almost rubbed out ; sometimes in the
spacious old-fashioned gardens, which I had almost
to myself, unless when now and then a solitary
gardening man would cross me ; and how the
nectarines and peaches hung upon the walls, without
my ever offering to pluck them, because they were for-
bidden fruit, unless now and then ; and because I had
more pleasure in strolling about among the old melancholy-looking yew-trees, or the firs, and picking up

the red berries, and the fir-apples, which were good
for nothing but to.look at—or in lying about upon the
fresh grass with all the fine garden smells around
me—or basking in the orangery, till I could almost
fancy myself ripening too along with the oranges and
the limes in that grateful warmth—or in watching the
dace that darted to and fro in the fish-pond at the
bottom of the garden, with here and there a great
sulky pike hanging midway down the water in silent
state, as if it mocked at their impertinent friskings,—
I had more pleasure in these busy-idle diversions than
in all the sweet flavours of peaches, nectarines,
oranges, and such-like common baits for children.
Here John slyly deposited back upon the plate a bunch
of grapes, which, not unobserved by Alice, he had
meditated dividing with her, and both seemed willing
to relinquish them for the present as irrelevant.
Then, in somewhat a more heightened tone, I told
how, though their great-grandmother Field loved all
her grandchildren, yet in an especial manner she
might be said to love their uncle, John L——, because
he was so handsome and spirited a youth, and a king
to the rest of us; and, instead of moping about in
solitary corners, like some of us, he would mount
the most mettlesome horse he could get, when but an
imp no bigger than themselves, and make it carry
him half over the county in a morning, and join the
hunters when there were any out ; (and yet he loved
the old great house and gardens too, but had too much
spirit to be always pent up within their boundaries ;)
and how their uncle grew up to man's estate as brave
as he was handsome, to the admiration of every body,
but of their great-grandmother Field most especially ;
and how he used to carry me upon his back when I

was a lame-footed boy, (for he was a good bit older
than I,) many a mile when I could not walk for pain ;
and how in after life he became lame-footed too, and
I did not always, I fear, make allowances enough for
him when he was impatient, and in pain, nor remember sufficiently how considerate he had been to me
when I was lame-footed ; and how when he died,
though he had not been dead an hour, it seemed as if
he had died a great while ago, such a distance there
is betwixt life and death ; and how I bore his death
as I thought pretty well at first, but afterwards it
haunted and haunted me ; and though I did not cry
or take it to heart as some do, and as I think he would
have done if I had died, yet I missed him all day
long, and knew not till then how much I had loved
him.   I missed his kindness, and I missed his cross-
ness, and wished him to be alive again, to be quarrel-
ling with him, (for we quarrelled sometimes,) rather
than not have him again, and was as uneasy without
him as he. their poor uncle, must have been when the
doctor took off his limb.—Here the children fell a
crying, and asked if their little mourning which they
had on was not for Uncle John, and they looked up,
and prayed me not to go on about their uncle, but to
tell them some stories about their pretty dead mother.
Then I told how for seven long years, in hope sometimes, sometimes in despair, yet persisting ever, I
courted the fair Alice W——n ; and, as much as
children could understand, I explained to them what
coyness, and difficulty, and denial, meant in maidens—
when suddenly, turning to Alice, the soul of the first
Alice looked out at her eyes with such a reality of
re-presentment, that I became in doubt which of them
stood there before me, or whose that bright hair was ;

and while I stood gazing, both the children gradually
grew fainter to my view, receding, and still receding,
till nothing at last but two mournful features were
seen in the uttermost distance, which, without speech,
strangely impressed upon me the effects of speech :
" We are not of Alice, nor of thee, nor are we children
at all.   The children of Alice call Bartrum[1] father.
We are nothing; less than nothing, and dreams.
We are only what might have been, and must wait
upon the tedious shores of Lethe millions of ages
before we have existence and a name"———and
immediately awaking, I found myself quietly seated
in my bachelor arm-chair, where I had fallen asleep,
with the faithful Bridget unchanged by my side ; but
John L. (or James Elia) was gone for ever.

DISTANT CORRESPONDENTS.

IN A LETTER TO B—— F——, ESQ., AT SYDNEY, NEW SOUTH WALES.

MY DEAR F——.   When I think how welcome the
sight of a letter from the world where you were born
must be to you in that strange one to which you have
been transplanted, I feel some compunctious visitings
at my long silence.   But indeed it is no easy effort to
set about a correspondence at our distance.   The
weary world of waters between us oppresses the
imagination.   It is difficult to conceive how a scrawl
of mine should ever stretch across it.   It is a sort of

presumption to expect that one's thoughts should live so far. It is like writing for posterity ; and reminds me of one of Mrs. Rowe's superscriptions, "Alcander to Strephon in the shades." Cowley's Post-Angel is no more than would be expedient in such an intercourse. One drops a packet at Lombard Street, and in twenty-four hours a friend in Cumberland gets it as fresh as if it came in ice. It is only like whispering through a long trumpet. But suppose a tube let down from the moon, with yourself at one end and *the man* at the other; it would be some balk to the spirit of conversation, if you knew that the dialogue exchanged with that interesting theosophist would take two or three revolutions of a higher luminary in its passage. Yet, for aught I know, you may be some parasangs nigher that primitive idea—Plato's man— than we in England here have the honour to reckon ourselves.

Epistolary matter usually compriseth three topics,— news, sentiment, and puns. In the latter, I include all non-serious subjects ; or subjects serious in themselves, but treated after my fashion, non-seriously.— And first, for news. In them the most desirable circumstance, I suppose, is that they shall be true. But what security can I have that what I now send you for truth shall not, before you get it, unaccountably turn into a lie ? For instance, our mutual friend P. is at this present writing (*my Now*) in good health, and enjoys a fair share of worldly reputation. You are glad to hear it. This is natural and friendly. But at this present reading (*your Now*) he may possibly be in the Bench, or going to be hanged, which in reason ought to abate something of your transport, (*i. e.* at hearing he was well, &c.,) or at least considerably to modify it. I am going to the play this evening, to have a laugh with Munden. You have no theatre, I think you told me, in your land of d——d realities. You naturally lick your lips, and envy me my felicity. Think but a moment, and you will correct the hateful emotion. Why it is Sunday morning with you, and 1823. This confusion of tenses, this grand solecism of *two presents*, is in a degree common to all postage. But if I sent you word to Bath or Devizes, that I was expecting the aforesaid treat this evening, though at the moment you received the intelligence my full feast of fun would be over, yet there would be for a day or two after, as you would well know, a smack, a relish left upon my mental palate, which would give rational encouragement for you to foster a portion, at least, of the disagreeable passion, which it was in part my intention to produce. But ten months hence, your envy or your sympathy would be as useless as a passion spent upon the dead. Not only does Truth in these long intervals un-essence herself, but (what is harder) one cannot venture a crude fiction, for the fear that it may ripen into a truth upon the voyage. What a wild improbable banter I put upon you, some three years since,—of Will Weatherall having married a servant maid ! I remember gravely consulting you how we were to receive her, (for Will's wife was in no case to be rejected,) and your no less serious replication in the matter ; how tenderly you advised an abstemious introduction of literary topics before the lady, with a caution not to be too forward in bringing on the carpet matters more within the sphere of her intelligence; your deliberate judgment, or rather wise suspension of sentence, how far jacks, and spits, and

mops, could with propriety be introduced as subjects ;
whether the conscious avoiding of all such matters in
discourse would not have a worse look than the taking
of them casually in our way ; in what manner we
should carry ourselves to our maid Becky, Mrs.
William Weatherall being by ; whether we should
show more delicacy, and a truer sense of respect for
Will's wife, by treating Becky with our customary
chiding before her, or by an unusual deferential
civility paid to Becky, as to a person of great worth,
but thrown by the caprice of fate into an humble
station.   There were difficulties, I remember, on both
sides, which you did me the favour to state with the
precision of a lawyer, united to the tenderness of a
friend.   I laughed in my sleeve at your solemn plead-
ings, when lo ! while I was valuing myself upon this
flam put upon you in New South Wales, the devil in
England, jealous possibly of any lie-children not his
own, or working after my copy, has actually instigated
our friend (not three days since) to the commission
of a matrimony, which I had only conjured up for
your diversion.   William Weatherall has married
Mrs. Cotterel's maid.   But to take it in its truest sense,
you will see, my dear Field, that news from me must
become history to you ; which I neither profess to
write, nor indeed care much for reading.   No person,
under a diviner, can, with any prospect of veracity,
conduct a correspondence at such an arm's length.
Two prophets, indeed, might thus interchange intelligence with effect ; the epoch of the writer (Habakkuk)
falling in with the true present time of the receiver
(Daniel) ; but then we are no prophets.

Then as to sentiment : it fares little better with
that.   This kind of dish, above all, requires to be

served up hot, or sent off in water-plates, that your friend may have it almost as warm as yourself. If it have time to cool, it is the most tasteless of all cold meats. I have often smiled at a conceit of the late Lord C. It seems that travelling somewhere about Geneva, he came to some pretty green spot, or nook, where a willow, or something, hung so fantastically and invitingly over a stream, (was it a stream, or a rock?—no matter,) that the stillness and the repose, after a weary journey, 'tis likely, in a languid moment of his Lordship's hot, restless life, so took his fancy that he could imagine no place so proper, in the event of his death, to lay his bones in. This was all very natural and excusable as a sentiment, and shows his character in a very pleasing light. But when from a passing sentiment it came to be an act; and when, by a positive testamentary disposal, his remains were actually carried all that way from England ; who was there, some desperate sentimentalists excepted, that did not ask the question, Why could not his Lordship have found a spot as solitary, a nook as romantic, a tree as green and pendent, with a stream as emblematic to his purpose, in Surrey, in Dorset, or in Devon ? Conceive the sentiment boarded up, freighted, entered at the Custom House (startling the tide-waiters with the novelty), hoisted into a ship. Conceive it pawed about and handled between the rude jests of tarpawlin ruffians—a thing of its delicate texture—the salt bilge wetting it till it became as vapid as a damaged lustring. Suppose it in material danger (mariners have some superstition about sentiments) of being tossed over in a fresh gale to some propitiatory shark, (spirit of Saint Gothard, save us from a quietus so foreign to the deviser's purpose !)

but it has happily evaded a fishy consummation.
Trace it then to its lucky landing, (at Lyons shall we
say ?—I have not the map before me,) jostled upon four
men's shoulders; baiting at this town; stopping to
refresh at t'other village; waiting a passport here, a
license there; the sanction of the magistracy in this
district, the concurrence of the ecclesiastics in that
canton; till at length it arrives at its destination,
tired out and jaded, from a brisk sentiment into a
feature of silly pride or tawdry senseless affectation.
How few sentiments, my dear F——, I am afraid
we can set down, in the sailor's phrase, as quite sea-
worthy.

Lastly, as to the agreeable levities, which, though
contemptible in bulk, are the twinkling corpuscula
which should irradiate a right friendly epistle—your
puns and small jests are, I apprehend, extremely
circumscribed in their sphere of action. They are so
far from a capacity of being packed up and sent beyond sea, that they will scarce endure to be trans-
ported by hand from this room to the next. Their
vigour is at the instant óf their birth. Their nutri-
ment for their brief existence is the intellectual
atmosphere of the by-standers : or this last is the fine
slime of Nilus—the *melior lutus*—whose maternal
recipiency is as necessary as the *sol pater* to their
equivocal generation. A pun hath a hearty kind of
present ear-kissing smack with it; you can no more
transmit it in its pristine flavour than you can send a
kiss. Have you not tried in some instances to palm
off a yesterday's pun upon a gentleman, and has it
answered ? Not but it was new to his hearing, but
it did not seem to come new from you. It did not
hitch in. It was like picking up at a village ale-house

a two-days-old newspaper. You have not seen it
before, but you resent the stale thing as an affront.
This sort of merchandise above all requires a quick
return. A pun, and its recognitory laugh, must be
co-instantaneous. The one is the brisk lightning,
the other the fierce thunder. A moment's interval,
and the link is snapped. A pun is reflected from a
friend's face as from a mirror. Who would consult
his sweet visnomy, if the polished surface were two
or three minutes (not to speak of twelve months, my
dear F—— in giving back its copy?

I cannot image to myself whereabout you are.
When I try to fix it, Peter Wilkins's island comes
across me. Sometimes you seem to be in the *Hades*
of *Thieves*. I see Diogenes prying among you with
his perpetual fruitless lantern. What must you be
willing by this time to give for the sight of an honest
man! You must almost have forgotten how *we* look.
And tell me what your Sydneyites do? Are they
th**v*ng all day long? Merciful heaven! what property can stand against such a depredation! The
kangaroos—your Aborigines—do they keep their primitive simplicity un-Europe-tainted, with those little
short fore puds, looking like a lesson framed by
Nature to the pickpocket! Marry, for diving into
fobs they are rather lamely provided *à priori;* but if
the hue and cry were once up, they would show as
fair a pair of hind-shifters as the expertest loco-motor
in the colony. We hear the most improbable tales
at this distance. Pray is it true that the young
Spartans among you are born with six fingers, which
spoils their scanning?—It must look very odd, but
use reconciles. For their scansion, it is less to be
regretted; for if they take it into their heads to be

poets, it is odds but they turn out, the greater part of them, vile plagiarists. Is there much difference to see, too, between the son of a th**f and the grand-son? or where does the taint stop? Do you bleach in three or in four generations? I have many ques-tions to put, but ten Delphic voyages can be made in a shorter time than it will take to satisfy my scruples. Do you grow your own hemp?—What is your staple trade,—exclusive of the national profession, I mean? Your locksmiths, I take it, are some of your great capitalists.

I am insensibly chatting to you as familiarly as when we used to exchange good-morrows out of our old contiguous windows, in pump-famed Hare Court in the Temple. Why did you ever leave that quiet corner?—Why did I?—with its complement of four poor elms, from whose smoke-dyed barks, the theme of jesting ruralists, I picked my first lady-birds! My heart is as dry as that spring sometimes proves in a thirsty August, when I revert to the space that is between us; a length of passage enough to render obsolete the phrases of our English letters before they can reach you. But while I talk I think you hear me,—thoughts dallying with vain surmise—

> Ay me! while thee the seas and sounding shores
> Hold far away.

Come back, before I am grown into a very old man, so as you shall hardly know me. Come, before Bridget walks on crutches. Girls whom you left children have become sage matrons while you are tarrying there. The blooming Miss W——r (you remember Sally W——r) called upon us yeterday, an aged crone. Folks whom you knew die off every year. Formerly, I thought that death was wearing out,—I stood ramparted about with' so many healthy friends. The departure of J—— W——, two Springs back, corrected my delusion. Since then the old divorcer has been busy. If you do not make haste to return, there will be little left to greet you, of me, **or** mine.

THE PRAISE OF CHIMNEY-SWEEPERS.

I LIKE to meet a sweep ; understand me,—not a grown sweeper, (old chimney-sweepers are by no means attractive,) but one of those tender novices, blooming through their first nigritude, the maternal washings not quite effaced from the cheek : such as come forth with the dawn, or somewhat earlier, with their little professional notes sounding like the *peep peep* of a young sparrow ; or liker to the matin lark should I pronounce them, in their aërial ascents not seldom anticipating the sun-rise ?

I have a kindly yearning toward these dim specks —poor blots—innocent blacknesses.

I reverence these young Africans of our own growth, —these almost clergy imps, who sport their cloth without assumption ; and from their little pulpits, (the tops of chimneys,) in the nipping air of a December morning, preach a lesson of patience to mankind.

When a child, what a mysterious pleasure it was to

X 2

witness their operation! to see a chit no bigger than
one's-self, enter, one knew not by what process, into
what seemed the *fauces Averni,*—to pursue him in
imagination, as he went sounding on through so
many dark stifling caverns, horrid shades!—to shudder
with the idea that "now, surely, he must be lost for
ever!"—to revive at hearing his feeble shout of discovered day-light—and then (O fulness of delight!)
running out of doors, to come just in time to see the
sable phenomenon emerge in safety, the brandished
weapon of his art victorious like some flag waved
over a conquered citadel! I seem to remember
having been told that a bad sweep was once left in a
stack with his brush, to indicate which way the wind
blew. It was an awful spectacle certainly; not much
unlike the old stage direction in Macbeth, where the
"Apparition of a child crowned, with a tree in his
hand, rises."

Reader, if thou meetest one of these small gentry
in thy early rambles, it is good to give him a penny.
It is better to give him twopence. If it be starving
weather, and to the proper troubles of his hard occupation a pair of kibed heels (no unusual accompaniment) be superadded, the demand on thy humanity
will surely rise to a tester.

There is a composition, the ground-work of which
I have understood to be the sweet wood 'yclept
sassafras. This wood boiled down to a kind of tea,
and tempered with an infusion of milk and sugar,
hath to some tastes a delicacy beyond the China
luxury. I know not how thy palate may relish it; for
myself, with every deference to the judicious Mr.
Read, who hath time out of mind kept open a shop
(the only one he avers in London) for the vending of

this "wholesome and pleasant beverage," on the
south side of Fleet Street, as thou approachest Bridge
Street—*the only Salopian house*—I have never yet
adventured to dip my own particular lip in a basin of
his commended ingredients; a cautious premonition
to the olfactories constantly whispering to me, that
my stomach must infallibly, with all due courtesy,
decline it.   Yet I have seen palates, otherwise not
uninstructed in dietetical elegancies, sup it up with
avidity.

I know not by what particular conformation of the
organ it happens, but I have always found that this
composition is surprisingly gratifying to the palate of
a young chimney-sweeper—whether the oily particles
(sassafras is slightly oleaginous) do attenuate and
soften the fuliginous concretions which are sometimes found (in dissections) to adhere to the roof of
the mouth in these unfledged practitioners;   or
whether Nature, sensible that she had mingled too
much of bitter wood in the lot of these raw victims,
caused to grow out of the earth her sassafras for a
sweet lenitive ;   but so it is, that no possible taste or
odour to the senses of a young chimney-sweeper can
convey a delicate excitement comparable to this mixture.   Being penniless, they will yet hang their black
heads over the ascending steam, to gratify one sense
if possible, seemingly no less pleased than those
domestic animals—cats—when they purr over a new-
found sprig of valerian.   There is something more in
these sympathies than philosophy can inculcate.

Now albeit Mr. Read boasteth, not without reason,
that his is the *only Salopian house ;* yet be it known
to thee, reader,—if thou art one who keepest what are
called good hours. thou art haply ignorant of the fact,—

he hath a race of industrious imitators, who from stalls, and under open sky, dispense the same savoury mess to humbler customers, at that dead time of the dawn, when (as extremes meet) the rake, reeling home from his midnight cups, and the hard-handed artisan leaving his bed to resume the premature labours of the day, jostle, not unfrequently to the manifest disconcerting of the former, for the honours of the pavement. It is the time when, in Summer, between the expired and the not yet relumined kitchen fires, the kennels of our fair metropolis give forth their least satisfactory odours. The rake, who wisheth to dissipate his o'ernight vapours in more grateful coffee, curses the ungenial fume as he passeth; but the artisan stops to taste, and blesses the fragrant breakfast.

This is *saloop*—the precocious herb-woman's darling—the delight of the early gardener, who transports his smoking cabbages by break of day from Hammersmith to Covent Garden's famed piazzas;—the delight, and oh! I fear, too often the envy, of the unpennied sweep. Him shouldst thou haply encounter, with his dim visage pendent over the grateful steam, regale him with a sumptuous basin (it will cost thee but three-halfpennies) and a slice of delicate bread and butter (an added halfpenny); so may thy culinary fires, eased of the o'er-charged secretions from thy worse-placed hospitalities, curl up a lighter volume to the welkin; so may the descending soot never taint thy costly well-ingredienced soups, nor the odious cry, quick-reaching from street to street, of the *fired chimney*, invite the rattling engines from ten adjacent parishes, to disturb for a casual scintillation thy peace and pocket !

I am by nature extremely susceptible of street affronts; the jeers and taunts of the populace; the low-bred triumph they display over the casual trip or splashed stocking of a gentleman. Yet can I endure the jocularity of a young sweep with something more than forgiveness. In the last Winter but one, pacing along Cheapside with my accustomed precipitation when I walk Westward, a treacherous slide brought me upon my back in an instant. I scrambled up with pain and shame enough, yet outwardly trying to face it down, as if nothing had happened, when the roguish grin of one of these young wits encountered me. There he stood, pointing me out with his dusky finger to the mob, and to a poor woman (I suppose his mother) in particular, till the tears for the exquisiteness of the fun (so he thought it) worked themselves out at the corners of his poor red eyes, red from many a previous weeping, and soot-inflamed, yet twinkling through all with such a joy, snatched out of desolation, that Hogarth———but Hogarth has got him already (how could he miss him?) in the March to Finchley, grinning at the pieman. There he stood, as he stands in the picture, irremovable, as if the jest was to last for ever, with such a maximum of glee and minimum of mischief in his mirth, (for the grin of a genuine sweep hath absolutely no malice in it,) that I could have been content, if the honour of a gentleman might endure it, to have remained his butt and his mockery till midnight.

I am by theory obdurate to the seductiveness of what are called a fine set of teeth. Every pair of rosy lips (the ladies must pardon me) is a casket presumably holding such jewels; but, methinks, they should take leave to " air" them as frugally as possible. The

fine ladies, or fine gentlemen, who show me their
teeth, show me bones. Yet must I confess, that from
the mouth of a true sweep a display (even to ostentation) of those white and shining ossifications, strikes
me as an agreeable anomaly in manners, and an
allowable piece of foppery. It is as when

> A sable cloud
> Turns forth her silver lining on the night.

It is like some remnant of gentry not quite extinct ;
a badge of better days ; a hint of nobility : and, doubtless, under the obscuring darkness and double night
of their forlorn disguisement, oftentimes lurketh good
blood, and gentle conditions, derived from lost
ancestry and a lapsed pedigree. The premature
apprenticements of these tender victims give but too
much encouragement, I fear, to clandestine and almost
infantile abductions; the seeds of civility and true
courtesy, so often discernible in these young grafts,
(not otherwise to be accounted for,) plainly hint at
some forced adoptions. Many noble Rachels mourning for their children, even in our days, countenance
the fact ; the tales of fairy-spiriting may shadow a
lamentable verity, and the recovery of the young
Montagu be but a solitary instance of good fortune
out of many irreparable and hopeless *defiliations*.

In one of the state-beds at Arundel Castle, a few
years since, under a ducal canopy, (that seat of the
Howards is an object of curiosity to visitors, chiefly
for its beds, in which the late duke was especially a
connoisseur,) encircled with curtains of delicatest
crimson, with starry coronets inwoven, folded between
a pair of sheets whiter and softer than the lap where
Venus lulled Ascanius, was discovered by chance,

after all methods of search had failed, at noon-day, fast asleep, a lost chimney-sweeper.   The little creature, having somehow confounded his passage among the intricacies of those lordly chimneys, by some unknown aperture had alighted upon this magnificent chamber; and, tired with his tedious explorations, was unable to resist the delicious invite-ment to repose, which he there saw exhibited ; so creeping between the sheets very quietly, laid his black head upon the pillow, and slept like a young Howard.

Such is the account given to the visitors at the Castle.   But I cannot help seeming to perceive a confirmation of what I had just hinted at in this story. A high instinct was at work in the case, or I am mis-taken.   Is it probable that a poor child of that description, with whatever weariness he might be visited, would have ventured, under such a penalty as he would be taught to expect, to uncover the sheets of a Duke's bed, and deliberately to lay himself down between them, when the rug, or the carpet, presented an obvious couch still far above his pretensions ?   Is this probable, I would ask, if the great power of nature, which I contend for, had not been manifested within him, prompting to the adventure ?   Doubtless this young nobleman (for such my mind misgives me that he must be) was allured by some memory, not amounting to full consciousness, of his condition in infancy, when he was used to be lapped by his mother, or his nurse, in just such sheets as he there found, into which he was now but creeping back as into his proper *incunabula* and resting-place.   By no other theory than by this sentiment of a pre-existent state (as I may call it), can I explain a deed so

venturous, and indeed upon any other system, so
indecorous, in this tender but unseasonable sleeper.

My pleasant friend JEM WHITE was so impressed
with a belief of metamorphoses like this frequently
taking place, that in some sort to reverse the wrongs
of fortune in these poor changelings, he instituted an
annual feast of chimney-sweepers, at which it was his
pleasure to officiate as host and waiter. It was a
solemn supper held in Smithfield, upon the yearly
return of the fair of St. Bartholomew. Cards were
issued a week before to the master-sweeps in and
about the metropolis, confining the invitation to their
younger fry.   Now and then an elderly stripling
would get in among us, and be goodnaturedly winked
at; but our main body were infantry.   One unfortunate wight, indeed, who, relying upon his dusky suit
had intruded himself into our party, but by tokens was
providentially discovered in time to be no chimney-
sweeper, (all is not soot which looks so,) was quoited
out of the presence with universal indignation, as not
having on the wedding garment ; but in general the
greatest harmony prevailed.   The place chosen was
a convenient spot among the pens, at the north side
of the fair, not so far distant as to be impervious to
the agreeable hubbub of that vanity, but remote
enough not to be obvious to the interruption of every
gaping spectator in it.   The guests assembled about
seven.   In those little temporary parlours three tables
were spread with napery, not so fine as substantial,
and at every board a comely hostess presided with
her pan of hissing sausages. The nostrils of the
young rogues dilated at the savour. JAMES WHITE,
as head waiter, had charge of the first table ; and
myself, with our trusty companion BIGOD, ordinarily

ministered to the other two.   There was clambering
and jostling, you may be sure, who should get at the
first table ; for Rochester in his maddest days could
not have done the humours of the scene with more
spirit than my friend.   After some general expression
of thanks for the honour the company had done him,
his inaugural ceremony was to clasp the greasy waist
of old dame Ursula (the fattest of the three), that
stood frying and fretting, half-blessing, half-cursing
" the gentleman," and imprint upon her chaste lips a
tender salute, whereat the universal host would set up
a shout that tore the concave, while hundreds of
grinning teeth startled the night with their brightness.   O it was a pleasure to see the sable younkers
lick in the unctuous meat, with *his* more unctuous
sayings—how he would fit the tit-bits to the puny
mouths, reserving the lengthier links for the seniors—
how he would intercept a morsel even in the jaws of
some young desperado, declaring it " must to the pan
again to be browned, for it was not fit for a gentleman's eating"—how he would recommend this slice
of white bread, or that piece of kissing-crust, to a
tender juvenile, advising them all to have a care of
cracking their teeth, which were their best patri-
mony,—how genteelly he would deal about the small
ale, as if it were wine, naming the brewer, and pro-
testing, if it were not good, he should lose their
custom ; with a special recommendation to wipe the
lip before drinking.   Then we had our toasts—" The
King,"—" the Cloth,"—which, whether they understood or not, was equally diverting and flattering ;—
and for a crowning sentiment, which never failed,
" May the Brush supersede the Laurel ! "   All these,
and fifty other fancies, which were rather felt than

comprehended by his guests, would he utter, standing
upon tables, and prefacing every sentiment with—
" Gentlemen, give me leave to propose so and so,"
which was a prodigious comfort to those young
orphans ; every now and then stuffing into his mouth
(for it did not do to be squeamish on these occasions)
indiscriminate pieces of those reeking sausages,
which pleased them mightily, and was the savouriest
part, you may believe, of the entertainment.

> Golden lads and lasses must,
> As chimney-sweepers, come to dust.

JAMES WHITE is extinct, and with him these suppers
have long ceased. He carried away with him half
the fun of the world when he died—of my world at
least. His old clients look for him among the pens ;
and missing him, reproach the altered feast of St.
Bartholomew, and the glory of Smithfield departed
for ever.

A COMPLAINT OF THE DECAY OF BEGGARS
IN THE METROPOLIS.

THE all-sweeping besom of societarian reformation—
your only modern Alcides' club to rid the time of its
abuses—is uplift with many-handed sway to extirpate
the last fluttering tatters of the bugbear MENDICITY
from the metropolis. Scrips, wallets, bags—staves,
dogs, and crutches—the whole mendicant fraternity,
with all their baggage, are fast posting out of the
purlieus of this eleventh persecution. From the

crowded crossing, from the corners of streets and turnings of alleys, the parting Genius of Beggary is " with sighing sent."

I do not approve of this wholesale going to work, this impertinent crusado, or *bellum ad exterminationem*, proclaimed against a species. Much good might be sucked from these Beggars.

They were the oldest and the honourablest form of pauperism. Their appeals were to our common nature ; less revolting to an ingenuous mind than to be a suppliant to the particular humours or caprice of any fellow creature, or set of fellow-creatures, parochial or societarian. Theirs were the only rates uninvidious in the levy, ungrudged in the assessment.

There was a dignity springing from the very depth of their desolation ; as to be naked is to be so much nearer to the being a man than to go in livery.

The greatest spirits have felt this in their reverses ; and when Dionysius from king turned schoolmaster, do we feel any thing towards him but contempt ? Could Vandyke have made a picture of him, swaying a ferula for a sceptre, which would have affected our minds with the same heroic pity, the same compassionate admiration, with which we regard his Belisarius begging for an *obolum* ? Would the moral have been more graceful, more pathetic ?

The Blind Beggar in the legend, the father of pretty Bessy—whose story doggrel rhymes and ale-house signs cannot so degrade or attenuate but that some sparks of a lustrous spirit will shine through the disguisements—this noble Earl of Cornwall (as indeed he was) and memorable sport of Fortune, fleeing from the unjust sentence of his liege lord, stript of all, and seated on the flowering green of Bethnal, with his more fresh and springing daughter by his side, illumining his rags and his beggary—would the child and parent have cut a better figure doing the honours of a counter, or expiating their fallen condition upon the three-foot eminence of some sempstering shop-board ?

In tale or history your Beggar is ever the just antipode to your King. The poets and romancical writers, (as dear Margaret Newcastle would call them,) when they would most sharply and feelingly paint a reverse of fortune, never stop till they have brought down their hero in good earnest to rags and the wallet. The depth of the descent illustrates the height he falls from. There is no medium which can be presented to the imagination without offence. There is no breaking the fall. Lear, thrown from his palace, must divest him of his garments, till he answer " mere nature ;" and Cresseid, fallen from a prince's love, must extend her pale arms, pale with other whiteness than of beauty, supplicating lazar arms with bell and clap-dish.

The Lucian wits knew this very well ; and, with a converse policy, when they would express scorn of greatness without the pity, they show us an Alexander in the shades cobbling shoes, or a Semiramis getting up foul linen.

How would it sound in song, that a great monarch had declined his affections upon the daughter of a baker ! yet do we feel the imagination at all violated when we read the " true ballad," where King Cophetua woos the beggar maid ?

Pauperism, pauper, poor man, are expressions of pity, but pity alloyed with contempt. No one properly contemns a Beggar. Poverty is a comparative thing, and each degree of it is mocked by its " neigh-bour grice." Its poor rents and comings-in are soon summed up and told. Its pretences to property are almost ludicrous. Its pitiful attempts to save excite a smile. Every scornful companion can weigh his trifle-bigger purse against it. Poor man reproaches poor man in the street with impolitic mention of his condition, his own being a shade better, while the rich pass by and jeer at both. No rascally compara-tive insults a Beggar, or thinks of weighing purses with him. He is not in the scale of comparison. He is not under the measure of property. He confessedly hath none, any more than a dog or a sheep. No one twitteth him with ostentation above his means. No one accuses him of pride, or upbraideth him with mock humility. None jostle with him for the wall, or pick quarrels for precedency. No wealthy neigh-bour seeketh to eject him from his tenement. No man sues him. No man goes to law with him. If I were not the independent gentleman that I am, rather than I would be a retainer to the great, a led captain, or a poor relation, I would choose, out of the delicacy and true greatness of my mind, to be a Beggar.

Rags, which are the reproach of poverty, are the Beggar's robes, and graceful *insignia* of his profession, his tenure, his full dress, the suit in which he is ex-pected to show himself in public. He is never out of the fashion, or limpeth awkwardly behind it. He is not required to put on Court mourning. He weareth all colours, fearing none. His costume hath under-gone less change than the Quaker's. He is the only man in the universe who is not obliged to study ap-pearances. The ups and downs of the world concern

him no longer. He alone continueth in one stay.
The price of stock or land affecteth him not. The
fluctuations of agricultural or commercial prosperity
touch him not, or at worst but change his customers.
He is not expected to become bail or surety for any
one.   No man troubleth him with questioning his
religion or politics. He is the only free man in the
universe.

The Mendicants of this great city were so many of
her sights, her lions.   I can no more spare them than
I could the Cries of London.   No corner of a street
is complete without them.   They are as indispensable
as the Ballad Singer; and in their picturesque attire
as ornamental as the signs of old London.   They
were the standing morals, emblems, mementos, dial-
mottos, the spital sermons, the books for children,
the salutary checks and pauses to the high and rush-
ing tide of greasy citizenry—

———— Look
Upon that poor and broken bankrupt there!

Above all, those old blind Tobits that used to line the
wall of Lincoln's Inn Garden, before modern fastidiousness had expelled them, casting up their ruined
orbs to catch a ray of pity, and (if possible) of light,
with their faithful Dog Guide at their feet,—whither
are they fled? or into what corners, blind as themselves, have they been driven, out of the wholesome
air and sun-warmth? immersed between four walls, in
what withering poor-house do they endure the penalty
of double darkness, where the chink of the dropt halfpenny no more consoles their forlorn bereavement,
far from the sound of the cheerful and hope-stirring
tread of the passenger?   Where hang their useless

staves? and who will farm their dogs?—Have the overseers of St. L—— caused them to be shot? or were they tied up in sacks and dropt into the Thames, at the suggestion of B——, the mild rector of ——?

Well fare the soul of unfastidious Vincent Bourne, most classical, and at the same time most English of the Latinists!—who has treated of this human and quadrupedal alliance, this dog and man friendship, in the sweetest of his poems, the *Epitaphium in Canem ;* or, *Dog's Epitaph*. Reader, peruse it ; and say, if customary sights, which could call up such gentle poetry as this, were of a nature to do more harm or good to the moral sense of the passengers through the daily thoroughfares of a vast and busy metropolis.

> Pauperis hic Iri requiesco Lyciscus, herilis,
> Dum vixi, tutela vigil columenque senectæ,
> Dux cæco fidus : nec, me ducente, solebat,
> Prætenso hinc atque hinc baculo, per iniqua locorum
> Incertam explorare viam ; sed fila secutus,
> Quæ dubios regerent passûs, vestigia tuta
> Fixit inoffenso gressu ; gelidumque sedile
> In nudo nactus saxo, quâ prætereuntium
> Unda frequens confluxit, ibi miserisque tenebras
> Lamentis, noctemque oculis ploravit obortam.
> Ploravit nec frustra ; obolum dedit alter[1] et alter,
> Queis corda et mentem indiderat[2] natura benignam.
> Ad latus interea jacui sopitus herile,
> Vel mediis vigil in somnis ; ad herilia jussa
> Auresque atque animum arrectus, seu frustula amice
> Porrexit sociasque dapes, seu longa diei
> Tædia perpessus, reditum sub nocte parabat.[3]
> Hi mores, hæc vita fuit, dum fata sinebant,
> Dum neque languebam morbis, nec inerte senectâ,
> Quæ tandem obrepsit, veterique satellite cæcum
> Orbavit dominum : prisci sed gratia facti
> Ne tota intereat, longos deleta per annos,
> Exiguum hunc Irus tumulum de cespite fecit,
> Etsi inopis, non ingratæ, munuscula dextræ ;

Carmine signavitque brevi, dominumque canemque
Quod memoret, fidumque canem dominumque benignum.

Poor Irus' faithful wolf-dog here I lie,
That wont to tend my old blind master's steps,
His guide and guard; nor, while my service lasted,
Had he occasion for that staff, with which
He now goes picking out his path in fear
Over the highways and crossings; but would plant,
Safe in the conduct of my friendly string,
A firm foot forward still, till he had reach'd
His poor seat on some stone, nigh where the tide
Of passers by in thickest confluence flow'd:
To whom with loud and passionate laments
From morn to eve his dark estate he wail'd.
Nor wail'd to all in vain: some here and there,
The well-disposed and good, their pennies gave.
I meantime at his feet obsequious slept;
Not all-asleep in sleep, but heart and ear
Prick'd up at his least motion; to receive
At his kind hand my customary crumbs,
And common portion in his feast of scraps;
Or when night warn'd us homewards, tired and spent
With our long day and tedious beggary.
These were my manners, this my way of life
Till age and slow disease me overtook,
And sever'd from my sightless master's side.
But lest the grace of so good deeds should die,
Through tract of years in mute oblivion lost,
This slender tomb of turf hath Irus rear'd
Cheap monument of no ungrudging hand,
And with short verse inscribed it, to attest,
In long and lasting union to attest,
The virtues of the Beggar and his Dog.

These dim eyes have in vain explored for some
months past a well-known figure, or part of the figure,
of a man, who used to glide his comely upper half
over the pavements of London, wheeling along with
most ingenious celerity, upon a machine of wood ; a

spectacle to natives, to foreigners, and to children. He was of a robust make, with a florid sailor-like complexion, and his head was bare to the storm and sunshine. He was a natural curiosity, a speculation to the scientific, a prodigy to the simple. The infant would stare at the mighty man brought down to his own level. The common cripple would despise his own pusillanimity, viewing the hale stoutness and hearty heart of this half-limbed giant. Few but must have noticed him; for the accident which brought him low took place during the riots of 1780, and he has been a groundling so long. He seemed earth-born, an Antæus, and to suck in fresh vigour from the soil which he neighboured. He was a grand fragment; as good as an Elgin marble. The nature, which should have recruited his reft legs and thighs, was not lost, but only retired into his upper parts, and he was half a Hercules. I heard a tremendous voice thundering and growling, as before an earthquake, and casting down my eyes, it was this mandrake reviling a steed that had started at his portentous appearance. He seemed to want but his just stature to have rent the offending quadruped in shivers. He was as the man-part of a centaur, from which the horse-half had been cloven in some dire Lapithan controversy. He moved on, as if he could have made shift with yet half of the body-portion which was left him. The *os sublime* was not wanting; and he threw out yet a jolly countenance upon the heavens. Forty-and-two years had he driven this out-of-door trade, and now that his hair is grizzled in the service, but his good spirits no way impaired, because he is not content to exchange his free air and exercise for the restraints of a poor-house, he is ex-

piating his contumacy in one of those houses (ironi-
cally christened) of Correction.

Was a daily spectacle like this to be deemed a
nuisance, which called for legal interference to remove? or not rather a salutary and a touching object
to the passers-by in a great city? Among her shows,
her museums, and supplies for ever-gaping curiosity,
(and what else but an accumulation of sights—endless
sights—*is* a great city; or for what else is it desirable?)
was there not room for one *Lusus* (not *Naturæ*,
indeed, but) *Accidentium?* What if in forty-and-two-
years' going about, the man had scraped together
enough to give a portion to his child (as the rumour
ran) of a few hundreds—whom had he injured?—
whom had he imposed upon? The contributors had
enjoyed their *sight* for their pennies. What if after
being exposed all day to the heats, the rains, and the
frosts of heaven—shuffling his ungainly trunk along
in an elaborate and painful motion—he was enabled
to retire at night to enjoy himself at a club of his
fellow cripples over a dish of hot meat and vegetables,
as the charge was gravely brought against him by a
clergyman deposing before a House of Commons'
Committee—was *this*, or was his truly paternal consideration, which (if a fact) deserved a statue rather
than a whipping-post, and is inconsistent at least
with the exaggeration of nocturnal orgies which he
has been slandered with—a reason that he should be
deprived of his chosen, harmless, nay edifying, way
of life, and be committed in hoary age for a sturdy
vagabond?—

There was a Yorick once, whom it would not have
shamed to have sate down at the cripples' feast, and
to have thrown in his benediction, ay, and his mite

too, for a companionable symbol. " Age, thou hast
lost thy breed."

Half of these stories about the prodigious fortunes
made by begging are (I verily believe) misers' calum-
nies. One was much talked of in the public papers
some time since, and the usual charitable inferences
deduced. A clerk in the Bank was surprised with
the announcement of a five-hundred pound legacy
left him by a person whose name he was a stranger
to. It seems that in his daily morning walks from
Peckham, (or some village thereabouts,) where he
lived, to his office, it had been his practice for the
last twenty years to drop his halfpenny duly into the
hat of some blind Bartimeus, that sate begging alms
by the way-side in the Borough. The good old
beggar recognised his daily benefactor by the voice
only; and, when he died, left all the amassings of
his alms (that had been half a century perhaps in
the accumulating) to his old Bank friend. Was this
a story to purse up people's hearts, and pennies,
against giving an alms to the blind ?—or not rather a
beautiful moral of well-directed charity on the one
part, and noble gratitude upon the other ?—

I sometimes wish I had been that Bank clerk.

I seem to remember a poor old grateful kind of
creature, blinking, and looking up with his no eyes in
the sun.—

Is it possible I could have steeled my purse against
him ?

Perhaps I had no small change.

Reader, do not be frightened at the hard words
" imposition," " imposture." *Give, and ask no questions.* Cast thy bread upon the waters. Some have
unawares (like this Bank clerk) entertained angels

Shut not thy purse-strings always against painted distress. Act a charity sometimes. When a poor creature (outwardly and visibly such) comes before thee, do not stay to inquire whether the " seven small children," in whose name he implores thy assistance, have a veritable existence. Rake not into the bowels of unwelcome truth to save a halfpenny. It is good to believe him. If he be not all that he pretendeth, *give*, and under a personate father of a family, think (if thou pleasest) that thou hast relieved an indigent bachelor. When they come with their conterfeit looks, and mumping tones, think them players. You pay your money to see a comedian feign these things, which, concerning these poor people, thou canst not certainly tell whether they are feigned or not.

A DISSERTATION UPON ROAST PIG.

———

MANKIND, says a Chinese manuscript, which my
friend M——— was obliging enough to read and
explain to me, for the first seventy thousand ages ate
their meat raw, clawing or biting it from the living
animal, just as they do in Abyssinia to this day.
This period is not obscurely hinted at by their great
Confucius in the second chapter of his Mundane
Mutations, where he designates a kind of golden age
by the term Cho-fang, literally the Cooks' Holiday.
The manuscript goes on to say, that the art of roasting, or rather broiling (which I take to be the elder
brother) was accidentally discovered in the manner
following.   The swine-herd Ho-ti, having gone out
into the woods one morning, as his manner was,
to collect mast for his hogs, left his cottage in the
care of his eldest son, Bo-bo, a great lubberly boy, who
being fond of playing with fire, as younkers of his
age commonly are, let some sparks escape into a
bundle of straw, which kindling quickly, spread the
conflagration over every part of their poor mansion,
till it was reduced to ashes.   Together with the
cottage, (a sorry antediluvian make-shift of a building,
you may think it,) what was of much more importance,
a fine litter of new-farrowed pigs, no less than nine in

number, perished. China pigs have been esteemed
a luxury all over the East, from the remotest periods
that we read of. Bo-bo was in the utmost consternation, as you may think, not so much for the sake of
the tenement, which his father and he could easily
build up again with a few dry branches, and the
labour of an hour or two at any time, as for the loss of
the pigs. While he was thinking what he should say
to his father, and wringing his hands over the smoking remnants of one of those untimely sufferers, an
odour assailed his nostrils, unlike any scent which he
had before experienced. What could it proceed
from ? Not from the burnt cottage : he had smelt
that smell before ; indeed this was by no means the
first accident of the kind which had occurred through
the negligence of this unlucky young fire-brand.
Much less did it resemble that of any known herb,
weed, or flower. A premonitory moistening at the
same time overflowed his nether lip. He knew not
what to think. He next stooped down to feel the
pig, if there were any signs of life in it. He burnt
his fingers, and to cool them he applied them in his
booby fashion to his mouth. Some of the crumbs of
the scorched skin had come away with his fingers,
and for the first time in his life, (in the world's life
indeed, for before him no man had known it,) he
tasted *crackling* ! Again he felt and fumbled at the
pig. It did not burn him so much now, still he licked
his fingers from a sort of habit. The truth at length
broke into his slow understanding, that it was the pig
that smelt so, and the pig that tasted so delicious ;
and surrendering himself up to the new-born pleasure,
he fell to tearing up whole handfulls of the scorched
skin with the flesh next it, and was cramming it

down his throat in his beastly fashion, when his sire
entered amid the smoking rafters, armed with retri-
butory cudgel, and finding how affairs stood, began to
rain blows upon the young rogue's shoulders as thick
as hail-stones, which Bo-bo heeded not any more
than if they had been flies.   The tickling pleasure
which he experienced in his lower regions had rendered him quite callous to any inconveniences he
might feel in those remote quarters.   His father
might lay on, but he could not beat him from his pig,
till he had fairly made an end of it, when, becoming a
little more sensible of his situation, something like
the following dialogue ensued :—

"You graceless whelp, what have you got there
devouring ? Is it not enough that you have burnt
me down three houses with your dog's tricks, and be
hanged to you ! but you must be eating fire, and I
know not what.   What have you got there, I say ?"

"O father, the pig, the pig ! do come and taste how
nice the burnt pig eats."

The ears of Ho-ti tingled with horror.   He cursed
his son, and he cursed himself that ever he should
beget a son that should eat burnt pig.

Bo-bo, whose scent was wonderfully sharpened
since morning, soon raked out another pig, and fairly
rending it asunder, thrust the lesser half by main force
into the fists of Ho-ti, still shouting out, "Eat, eat,
eat the burnt pig, father, only taste—O Lord !"—with
such-like barbarous ejaculations, cramming all the
while as if he would choke.

Ho-ti trembled every joint while he grasped the
abominable thing, wavering whether he should not
put his son to death for an unnatural young monster,
when the crackling scorching his fingers, as it had

done his son's, and applying the same remedy to them, he in his turn tasted some of its flavour, which, make what sour mouths he would for a pretence, proved not altogether displeasing to him. In conclusion, (for the manuscript here is a little tedious,) both father and son fairly sat down to the mess, and never left off till they had despatched all that remained of the litter.

Bo-bo was strictly enjoined not to let the secret escape, for the neighbours would certainly have stoned them for a couple of abominable wretches, who could think of improving upon the good meat which God had sent them. Nevertheless, strange stories got about. It was observed that Ho-ti's cottage was burnt down now more frequently than ever. Nothing but fires from this time forward. Some would break out in broad day, others in the night-time. As often as the sow farrowed, so sure was the house of Ho-ti to be in a blaze; and Ho-ti himself, which was the more remarkable, instead of chastising his son, seemed to grow more indulgent to him than ever. At length they were watched, the terrible mystery discovered, and father and son summoned to take their trial at Pekin, then an inconsiderable assize town. Evidence was given, the obnoxious food itself produced in court, and verdict about to be pronounced, when the foreman of the jury begged that some of the burnt pig, of which the culprits stood accused, might be handed into the box. He handled it, and they all handled it; and burning their fingers, as Bo-bo and his father had done before them, and nature prompting to each of them the same remedy, against the face of all the facts, and the clearest charge which judge had ever given,—to the surprise of the whole court, townsfolk, strangers, reporters, and all present—without leaving the box, or any manner of consultation whatever, they brought in a simultaneous verdict of Not Guilty.

The judge, who was a shrewd fellow, winked at the manifest iniquity of the decision : and when the court was dismissed, went privily and bought up all the pigs that could be had for love or money.   In a few days his lordship's town-house was observed to be on fire.   The thing took wing, and now there was nothing to be seen but fire in every direction.   Fuel and pigs grew enormously dear all over the district. The insurance-offices, one and all, shut up shop. People built slighter and slighter every day, until it was feared that the very science of architecture would in no long time be lost to the world.   Thus this custom of firing houses continued, till in process of time, says my manuscript, a sage arose, like our Locke, who made a discovery that the flesh of swine, or indeed of any other animal, might be cooked (*burnt*, as they called it,) without the necessity of consuming a whole house to dress it.   Then first began the rude form of a gridiron.   Roasting by the string or spit came in a century or two later, I forget in whose dynasty.   By such slow degrees, concludes the manuscript, do the most useful, and seemingly the most obvious, arts make their way among mankind.

Without placing too implicit faith in the account above given, it must be agreed that if a worthy pretext for so dangerous an experiment as setting houses on fire (especially in these days) could be assigned in favour of any culinary object, that pretext and excuse might be found in ROAST PIG.

Of all the delicacies in the whole *mundus edibilis*, I

will maintain it to be the most delicate—*princeps obsoniorum.*

I speak not of your grown porkers—things between pig and pork, those hobbydehoys—but a young and tender suckling, under a moon old, guiltless as yet of the sty, with no original speck of the *amor immunditiæ*, the hereditary failing of the first parent, yet manifest—his voice as yet not broken, but something between a childish treble and a grumble—the mild forerunner or *præludium* of a grunt.

He must be roasted.   I am not ignorant that our ancestors ate them seethed, or boiled; but what a sacrifice of the exterior tegument !

There is no flavour comparable, I will contend, to that of the crisp, tawny, well-watched, not over-roasted, *crackling*, as it is well called.   The very teeth are invited to their share of the pleasure at this banquet in overcoming the coy, brittle resistance—with the adhesive oleaginous—O call it not fat ! but an indefinable sweetness growing up to it—the tender blossoming of fat—fat cropped in the bud—taken in the shoot—in the first innocence—the cream and quintessence of the child-pig's yet pure food—the lean, no lean, but a kind of animal manna—or, rather, fat and lean (if it must be so) so blended and running into each other, that both together make but one ambrosian result, or common substance.

Behold him, while he is "doing"—it seemeth rather a refreshing warmth than a scorching heat that he is so passive to.   How equably he twirleth round the string !—Now he is just done.   To see the extreme sensibility of that tender age ! he hath wept out his pretty eyes—radiant jellies—shooting stars.—

See him in the dish, his second cradle, how meek

he lieth !—Wouldst thou have had this innocent grow
up to the grossness and indocility which too often
accompany maturer swinehood ?   Ten to one he
would have proved a glutton, a sloven, an obstinate,
disagreeable animal, wallowing in all manner of filthy
conversation.   From these sins he is happily snatched
away.

> Ere sin could blight or sorrow fade,
> Death came with timely care.

His memory is odoriferous.   No clown curseth, while
his stomach half rejecteth, the rank bacon ; no coal-
heaver bolteth him in reeking sausages ; he hath a
fair sepulchre in the grateful stomach of the judicious epicure, and for such a tomb might be content
to die.

He is the best of sapors.   Pine-apple is great.   She
is indeed almost too transcendent,—a delight, if not
sinful, yet so like to sinning that really a tender-
conscienced person would do well to pause,—too
ravishing for mortal taste, she woundeth and exco-
riateth the lips that approach her.   Like lovers' kisses,
she biteth : she is a pleasure bordering on pain from
the fierceness and insanity of her ·relish ; but she
stoppeth at the palate ; she meddleth not with the
appetite ; and the coarsest hunger might barter her
consistently for a mutton-chop.

Pig (let me speak his praise) is no less provocative
of the appetite than he is satisfactory to the critical-
ness of the censorious palate.   The strong man may
batten on him, and the weakling refuseth not his mild
juices.

Unlike to mankind's mixed characters, a bundle of
virtues and vices, inexplicably intertwisted, and not
to be unravelled without hazard, he is good through-

out. No part of him is better or worse than another.
He helpeth, as far as his little means extend, all
around. He is the least envious of banquets. He is
all neighbours' fare.

I am one of those who freely and ungrudgingly impart a share of the good things of this life which fall
to their lot (few as mine are in this kind) to a friend.
I protest I take as great an interest in my friend's
pleasures, his relishes, and proper satisfactions, as in
mine own. "Presents," I often say, "endear Absents."
Hares, pheasants, partridges, snipes, barn-door
chickens, (those "tame villatic fowl,") capons, plovers,
brawn, barrels of oysters, I dispense as freely as I
receive them. I love to taste them, as it were, upon
the tongue of my friend. But a stop must be put
somewhere. One would not, like Lear, " give every
thing." I make my stand upon pig. Methinks it is
an ingratitude to the giver of all good flavours to
extra-domiciliate, or send out of the house slightingly
(under pretext of friendship, or I know not what,)
a blessing so particularly adapted, predestined, I may
say, to my individual palate.—It argues an insensibility.

I remember a touch of conscience in this kind at
school. My good old aunt, who never parted from
me at the end of a holiday without stuffing a sweet-
meat, or some nice thing into my pocket, had dismissed me one evening with a smoking plum-cake,
fresh from the oven. In my way to school (it was
over London bridge) a grey-headed old beggar saluted
me. (I have no doubt, at this time of day, that he was
a counterfeit.) I had no pence to console him with,
and in the vanity of self-denial, and the very coxcombry of charity, schoolboy-like, I made him a

present of the whole cake.   I walked on a little, buoyed up, as one is on such occasions, with a sweet soothing of self-satisfaction; but before I had got to the end of the bridge my better feelings returned, and I burst into tears, thinking how ungrateful I had been to my good aunt, to go and give her good gift away to a stranger that I had never seen before, and who might be a bad man for aught I knew; and then I thought of the pleasure my aunt would be taking in thinking that I (I myself, and not another) would eat her nice cake.   And what should I say to her the next time I saw her?—how naughty I was to part with her pretty present!—and the odour of that spicy cake came back upon my recollection, and the pleasure and the curiosity I had taken in seeing her make it, and her joy when she sent it to the oven, and how disappointed she would feel that I had never had a bit of it in my mouth at last.   And I blamed my impertinent spirit of alms-giving, and out-of-place hypocrisy of goodness; and above all, I wished never to see the face again of that insidious, good-for-nothing, old grey impostor.

Our ancestors were nice in their method of sacrificing these tender victims.   We read of pigs whipt to death with something of a shock, as we hear of any other obsolete custom.   The age of discipline is gone by, or it would be curious to inquire (in a philosophical light merely) what effect this process might have towards intenerating and dulcifying a substance naturally so mild and dulcet as the flesh of young pigs.   It looks like refining a violet.   Yet we should be cautious, while we condemn the inhumanity, how we censure the wisdom of the practice.   It might impart a gusto.

I remember an hypothesis, argued upon by the young students when I was at St. Omer's, and maintained with much learning and pleasantry on both sides, " Whether, supposing that the flavour of a pig who obtained his death by whipping (*per flagellationem extremam*) superadded a pleasure upon the palate of a man more intense than any possible suffering we can conceive in the animal, is man justified in using that method of putting the animal to death ?" I forget the decision.

His sauce should be considered : decidedly, a few bread crumbs, done up with his liver and brains, and a dash of mild sage. But banish, dear Mrs. Cook, I beseech you, the whole onion tribe. Barbecue your whole hogs to your palate, steep them in shalots, stuff them out with plantations of the rank and guilty garlic ; you cannot poison them, or make them stronger than they are ; but consider, he is a weakling,—a flower.

A BACHELOR'S COMPLAINT OF THE BE-HAVIOUR OF MARRIED PEOPLE.

As a single man, I have spent a good deal of my time in noting down the infirmities of Married People, to console myself for those superior pleasures which they tell me I have lost by remaining as I am.

I cannot say that the quarrels of men and their wives ever made any great impression upon me, or had much tendency to strengthen me in those anti-social resolutions which I took up long ago upon more substantial considerations. What oftenest offends me at the houses of married persons where I visit, is an error of quite a different description ;—it is that they are too loving.

Not too loving neither: that does not explain my meaning. Besides, why should that offend me ? The very act of separating themselves from the rest of the world, to have the fuller enjoyment of each other's society, implies that they prefer one another to all the world.

But what I complain of is, that they carry this preference so undisguisedly, they perk it up in the faces of us single people so shamelessly, you cannot be in their company a moment without being made to feel, by some indirect hint or open avowal, that *you* are not the object of this preference. Now there are some things which give no offence, while implied or taken for granted .merely ; but expressed, there is much offence in them. If a man were to accost the first homely-featured or plain-dressed young woman of his acquaintance, and tell her bluntly that she was not handsome or rich enough for him, and he could not marry her, he would deserve to be kicked for his ill manners ; yet no less is implied in the fact, that having access and opportunity of putting the question to her, he has never yet thought fit to do it. The young woman understands this as clearly as if it were put into words ; but no reasonable young woman would think of making this the ground of a quarrel. Just as little right have a married couple to tell me by speeches, and looks that are scarce less plain than speeches, that I am not the happy man,—the lady's choice. It is enough that I know I am not: I do not want this perpetual reminding.

The display of superior knowledge or riches may
be made sufficiently mortifying ; but these admit of a
palliative. The knowledge which is brought out to
insult me, may accidentally improve me ; and in the
rich man's houses and pictures, his parks and
gardens, I have a temporary usufruct at least. But
the display of married happiness has none of these
palliatives : it is throughout pure, unrecompensed,
unqualified insult.

Marriage by its best title is a monopoly, and not of
the least invidious sort. It is the cunning of most
possessors of any exclusive privilege to keep their
advantage as much out of sight as possible, that their
less favoured neighbours, seeing little of the benefit,
may the less be disposed to question the right. But
these married monopolists thrust the most obnoxious
part of their patent into our faces.

Nothing is to me more distasteful than that entire
complacency and satisfaction which beam in the
countenances of a new-married couple,—in that of
the lady particularly : it tells you that her lot is
disposed of in this world : that *you* can have no
hopes of her. It is true, I have none : nor wishes
either, perhaps ; but this is one of those truths which
ought, as I said before, to be taken for granted, not
expressed.

The excessive airs which those people give themselves, founded on the ignorance of us unmarried
people, would be more offensive if they were less
irrational. We will allow them to understand the
mysteries belonging to their own craft better than we,
who have not had the happiness to be made free of
the company : but their arrogance is not content
within these limits. If a single person presume to

offer his opinion in their presence, though upon the most indifferent subject, he is immediately silenced as an incompetent person. Nay, a young married lady of my acquaintance, who, the best of the jest was, had not changed her condition above a fortnight before, in a question on which I had the misfortune to differ from her, respecting the properest mode of breeding oysters for the London market, had the assurance to ask with a sneer, how such an old Bachelor as I could pretend to know any thing about such matters.

But what I have spoken of hitherto is nothing to the airs which these creatures give themselves when they come, as they generally do, to have children. When I consider how little of a rarity children are,— that every street and blind alley swarms with them,— that the poorest people commonly have them in most abundance,—that there are few marriages that are not blest with at least one of these bargains,—how often they turn out ill, and defeat the fond hopes of their parents, taking to vicious courses, which end in poverty, disgrace, the gallows, &c.,—I cannot for my life tell what cause for pride there can possibly be in having them. If they were young phœnixes, indeed, that were born but one in a year, there might be a pretext. But when they are so common——

I do not advert to the insolent merit which they assume with their husbands on these occasions. Let *them* look to that. But why *we*, who are not their natural-born subjects, should be expected to bring our spices, myrrh, and incense,—our tribute and homage of admiration,—I do not see.

" Like as the arrows in the hand of the giant, even so are the young children : " so says the excellent office in our Prayer Book appointed for the churching of women. "Happy is the man that hath his quiver full of them." So say I; but then don't let him discharge his quiver upon us that are weaponless; let them be arrows, but not to gall and stick us. I have generally observed that these arrows are double-headed: they have two forks, to be sure to hit with one or the other. As for instance, when you come into a house which is full of children, if you happen to take no notice of them, (you are thinking of something else, perhaps, and turn a deaf ear to their innocent caresses,) you are set down as untractable, morose, a hater of children. On the other hand, if you find them more than usually engaging, if you are taken with their pretty manners, and set about in earnest to romp and play with them, some pretext or other is sure to be found for sending them out of the room; they are too noisy or boisterous, or Mr. ——— does not like children. With one or other of these folks the arrow is sure to hit you.

I could forgive their jealousy, and dispense with toying with their brats, if it gives them any pain; but I think it unreasonable to be called upon to *love* them, where I see no occasion; to love a whole family, perhaps eight, nine, or ten, indiscriminately; to love all the pretty dears, because children are so engaging!

I know there is a proverb, "Love me, love my dog:" that is not always so very practicable, particularly if the dog be set upon you to tease you or snap at you in sport. But a dog, or a lesser thing—any inanimate substance, as a keepsake, a watch or a ring, a tree, or the place where we last parted when my friend went away upon a long absence, I can make shift to love, because I love him, and any thing that reminds me of him ; provided it be in its nature indifferent, and apt to receive whatever hue fancy can give it. But children have a real character, and an essential being of themselves : they are amiable or unamiable *per se ;* I must love or hate them as I see cause for either in their qualities. A child's nature is too serious a thing to admit of its being regarded as a mere appendage to another being, and to be loved or hated accordingly: they stand with me upon their own stock, as much as men and women do. Oh, but you will say, sure it is an attractive age,— there is something in the tender years of infancy that of itself charms us. That is the very reason why I am more nice about them. I know that a sweet child is the sweetest thing in nature, not even excepting the delicate creatures which bear them : but the prettier the kind of a thing is, the more desirable it is that it should be pretty of its kind. One daisy differs not much from another in glory; but a violet should look and smell the daintiest. I was always rather squeamish in my women and children.

But this is not the worst : one must be admitted into their familiarity at least, before they can complain of inattention. It implies visits and some kind of intercourse. But if the husband be a man with whom you have lived on a friendly footing before marriage—if you did not come in on the wife's side —if you did not sneak into the house in her train, but were an old friend in fast habits of intimacy before their courtship was so much as thought on,— look about you—your tenure is precarious : before a twelvemonth shall roll over your head you shall find

your old friend gradually grow cool and altered towards you, and at last seek opportunities of breaking
with you. I have scarce a married friend of my acquaintance, upon whose firm faith I can rely, whose
friendship did not commence *after the period of his
marriage*. With some limitations, they can endure
that ; but that the good man should have dared to
enter into a solemn league of friendship in which
they were not consulted, though it happened before
they knew him,—before they that are now man and
wife ever met,—this is intolerable to them. Every
long friendship, every old authentic intimacy, must
be brought into their office to be new stamped with
their currency, as a sovereign prince calls in the good
old money that was coined in some reign before he
was born or thought of, to be new marked and minted
with the stamp of his authority, before he will let it
pass current in the world. You may guess what luck
generally befalls such a rusty piece of metal as I am
in these *new mintings*.

Innumerable are the ways which they take to insult
and worm you out of their husband's confidence.
Laughing at all you say with a kind of wonder, as if
you were a queer kind of fellow that said good things,
but an oddity, is one of the ways ; they have a particular kind of stare for the purpose ; till at last the
husband, who used to defer to your judgment, and
would pass over some excrescences of understanding
and manner for the sake of a general vein of observation (not quite vulgar) which he perceived in you,
begins to suspect whether you are not altogether a
humourist,—a fellow well enough to have consorted
with in his bachelor days, but not quite so proper to
be introduced to ladies. This may be called the

staring way ; and is that which has oftenest been put
in practice against me.

Then there is the exaggerating way, or the way of
irony ; that is, where they find you an object of
special regard with their husband, who is not so
easily to be shaken from the lasting attachment
founded on esteem which he has conceived towards
you, by never qualified exaggerations to cry up all
that you say or do, till the good man, who understands
well enough that it is all done in compliment to him,
grows weary of the debt of gratitude which is due to
so much candour, and by relaxing a little on his part,
and taking down a peg or two in his enthusiasm,
sinks at length to the kindly level of moderate esteem
—that " decent affection and complacent kindness "
towards you, where she herself can join in sympathy
with him without much stretch and violence to her
sincerity.

Another way (for the ways they have to accomplish
so desirable a purpose are infinite) is, with a kind of
innocent simplicity, continually to mistake what it
was which first made their husband fond of you. If
an esteem for something excellent in your moral
character was that which riveted the chain which she
is to break, upon any imaginary discovery of a want
of poignancy in your conversation, she will cry, " I
thought my dear you described your friend, Mr. ——
as a great wit ! " If, on the other hand, it was for
some supposed charm in your conversation that he
first grew to like you, and was content for this to
overlook some trifling irregularities in your moral
deportment, upon the first notice of any of these she
as readily exclaims, " This, my dear, is your good
Mr. —— ! ' One good lady whom I took the liberty

of expostulating with for not showing me quite so
much respect as I thought due to her husband's old
friend, had the candour to confess to me that she had
often heard Mr. —— speak of me before marriage, and
that she had conceived a great desire to be acquainted
with me, but that the sight of me had very much
disappointed her expectations; for from her husband's
representations of me, she had formed a notion that
she was to see a fine, tall, officer-like-looking man,
(I use her very words,) the very reverse of which
proved to be the truth.   This was candid; and I
had the civility not to ask her, in return, how she
came to pitch upon a standard of personal accomplishments for her husband's friends which differed
so much from his own; for my friend's dimensions as
near as possible approximate to mine ; he standing
five feet five in his shoes, in which I have the advantage of him by about half an inch ; and he no more than
myself exhibiting any indications of a martial character in his air or countenance.

These are some of the mortifications which I have
encountered in the absurd attempt to visit at their
houses. To enumerate them all would be a vain
endeavour; I shall therefore just glance at the very
common impropriety of which married ladies are
guilty,—of treating us as if we were their husbands,
and *vice versâ*. I mean when they use us with familiarity, and their husbands with ceremony. *Testacea*,
for instance, kept me the other night two or three
hours beyond my usual time of supping, while she
was fretting because Mr. —— did not come home till
the oysters were all spoiled, rather than she would
be guilty of the impoliteness of touching one in his
absence. This was reversing the point of good

manners : for ceremony is an invention to take off
the uneasy feeling which we derive from knowing
ourselves to be less the object of love and esteem
with a fellow creature than some other person is.   It
endeavours to make up by superior attentions in little
points for the invidious preference which it is forced
to deny in the greater. Had *Testacea* kept the oysters
back for me, and withstood her husband's importuni-
ties to go to supper, she would have acted according
to the strict rules of propriety.   I know no ceremony that ladies are bound to observe to their
husbands, beyond the point of a modest behaviour
and decorum ; therefore I must protest against the
vicarious gluttony of *Cerasia,* who at her own table
sent away a dish of Morellas, which I was applying
to with great good-will, to her husband at the other
end of the table, and recommended a plate of less
extraordinary gooseberries to my unwedded palate
in their stead.   Neither can I excuse the wanton
affront of ——

But I am weary of stringing up of all my married
acquaintance by Roman denominations. Let them
amend and change their manners, or I promise to
record the full-length English of their names, to the
terror of all such desperate offenders in future.

ON SOME OF THE OLD ACTORS.

THE casual sight of an old Play Bill, which I picked up the other day—I know not by what chance it was preserved so long—tempts me to call to mind a few of the Players who make the principal figure in it. It presents the cast of parts in the *Twelfth Night*, at the old Drury Lane Theatre two-and-thirty years ago. There is something very touching in these old remembrances. They make us think how we *once* used to read a Play Bill—not, as now peradventure, singling out a favourite performer, and casting a negligent eye over the rest ; but spelling out every name, down to the very mutes and servants of the scene ; when it was a matter of no small moment to us whether Whitfield, or Packer, took the part of Fabian ; when Benson, and Burton, and Phillimore—names of small account—had an importance beyond what we can be content to attribute now to the time's best actors. " Orsino, by Mr. Barrymore." What a full Shaksperian sound it carries ! how fresh to memory arise the image and the manner of the gentle actor!

Those who have only seen Mrs. Jordan within the last ten or fifteen years can have no adequate notion of her performance of such parts as Ophelia; Helena, in *All's Well that Ends Well;* and Viola in this play. Her voice had latterly acquired a coarseness, which suited well enough with her Nells and Hoydens, but in those days it sank, with her steady, melting eye, into the heart.   Her joyous parts, in which her memory now chiefly lives, in her youth were outdone by her plaintive ones.   There is no giving an account how she delivered the disguised story of her love for Orsino.   It was no set speech, that she had foreseen, so as to weave it into an harmonious period, line necessarily, following line, to make up the music—yet I have heard it so spoken, or rather *read*, not without its grace and beauty—but, when she had declared her sister's history to be a "blank," and that she "never told her love," there was a pause, as if the story had ended—and then the image of the "worm in the bud," came up as a new suggestion—and the heightened image of "Patience" still followed after that, as by some growing (and not mechanical) process, thought springing up after thought, I would almost say, as they were watered by her tears.   So in those fine lines—

> Right loyal cantos of contemned love—
> Hollow your name to the reverberate hills—

there was no preparation made in the foregoing image for that which was to follow.   She used no rhetoric in her passion ; or it was Nature's own rhetoric, most legitimate then, when it seemed altogether without rule or law.

Mrs. Powel (now Mrs. Renard), then in the pride of her beauty, made an admirable Olivia.   She was particularly excellent in her unbending scenes in conversation with the Clown.   I have seen some Olivias—

and those very sensible actresses too—who in these interlocutions have seemed to set their wits at the jester, and to vie conceits with him in downright emulation. But she used him for her sport, like what he was, to trifle a leisure sentence or two with, and then to be dismissed, and she to be the Great Lady still. She touched the imperious fantastic humour of the character with nicety. Her fine spacious person filled the scene.

The part of Malvolio has, in my judgment, been so often misunderstood, and the *general merits* of the actor, who then played it, so unduly appreciated, that I shall hope for pardon if I am a little prolix upon these points.

Of all the actors who flourished in my time—a melancholy phrase if taken aright, reader—Bensley had most of the swell of soul, was greatest in the delivery of heroic conceptions, the emotions consequent upon the presentment of a great idea to the fancy. He had the true poetical enthusiasm—the rarest faculty among players. None that I remember possessed even a portion of that fine madness which he threw out in Hotspur's famous rant about glory, or the transports of the Venetian incendiary at the vision of the fired city. His voice had the dissonance, and at times the inspiriting effect, of the trumpet. His gait was uncouth and stiff, but no way embarrassed by affectation; and the thorough-bred gentleman was uppermost in every movement. He seized the moment of passion with greatest truth; like a faithful clock, never striking before the time; never anticipating or leading you to anticipate. He was totally destitute of trick and artifice. He seemed come upon the stage to do the poet's message simply,

and he did it with as genuine fidelity as the nuncios
in Homer deliver the errands of the gods.   He let
the passion or the sentiment do its own work without
prop or bolstering.   He would have scorned to
mountebank it ; and betrayed none of that *cleverness*
which is the bane of serious acting.   For this reason,
his Iago was the only endurable one which I remember to have seen.   No spectator, from his action,
could divine more of his artifice than Othello was
supposed to do.   His confessions in soliloquy alone
put you in possession of the mystery.   There were
no by-intimations to make the audience fancy their
own discernment so much greater than that of the
Moor—who commonly stands like a great helpless
mark, set up for mine Ancient, and a quantity of
barren spectators, to shoot their bolts at.   The Iago
of Bensley did not go to work so grossly.   There was
a triumphant tone about the character, natural to a
general consciousness of power; but none of that
petty vanity which chuckles and cannot contain
itself upon any little successful stroke of its knavery—
as is common with your small villains, and green
probationers in mischief.   It did not clap or crow
before its time.   It was not a man setting his wits at
a child, and winking all the while at other children,
who are mightily pleased at being let into the secret ;
but a consummate villain entrapping a noble nature
into toils, against which no discernment was avail-
able, where the manner was as fathomless as the
purpose seemed dark, and without motive.   The part
of Malvolio, in the *Twelfth Night*, was performed by
Bensley with a richness and a dignity of which (to
judge from some recent castings of that character)
the very tradition must be worn out from the stage.   No

manager in those days would have dreamed of giving it to Mr. Baddeley or Mr. Parsons ; when Bensley was occasionally absent from the theatre, John Kemble thought it no derogation to succeed to the part.   Malvolio is not essentially ludicrous.   He becomes comic but by accident.   He is cold, austere, repelling ; but dignified, consistent, and, for what appears, rather of an over-stretched morality.   Maria describes him as a sort of Puritan ; and he might have worn his gold chain with honour in one of our old round-head families, in the service of a Lambert or a Lady Fairfax.   But his morality and his manners are misplaced in Illyria.   He is opposed to the proper *levities* of the piece, and falls in the unequal contest.   Still his pride, or his gravity, (call it which you will,) is inherent, and native to the man, not mock or affected, which latter only are the fit objects to excite laughter. His quality is at the best unlovely, but neither buffoon nor contemptible.   His bearing is lofty, a little above his station, but probably not much above his deserts. We see no reason why he should not have been brave, honourable, accomplished.   His careless committal of the ring to the ground (which he was commissioned to restore to Cesario) bespeaks a generosity of birth and feeling.   His dialect on all occasions is that of a gentleman and a man of education.   We must not confound him with the eternal old, low steward of comedy.   He is master of the household to a great princess ; a dignity probably conferred upon him for other respects than age or length of service.   Olivia, at the first indication of his supposed madness, declares that she " would not have him miscarry for half of her dowry."   Does this look as if the character was meant to appear little or insignificant? Once, indeed, she accuses him to his face—of what?—of being "sick of self-love,"—but with a gentleness and considerateness which could not have been if she had not thought that this particular infirmity shaded some virtues. His rebuke to the knight and his sottish revellers is sensible and spirited; and when we take into consideration the unprotected condition of his mistress, and the strict regard with which her state of real or dissembled mourning would draw the eyes of the world upon her house-affairs, Malvolio might feel the honour of the family in some sort in his keeping; as it appears not that Olivia had any more brothers or kinsmen to look to it—for Sir Toby had dropped all such nice respects at the buttery-hatch. That Malvolio was meant to be represented as possessing estimable qualities, the expression of the Duke, in his anxiety to have him reconciled, almost infers: "Pursue him, and entreat him to a peace." Even in his abused state of chains and darkness, a sort of greatness seems never to desert him. He argues highly and well with the supposed Sir Topas, and philosophises gallantly upon his straw.[1] There must have been some shadow of worth about the man; he must have been something more than a mere vapour—a thing of straw, or Jack in office—before Fabian and Maria could have ventured sending him upon a courting errand to Olivia. There was some consonancy (as he would say) in the undertaking, or the jest would nave been too bold even for that house of misrule.

---

[1] *Clown.* What is the opinion of Pythagoras concerning wild fowl?
Mal. That the soul of our grandam might haply inhabit a bird.
Clown. What thinkest thou of his opinion?
Mal. I think nobly of the soul, and no way approve his opinion.

Bensley, accordingly, threw over the part an air of Spanish loftiness. He looked, spake, and moved like an old Castilian. He was starch, spruce, opinionated, but his superstructure of pride seemed bottomed upon a sense of worth. There was something in it beyond the coxcomb. It was big and swelling, but you could not be sure that it was hollow. You might wish to see it taken down, but you felt that it was upon an elevation. He was magnificent from the outset; but when the decent sobrieties of the character began to give way, and the poison of self-love, in his conceit of the Countess's affection, gradually to work, you would have thought that the hero of La Mancha in person stood before you. How he went smiling to himself! With what ineffable carelessness would he twirl his gold chain! What a dream it was! You were infected with the illusion, and did not wish that it should be removed. You had no room for laughter. If an unseasonable reflection of morality obtruded itself, it was a deep sense of the pitiable infirmity of man's nature, that can lay him open to such frenzies; but, in truth, you rather admired than pitied the lunacy while it lasted; you felt that an hour of such mistake was worth an age with the eyes open. Who would not wish to live but for a day in the conceit of such a lady's love as Olivia? Why, the Duke would have given his principality but for a quarter of a minute, sleeping or waking, to have been so deluded. The man seemed to tread upon air, to taste manna, to walk with his head in the clouds, to mate Hyperion. O shake not the castles of his pride; endure yet for a season bright moments of confidence; "stand still, ye watches of the element," that Malvolio may be still in fancy fair Olivia's lord!—but

fate and retribution say " no." I hear the mischievous
titter of Maria—the witty taunts of Sir Toby—the
still more insupportable triumph of the foolish knight
—the counterfeit Sir Topas is unmasked—and " thus
the whirligig of time," as the true clown hath it,
" brings in his revenges." I confess that I never
saw the catastrophe of this character, while Bensley
played it, without a kind of tragic interest. There
vas good foolery too. Few now remember Dodd.
What an Aguecheek the stage lost in him ! Love-
grove, who came nearest to the old actors, revived
the character some few seasons ago, and made it
sufficiently grotesque ; but Dodd was *it*, as it came
out of Nature's hands. It might be said to remain
in puris naturalibus. In expressing slowness of
apprehension, this actor surpassed all others. You
could see the first dawn of an idea stealing slowly
over his countenance, climbing up by little and little,
with a painful process, till it cleared up at last to the
fulness of a twilight conception—its highest meridian.
He seemed to keep back his intellect, as some have
had the power to retard their pulsation. The balloon
takes less time in filling than it took to cover the
expansion of his broad moony face over all its quarters with expression. A glimmer of understanding
would appear in a corner of his eye, and for lack of
fuel go out again. A part of his forehead would
catch a little intelligence, and be a long time in com-
municating it to the remainder.

I am ill at dates, but I think it is now better than
five-and-twenty years ago, that walking in the gardens
of Gray's Inn,—they were then far finer than they are
now; the accursed Verulam Buildings had not en-
croached upon all the east side of them, cutting out

delicate green crankles, and shouldering away one of
two of the stately alcoves of the terrace—the survivor
stands gaping and relationless as if it remembered its
brother—they are still the best gardens of any of the
Inns of Court, my beloved Temple not forgotten—
have the gravest character; their aspect being altogether reverend and law-breathing; Bacon has left
the impress of his foot upon their gravel walks;—
taking my afternoon solace on a Summer day upon
the aforesaid terrace, a comely sad personage came
towards me, whom, from his grave air and deportment, I judged to be one of the old Benchers of the
Inn.   He had a serious, thoughtful forehead, and
seemed to be in meditations of mortality.   As I have
an instinctive awe of old Benchers, I was passing
him with that sort of sub-indicative token of respect
which one is apt to demonstrate towards a venerable
stranger, and which rather denotes an inclination to
greet him, than any positive motion of the body to
that effect, (a species of humility and will-worship
which I observe, nine times out of ten, rather puzzles
than pleases the person it is offered to,) when the
face, turning full upon me, strangely identified itself
with that of Dodd.   Upon close inspection I was not
mistaken.   But could this sad thoughtful countenance
be the same vacant face of folly which I had hailed
so often under circumstances of gaiety; which I had
never seen without a smile, or recognised but as the
usher of mirth; that looked out so formally flat in
Foppington, so frothily pert in Tattle, so impotently
busy in Backbite; so blankly divested of all meaning,
or resolutely expressive of none, in Acres, in Fribble,
and a thousand agreeable impertinences?   Was this
the face, full of thought and carefulness, that had so

often divested itself at will of every trace of either to
give me diversion, to clear my cloudy face for two or
three hours at least of its furrows ? Was this the
face—manly, sober, intelligent—which I had so often
despised, made mocks at, made merry with ? The
remembrance of the freedoms which I had taken with
it came upon me with a reproach of insult. I could
have asked it pardon. I thought it looked upon me
with a sense of injury. There is something strange
as well as sad in seeing actors, your pleasant fellows
particularly, subjected to and suffering the common
lot ; their fortunes, their casualties, their deaths,
seem to belong to the scene, their actions to be
amenable to poetic justice only. We can hardly connect them with more awful responsibilities. The
death of this fine actor took place shortly after this
meeting. He had quitted the stage some months ;
and, as I learned afterwards, had been in the habit of
resorting daily to these gardens, almost to the day of
his decease. In these serious walks, probably, he was
divesting himself of many scenic and some real
vanities—weaning himself from the frivolities of the
lesser and the greater theatre—doing gentle penance
for a life of no very reprehensible fooleries—taking
off by degrees the buffoon mask, which he might feel
he had worn too long—and rehearsing for a more
solemn cast of part. Dying, he " put on the weeds
of Dominic."[1]

---

[1] Dodd was a man of reading, and left at his death a choice collection of old English literature. I should judge him to have been a man
of wit.   I know one instance of an impromptu which no length of
study could have bettered.   My merry friend, Jem White, had seen
Dodd one evening in Aguecheek, and recognising him the next day in
Fleet Street, was irresistibly impelled to take off his hat and salute him
as the identical Knight of the preceding evening with a " Save you,

If few can remember Dodd, many yet living will not easily forget the pleasant creature who in those days enacted the part of the Clown to Dodd's Sir Andrew. Richard, or rather Dicky Suett—for so in his life-time he delighted to be called, and time hath ratified the appellation—lieth buried on the north side of the cemetery of Holy Paul, to whose service his nonage and tender years were dedicated. There are who do yet remember him at that period—his pipe clear and harmonious. He would often speak of his chorister days, when he was " cherub Dicky."

What clipped his wings, or made it expedient that he should exchange the holy for the profane state ; whether he had lost his good voice, (his best recommendation to that office,) like Sir John, " with hallooing and singing of anthems ; " or whether he was adjudged to lack something, even in those early years, of the gravity indispensable to an occupation which professeth to " commerce with the skies,"—I could never rightly learn ; but we find him, after the probation of a twelvemonth or so, reverting to a secular condition, and become one of us.

I think he was not altogether of that timber out of which cathedral seats and sounding-boards are hewed. But if a glad heart—kind, and therefore glad—be any part of sanctity, then might the robe of Motley, with which he invested himself with so much humility after his deprivation, and which he wore so long with so much blameless satisfaction to himself and to the public, be accepted for a surplice—his white stole, and *albe.*

Sir Andrew." Dodd, not at all disconcerted at this unusual address from a stranger, with a courteous half-rebuking wave of the hand, put him off with an " Away, *Fool !* "

The first-fruits of his secularisation was an engagement upon the boards of Old Drury, at which theatre
he commenced, as I have been told, with adopting the
manner of Parsons in old men's characters.   At the
period in which most of us knew him, he was no more
an imitator than he was in any true sense himself
imitable.

He was the Robin Goodfellow of the stage.   He
came in to trouble all things with a welcome perplexity, himself no whit troubled for the matter.   He
was known, like Puck, by his note—*Ha ! Ha ! Ha !*—
sometimes deepening to *Ho ! Ho ! Ho !* with an
irresistible accession, derived, perhaps, remotely from
his ecclesiastical education, foreign to his prototype
of—*O La !*   Thousands of hearts yet respond to the
chuckling *O La !* of Dickey Suett, brought back to
their remembrance by the faithful transcript of his
friend Mathew's mimicry.   The " force of nature
could no further go."   He drolled upon the stock of
these two syllables richer than the cuckoo.

Care, that troubles all the world, was forgotten in
his composition.   Had he had but two grains (nay,
half a grain) of it, he could never have supported
himself upon those two spider's strings, which served
him (in the latter part of his unmixed existence) as
legs.   A doubt or a scruple must have made him
totter, a sigh have puffed him down ; the weight of a
frown had staggered him, a wrinkle made him lose
his balance.   But on he went, scrambling upon those
airy stilts of his, with Robin Goodfellow, " through
brake, through briar," reckless of a scratched face or
a torn doublet.

Shakspeare foresaw him, when he framed his fools
and jesters.   They have all the true Suett stamp, a

loose and shambling gait, a slippery tongue, this last
the ready midwife to a without-pain-delivered jest; in
words, light as air, venting truths deep as the centre ;
with idlest rhymes tagging conceit when busiest,
singing with Lear in the tempest, or Sir Toby at the
buttery-hatch.

Jack Bannister and he had the fortune to be more
of personal favourites with the town than any actors
before or after.   The difference, I take it, was this :—
Jack was more *beloved* for his sweet, good-natured,
moral pretensions.   Dicky was more *liked* for his
sweet, good-natured, no pretensions at all.   Your
whole conscience stirred with Bannister's performance
of Walter in the *Children in the Wood ;* but Dicky
seemed like a thing, as Shakspeare says of Love, too
young to know what conscience is.   He put us into
Vesta's days.   Evil fled before him—not as from
Jack, as from an antagonist,—but because it could
not touch him, any more than a cannon ball a fly.
He was delivered from the burthen of that death ;
and, when Death came himself, not in metaphor, to
fetch Dicky, it is recorded of him by Robert Palmer,
who kindly watched his exit, that he received the last
stroke, neither varying his accustomed tranquillity,
nor tune, with the simple exclamation, worthy to have
been recorded in his epitaph—*O La ! O La ! Bobby !*

The elder Palmer (of stage-treading celebrity)
commonly played Sir Toby in those days ; but there
is a solidity of wit in the jests of that half-Falstaff
which he did not quite fill out.   He was as much too
showy as Moody (who sometimes took the part) was
dry and sottish.   In sock or buskin there was an air
of swaggering gentility about Jack Palmer.   He was
a *gentleman* with a slight infusion of *the footman*.

His brother Bob, (of recenter memory,) who was his
shadow in every thing while he lived, and dwindled
into less than a shadow afterwards, was a *gentleman*
with a little stronger infusion of the *latter ingredient ;*
that was all.   It is amazing how a little of the more
or less makes a difference in these things.   When you
saw Bobby in the Duke's Servant,[1] you said "What
a pity such a pretty fellow was only a servant !"
When you saw Jack figuring in Captain Absolute,
you thought you could trace his promotion to some
lady of quality who fancied the handsome fellow in
his topknot, and had bought him a commission.
Therefore Jack in Dick Amlet was insuperable.

Jack had two voices, both plausible, hypocritical,
and insinuating; but his secondary or supplemental
voice still more decisively histrionic than his common
one.   It was reserved for the spectator ; and the
dramatis personæ were supposed to know nothing at
all about it.   The *lies* of Young Wilding, and the
sentiments in Joseph Surface, were thus marked out
in a sort of italics to the audience.   This secret
correspondence with the company before the curtain
(which is the bane and death of tragedy) has an extremely happy effect in some kinds of comedy, in the
more highly artificial comedy of Congreve or of
Sheridan especially, where the absolute sense of
reality (so indispensable to scenes of interest) is not
required, or would rather interfere to diminish your
pleasure.   The fact is, you do not believe in such
characters as Surface—the villain of artificial
comedy—even while you read or see them.   If you
did, they would shock and not divert you.   When

---

[1] *High Life Below Stairs.*

Ben, in *Love for Love*, returns from sea, the following
exquisite dialogue occurs at his first meeting with his
father :—

Sir Sampson. Thou hast been many a weary league, Ben, since I
saw thee.

Ben. Ey, ey, been? Been far enough, and that be all. Well,
father, and how do all at home? how does brother Dick, and
brother Val?

Sir Sampson. Dick! body o' me, Dick has been dead these two
years. I writ you word when you were at Leghorn.

Ben. Mess, that's true : marry, I had forgot. Dick is dead, as
you say. Well, and how, I have a many questions to ask you.

Here is an instance of insensibility which in real
life would be revolting, or rather in real life could not
have co-existed with the warm-hearted temperament
of the character. But when you read it in the spirit
with which such playful selections and specious combinations rather than strict *metaphrases* of nature
should be taken, or when you saw Bannister play it,
it neither did, nor does, wound the moral sense at
all. For what is Ben—the pleasant sailor which
Bannister gives us—but a piece of satire—a creation
of Congreve's fancy—a dreamy combination of all the
accidents of a sailor's character—his contempt of
money—his credulity to women—with that necessary
enstrangement from home which it is just within the
verge of credibility to suppose *might* produce such an
hallucination as is here described. We never think
the worse of Ben for it, or feel it as a stain upon his
character. But when an actor comes, and instead of
the delightful phantom—the creature dear to half-
belief, which Bannister exhibited—displays before our
eyes a downright concretion of a Wapping sailor,
a jolly warm-hearted Jack Tar, and nothing else ;

when instead of investing it with a delicious con-
fusedness of the head, and a veering undirected
goodness of purpose, he gives to it a downright day-
light understanding, and a full consciousness of its
actions; thrusting forward the sensibilities of the
character with a pretence as if it stood upon nothing
else, and was to be judged by them alone—we feel
the discord of the thing; the scene is disturbed; a
real man has got in among the dramatis personæ,
and puts them out.   We want the sailor turned out.
We feel that his true place is not behind the curtain,
but in the first or second gallery.

ON THE ARTIFICIAL COMEDY OF THE
LAST CENTURY.

THE artificial Comedy, or Comedy of manners, is
quite extinct on our stage.   Congreve and Farquhar
show their heads once in seven years only, to be
exploded and put down instantly.   The times cannot
bear them.   Is it for a few wild speeches, an occasional licence of dialogue ?   I think not altogether.
The business of their dramatic characters will not
stand the moral test.   We screw every thing up to
that.   Idle gallantry in a fiction, a dream, the passing
pageant of an evening, startles us in the same way as
the alarming indications of profligacy in a son or
ward in real life should startle a parent or guardian.
We have no such middle emotions as dramatic
interests left.   We see a stage libertine playing his

loose pranks of two hours' duration, and of no after
consequence, with the severe eyes which inspect real
vices with their bearings upon two worlds.   We are
spectators to a plot or intrigue, (not reducible in life
to the point of strict morality,) and take it all for
truth.   We substitute a real for a dramatic person,
and judge him accordingly.   We try him in our
courts, from which there is no appeal to the *dramatis
personæ*, his peers.   We have been spoiled with—not
sentimental comedy—but a tyrant far more pernicious
to our pleasures which has succeeded to it, the
exclusive and all-devouring drama of common life ;
where the moral point is every thing ; where, instead
of the fictitious half-believed personages of the stage,
(the phantoms of old comedy,) we recognise ourselves, our brothers, aunts, kinsfolk, allies, patrons,
enemies,—the same as in life,—with an interest in
what is going on so hearty and substantial, that we
cannot afford our moral judgment, in its deepest and
most vital results, to compromise or slumber for a
moment.   What is *there* transacting, by no modifica-
tion is made to affect us in any other manner than the
same events or characters would do in our relationships of life.   We carry our fire-side concerns to the
theatre with us.   We do not go thither like our
ancestors, to escape from the pressure of reality, so
much as to confirm our experience of it; to make
assurance double, and take a bond of fate.   We must
live our toilsome lives twice over, as it was the
mournful privilege of Ulysses to descend twice to the
shades.   All that neutral ground of character, which
stood between vice and virtue ; or which in fact was
indifferent to neither, where neither properly was
called in question ; that happy breathing-place from

the burthen of a perpetual moral questioning—the sanctuary and quiet Alsatia of hunted casuistry—is broken up and disfranchised, as injurious to the interests of society. The privileges of the place are taken away by law. We dare not dally with images, or names, of wrong. We bark like foolish dogs at shadows. We dread infection from the scenic representation of disorder, and fear a painted pustule. In our anxiety that our morality should not take cold, we wrap it up in a great blanket surtout of precaution against the breeze and sunshine.

I confess for myself that (with no great delinquencies to answer for) I am glad for a season to take an airing beyond the diocese of the strict conscience,— not to live always in the precincts of the Law Courts,— but now and then, for a dream-while or so, to imagine a world with no meddling restrictions—to get into recesses, whither the hunter cannot follow me—

> —————Secret shades
> Of woody Ida's inmost grove,
> While yet there was no fear of Jove.

I come back to my cage and my restraint the fresher and more healthy for it. I wear my shackles more contentedly for having respired the breath of an imaginary freedom. I do not know how it is with others, but I feel the better always for the perusal of one of Congreve's—nay, why should I not add even of Wycherley's—comedies. I am the gayer at least for it; and I could never connect those sports of a witty fancy in any shape with any result to be drawn from them to imitation in real life. They are a world of themselves almost as much as fairy-land. Take one of their characters, male or female, (with few

exceptions they are alike,) and place it in a modern
play, and my virtuous indignation shall rise against
the profligate wretch as warmly as the Catos of the
pit could desire ; because in a modern play I am to
judge of the right and the wrong. The standard of
police is the measure of *political justice.* The
atmosphere will blight it ; it cannot live here. It has
got into a moral world, where it has no business,
from which it must needs fall headlong ; as dizzy,
and incapable of making a stand, as a Swedenborgian
bad spirit that has wandered unawares into the sphere
of one of his Good Men, or Angels. But in its own
world do we feel the creature is so very bad ?—The
Fainalls and the Mirabels, the Dorimants and the
Lady Touchwoods, in their own sphere, do not offend
my moral sense ; in fact they do not appeal to it at
all. They seem engaged in their proper element.
They break through no laws, or conscientious
restraints. They know of none. They have got out
of Christendom into the land—what shall I call it ?—
of cuckoldry—the Utopia of gallantry, where pleasure
is duty, and the manners perfect freedom. It is altogether a speculative scene of things, which has no
reference whatever to the world that is. No good
person can be justly offended as a spectator, because
no good person suffers on the stage. Judged morally,
every character in these plays—the few exceptions
only are *mistakes*—is alike essentially vain and worth-
less. The great art of Congreve is especially shown
in this, that he has entirely excluded from his scenes
(some little generosities in the part of Angelica
perhaps excepted) not only any thing like a faultless
character, but any pretensions to goodness or good
feelings whatsoever. Whether he did this designedly,

or instinctively, the effect is as happy as the design (if design) was bold.   I used to wonder at the strange power which his Way of the World in particular possesses of interesting you all along in the pursuits of characters, for whom you absolutely care nothing—for you neither hate nor love his personages—and I think it is owing to this very indifference for any that you endure the whole.   He has spread a privation of moral light, I will call it, rather than by the ugly name of palpable darkness, over his creations ; and his shadows flit before you without distinction or preference.   Had he introduced a good character, a single gush of moral feeling, a revulsion of the judgment to actual life and actual duties, the impertinent Goshen would have only lighted to the discovery of deformities, which now are none, because we think them none.

Translated into real life, the characters of his and his friend Wycherley's dramas are profligates and strumpets,—the business of their brief existence, the undivided pursuit of lawless gallantry.   No other spring of action, or possible motive of conduct, is recognised ; principles which, universally acted upon, must reduce this frame of things to a chaos.   But we do them wrong in so translating them.   No such effects are produced, in *their* world.   When we are among them, we are amongst a chaotic people.   We are not to judge them by our usages.   No reverend institutions are insulted by their proceedings, for they have none among them.   No peace of families is violated, for no family ties exist among them.   No purity of the marriage bed is stained, for none is supposed to have a being.   No deep affections are disquieted, no holy wedlock bands are snapped asunder, for affection's depth and wedded faith are not of the growth of that soil. There is neither right nor wrong, gratitude or its opposite, claim or duty, paternity or sonship. Of what consequence is it to Virtue, or how is she at all concerned about it, whether Sir Simon or Dapperwit steals away Miss Martha ; or who is the father of Lord Froth's or Sir Paul Pliant's children ?

The whole is a passing pageant, where we should sit as unconcerned at the issues, for life or death, as at a battle of the frogs and mice. But, like Don Quixote, we take part against the puppets, and quite as impertinently. We dare not contemplate an Atlantis, a scheme out of which our coxcombical moral sense is for a little transitory ease excluded. We have not the courage to imagine a state of things for which there is neither reward nor punishment. We cling to the painful necessities of shame and blame. We would indict our very dreams.

Amidst the mortifying circumstances attendant upon growing old, it is something to have seen the *School for Scandal* in its glory. This comedy grew out of Congreve and Whycherley, but gathered some allays of the sentimental comedy which follow theirs. It is impossible that it should be now *acted*, though it continues, at long intervals, to be announced in the bills. Its hero, when Palmer played it at least, was Joseph Surface. When I remember the gay boldness, the graceful solemn plausibility, the measured step, the insinuating voice, (to express it in a word,) the downright *acted* villany of the part, so different from the pressure of conscious actual wickedness, the hypocritical assumption of hypocrisy, which made Jack so deservedly a favourite in that

character, I must needs conclude the present generation of playgoers more virtuous than myself, or more
dense. I freely confess that he divided the palm with
me with his better brother; that, in fact, I like him
quite as well. Not but there are passages, like that,
for instance, where Joseph is made to refuse a pittance
to a poor relation,—incongruities which Sheridan
was forced upon by the attempt to join the artificial
with the sentimental comedy, either of which must
destroy the other: but over these obstructions Jack's
manner floated him so lightly, that a refusal from him
no more shocked you, than the easy compliance of
Charles gave you in reality any pleasure; you got
over the paltry question as quickly as you could, to
get back into the regions of pure comedy, where no
cold moral reigns. The highly artificial manner of
Palmer in this character counteracted every disagreeable impression which you might have received from
the contrast, supposing them real, between the two
brothers. You did not believe in Joseph with the
same faith with which you believed in Charles. The
latter was a pleasant reality, the former a no less
pleasant poetical foil to it. The comedy, I have said,
is incongruous; a mixture of Congreve with sentimental incompatibilities; the gaiety upon the whole
is buoyant; but it required the consummate art of
Palmer to reconcile the discordant elements.

A player with Jack's talents, if we had one now,
would not dare to do the part in the same manner.
He would instinctively avoid every turn which might
tend to unrealise, and so to make the character fas-
cinating. He must take his cue from his spectators,
who would expect a bad man and a good man as
rigidly opposed to each other as the death-beds of

those geniuses are contrasted in the prints, which 1
am sorry to say have disappeared from the windows
of my old friend Carrington Bowles, of St. Paul's
Churchyard memory—(an exhibition as venerable
as the adjacent cathedral, and almost coeval)
of the bad and good man at the hour of death,
where the ghastly apprehensions of the former, and
truly the grim phantom with his reality of a toasting-
fork is not to be despised, so finely contrast with the
meek complacent kissing of the rod,—taking it in
like honey and butter,—with which the latter submits
to the scythe of the gentle bleeder Time, who wields
his lancet with the apprehensive finger of a popular
young ladies' surgeon. What flesh, like loving grass,
would not covet to meet half-way the stroke of such
a delicate mower? John Palmer was twice an actor
in this exquisite part. He was playing to you all
the while that he was playing upon Sir Peter and his
lady. You had the first intimation of a sentiment
before it was on his lips. His altered voice was
meant for you, and you were to suppose that his
fictitious co-flutterers on the stage perceived nothing
at all of it. What was it to you if that half reality,
the husband, was over-reached by the puppetry, or
the thin thing (Lady Teazle's reputation) was persuaded it was dying of a plethory? The fortunes of
Othello and Desdemona were not concerned in it.
Poor Jack has passed from the stage in good time,
that he did not live to this our age of seriousness.
The pleasant old Teazle *King*, too, is gone in good
time. His manner would scarce have passed current
in our day. We must love or hate, acquit or condemn, censure or pity, exert our detestable coxcombry
of moral judgment upon every thing. Joseph Surface,

to go down now, must be a downright revolting villain—no compromise; his first appearance must shock and give horror; his specious plausibilities, which the pleasurable faculties of our fathers welcomed with such hearty geetings, knowing that no harm (dramatic harm even) could come, or was meant to come of them, must inspire a cold and killing aversion. Charles, the real canting person of the scene, (for the hypocrisy of Joseph has its ulterior legitimate ends, but his brother's professions of a good heart centre in downright self-satisfaction,) must be *loved*, and Joseph *hated*. To balance one disagreeable reality with another, Sir Peter Teazle must be no longer the comic idea of a fretful old bachelor bridegroom, whose teasings (while King acted it) were evidently as much played off at you as they were meant to concern any body on the stage,—he must be a real person, capable in law of sustaining an injury—a person towards whom duties are to be acknowledged—the genuine crim. con. antagonist of the villanous seducer Joseph. To realise him more, his sufferings under his unfortunate match must have the downright pungency of life—must (or should) make you not mirthful but uncomfortable, just as the same predicament would move you in a neighbour or old friend. The delicious scenes which give the play its name and zest, must affect you in the same serious manner as if you heard the reputation of a dear female friend attacked in your real presence. Crabtree and Sir Benjamin—those poor snakes that live but in the sunshine of your mirth—must be ripened by this hot-bed process of realisation into asps or amphisbænas; and Mrs. Candour (O frightful!) become a hooded serpent. Oh! who that remembers Parsons

and Dodd—the wasp and butterfly of the School
for Scandal—in those two characters, and charming
natural Miss Pope, the perfect gentlewoman as distinguished from the fine lady of comedy, in this latter
part, would forego the true scenic delight, the escape
from life, the oblivion of consequences, the holiday
barring out of the pedant Reflection, those Satur-
nalia of two or three brief hours, well won from the
world, to sit instead at one of our modern plays, to
have his coward conscience (that forsooth must not
be left for a moment) stimulated with perpetual
appeals, dulled rather, and blunted, as a faculty without repose must be, and his moral vanity pampered
with images of notional justice, notional beneficence,
lives saved without the spectator's risk, and fortunes
given away that cost the author nothing?

No piece was perhaps ever so completely cast in
all its parts as this *manager's comedy*. Miss Farren
had succeeded to Mrs. Abington in Lady Teazle;
and Smith, the original Charles, had retired when I
first saw it. The rest of the characters, with very
slight exceptions, remained. I remember it was then
the fashion to cry down John Kemble, who took the
part of Charles after Smith, but I thought very
unjustly. Smith I fancy was more airy, and took
the eye with a certain gaiety of person. He brought
with him no sombre recollections of tragedy. He
had not to expiate the fault of having pleased beforehand in lofty declamation. He had no sins of
Hamlet or of Richard to atone for. His failure in
these parts was a passport to success in one of so
opposite a tendency. But, as far as I could judge,
the weighty sense of Kemble made up for more
personal incapacity than he had to answer for. His

harshest tones in this part came steeped and dulcified in good-humour. He made his defects a grace. His exact declamatory manner, as he managed it, only served to convey the points of his dialogue with more precision. It seemed to head the shafts to carry them deeper. Not one of his sparkling sentences was lost. I remember minutely how he delivered each in succession, and cannot by any effort imagine how any of them could be altered for the better. No man could deliver brilliant dialogue, the dialogue of Congreve or of Wycherley, because none understood it half so well as John Kemble. His Valentine, in *Love for Love*, was, to my recollection, faultless. He flagged sometimes in the intervals of tragic passion. He would slumber over the level parts of an heroic character. His Macbeth had been known to nod. But he always seemed to me to be particularly alive to pointed and witty dialogue. The relaxing levities of tragedy had not been touched by any since him; the playful court-bred spirit in which he condescended to the players in Hamlet—the sportive relief which he threw into the darker shades of Richard, dis-appeared with him. He had his sluggish moods, his torpors, but they were the halting-stones and resting-place of his tragedy—politic savings, and fetches of the breath—husbandry of the lungs, where Nature pointed him to be an economist, rather, I think, than errors of the judgment. They were, at worst, less painful than the eternal tormenting un-appeasable vigilance, the "lidless dragon eyes," of present fashionable tragedy.

ON THE ACTING OF MUNDEN.

Not many nights ago I had come home from seeing this extraordinary performer in *Cockletop;* and when I retired to my pillow his whimsical image still stuck by me in a manner as to threaten sleep. In vain I tried to divest myself of it, by conjuring up the most opposite associations. I resolved to be serious. I raised up the gravest topics of life; private misery, public calamity. All would not do:

——There the antic sate
Mocking our state——

his queer visnomy, his bewildering costume, all the strange things which he had raked together, his serpentine rod swagging about in his pocket, Cleopatra's tear, and the rest of his relics, O'Keefe's wild farce, and *his* wilder commentary, till the passion of laughter, like grief in excess, relieved itself by its own weight, inviting the sleep which in the first instance it had driven away.

But I was not to escape so easily. No sooner did I fall into slumbers, than the same image, only more perplexing, assailed me in the shape of dreams. Not one Munden, but five hundred, were dancing before me, like the faces which, whether you will or no, come when you have been taking opium—all the strange

Dawsons.Ph.-Sc.

Munden
With M.ʳˢ Orger, Miss Cubitt & M.ʳ Knight.
in Lock & Key.
From an engraving by Thos. Lupton,
after G. Clint A.R.A.

combinations, which this strangest of all strange mortals ever shot his proper countenance into, from the day he came commissioned to dry up the tears of the town for the loss of the now almost forgotten Edwin. Oh for the power of the pencil to have fixed them when I awoke! A season or two since, there was exhibited a Hogarth gallery. I do not see why there should not be a Munden Gallery. In richness and variety, the latter would not fall far short of the former.

There is one face of Farley, one face of Knight, one (but what a one it is!) of Liston; but Munden has none that you can properly pin down and call *his.* When you think he has exhausted his battery of looks, in unaccountable warfare with your gravity, suddenly he sprouts out an entirely new set of features, like Hydra. He is not one, but legion; not so much a comedian as a company. If his name could be multiplied like his countenance, it might fill a play-bill. He, and he alone, literally *makes faces:* applied to any other person, the phrase is a mere figure, denoting certain modifications of the human countenance. Out of some invisible wardrobe he dips for faces, as his friend Suett used for wigs, and fetches them out as easily. I should not be surprised to see him some day put out the head of a river-horse; or come forth a pewitt, or lapwing, some feathered metamorphosis.

I have seen this gifted actor in Sir Christopher Curry, in old Dornton, diffuse a glow of sentiment which has made the pulse of a crowded theatre beat like that of one man, when he has come in aid of the pulpit, doing good to the moral heart of a people. I have seen some faint approaches to this sort of excellence in other players. But in the grand grotesque of farce, Munden stands out as single and unaccompanied as Hogarth. Hogarth, strange to tell, had no followers. The school of Munden began, and must end, with himself.

Can any man *wonder* like he does? can any man *see ghosts* like he does? or *fight with his own shadow,* "SESSA," as he does in that strangely-neglected thing, *the Cobbler of Preston,* where his alterations from the Cobbler to the Magnifico, and from the Magnifico to the Cobbler, keep the brain of the spectator in as wild a ferment, as if some Arabian Night were being acted before him? Who like him can throw, or ever attempted to throw, a preternatural interest over the commonest daily life objects? A table or a joint stool, in his conception, rises into a dignity equivalent to Cassiopeia's chair. It is invested with constellatory importance. You could not speak of it with more deference, if it were mounted into the firmament. A beggar in the hands of Michael Angelo, says Fuseli, rose the Patriarch of Poverty. So the gusto of Munden antiquates and ennobles what it touches. His pots and his ladles are as grand and primal as the seething-pots and hooks seen in old prophetic vision. A tub of butter, contemplated by him, amounts to a Platonic idea. He understands a leg of mutton in its quiddity. He stands wondering, amid the common-place materials of life, like primæval man with the sun and stars about him.

THE LAST

ESSAYS OF ELIA.

BEING A SEQUEL TO ESSAYS PUBLISHED UNDER

THAT NAME.

PREFACE.

BY A FRIEND OF THE LATE ELIA.

———

THIS poor gentleman, who for some months past had been in a declining way, hath at length paid his final tribute to nature.

To say truth, it is time he were gone. The humour of the thing, if there was ever much in it, was pretty well exhausted: and a two years' and a half existence has been a tolerable duration for a phantom.

I am now at liberty to confess, that much which I have heard objected to my late friend's writings was well-founded. Crude they are, I grant you—a sort of unlicked, incondite things—villanously pranked in an affected array of antique modes and phrases. They had not been *his*, if they had been other than such; and better it is, that a writer should be natural in a self-pleasing quaintness, than to affect a naturalness (so called) that should be strange to him. Egotistical they have been pronounced by some who did not know, that what he tells us, as of himself, was often true only (historically) of another; as in a former Essay (to save many instances)—where under the *first person* (his favourite figure) he shadows forth

the forlorn estate of a country-boy placed at a London
school, far from his friends and connexions—in direct
opposition to his own early history. If it be egotism
to imply and twine with his own identity the griefs
and affections of another—making himself many, or
reducing many unto himself—then is the skilful
novelist, who all along brings in his hero, or heroine,
speaking of themselves, the greatest egotist of all;
who yet has never, therefore, been accused of that
narrowness. And how shall the intenser dramatist
escape being faulty, who doubtless, under cover of
passion uttered by another, oftentimes give blameless
vent to his most inward feelings, and expresses his
own story modestly?

My late friend was in many respects a singular
character. Those who did not like him, hated him;
and some, who once liked him, afterwards became
his bitterest haters. The truth is, he gave himself
too little concern what he uttered, and in whose
presence. He observed neither time nor place, and
would e'en out with what came uppermost. With
the severe religionists he would pass for a free-
thinker; while the other faction set him down for a
bigot, or persuaded themselves that he belied his sentiments. Few understood him; and I am not certain
that at all times he quite understood himself. He
too much affected that dangerous figure—irony. He
sowed doubtful speeches, and reaped plain, un-
equivocal hatred. He would interrupt the gravest
discussion with some light jest; and yet, perhaps,
not quite irrelevant in ears that could understand it.
Your long and much talkers hated him. The in-
formal habit of his mind, joined to an inveterate im-
pediment of speech, forbade him to be an orator;

and he seemed determined that no one else should play that part when he was present. He was *petit* and ordinary in his person and appearance. I have seen him sometimes in what is called good company, but where he has been a stranger, sit silent, and be suspected for an odd fellow; till some unlucky occasion provoking it, he would stutter our some senseless pun (not altogether senseless perhaps, if rightly taken), which has stamped his character for the evening. It was hit or miss with him; but nine times out of ten, he contrived by this device to send away a whole company his enemies. His conceptions rose kindlier than his utterance, and his happiest *impromptus* had the appearance of effort. He has been accused of trying to be witty, when in truth he was but struggling to give his poor thoughts articulation. He chose his companions for some individuality of character which they manifested.—Hence, not many persons of science, and few professed *literati*, were of his councils. They were, for the most part, persons of an uncertain fortune; and, as to such people commonly nothing is more obnoxious than a gentleman of settled (though moderate) income, he passed with most of them for a great miser. To my knowledge this was a mistake. His *intimados*, to confess a truth, were in the world's eye a ragged regiment. He found them floating on the surface of society; and the colour, or something else, in the weed pleased him. The burrs stuck to him—but they were good and loving burrs for all that. He never greatly cared for the society of what are called good people. If any of these were scandalised (and offences were sure to arise), he could not help it. When he has been remonstrated with for not making

more concessions to the feelings of good people, he
would retort by asking, what one point did these
good people ever concede to him? He was temperate in his meals and diversions, but always kept
a little on this side of abstemiousness. Only in the
use of the Indian weed he might be thought a little
excessive. He took it, he would say, as a solvent of
speech. Marry—as the friendly vapour ascended,
how his prattle would curl up sometimes with it! the
ligaments, which tongue-tied him, were loosened,
and the stammerer proceeded a statist!

I do not know whether I ought to bemoan or rejoice that my old friend is departed. His jests were
beginning to grow obsolete, and his stories to be
found out. He felt the approaches of age; and
while he pretended to cling to life, you saw how
slender were the ties left to bind him. Discoursing
with him latterly on this subject, he expressed
himself with a pettishness which I thought unworthy of him. In our walks about his suburban
retreat, as he called it, at Shacklewell, some children belonging to a school of industry had met
us, and bowed and curtseyed to us, as he thought,
in an especial manner to *him*. "They take me for
a visiting governor," he muttered earnestly. He
had a horror, which he carried to a foible, of looking
like anything important and parochial. He thought
that he approached nearer to that stamp daily. He
had a general aversion from being treated like a
grave or respectable character, and kept a wary eye
upon the advances of age that should so entitle him.
He herded always, while it was possible, with people
younger than himself. He did not conform to the
march of time, but was dragged along in the proces-

sion. His manners lagged behind his years. He was too much of the boy-man. The *toga virilis* never sate gracefully on his shoulders. The impressions of infancy had burnt into him, and he resented the impertinence of manhood. These were weaknesses ; but such as they were, they are a key to explicate some of his writings.

ESSAYS OF ELIA.

BLAKESMOOR IN H———SHIRE.

I DO not know a pleasure more affecting than to
range at will over the deserted apartments of some
fine old family mansion.   The traces of extinct
grandeur admit of a better passion than envy : and
contemplations on the great and good, whom we
fancy in succession to have been its inhabitants,
weave for us illusions, incompatible with the bustle
of modern occupancy, and vanities of foolish present
aristocracy.   The same difference of feeling, I think,
attends us between entering an empty and a crowded
church.   In the latter it is chance but some present
human frailty—an act of inattention on the part of
some of the auditory, or a trait of affectation, or worse,
vainglory on that of the preacher—puts us by our
best thoughts, disharmonizing the place and the
occasion.   But wouldst thou know the beauty of
holiness, go alone on some week-day, borrowing the

keys of good Master Sexton, traverse the cool aisles of some country church, think of the piety that has kneeled there—the congregations, old and young, that have found consolation there—the meek pastor— the docile parishioner.   With no disturbing emotions, no cross conflicting comparisons, drink in the tranquillity of the place, till thou thyself become as fixed and motionless as the marble effigies that kneel and weep around thee.

Journeying northward lately, I could not resist going some few miles out of my road to look upon the remains of an old great house with which I had been impressed in this way in infancy.   I was apprised that the owner of it had lately pulled it down : still I had a vague notion that it could not all have perished, that so much solidity with magnificence could not have been crushed all at once into the mere dust and rubbish which I found it.

The work of ruin had proceeded with a swift hand indeed, and the demolition of a few weeks had reduced it to an antiquity.

I was astonished at the indistinction of every thing. Where had stood the great gates ?   What bounded the court-yard ?   Whereabout did the out-houses commence ?   A few bricks only lay as representatives of that which was so stately and so spacious.

Death does not shrink up his human victim at this rate.   The burnt ashes of a man weigh more in their proportion.

Had I seen these brick-and-mortar knaves at their process of destruction, at the plucking of every panel I should have felt the varlets at my heart.   I should have cried out to them to spare a plank at least out of

the cheerful store-room, in whose hot window-seat I
used to sit and read Cowley, with the grass-plot
before, and the hum and flappings of that one solitary
wasp that ever haunted it about me : it is in mine
ears now, as oft as Summer returns ; or a panel of
the yellow room.

Why, every plank and panel of that house for me
had magic in it. The tapestried bed-rooms—tapestry
so much better than painting—not adorning merely,
but peopling the wainscots—at which childhood ever
and anon would steal a look, shifting its coverlid
(replaced as quickly) to exercise its tender courage in
a momentary eye-encounter with those stern bright
visages, staring reciprocally—all Ovid on the walls,
in colours vivider than his descriptions : Actæon in
mid sprout, with the unappeasable prudery of Diana ;
and the still more provoking, and almost culinary
coolness of Dan Phœbus, eel-fashion, deliberately
divesting of Marsyas.

Then, that haunted room, in which old Mrs. Battle
died, whereinto I have crept, but always in the day-
time, with a passion of fear, and a sneaking curiosity,
terror-tainted, to hold communication with the past :
How shall they build it up again ?

It was an old deserted place, yet not so long
deserted but that traces of the splendour of past
inmates were everywhere apparent. Its furniture
was still standing, even to the tarnished gilt leather
battledores, and crumbling feathers of shuttlecocks in
the nursery, which told that children had once played
there. But I was a lonely child, and had the range
at will of every apartment, knew every nook and
corner, wondered and worshipped everywhere.

The solitude of childhood is not so much the

mother of thought as it is the feeder of love, and
silence, and admiration.   So strange a passion for
the place possessed me in those years, that, though
there lay (I shame to say how few roods distant from
the mansion) half hid by trees what I judged some
romantic lake, such was the spell which bound me to
the house, and such my carefulness not to pass its
strict and proper precincts, that the idle waters lay
unexplored for me ; and not till late in life, curiosity
prevailing over elder devotion, I found, to my
astonishment, a pretty brawling brook had been the
Lacus Incognitus of my infancy. Variegated views,
extensive prospects, and those at no great distance
from the house, (I was told of such,) what were they to
me, being out of the boundaries of my Eden ? So far
from a wish to roam, I would have drawn, methought,
still closer the fences of my chosen prison ; and have
been hemmed in by a yet securer cincture of those
excluding garden walls.   I could have exclaimed with
that garden-loving poet—

> Bind me, ye woodbines, in your twines
> Curl me about, ye gadding vines ;
> And oh so close your circles lace,
> That I may never leave this place
> But, lest your fetters prove too weak,
> Ere I your silken bondage break,
> Do you, O brambles, chain me too,
> And, courteous briars, nail me through.

I was here as in a holy temple. Snug fire-sides—
the low-built roof—parlours ten feet by ten—frugal
boards, and all the homeliness of home—these were
the condition of my birth, the wholesome soil which
I was planted in.   Yet, without impeachment to their
tenderest lessons, I am not sorry to have had glances

of something beyond; and to have taken, if but a
peep, in childhood, at the contrasting accidents of a
great fortune.

To have the feeling of gentility, it is not necessary
to have been born gentle. The pride of ancestry may
be had on cheaper terms than to be obliged to an
importunate race of ancestors; and the coatless
antiquary in his unemblazoned cell, revolving the
long line of a Mowbray's or De Clifford's pedigree, at
those sounding names may warm himself into as gay
a vanity as these who do inherit them. The claims
of birth are ideal merely; and what herald shall go
about to strip me of an idea? Is it trenchant to
their swords? Can it be hacked off as a spur can? or
torn away like a tarnished garter?

What else were the families of the great to us?
What pleasure should we take in their tedious genea-
logies, or their capitulatory brass monuments? What
to us the uninterrupted current of their bloods, if our
own did not answer within us to a cognate and
correspondent elevation?

Or wherefore else, O tattered and diminished
'Scutcheon that hung upon the time-worn walls of
thy princely stairs, BLAKESMOOR, have I in childhood
so oft stood poring upon the mystic characters—thy
emblematic supporters, with their prophetic " Resur-
gam"—till, every dreg of peasantry purging off, I
received into myself Very Gentility? Thou wert
first in my mourning eyes; and of nights hast detained
my steps from bedward, till it was but a step from
gazing at thee to dreaming on thee.

This is the only true gentry by adoption; the
veritable change of blood, and not, as empirics have
fabled, by transfusion.

2 C 2

Who it was by dying that had earned the splendid trophy, I know not, I inquired not ; but its fading rags, and colours cobweb-stained, told that its subject was of two centuries back.

And what if my ancestor at that date was some Damœtas, feeding flocks, not his own, upon the hills of Lincoln,—did I in less earnest vindicate to myself the family trappings of this once proud Ægon ? repaying by a backward triumph the insults he might possibly have heaped in his life-time upon my poor pastoral progenitor.

If it were presumption so to speculate, the present owners of the mansion had least reason to complain. They had long forsaken the old house of their fathers for a newer trifle ; and I was left to appropriate to myself what images I could pick up, to raise my fancy or to soothe my vanity.

I was the true descendant of those old W——s, and not of the present family of that name, who had fled the old waste places.

Mine was that gallery of good old family portraits, which as I have gone over, giving them in fancy my own family name, one—and then another—would seem to smile, reaching forward from the canvas, to recognise the new relationship ; while the rest looked grave, as it seemed, at the vacancy in their dwelling, and thoughts of fled posterity.

The Beauty with the cool blue pastoral drapery, and a lamb, that hung next the great bay window, with the bright yellow H——shire hair, and eye of watchet hue, (so like my Alice !) I am persuaded she was a true Elia—Mildred Elia, I take it.

Mine, too, BLAKESMOOR, was thy noble Marble Hall, with its mosaic pavements, and its Twelve

Cæsars—stately busts in marble—ranged round ; of whose countenances, young reader of faces as I was, the frowning beauty of Nero, I remember, had most of my wonder : but the mild Galba had my love. There they stood in the coldness of death, yet freshness of immortality.

Mine, too, thy lofty Justice Hall, with its one chair of authority, high-backed and wickered, once the terror of luckless poacher or self-forgetful maiden ; so common since, that bats have roosted in it.

Mine, too,—whose else ?—thy costly fruit-garden, with its sun-baked southern wall ; the ampler pleasure-garden, rising backwards from the house in triple terraces, with flower-pots now of palest lead, save that a speck here and there, saved from the elements, bespake their pristine state to have been gilt and glittering ; the verdant quarters backwarder still ; and stretching still beyond, in old formality, thy firry wilderness, the haunt of the squirrel, and the day-long murmuring wood-pigeon, with that antique image in the centre, God or Goddess I wist not : but child of Athens or old Rome paid never a sincerer worship to Pan or to Sylvanus in their native groves, than I to that fragmental mystery.

Was it for this that I kissed my childish hands too fervently in your idol-worship, walks and windings of BLAKESMOOR ! For this, or what sin of mine, has the plough passed over your pleasant places ? I sometimes think that as men, when they die, do not die all, so of their extinguished habitations there may be a hope—a germ to be revivified.

POOR RELATIONS.

——

A Poor Relation is the most irrelevant thing in nature,—a piece of impertinent correspondency,—an odious approximation,—a haunting conscience,—a preposterous shadow, lengthening in the noon-tide of our prosperity,—an unwelcome remembrancer,—a perpetually recurring mortification,—a drain on your purse, a more intolerable dun upon your pride,—a drawback upon success,—a rebuke to your rising,—a stain in your blood,—a blot on your 'scutcheon,—a rent in your garment,—a death's-head at your banquet,—Agathocles's pot,—a Mordecai in your gate, a Lazarus at your door,—a lion in your path,—a frog in your chamber,—a fly in your ointment,—a mote in your eye,—a triumph to your enemy, an apology to your friends,—the one thing not needful,—the hail in harvest,—the ounce of sour in a pound of sweet.

He is known by his knock. Your heart telleth you "That is Mr. ——." A rap between familiarity and respect, that demands, and at the same time seems to despair of, entertainment. He entereth smiling and embarrassed. He holdeth out his hand to you to shake, and draweth it back again. He casually looketh in about dinner time, when the table is full.

He offereth to go away, seeing you have company, but is induced to stay. He filleth a chair, and your visitor's two children are accommodated at a side-table. He never cometh upon open days, when your wife says, with some complacency, "My dear, perhaps Mr. —— will drop in to-day." He remembereth birth-days, and professeth he is fortunate to have stumbled upon one. He declareth against fish, the turbot being small, yet suffereth himself to be importuned into a slice, against his first resolution. He sticketh by the port, yet will be prevailed upon to empty the remainder glass of claret, if a stranger press it upon him. He is a puzzle to the servants, who are fearful of being too obsequious or not civil enough to him. The guests think "they have seen him before." Every one speculateth upon his condition ; and the most part take him to be a tide-waiter. He calleth you by your Christian name, to imply that his other is the same with your own. He is too familiar by half, yet you wish he had less diffidence. With half the familiarity, he might pass for a casual dependant ; with more boldness, he would be in no danger of being taken for what he is. He is too humble for a friend ; yet taketh on him more state than befits a client. He is a worse guest than a country tenant, inasmuch as he bringeth up no rent ; yet 'tis odds, from his garb and demeanour, that your guests take him for one. He is asked to make one at the whist table ; he refuseth on the score of poverty, and resents being left out. When the company break up, he proffereth to go for a coach, and lets the servant go. He recollects your grandfather ; and will thrust in some mean and quite unimportant anecdote of the family. He knew it when it was not quite so

flourishing as "he is blest in seeing it now." He
reviveth past situations, to institute what he calleth
"favourable comparisons." With a reflecting sort of
congratulation he will inquire the price of your furniture, and insults you with a special commendation of
your window-curtains. He is of opinion that the urn
is the more elegant shape; but, after all, there was
something more comfortable about the old tea-kettle,
which you must remember. He dares say you must
find a great convenience in having a carriage of your
own, and appealeth to your lady if it is not so. He
inquireth if you have had your arms done on vellum
yet; and did not know, till lately, that such-and-such
had been the crest of the family. His memory is unseasonable; his compliments are perverse; his talk
is a trouble; his stay pertinacious; and when he
goeth away, you dismiss his chair into a corner, as
precipitately as possible, and feel fairly rid of two
nuisances.

There is a worse evil under the sun, and that is a
female Poor Relation. You may do something with
the other; you may pass him off tolerably well; but
your indigent she-relative is hopeless. "He is an
old humourist," you may say, "and affects to go
threadbare. His circumstances are better than folks
would take them to be. You are fond of having a
Character at your table, and truly he is one." But in
the indications of female poverty there can be no
disguise. No woman dresses below herself from
caprice. The truth must out without shuffling. "She
is plainly related to the L——s; or what does she at
their house?" She is, in all probability, your wife's
cousin. Nine times out of ten, at least, this is the
case. Her garb is something between a gentle-

woman's and a beggar's, yet the former evidently predominates. She is most provokingly humble, and ostentatiously sensible to her inferiority. He may require to be repressed sometimes—*aliquando sufflaminandus erat*—but there is no raising her. You send her soup at dinner, and she begs to be helped after the gentlemen. Mr. —— requests the honour of taking wine with her; she hesitates between Port and Madeira, and chooses the former, because he does. She calls the servant *Sir;* and insists on not troubling him to hold her plate. The housekeeper patronizes her. The children's governess takes upon her to correct her when she has mistaken the piano for a harpsichord.

Richard Amlet, Esq., in the play, is a notable instance of the disadvantages to which this chimerical notion of *affinity constituting a claim to acquaintance,* may subject the spirit of a gentleman. A little foolish blood is all that is betwixt him and a lady with a great estate. His stars are perpetually crossed by the malignant maternity of an old woman, who persists in calling him "her son Dick." But she has wherewithal in the end to recompense his indignities, and float him again upon the brilliant surface, under which it had been her seeming business and pleasure all along to sink him. All men, besides, are not of Dick's temperament. I knew an Amlet in real life, who, wanting Dick's buoyancy, sank indeed. Poor W—— [Favell] was of my own standing at Christ's, a fine classic, and a youth of promise. If he had a blemish, it was too much pride; but its quality was inoffensive; it was not of that sort which hardens the heart, and serves to keep inferiors at a distance; it only sought to ward off derogation from itself. It was the principle of self-respect carried as far as it could go, without infringing upon that respect which he would have every one else equally maintain for himself. He would have you to think alike with him on this topic. Many a quarrel have I had with him, when we were rather older boys, and our tallness made us much more obnoxious to observation in the blue clothes, because I would not thread the alleys and blind ways of the town with him to elude notice, when we have been out together on a holiday in the streets of this sneering and prying metropolis. W—— went, sore with these notions, to Oxford, where the dignity and sweetness of a scholar's life, meeting with the alloy of an humble introduction, wrought in him a passionate devotion to the place, with a profound aversion from the society. The servitor's gown (worse than his school array) clung to him with Nessian venom. He thought himself ridiculous in a garb under which Latimer must have walked erect, and in which Hooker, in his young days, possibly flaunted in a vein of no discommendable vanity. In the depth of college shades, or in his lonely chamber, the poor student shrunk from observation. He found shelter among books, which insult not; and studies, that ask no questions of a youth's finances. He was lord of his library, and seldom cared for looking out beyond his domains. The healing influence of studious pursuits was upon him, to soothe and to abstract. He was almost a healthy man, when the waywardness of his fate broke out against him with a second and worse malignity. The father of W—— had hitherto exercised the humble profession of house-painter at N——, near Oxford. A supposed interest with some of the heads of colleges had now induced him to take up his abode in that city, with the hope of being employed upon some public works which were talked of. From that moment I read in the countenance of the young man the determination which at length tore him from academical pursuits for ever. To a person unacquainted with our universities, the distance between the gownsmen and the townsmen, as they are called —the trading part of the latter especially—is carried to an excess that would appear harsh and incredible. The temperament of W——'s father was diametrically the reverse of his own. Old W—— was a little, busy, cringing tradesman, who, with his son upon his arm, would stand bowing and scraping, cap in hand, to any thing that wore the semblance of a gown— insensible to the winks and opener remonstrances of the young man, to whose chamber-fellow, or equal in standing, perhaps, he was thus obsequiously and gratuitously ducking. Such a state of things could not last. W—— must change the air of Oxford, or be suffocated. He chose the former; and let the sturdy moralist, who strains the point of the filial duties as high as they can bear, censure the dereliction; he cannot estimate the struggle. I stood with W——, the last afternoon I ever saw him, under the eaves of his paternal dwelling. It was in the fine lane leading from the High Street to the back of * * * college, where W—— kept his rooms. He seemed thoughtful and more reconciled. I ventured to rally him—finding him in a better mood—upon a representation of the Artist Evangelist, which the old man, whose affairs were beginning to flourish, had caused to be set up in a splendid sort of frame over his really handsome shop; either as a token of prosperity or badge

of gratitude to his saint. W—— looked up at the
Luke, and, like Satan, "knew his mounted sign—
and fled." A letter on his father's table, the next
morning, announced that he had accepted a commission in a regiment about to embark for Portugal. He
was among the first who perished before the walls of
St. Sebastian.

Upon a subject which I began with treating half
seriously, I do not know how I should have fallen
upon a recital so eminently painful ; but this theme of
poor relationship is replete with so much matter for
tragic as well as comic associations, that it is difficult
to keep the account distinct without blending. The
earliest impressions which I received on this matter
are certainly not attended with any thing painful, or very humiliating in the recalling. At my
father's table (no very splendid one) was to be found,
every Saturday, the mysterious figure of an aged
gentleman, clothed in neat black, of a sad yet comely
appearance. His deportment was of the essence of
gravity ; his words were few or none ; and I was not
to make a noise in his presence. I had little inclination to do so, for my cue was to admire in silence.
A particular elbow-chair was appropriated to him,
which was in no case to be violated. A peculiar sort
of sweet pudding, which appeared on no other occasion, distinguished the days of his coming. I used
to think him a prodigiously rich man. All I could
make out of him was, that he and my father had
been schoolfellows, a world ago, at Lincoln, and that
he came from the Mint. The Mint I knew to be a
place where all the money was coined, and I thought
he was the owner of all that money. Awful ideas of
the Tower twined themselves about his presence.

He seemed above human infirmities and passions. A sort of melancholy grandeur invested him. From some inexplicable doom I fancied him obliged to go about in an eternal suit of mourning; a captive; a stately being let out of the Tower on Saturdays. Often have I wondered at the temerity of my father, who, in spite of an habitual general respect which we all in common manifested towards him, would venture now and then to stand up against him in some argument touching their youthful days. The houses of the ancient city of Lincoln are divided (as most of my readers know) between the dwellers on the hill and in the valley. This marked distinction formed an obvious division between the boys who lived above (however brought together in a common school) and the boys whose paternal residence was on the plain; a sufficient cause of hostility in the code of these young Grotiuses. My father had been a leading Mountaineer; and would still maintain the general superiority, in skill and hardihood, of the *Above Boys* (his own faction) over the *Below Boys* (so were they called), of which party his contemporary had been a chieftain. Many and hot were the skirmishes on this topic, the only one upon which the old gentleman was ever brought out; and bad blood bred, even sometimes almost to the recommencement (so I expected) of actual hostilities. But my father, who scorned to insist upon advantages, generally contrived to turn the conversation upon some adroit by-commendation of the old Minster; in the general preference of which, before all other cathedrals in the island, the dweller on the hill, and the plain-born, could meet on a conciliating level, and lay down their less important differences. Once only I saw the old gentleman really

ruffled, and I remembered with anguish the thought
that came over me : "perhaps he will never come
here again." He had been pressed to take another
plate of the viand, which I have already mentioned
as the indispensable concomitant of his visits. He
had refused with a resistance amounting to rigour,
when my aunt, an old Lincolnian, but who had some
thing of this, in common with my cousin Bridget,
that she would sometimes press civility out of
season, uttered the following memorable application :
" Do take another slice, Mr. Billet, for you do not
get pudding every day." The old gentleman said
nothing at the time ; but he took occasion in the
course of the evening, when some argument had
intervened between them, to utter with an emphasis
which chilled the company, and which chills me
now as I write it, "Woman, you are superan-
nuated !" John Billet did not survive long after the
digesting of this affront: but he survived long enough
to assure me that peace was actually restored ! and,
if I remember aright, another pudding was discreetly
substituted in the place of that which had occasioned
the offence. He died at the Mint, (anno 1781,) where
he had long held, what he accounted, a comfortable
independence ; and with five pounds, fourteen shillings, and a penny, which were found in his escrutoire
after his decease, he left the world, blessing God
that he had enough to bury him, and that he had
never been obliged to any man for a sixpence. This
was a Poor Relation.

DETACHED THOUGHTS ON BOOKS AND READING.

To mind the inside of a book is to entertain one's self with the forced product of another man's brain. Now I think a man of quality and breeding may be much amused with the natural sprouts of his own. *Lord Foppington, in the Relapse.*

AN ingenious acquaintance of my own was so much struck with this bright sally of his Lordship, that he has left off reading altogether, to the great improvement of his originality. At the hazard of losing some credit on this head, I must confess that I dedicate no inconsiderable portion of my time to other people's thoughts. I dream away my life in others' speculations. I love to lose myself in other men's minds. When I am not walking I am reading; I cannot sit and think. Books think for me.

I have no repugnances. Shaftesbury is not too genteel for me, nor Jonathan Wild too low. I can read any thing which I call *a book*. There are things in that shape which I cannot allow for such.

In this catalogue of *books which are no books—biblia a-biblia*, I reckon Court Calendars, Directories, Pocket Books, Draught Boards bound and lettered on the back, Scientific Treatises, Almanacks, Statutes at Large: the works of Hume, Gibbon, Robertson, Beattie, Soame Jenyns, and generally all those volumes which "no gentleman's library should be without:" the Histories of Flavius Josephus (that learned Jew), and Paley's Moral Philosophy. With these exceptions I can read almost any thing. I bless my stars for a taste so catholic, so unex-cluding.

I confess that it moves my spleen to see these *things in books' clothing* perched upon shelves, like false saints, usurpers of true shrines, intruders into the sanctuary, thrusting out the legitimate occupants. To reach down a well-bound semblance of a volume, and hope it some kind-hearted play-book, then, open-ing what "seem its leaves," to come bolt upon a withering Population Essay. To expect a Steele or a Farquhar, and find Adam Smith. To view a well-arranged assortment of block-headed Encyclo-pædias (Anglicanas or Metropolitanas) set out in an array of russia or morocco, when a tithe of that good leather would comfortably re-clothe my shiver-ing folios—would renovate Paracelsus himself, and enable old Raymund Lully to look like himself again in the world. I never see these impostors but I long to strip them, to warm my ragged vete-rans in their spoils.

To be strong-backed and neat-bound is the desi-deratum of a volume. Magnificence comes after. This, when it can be afforded, is not to be lavished upon all kinds of books indiscriminately. For in-stance, I would not dress a set of Magazines in full suit. The dishabille, or half binding, (with russia backs ever,) is *our* costume. A Shakspeare or a Milton (unless the first editions) it were mere foppery to trick out in gay apparel. The possession of them confers no distinction. The exterior of them, (the things themselves being so common), strange to say, raises no sweet emotions, no tickling sense of property in the owner. Thomson's Seasons, again, looks best (I maintain it) a little torn and dog's-eared. How beautiful to a genuine lover of reading are the sullied leaves and worn-out appearance, nay, the very odour, (beyond russia,) if we would not forget kind feelings in fastidiousness, of an old "Circulating Library" Tom Jones, or Vicar of Wakefield! How they speak of the thousand thumbs that have turned over their pages with delight! of the lone sempstress, whom they may have cheered (milliner, or harder-working mantua-maker) after her long day's needle-toil, running far into midnight, when she has snatched an hour, ill spared from sleep, to steep her cares, as in some Lethean cup, in spelling out their enchanting contents! Who would have them a whit less soiled? What better condition could we desire to see them in?

In some respects the better a book is, the less it demands from binding. Fielding, Smollett, Sterne, and all that class of perpetually self-reproductive volumes—Great Nature's Stereotypes—we see them individually perish with less regret, because we know the copies of them to be "eterne." But where a book is at once both good and rare, where the individual is almost the species, and when *that* perishes,

> We know not where is that Promethean torch
> That can its light relumine;

such a book, for instance, as the Life of the Duke of Newcastle, by his Duchess: no casket is rich enough, no casing sufficiently durable, to honour and keep safe such a jewel.

Not only rare volumes of this description, which seem hopeless ever to be reprinted, but old editions of writers, such as Sir Philip Sydney, Bishop Taylor, Milton in his prose works, Fuller, (of whom we *have* reprints, yet the books themselves, though they go about, and are talked of here and there, we know have not endenizened themselves, nor possibly ever will, in the national heart, so as to become stock books,) it is good to possess these in durable and costly covers. I do not care for a First Folio of Shakspeare. I rather prefer the common editions of Rowe and Tonson, without notes, and with *plates*, which, being so execrably bad, serve as maps or modest remembrancers to the text; and without pretending to any supposable emulation with it, are so much better than the Shakspeare *engravings*, which *did*. I have a community of feeling with my countryman about his Plays, and I like those editions of him best which have been oftenest tumbled about and handled. On the contrary, I cannot read Beaumont and Fletcher but in Folio. The Octavo editions are painful to look at. I have no sympathy with them. If they were as much read as the current editions of the other poet, I should prefer them in that shape to the older one. I do not know a more heartless sight than the reprint of the "Anatomy of Melancholy." What need was there of unearthing the bones of that fantastic old great man, to expose them in a winding-sheet of the newest fashion to modern censure ? What hapless stationer could dream of Burton ever becoming popular ? The wretched Malone could not do worse, when he bribed the sexton of Stratford Church to let him white-wash the painted effigy of old Shakspeare, which stood there, in rude but lively fashion depicted, to the very colour of the cheek, the eye, the eyebrow, hair, the very dress he used to wear,—the only authentic testimony we had, however imperfect, of these curious parts and parcels of him. They covered him over with a coat of white paint. By ——, if I had been a justice of peace for Warwickshire, I would have clapped both commentator and sexton fast in the stocks, for a pair of meddling sacrilegious varlets.

I think I see them at their work, these sapient trouble-tombs !

Shall I be thought fantastical if I confess that the names of some of our poets sound sweeter, and have a finer relish to the ear, (to mine at least,) than that of Milton or of Shakspeare ? It may be that the latter are more staled and rung upon in common discourse. The sweetest names, and which carry a perfume in the mention, are Kit Marlowe, Drayton, Drummond of Hawthornden, and Cowley.

Much depends upon *when* and *where* you read a book. In the five or six impatient minutes before the dinner is quite ready, who would think of taking up the " Fairy Queen " for a stop-gap, or a volume of Bishop Andrewes's sermons ?

Milton almost requires a solemn service of music to be played before you enter upon him. But he brings his music; to which, who listens, had need bring docile thoughts and purged ears.

Winter evenings—the world shut out—with less of ceremony the gentle Shakspeare enters. At such a season the *Tempest,* or his own *Winter's Tale.*

These two poets you cannot avoid reading aloud— to yourself, or (as it chances) to some single person

2 D 2

listening. More than one, and it degenerates into an audience.

Books of quick interest, that hurry on for incidents, are for the eye to glide over only. It will not do to read them out. I could never listen to even the better kind of modern novels without extreme irksomeness.

A newspaper read out is intolerable. In some of the Bank offices it is the custom (to save so much individual time) for one of the clerks, who is the best scholar, to commence upon the *Times*, or the *Chronicle*, and recite its entire contents aloud, *pro bono publico*. With every advantage of lungs and elocution, the effect is singularly vapid. In barbers' shops and public-houses a fellow will get up and spell out a paragraph, which he communicates as some discovery. Another follows with *his* selection. So the entire journal transpires at length by piece-meal. Seldom-readers are slow readers, and without this expedient no one in the company would probably ever travel through the contents of a whole paper.

Newspapers always excite curiosity. No one ever lays one down without a feeling of disappointment.

What an eternal time that gentleman in black, at Nando's, keeps the paper ! I am sick of hearing the waiter bawling out incessantly, " The *Chronicle* is in hand, Sir."

Coming into an inn at night—having ordered your supper—what can be more delightful than to find lying in the window-seat, left there time out of mind by the carelessness of some former guest, two or three numbers of the old *Town and Country Magazine*, with its amusing *tête-à-tête* pictures—" The Royal Lover and Lady G—— ;" " The Melting Platonic and the old Beau,"—and such-like antiquated scandal? Would you exchange it—at that time, and in that place—for a better book?

Poor Tobin, who latterly fell blind, did not regret it so much for the weightier kinds of reading, (the " Paradise Lost," or " Comus," he could have *read* to him,) but he missed the pleasure of skimming over with his own eye a magazine, or a light pamphlet.

I should not care to be caught in the serious avenues of some cathedral alone, and reading *Candide*.

I do not remember a more whimsical surprise than having been once detected, by a familiar damsel, reclined at my ease upon the grass, on Primrose Hill, (her Cythera,) reading *Pamela*. There was nothing in the book to make a man seriously ashamed at the exposure; but as she seated herself down by me, and seemed determined to read in company, I could have wished it had been any other book. We read on very sociably for a few pages; but not finding the author much to her taste she got up and went away. Gentle casuist, I leave it to thee to conjecture, whether the blush (for there was one between us) was the property of the nymph or the swain in this dilemma. From me you shall never get the secret.

I am not much a friend to out-of-doors reading. I cannot settle my spirits to it. I knew a Unitarian minister, who was generally to be seen upon Snow Hill, (as yet Skinner's Street *was not*,) between the hours of ten and eleven in the morning, studying a volume of Lardner. I own this to have been a strain of abstraction beyond my reach. I used to admire how he sidled along, keeping clear of secular contacts. An illiterate encounter with a porter's knot or a bread-

basket would have quickly put to flight all the
theology I am master of, and have left me worse than
indifferent to the five points.

There is a class of street readers whom I can never
contemplate without affection,—the poor gentry,
who, not having wherewithal to buy or hire a book,
filch a little learning at the open stalls ; the owner,
with his hard eye, casting envious looks at them all
the while, and thinking when they will have done.
Venturing tenderly, page after page, expecting every
moment when he shall interpose his interdict, and yet
unable to deny themselves the gratification, they
" snatch a fearful joy."   Martin B————, in this
way, by daily fragments, got through two volumes of
" Clarissa," when the stall-keeper damped his laudable
ambition, by asking him (it was in his younger days)
whether he meant to purchase the work.   M——
declares, that under no circumstance in his life did he
ever peruse a book with half the satisfaction which he
took in those uneasy snatches.   A quaint poetess of
our day has moralised upon this subject in two very
touching but homely stanzas :—

> " I saw a boy with eager eye
> Open a book upon a stall,
> And read, as he'd devour it all ;
> Which when the stall-man did espy,
> Soon to the boy I heard him call,
> ' You Sir, you never buy a book,
> Therefore in one you shall not look.'
> The boy pass'd slowly on, and with a sigh
> He wish'd he never had been taught to read.
> Then of the old churl's books he should have had no need.
>
> Of sufferings the poor have many,
> Which never can the rich annoy :
> I soon perceived another boy,

Who look'd as if he had not any
Food—for that day at least—enjoy
The sight of cold meat in a tavern larder.
This boy's case, then thought I, is surely harder,
Thus hungry, longing, thus without a penny,
Beholding choice of dainty-dressed meat :
No wonder if he wish he ne'er had learn'd to eat."

STAGE ILLUSION.

A PLAY is said to be well or ill acted in proportion to
the scenical illusion produced.   Whether such illusion
can in any case be perfect, is not the question.   The
nearest approach to it, we are told, is when the actor
appears wholly unconscious of the presence of
spectators.   In tragedy—in all which is to affect the
feelings—this undivided attention to his stage
business seems indispensable.   Yet it is, in fact,
dispensed with every day by our cleverest tragedians ;
and while these references to an audience, in the shape
of rant or sentiment, are not too frequent or palpable,
a sufficient quantity of illusion for the purposes of
dramatic interest may be said to be produced in spite
of them.   But, tragedy apart, it may be inquired
whether, in certain characters in comedy, especially
those which are a little extravagant, or which involve
some notion repugnant to the moral sense, it is not a
proof of the highest skill in the comedian when, without absolutely appealing to an audience, he keeps up
a tacit understanding with them ; and makes them,
unconsciously to themselves, a party in the scene.
The utmost nicety is required in the mode of doing

this ; but we speak only of the great artists in the profession.

The most mortifying infirmity in human nature, to feel in ourselves, or to contemplate in another, is perhaps cowardice. To see a coward *done to the life* upon a stage would produce any thing but mirth. Yet we most of us remember Jack Bannister's cowards. Could any thing be more agreeable, more pleasant ? We loved the rogues. How was this effected but by the exquisite art of the actor in a perpetual sub-insinuation to us, the spectators, even in the extremity of the shaking fit, that he was not half such a coward as we took him for ? We saw all the common symptoms of the malady upon him,—the quivering lip, the cowering knees, the teeth chattering,—and could have sworn "that man was frightened." But we forgot all the while—or kept it almost a secret to ourselves—that he never once lost his self-possession ; that he let out, by a thousand droll looks and gestures—meant at *us*, and not at all supposed to be visible to his fellows in the scene— that his confidence in his own resources had never once deserted him. Was this a genuine picture of a coward ?—or not rather a likeness, which the clever artist contrived to palm upon us instead of an original ; while we secretly connived at the delusion for the purpose of greater pleasure than a more genuine counterfeiting of the imbecility, helplessness, and utter self desertion, which we know to be concomitants of cowardice in real life, could have given us ?

Why are misers so hateful in the world, and so endurable on the stage, but because the skilful actor, by a sort of sub-reference, rather than direct appeal to us, disarms the character of a great deal of its odious-ness, by seeming to engage *our* compassion for the insecure tenure by which he holds his money-bags and parchments ? By this subtle vent half of the hatefulness of the character—the self-closeness with which in real life it coils itself up from the sympathies of men—evaporates. The miser becomes sympathetic ; *i. e.* is no genuine miser. Here again a diverting likeness is substituted for a very disagreeable reality.

Spleen, irritability—the pitiable infirmities of old men, which produce only pain to behold in the realities—counterfeited upon a stage, divert not altogether for the comic appendages to them, but in part from an inner conviction that they are *being acted* before us ; that a likeness only is going on, and not the thing itself. They please by being done under the life, or beside it ; not *to the life*. When Gattie acts an old man, is he angry indeed ? or only a pleasant counterfeit, just enough of a likeness to recognise, without pressing upon us the uneasy sense of a reality ?

Comedians, paradoxical as it may seem, may be too natural. It was the case with a late actor. Nothing could be more earnest or true than the manner of Mr. Emery; this told excellently in his Tyke, and characters of a tragic cast. But when he carried the same rigid exclusiveness of attention to the stage business, and wilful blindness and oblivion of every thing before the curtain into his comedy, it produced a harsh and dissonant effect. He was out of keeping with the rest of the *Personæ Dramatis*. There was as little link between him and them, as betwixt himself and the audience. He was a third estate, dry, repulsive, and unsocial to all. Individually considered, his execution was masterly. But comedy is not this unbending thing; for this reason, that the same degree of credibility is not required of it as to serious scenes. The degrees of credibility demanded to the two things, may be illustrated by the different sort of truth which we expect when a man tells us a mournful or a merry story. If we suspect the former of falsehood in any one tittle, we reject it altogether. Our tears refuse to flow at a suspected imposition. But the teller of a mirthful tale has latitude allowed him. We are content with less than absolute truth. 'Tis the same with dramatic illusion. We confess we love in comedy to see an audience naturalized behind the scenes, taken into the interest of the drama, welcomed as bystanders however. There is something ungracious in a comic actor holding himself aloof from all participation or concern with those who are come to be diverted by him. Macbeth must see the dagger, and no ear but his own be told of it; but an old fool in farce may think he *sees something*, and by conscious words and looks express it, as plainly as he can speak, to pit, box, and gallery. When an impertinent in tragedy—an Osric, for instance—breaks in upon the serious passions of the scene, we approve of the contempt with which he is treated. But when the pleasant impertinent of comedy, in a piece purely meant to give delight, and raise mirth out of whimsical perplexities, worries the studious man with taking up his leisure, or making his house his home, the same sort of contempt expressed (however *natural*) would destroy the balance of delight in the spectators. To make the intrusion comic, the actor who plays the annoyed man must a little desert nature ; he must, in short, be thinking of

the audience, and express only so much dissatisfac-
tion and peevishness as is consistent with the pleasure
of comedy. In other words, his perplexity must
seem half put on. If he repel the intruder with the
sober set face of a man in earnest, and more especially if he deliver his expostulations in a tone which
in the world must necessarily provoke a duel, his
real-life manner will destroy the whimsical and purely
dramatic existence of the other character, (which to
render it comic demands an antagonist comicality on
the part of the character opposed to it,) and convert
what was meant for mirth, rather than belief, into a
downright piece of impertinence indeed, which would
raise no diversion in us, but rather stir pain, to see
inflicted in earnest upon any unworthy person. A
very judicious actor (in most of his parts) seems to
have fallen into an error of this sort in his playing
with Mr. Wrench in the farce of *Free and Easy.*

Many instances would be tedious: these may
suffice to show that comic acting at least does not
always demand from the performer that strict abstraction from all reference to an audience which is exacted
of it; but that in some cases a sort of compromise
may take place, and all the purposes of dramatic delight be attained by a judicious understanding, not
too openly announced, between the ladies and gentlemen on both sides of the curtain.

TO THE SHADE OF ELLISTON.

J OYOUSEST of once embodied spirits, whither at length
hast thou flown ? To what genial region are we permitted to conjecture that thou hast flitted ?

Art thou sowing thy WILD OATS yet (the harvest
time was still to come with thee) upon casual sands
of Avernus ? or art thou enacting ROVER (as we would
gladlier think) by wandering Elysian streams ?

This mortal frame, while thou didst play thy brief
antics amongst us, was in truth any thing but a prison
to thee, as the vain Platonist dreams of this *body* to
be no better than a county gaol, forsooth, or some
house of durance vile, whereof the five senses are the
fetters. Thou knewest better than to be in a hurry
to cast off those gyves ; and had notice to quit, I fear,
before thou wert quite ready to abandon this fleshly
tenement. It was thy Pleasure House, thy Palace
of Dainty Devices ; thy Louvre, or thy White Hall.

What new mysterious lodgings dost thou tenant
now ? or when may we expect thy aërial house-
warming ?

Tartarus we know, and we have read of the Blessed
Shades ; now cannot I intelligibly fancy thee in
either.

Is it too much to hazard a conjecture that (as the
Schoolmen admitted a receptacle apart for Patriarchs
and un-chrisom babes) there may exist—not far perchance from that store-house of all vanities, which

Milton saw in a vision—a LIMBO somewhere for
PLAYERS? and that

> Up thither like aërial vapours fly
> Both all Stage things, and all that in Stage things
> Built their fond hopes of glory, or lasting fame?
> All the unaccomplish'd works of Authors' hands,
> Abortive, monstrous, or unkindly mix'd,
> Damn'd upon earth, fleet thither—
> Play, Opera, Farce, with all their trumpery.—

There, by the neighbouring moon, (by some not
improperly supposed thy Regent Planet upon earth,)
mayst thou not still be acting thy managerial pranks,
great disembodied lessee? but lessee still, and still
a manager.

In green-rooms, impervious to mortal eye, the muse
beholds thee wielding posthumous empire.

Thin ghosts of figurantes (never plump on earth)
circle thee in endlessly, and still their song is *Fie on
sinful phantasy!*

Magnificent were thy capriccios on this globe of
earth, ROBERT WILLIAM ELLISTON! for as yet we
know not thy new name in heaven.

It irks me to think, that, stript of thy regalities,
thou shouldst ferry over, a poor forked shade, in crazy
Stygian wherry. Methinks I hear the old boatman,
paddling by the weedy wharf, with raucid voice,
bawling "SCULLS, SCULLS!" to which, with waving
hand and majestic action, thou deignest no reply,
other than in two curt monosyllables, "No:
Oars."

But the laws of Pluto's kingdom know small difference between king and cobbler, manager and call-boy;
and if haply your dates of life were conterminate, you
are quietly taking your passage, cheek by cheek (O

ignoble levelling of Death!) with the shade of some
recently departed candle-snuffer.

But mercy! what strippings, what tearing off of
histrionic robes and private vanities! what denuda-
tions to the bone, before the surly Ferryman will
admit you to set a foot within his battered lighter!

Crowns, sceptres, shield, sword, and truncheon,
thy own coronation robes, (for thou hast brought the
whole property-man's wardrobe with thee, enough to
sink a navy,) the judge's ermine, the coxcomb's wig,
the snuffbox *à la Foppington*,—all must overboard,
he positively swears; and that Ancient Mariner
brooks no denial; for, since the tiresome monodrame
of the old Thracian Harper, Charon, it is to be believed, hath shown small taste for theatricals.

Ay, now 'tis done. You are just boat-weight; *pura
et puta anima.*

But, bless me, how *little* you look!

So shall we all look—kings and keysars[1]—stripped
for the last voyage.

But the murky rogue pushes off. Adieu, pleasant,
and thrice pleasant shade! with my parting thanks
for many a heavy hour of life lightened by thy harmless extravaganzas, public or domestic.

Rhadamanthus, who tries the lighter causes below,
leaving to his two brethren the heavy calendars—
honest Rhadamanth, always partial to players, weighing their parti-coloured existence here upon earth,—
making account of the few foibles that may have
shaded thy *real life*, as we call it, (though, substan-
tially, scarcely less a vapour than thy idlest vagaries
upon the boards of Drury,) as but of so many echoes,
natural re-percussions, and results to be expected
from the assumed extravagancies of thy *secondary* or

mock life, nightly upon a stage—after a lenient casti-
gation, with rods lighter than of those Medusean
ringlets, but just enough to "whip the offending
Adam out of thee," shall courteously dismiss thee at
the right hand gate—the o. p. side of Hades—that
conducts to masques and merry-makings in the
Theatre Royal of Proserpine.

PLAUDITO, ET VALETO.

NOTES

TO THE

ESSAYS OF ELIA.

Most of the "Elia" Essays appeared in the "London Magazine," Lamb's first contribution being "Oxford in the Vacation" in October, 1820, and his last, "The last Peach," in April, 1825. A portion was issued in a volume in 1823, under the title of "ELIA: Essays which have appeared under that name in the 'London Magazine,'" Lamb having adopted as his signature the name of a young foreigner, then dead, who had been his fellow Clerk at the India Office. Elia it would seem is the Italian for Elijah; in strictness, therefore, it should be pronounced Elīa, not as it usually is, Elīa. The sale was slow, a second edition not being called for until eleven years later. The second series was issued not long before his death, in 1833, under the title of "THE LAST ESSAYS OF ELIA," and comprised papers from the "London Magazine;" the "Reflector;" the "Englishman;" the "Champion;" and the "New Monthly." By this time he had grown heartily tired of the signature, which he spoke of as "the sickening Elia at the bottom," &c. It will be seen that the author introduced for the second, or even the third time, some favourite pieces, which had already travelled the public highway in more obscure vehicles.

THE SOUTH SEA HOUSE.

"At the north-east extremity of Threadneedle Street, is situated the South Sea House. The back front was formerly the Excise Office: then the South Sea House. The new Building, in which the Company's affairs are now transacted, is a magnificent structure of brick and stone, about a quadrangle supported by pillars of the Tuscan order. which form a fine Piazza." Northonck in his *History of London*, thus describes the building as it appeared in Lamb's day.

"*His fine official suite of rooms . . . I know not who is the occupier of them now.*" On this passage there was originally a note :—

"I have since been informed that the present tenant of them is Mr. Lamb, a gentleman who is happy in the possession of some choice pictures, and among them a rare portrait of Milton, which I mean to do myself the pleasure of going to see, and at the same time to refresh my memory with the sight of old scenes. Mr. Lamb has the character of a right courteous and communicative collector."

His brother, John Lamb, is intended. The South Sea House, after the business had been discontinued, was let out in "Private Chambers," John Lamb, one of its retired officials, naturally becoming a tenant. The old building itself was burnt down in 1826.

"*Walter Plumer, ... summoned before the House of Commons about a business of franks,*" &c. A slight mistake. It was Cave the Printer that was brought before the House for too conscientiously exercising his inspection of Mr. Plumer's franks.

"*The very names are fantastic, like Henry Pimpernel and old John Naps of Greece.*"
Compare "Taming of the Shrew," Induc. Sec. 2. *3rd Serv.* to Sly. "Why, sir, you know no house, nor no such maid, nor no such men, as you have reckoned up. As Stephen Sly and old John Naps of Greece, and Peter Turf, and Henry Pimpernell, and twenty more such names and men as these, which never were, nor no man ever saw."
[*Lond. Mag.,* Aug., 1820.]

OXFORD IN THE VACATION.

"*The Elder Repose of MS.*" Here was a note suppressed in the "Essays:"—

"There is something to me repugnant at any time in written hand. The text never seems determinate. Print settles it. I had thought of the Lycidas as of a full-grown beauty—as springing up with all its parts absolute—till, in an evil hour, I was shown the original written copy of it, together with the other minor poems of its author, in the Library of Trinity, kept like some treasure to be proud of. I wish they had thrown them in the Cam, or sent them after the latter cantos of Spenser into the Irish Channel. How it staggered me to see the fine things in thin ore! interlined, corrected! as if their words were mortal, alterable, displaceable, at pleasure! as if they might have been otherwise and just as good! as if inspiration were made up of parts, and those fluctuating, successive, indifferent! I will never go into the workshop of any great artist again, nor desire a sight of his picture till it is fairly off the easel. No, not if Raphael were to be alive again, and painting another Galatea."

" None thinks of offering violence or injustice." Here was a note:—

"Violence or injustice, certainly none, Mr. Elia. But you will acknowledge that the charming unsuspectingness of our friend has sometimes laid him open to attacks, which, tho' savouring (we hope) more of waggery than of malice, such is our unfeigned respect for G. D., might we think, much better have been omitted. Such was that silly joke of L——, who at the time the question of the Scotch novels was first agitated, gravely assured our friend— who as gravely went about repeating it in all companies—that Lord Castlereagh had acknowledged himself to be the author of Waverley!

" D. . . has lately lit upon a MS. Collection of Charters relative to C. . . . " The eccentric George Dyer, besides his better

known "History of Cambridge," published the Charters here alluded to, not without long delay and intervals, for which he was repeatedly brought to account by the subscribers.

"*He made a call at our friend M's, in Bedford Square.*" Mr. Basil Montague's. . . Mr. Procter vouches for the truth of this instance; and adds another, "of his emptying his snuff-box into the teapot when he was preparing breakfast for a hungry friend."

"*Pretty A. S.*" Anne Skipper, now (1875) Mrs. Procter.

After the paragraph ending "*Obtruded personal presence*," came originally these two passages :—

"D. commenced life after a course of hard study in the house of "pure Emanuel" as usher to a knavish fanatic schoolmaster at * * *, at a salary of eight pounds per annum, with board and lodging. Of this poor stipend he never received above half in all the laborious years he served this man. He tells a pleasant anecdote, that when poverty, staring out at his ragged knees, has sometimes compelled him, against the modesty of his nature, to hint at arrears, Dr. * * * would take no immediate notice, but after supper, when the school was called together to evensong, he would never fail to introduce some instructive homily against riches and the corruption of the heart occasioned thro' the desire of them; ending with, "Lord, keep thy servants above all things from the heinous sin of avarice. Having food and raiment let us therewithal be content. Give me Hagar's wish," and the like; which to the little auditory sounded like a doctrine full of Christian prudence and simplicity, but to poor D. was a receipt in full for that quarter's demand at least. And D. has been under-working for himself ever since : drudging at low rates for unappreciating booksellers; wasting his fine erudition in silent corrections of the Classics and in those, unostentatious but solid services to learning, which commonly fall to the lot of laborious scholars who have not the heart to sell themselves to the best advantage. He has published poems which do not sell, because their character is unobtrusive like his own, and because he has been too much absorbed in ancient literature to know what the popular mark in poetry is, even if he could have hit it. And, therefore, his verses are properly what he terms them : *crotchets*, voluntaries, odes to liberty, and spring effusions, little tributes and offerings left behind him upon tables and window-seats at parting from friends' houses, and from all the inns of hospitality where he has been courteously (or but tolerably) received in his pilgrimage. If his muse of kindness halt a little behind the strong lines in fashion in this excitement-loving age, his prose is the best of the sort in the world, and exhibits a faithful transcript of his own healthy, natural mind, and cheerful, innocent one of conversation.

Mr. Dyer was naturally dissatisfied with this sketch of peculiarities, which, even without the initials, were recognizable. His simple, kindly nature could hardly take offence; but he remonstrated; and his friend, in a letter, given in the Correspondence of the next number, hastened to make the *amende :*

Elia requests the Editor to inform W. K. that in his article on Oxford, under the initials G. D., it was his ambition to make more familiar to the public a character, which, for integrity and single-heartedness, he has long been accustomed to rank among the best patterns of his species. That, if he has failed in the end which he proposed, it was an error of judgment merely. That, if in pursuance of his purpose, he has drawn forth some personal peculiarities of his friend into notice, it was only from conviction that the

public, in living subjects especially, do not endure
pure panegyric. That the anecdotes which he produced were no more than he conceived necessary to
awaken attention to character, and were meant solely
to illustrate it. That it is an entire mistake to
suppose that he undertook in character to set off his
own wit or ingenuity. That, he conceives, a candid
interpreter might find something intended, beyond a
heartless jest. That G. D., however, having thought
it necessary to disclaim the anecdote respecting
Dr. ———, it becomes him, who can never for a
moment doubt the veracity of his friend, to account
for it from an imperfect remembrance of some story
he heard long ago, and which, happening to tally
with his argument, he set down too hastily to the
account of G. D. That from G. D.'s strong affirmations and proofs to the contrary, he is bound to
believe it belongs to no part of G. D.'s biography.
That the transaction, supposing it true, must have
taken place more than forty years ago. That, in
consequence, it is not likely to " meet the eye of
many who might be justly offended." Finally, that
what he has said of the Booksellers, referred to a
period of many years, in which he has had the
happiness of G. D.'s acquaintance; and can have
nothing to do with any present or prospective engagements of G. D. with those gentlemen, to the
nature of which, he professes himself an entire
stranger.

The Note, " *Januses of one face, Sir Thomas Brown,*" was added
when the Essays were collected.

In the " London Magazine," the Essay thus ended, Aug. 5, 1820 :
" *From my rooms, facing the Bodleian.*"

[*Lond Mag.*, Oct., 1820.]

CHRIST'S HOSPITAL FIVE AND THIRTY YEARS AGO.

" *A Magnificent Eulogy on my Old School.*" The "Works" were published in 1818, but the paper referred to had appeared so early as 1809. The present Essay illustrates one of Lamb's devices for giving variety to a subject, by treating it from another, or second point of view. He now writes in the character of Coleridge.

" *The present worthy Sub-Treasurer.*" Richard Norris, whose death-bed Lamb has elsewhere pathetically described, and who then held an office in Christ's Hospital.

" *Sweet Calne.*" Where Coleridge was born. He has detailed his desolate condition at the school in his " Biographia Literaria."

" *L.'s governor lived in a manner under the paternal roof.*" This alludes to Mr. Salt, the Bencher, to whom Lamb's father was clerk and servant.

" *The Monitors.*" Leigh Hunt also records instances of their tyranny.

The Rev. James Boyer." Boyer was long under-master, from 1767; and became upper-master in 1777.

" *Matthew Field.*"—" *A little dramatic effusion of his* . . . *Vertummus and Pomona, &c.*" Produced not by Garrick at Drury Lane, as Lamb states, but at Covent Garden, in 1782, after Garrick had retired.

" *Coleridge in his Literary Life,*" &c. He writes: " I fancy I can almost hear him exclaiming, Harp? Harp? Lyre? Pen and ink, boy, you mean. Muse, boy, muse? Your nurse's daughter, you mean. Pierian spring? O aye! The cloister pump, I suppose." Boyer retired in 1799, obtained a living of a thousand a year, and died in 1814. To this may be added Leigh Hunt's sketch: " His clothes were cut short, his hands hung out of the sleeve, with tight wristbands, as if ready for execution; and, he generally wore grey worsted stockings, very tight."

" *C. V. Le G.*" Charles Valentine Le Grice, afterwards Tutor, and Rector of a Cornwall Parish. Samuel was the " Junior Le Grice," who died of yellow fever in the West Indies.

Samuel Favell. " He left Cambridge," says Lamb, in the " Key to Elia," given by Mr. Hazlitt, " because he was ashamed of his father who was a House Painter there." The allusion is also explained, but with a change of initial to W, in the essay on "Poor Relations."

"*T——e.*" Trollope, who succeeded Boyer. Two lines before Stevens' name is given in full. Trollope's is thus disguised. Diplomatic office would seem about as conspicuous as that of a Colonial Bishop, yet "Th——" denotes the one, and "Thomas Fanshaw Middleton," the other.

"*There was one H——* . . . *in after days* . . . seen expiating *in the hulks.*" In the Key alluded to, Lamb supplies the name, Hodges.

"*Grecian with S. was Th——*" Thornton, afterwards Minister to Portugal.

"*Poor S——*" "Scott, died in Bedlam."—*Key.*

"*Ill-fated M——*" Maunder—dismissed school."—*Ibid.*

"*F—— dogged, faithful,*" &c. "Favelle."

Both he and Le Grice wrote from their College to the Duke of York for Commissions, who good-naturedly sent them.

"*Fr——*" "Franklin, Grammar Master at Hertford."—*Key.*

'*Marmaduke, T.*" "Marmaduke Thompson."—*Key.*

"*Bless thy handsome face.*" This is also related by Leigh Hunt, in his Autobiography.

[*Lond. Mag.*, Dec., 1820.]

THE TWO RACES OF MEN.

This essay seems to have been sent to the Editor under the title of "Two Sorts of Men;" the Editor saying "it" should be carefully considered.

Ralph Bigod. Fenwick, an unlucky adventurer and Proprietor of a Newspaper, &c.; one of whose disastrous ventures was the *Albion.* In his letters, Lamb describes him as "a living scoundrel, lurking about the Pothouses."

"*Comberbatch.*" The name assumed by Coleridge when he enlisted. He told Mr. Cottle that he had seen it over a door in Lincoln's Inn Fields, or the Temple. It might be thought from the distinction taken between "Comberbatch" and "S. T. C.," to whom the reader is expressly invited to lend his Books, that two different persons were intended. Both refer to Coleridge, as will be seen from Lamb's reproachful letter on the abstraction of what his maid called "Luster's Tables" (Luther's Table Talk).

"*Spiteful K.*" Originally "* * * Kenney, a dramatist, author of "Raising the Wind."—*Key.* Some of the touches in Bigod's character, suggest the eccentric Bibb, the hero of that amusing piece.

"*Thy wife, too, that part French, &c.*" Daughter of Mercier, author of the graphic *Tableau de Paris.*

Many are those precious MSS. of his, &c. In the Catalogue of some of Lamb's Books, offered for sale at New York, were some five works thus "enriched," Buncle, Donne, "God's Revenge," Commines, &c.

[*Lond. Mag.,* Dec., 1820.]

NEW YEAR'S EVE.

" *Alice W——n.*" His first love. In the Key he writes: "Alice W——n; feigned (Winterton)." Here is disguise upon disguise. According to Mr. W. C. Hazlitt, she married a pawnbroker in Princes Street, Leicester Square. It is improbable that his name should have been Bartrum, as Lamb mentions it in one of his Essays, "The children of Alice call Bartrum father." Mr. Allsop writes to me, that he recollects walking past the house, when Lamb said "Alice lives, or lived, there."

" *Old Dorrell.*" Compare the verses " Fine merry franions," and the suppressed lines in which he inveighs against this relation.

" *I know him to be a notorious * * *.*" In the Key, "no meaning."

[*Lond. Mag.,* Jan. 1821.]

MRS. BATTLE'S OPINIONS ON WHIST.

" *Old Sarah Battle.*" From the allusions to Mr. Plumer, to the pictures at Sandham, as well as from a sketch given in "Mrs. Leicester's School," it seems that Mrs. Field, his grandmother and Mr. Plumer's housekeeper, is intended.

" *A clean harth.*" On this word originally was a note:—

" This was before the introduction of rugs, reader. You must remember the intolerable crash of the unswept cinder betwixt your foot and the marble."

"*They like to win one game and lose another.*" Here was a note :

" As if a sportsman should tell you he liked to kill a fox one day and lose him the next."

"*To these puny objecters.*" Originally it ran :

" as nurturing the bad passions (dropping for awhile the speaking mask of old Sarah Battle) I would retort," &c.

The paper in its original shape closed at " esteeming them to be such." The rest followed as " P.S."
[*Lond. Mag.*, Feb. 1821.]

A CHAPTER ON EARS.

"*Quite unabashed.*" Here was a note :

" Earless on high stood unabashed Defoe."—*Dunciad.*

"*Mrs. S——.*" Mrs. Spinkes, according to the Key.

"*Party in a parlour,*" &c. Lines from Wordsworth's " Peter Bell."

"*Disappointing book in Patmos.*" Here was a reference : " Rev. chap. x. ver. 10."

"*They cannot resist.*" Here was a reference : " Anatomy of Melancholy."

"*Good Catholic friend Nov.*" Vincent Novello, father of Clara Novello, and of Mrs. Cowden Clarke.

"*Minor heavens.*" A note :

" I have been there and still would go,
'Tis like a little Heaven below."—*Dr. Watts.*

At the end of the Essay the following was added :—

" P.S.—A writer, whose real name it seems is Boldero, but who has been entertaining the town for the last twelve months with some very pleasant lucubrations under the assumed signature of Leigh Hunt,* in

---

* Clearly a fictitious appellation ; for, if we admit the latter of these names to be in a manner English, what is *Leigh?* Christian nomenclature knows no such.—(C. L.)

his ' Indicator' of the 31st January last has thought fit to insinuate that I, *Elia*, do not write the little sketches which bear my signature in this magazine, but that the true author of them is a Mr. L——b. Observe the critical period at which he has chosen to impute the calumny,—on the very eve of the publication of our last number,—affording no scope for explanation for a full month ; during which time I must needs lie writhing and tossing under the cruel imputation of nonentity. Good Heavens! that a plain man must not be allowed *to be*——

" They call this an age of personality ; but surely this spirit of anti-personality (if I may so express it) is something worse.

" Take away my moral reputation,—I may live to discredit that calumny ; injure my literary fame,—I may write that up again ; but, when a gentleman is robbed of his identity, where is he ?

"Other murderers stab but at our existence, a frail and perishing trifle at the best ; but here is an assassin who aims at our very essence ; who not only forbids us *to be* any longer, but *to have been* at all.   Let our ancestors look to it.

" Is the parish register nothing ? Is the house in Princes Street, Cavendish Square, where we saw the light six-and-forty years ago, nothing ? Were our progenitors from stately Genoa, where we flourished four centuries back, before the barbarous name of Boldero* was known to a European mouth, nothing ? Was the goodly scion of our name, transplanted into England in the reign of the seventh Henry, nothing ? Are the archives of the Steelyard, in succeeding reigns (if haply they survive the fury of our envious enemies), showing that we flourished in prime repute, as merchants, down to the period of the Commonwealth, nothing ?

" ' Why, then the world, and all that's in't, is nothing ;
The covering sky is nothing ; Bohemia nothing.'

" I am ashamed that this trifling writer should have power to move me so."

Leigh Hunt replied in the same merry vein : " They further corroborate what we have heard ; viz., that the family were obliged to fly from Genoa for saying that the Pope was the author of Rabelais ; and that Elia is not an anagram, as some have thought it, but the Judaico-Christian name of the writer before us, whose surname, we find, is not Lamb, but Lomb ;—Elia Lomb ! What a name ! He told a friend of ours so in company, and would have palmed himself upon him for a

---

* It is clearly of Transatlantic origin.—(C. L.)

Scotchman, but that his countenance betrayed him. We regret that
such a person should have had us at a disadvantage; and shall take care
in future how we panegyrise our betters in such a way, as to render
them liable to be confounded with their inferiors."

Boldero was the name of one of the Directors of the India House.

[*Lond. Mag.*, March, 1821.]

ALL FOOLS' DAY.

"*Raymond Lully, you look wise.*"   Originally it ran, " Mr.———
you look wise," &c.

" *Duns spare your definitions,*" stood, " Mr. Hazlitt I cannot indulge
you in your definition."

On " *Empedocles.*"   A note:

> " He who to be deem'd
> A god, leap'd fondly into Ætna's flame."

On " *Cleombrotis*"—

> " He who to enjoy
> Plato's Elysium leap'd into the sea."

On " *Babel*"—

> " The builders . . . of Babel on the plain of Shinar."

" *Ha! honest R———, my fine old librarian of Ludgate.*"
" Ramsay, London Library, Ludgate Street, now extinct," according to
the Key.

" *Granville S———.*"   " Granville Sharp."   Another instance of
Lamb's favourite *semi-revelation*.

The Essay was dated " April 1, 1821."

[*Lond. Mag.*, April, 1821.]

A QUAKERS' MEETING.

" *I have seen the reeling sea ruffian who wandered into your receptacle.*"   A reminiscence also given in a letter to Coleridge.

" *And I remembered . . . Fox in the bail-dock.*"   Lamb elsewhere acknowledges a little mistake in this passage. " I have quoted
George Fox in my ' Quakers' Meeting,' as having said he was ' lifted
up in spirit.' "

" *He had been a wit,*" &c.   Compare letter to Coleridge, Feb. 13,
1797.

[*Lond. Mag.*, April, 1821.]

THE OLD AND THE NEW SCHOOLMASTER.

" *A very dear friend.*" Barron Field.

" *My friend M———.*" Manning.

The schoolmaster's letter is clearly in Lamb's own language; the substance may have been supplied by his friend Mylius, a well-known teacher.

The Essay originally thus closed, after " Can I reproach her for it ?" " These kind of complaints are not often drawn from me. I am aware that I am a fortunate, I mean a prosperous man. My feelings prevent me from transcribing any further."

[*Lond. Mag.*, May, 1821.]

IMPERFECT SYMPATHIES.

Originally entitled " JEWS, QUAKERS, SCOTCHMEN, and other Imperfect Sympathies."

" *B———.*" " Braham, now a Christian." Lamb, in the Key.

" *A healthy book.*" This jest he repeated to Mr. Allsop, when he sat next to him at dinner.

" *I was travelling in a stage coach with three male Quakers.*" " The Quaker story did not happen to me," Lamb writes to Barton, March 11, 1823, " but to Carlisle, the surgeon, from whose mouth I have twice heard it."

[*Lond. Mag.*, August, 1821.]

WITCHES AND OTHER NIGHT FEARS.

" *T. H.*" Thornton, Leigh Hunt's child.

" *Lambeth Palace.*" Originally this passage followed :—

" When I awoke I came to a determination to write prose all the rest of my life ; and with submission to some of our young writers who are yet diffident of their powers, and balancing perhaps between verse and prose, they might not do unwisely to decide the preference by the texture of their natural dreams. If these are prosaic, they may depend upon it they have not much to expect in a creative way from their artificial ones. What dreams must not Spenser have had !"

VALENTINE'S DAY.

This Essay first appeared in the *Examiner*, very appropriately, on Feb, 14, 1819.

"*E. B.*" "Edward Burney, half-brother to Miss Burney."— Lamb's "Key."

MY RELATIONS.

"*James and Bridget Elia.*" John and Mary Lamb.

"*They are older than myself by twelve and ten years.*" Compare his sonnet :—

> "John, you were figuring in the gay career,
> Of blooming manhood with a young man's joy,
> When I was yet a little peevish boy."

"*Through the green plains of pleasant Hertfordshire.*" From an unpublished sonnet of Lamb's.

"*Society for the relief of . . . . &c.*" "Distres't Sailors," according to Lamb's "Key."

The Essay originally concluded, "Till then, Farewell!"

[*Lond. Mag.*, June, 1821.]

MACKERY END.

"*B. F.*" Barron Field.

"*I wish that I could throw into a heap.*" Originally all in Italics, as though to lend emphasis to the wish.

"*But thou, that didst appear so fair.*" Wordswoi th on "Yarrow Revisited."

[*Lond. Mag.*, July, 1821.]

MY FIRST PLAY.

"*Cross Court.*" Originally "Russell Court." " *At the north end of Cross Court . . .* the identical Pit entrance," &c. It still stands; a sort of huckster's shop, with a grimed pediment of " architectural pretensions," but disconnected with the theatre.

"*On her elopement with him from a boarding school.*" A slight mistake; Miss Linley set off from her own house.

"*The Way of the World.*" It was acted at Drury Lane on October 31st, 1780.

"*Gave me time to drop.*" Originally "crop." In Mr. Forster's copy of the article, this is altered in the author's own handwriting to " drop." As this may be taken to be a final correction, it has thus been corrected in the text.

[*Lond. Mag.*, Dec. 1821.]

MODERN GALLANTRY.

After " *point of gallantry*," came originally—

" As upon a thing altogether unknown to the old classic ages; this has been defined to consist in," &c.

"*James Paice,*" &c. A real personage, as Lamb states in one of his letters.

[*Lond. Mag.*, Nov., 1822.]

THE OLD BENCHERS OF THE INNER TEMPLE.

"*The cheerful Crown-office Row,*" Long since taken down and rebuilt.

"*J——ll.*" Jekyll, a Master in Chancery.

"*Samuel Salt.*" He told the author of the " Book for a Rainy Day," that he was one of the two persons that attended Sterne's funeral.

"*Susan P——.*" Pierson, according to the Key

"*B——d Row.*" Bedford Row.—*Ibid.*

"*His man Lovel.*" A sketch of Lamb's father.

"*Jackson—the omniscient Jackson, as he was called.*" Dr. Johnson was acquainted with him, but thought the title profane, and altered it to "all-knowing."

"*R. N.*" Richard Norris, Under-Treasurer of the Temple.

[*Lond. Mag.*, Sept., 1821.]

GRACE BEFORE MEAT.

"*C———.*" Coleridge, according to the Key.

"*Is there no Clergyman here?*" A story commonly related of Theodore Hook. See, among the Miscellaneous Pieces, Lamb's reply to "Peter Ball or Bell," a correspondent.

[*Lond. Mag.*, Nov., 1821.]

DREAM CHILDREN.

"*A great house in Norfolk.*" Blakesware, in Hertfordshire, is intended.

"*Their great-grandmother Field.*" Lamb's "Grandame."

"*The nectarines and peaches.*" Compare "The Last Peach."

"*How in after life he became lame-footed too.*" Compare the letter to Coleridge of October 3, 1796.

[*Lond. Mag.*, Jan., 1822.]

DISTANT CORRESPONDENTS.

"*B. F.*" Barron Field. "Brother of Frank."—*Key.* Late Chief Justice of Gibraltar. The same thoughts will be found in a letter to Field, dated September 22, 1822. The present letter appeared in the *Examiner*, as well as in the *London Magazine.*

"*Lord C.*" Lord Camelford. The curious story here related is true. His will directed that he should be interred in the neighbourhood of Berne.

"*Sally W———r.*" Winter, according to Lamb's Key.

"*J. W.*" Jim White. At the end was a postscript:—"Something of home matters I could add; but *that*, with certain remembrances, not to be omitted, I reserve for the grave postscript to this light epistle; which postscript, for weighty reasons, justificatory in any Court of feeling, I think better omitted in this first edition.

"London, March 1, 1822."

[*Lond. Mag.*, March, 1822.]

THE PRAISE OF CHIMNEY-SWEEPERS.

Originally there was the second title—" A May-day Effusion."

" *In one of the state beds at Arundel Castle*." No recollection of this legend is preserved in the family.

" *Cards were issued*," &c. Mrs. Montague anticipated " Jim White" in the idea of their gatherings, and gave an entertainment every May-day to the Sweeps at her house in Portman Square. A Climbing Boys' Bill was introduced three or four years after the appearance of the Essay.

" *James White is extinct*." He died in 1821.

[*Lond. Mag.*, May, 1822.]

A COMPLAINT OF THE DECAY OF BEGGARS.

" *Neighbour Grice*." Here was a reference, " Timon of Athens."

" *St. L——*." " *B—— the mild rector*." " No meaning."
—*Key*.

The following passage was retrenched when the Essays were collected ; no doubt as being too familiar in tone :—

" ' Pray God your honour, relieve me,' said a poor beadswoman to my friend L—— one day ; ' I have seen better days.' ' So have I, my good woman,' retorted he, looking up at the welkin, which was just then threatening a storm ; and the jest (he will have it) was as good to the beggar as a tester. It was, at all events, kinder than consigning her to the stocks or the parish beadle. But L—— had a way of viewing things in rather a paradoxical light on some occasions. P.S.—My friend Hume (not M.P.) has a curious manuscript in his possession—the original draft of the celebrated ' Beggar's Petition,' (who cannot say by heart the ' Beggar's Petition ?') as it was written by some school usher (as I remember), with corrections interlined from the pen of Oliver Goldsmith. As a specimen of the Doctor's improvement, I recollect one most judicious alteration :—

' A pamper'd menial drove me from the door.'

It stood originally :—

' A livery servant drove me,' &c.

Here is an instance of poetical or artificial language, properly subs tuted for the phrase of common conversation. Against Wordsworth, I think I must get H. to send it to the 'London,' as a corollary to the foregoing."

The reply to the beggar was Lamb's own, and it is repeated in the letter to Manning, of Jan. 2, 1810.

At the end came another familiar note:

"N.B.—I am glad to see Janus veering about to the old quarter. I feared he had been rust-bound. C, being asked why he did not like Gold's 'London' as well as ours—it was n poor S,'s time—replied, 'Because there is no WEATHERCOCK, and that's the reason why.'"

[*Lond. Mag.*, June, 1822.]

A DISSERTATION ON ROAST PIG.

"*Chinese Manuscript.*" Mr. W. C. Hazlitt has shown that this was an Italian poem by Bistonio, entitled "Gli elogi del Porco." Compare also the letter to Manning, of March 9, 1822.

[*Lond. Mag.*, Sept., 1822.]

A BACHELOR'S COMPLAINT.

"*As a single man.*" It began originally, "I am a single man, no quite turned of forty, and have," &c.

"*Morellas.*" Here was a note: "I don't know now to spell this word; I mean Morella cherries."

"*Record.*" In the last paragraph stood originally "send you," and there was added at the close: "P.S.—I hope you are not a married man, INNUPTUS." The paper first appeared in *The Reflector*. It closed: "Your humble servant, ELIA."

[*Lond. Mag.*, Sept., 1822.]

ON SOME OF THE OLD ACTORS.

There were originally two papers on this subject; the first of which, having the same title, opened with the passage, "Of all the actors that flourished in my time," and concluded with what now makes a separate Essay, "The Artificial Comedy;" a portion of this latter being discarded. The second paper, entitled "The Old Actors," opened with the graphic description of the theatrical portraits, which he afterwards altogether suppressed. Then followed the sketch of Suett, which thus began :—

" Mr. Suett.

" O for a slip-shod muse, to celebrate in numbers loose and shambling as himself, the merits and the person of Mr. Richard Suett, Comedian !

" Richard, or rather Dickey Suett," &c.

" *Your whole conscience stirred with Bannister's performance of Walter, in the Children in the Wood.*" Then was interposed : " How very beautiful it was !"

At the end of the paragraph, after the words " *O la ! Bobby !*" was introduced the sketch, later made a separate Essay, and called " On the Acting of Munden," but here entitled—

" Mr. Munden."

The first paper concluded with a notice, " To be resumed occasionally ;" so that he seems to have intended a series of these pleasantly discursive sketches.

" *The casual sight of an old Play-Bill . . . . two and thirty years ago.*" This was the performance of *Twelfth Night* on November 3, 1790, when the three players mentioned in the text appeared

" *His Iago was the only endurable one.*" This praise of Bensley is not endorsed by any of his contemporaries, who considered him a stilted performer.

" *He* (Suett) *received the last stroke with the simple exclamation, 'Oh la! Bobby !*'" One of Lamb's pleasant fictions. It was at Suett's funeral that one of the mourners made the exclamation, as related in Barham's Life of Hook.

[*Lond. Mag.*, Feb. 1822.]

ON THE ARTIFICIAL COMEDY, &c.

" *They break through no laws.*" This well-known fantastic theory of Lamb's, as to the morality of Wycherly and Congreve's plays, has been dealt with by Lord Macaulay in one of his Essays.

" *I am to judge of the right and the wrong. The standard,*" &c. Originally " right and wrong ; and the standard," &c.

" *Poor Jack has passed from the stage in good time.*" A tragic interest is attached to his fate, from his furnishing one of the rare instances of an actor dying on the stage.   This catastrophe took place at Liverpool, when he was acting in "The Stranger."

"*The fashion to cry down John Kemble*," *i.e.*, in Charles Surface. The jest ran that it was "Charles's martyrdom."

"*Disappeared with him.*"   Here was a sentence:

> "Tragedy is become a uniform dead weight.   They have fastened lead to her buskins.   She never pulls them off for the ease of a moment.   To insert a commonplace from Niobe, she never forgets herself to liquefaction."

"*The pleasant old Teazle, King.*"   Originally "the fidgety, pleasant old."

"*Exert one's detestable coxcombry.*"   In Mr. Forster's copy, Lamb has changed "coxcombry" to "impertinence."

The paper originally concluded with the humorous and, indeed, almost farcical, sketch of the production of Godwin's "Antonio," which will be found among the Miscellaneous Pieces.   It was out of keeping with the sober character of the rest, though, perhaps, suited to the familiar strain of the *London Magazine*.   It was besides highly personal, and Lamb's fastidious taste discarded it, when he came to collect and revise his Essays.

"*The fired city.*"   Here was a foot note:

> "How lovelily the Adriatic, when
>   Dress'd in her flames will shine—devouring flames;
>   Such as will burn her to her wat'ry bottom,
>   And hiss in her foundation."
>
> PIERRE, *in "Venice Preserved."*

Also on the words—

"*Birth and feeling,*" a note:

"VIOLA.   She took the ring from me; I'll none of it.

"MAL.   Come, sir, you peevishly threw it to her; and her will is it should be so returned.   If it be worth stooping for, then it lies in your eye; if not, be it his that finds it."

[*Lond. Mag.*, April, 1822.]

In the June number, *Elia* assures "his pleasant remembrancer * * * that he has not lost sight of the topic he recommended so warmly.   He has only put it off for a number or two."   Later he wished the readers to know that he was not the "Lion's Head," or editor of the olla podrida of answers to correspondents.

ON THE ACTING OF MUNDEN.

This Essay first appeared in the *Examiner*, then in the *Athenæum*, and finally in the *London Magazine* (October, 1822), before it was included in the collected Essays. This shows his appreciation of a little piece which it would be vain to praise. Originally it was in more colloquial shape, and began, " We had come home from," &c. ; " we" being substituted all through for " I." The paper in the *London Magazine* (July, 1824), " Munden's Farewell," has been attributed to Lamb, but though in imitation of his style, it is certainly by an inferior hand.

In the *Examiner* (Nov. 1, 1819), the Essay began :

" It is none of the least pleasant features in the improved management of Drury Lane Theatre, that so many pieces have been brought forward, which give scope to the admirable talents of this performer."

It thus concluded :

" This faint sketch we beg to be taken as a mere corollary to some admirable strictures on the character of this great performer, in a paper signed 'T. N. T.' which appeared some months ago in the *Champion*, *Non tam certandi cupidus quam te imitari aveo.*
          * * * *."

These four stars—Lamb's favourite signature in the *Examiner*—stand for " Elia."

" *The grand grotesque of farce.*" Originally, " In what has been truly denominated the sublime of farce."

PREFACE TO THE "LAST ESSAYS."

" A Character of the Late Elia," by a friend, was the original title of this piece, which will be found in its original shape among the Miscellaneous Pieces. It is not easy to see the object of this Farewell unless he was tired of the signature, " the sickening Elia," as he called it. He certainly did not mean to take leave of Essay writing, as there was a paper by him in the same number, and the editor took care to prevent any misapprehension in the matter. " Elia is dead ! at least so a *friend* says, but if he be dead, we have seen him in one of those hours ' when he is wont to walk,' and his *ghostship* has promised us very material assistance in our future numbers. We were greatly tempted to put the Irish question to him of ' Why did you die?' . . . . We could lay our finger upon the man we suspect as being guilty of Elia's death !"

This seems to point to one of the waggeries of "Janus Weathercock," which Lamb always relished. In the next number there was a paper called "The Literary Police Office," where "Charles Lamb was brought up, charged with the barbarous murder of the late Mr. Elia. There appears to have been no apparent motive for this horrible murder, unless the prisoner had an eye to poor Mr. Elia's situation on the *London Magazine*." In the same number the Editor promised a series of critical and miscellaneous pieces from his pen, and in the next appeared this notice:—" March, 1823. Elia is not dead ! We thought as much, and even hinted our thought in the number for January. The following letter, declaring Elia's existence, is in his own handwriting, and was left by his own hand. We never saw a man so extremely alive, as he was, to the injury done him.

" Elia returns his thanks to the facetious Janus Weathercock, who during his late unavoidable excursion to the Isles of Sark, Guernsey, and Jersey, took advantage of his absence to plot a sham account of his death, and to impose upon the town a posthumous Essay, signed by his Ghost; which how like it is to any of the undoubted Essays of the author, may be seen by comparing it with his volume just published. One or two former papers with his signature, which are not reprinted in the volume, he has reason to believe were pleasant forgeries by the same ingenious hand."

[*Lond. Mag.*, Jan. 1823.]

BLAKESMOOR, IN H———SHIRE.

The house described in this sketch is Gilston Park, the seat of Mr. Plumer Ward, as Mr. Patmore first pointed out. Here Lamb's grandmother Field had been housekeeper, and he himself, when a child, had played about its great chambers and gardens. The destruction described in the Essay is somewhat exaggerated, as the house appears to have been wrecked rather than demolished. In the " Dream Children" he puts it more correctly; describing how the house afterwards fell into decay, was *nearly* pulled down, and all its ornaments stripped and carried away to the owner's other house. " At Mr. Plumer Ward's death," says Mr. W. C. Hazlitt, "there was much litigation as to the succession to the property. His children by his former wife claimed it, as did also the relatives of Mrs. Plumer, who was granddaughter of the Earl of Abercorn. The consequence was, that the house was completely destroyed—each party being anxious that the other should not possess it. The furniture, the curious tapestry hangings described by Lamb—every thing was ruthlessly dragged out upon the lawn, and burnt. So great an amount of furniture was collected in the mansion, that the work of destruction was not completed in less than ten days, during which time many articles were saved from the flames by the farm-labourers around, whose cottages still contain the only remaining relics of Blakesware."

It was later restored by Mr. Plumer Ward, the statesman and novelist.

" *The garden-loving Poet.*" A reference was given : " Marvell on Appleton House to the Lord Fairfax."

" *De Mowbray and De Clifford.*" Mr. Plumer Ward wrote a novel with this latter title.

" *H——shire.*" Hertfordshire.

" *W——ds.*" Wards.

" *They had long forsaken the old house of their fathers for a newer trifle.*" Blakesware was the seat of Mr. Ward, who had married Mrs. Plumer.

" *That beauty with the cool blue pastoral drapery and a lamb.*" The owner, in his description of the place furnished to Mr. Patmore, mentions a portrait of the Countess of Abercorn as a Shepherdess. He also describes the noble octagon hall, " the twelve Cæsars," and the carving of the chimney-piece, representing a stag chase, which Lamb alludes to in his paper " Dream Children."

" *Mildred Elia, I take it.*" After these words followed :

" From her, and from my passion for her—for I first learned love from a picture—Bridget took the hint of those pretty whimsical lines, which thou may'st see, if haply thou hast never seen them, Reader, in the margin. But my Mildred grew not old, like the imaginary

Helen." In a note was given the little poem referred to: "Helen,"
by Miss Lamb.
    ⸢*Lond. Mag.*, Sept., 1824.]

POOR RELATIONS.

"*A pound of sweet.*" Here was originally added, "the bore *par excellence.*"

"*A female poor relation.*" Lamb had favourable opportunities of studying this genus, in Mrs. Reynolds and other dependants, whom he supported.

"*Richard Amlet in the Play.*" "The Confederacy."

"*Poor W——.*" Referring to Favelle before described; the scene being changed from Cambridge to Oxford.

    [*Lond. Mag.*, May, 1823.]

DETACHED THOUGHTS ON BOOKS AND READERS.

"*Pocket Books.*" After these words came a parenthesis, "(the 'Literary' excepted)". Lamb, with Leigh Hunt and some friends, was much interested in this venture, and supplied some contributions.

"*Indifferent to the five points.*" Originally this passage followed:—

"I was once amused—there is a pleasure in *affecting* affectation—at the indignation of a crowd that was jostling in with me at the pit-door of Covent Garden Theatre, to have a sight of Master Betty—then at once in his dawn and his meridian—in *Hamlet.* I had been invited, quite unexpectedly, to join a party, whom I met near the door of the playhouse, and I happened to have in my hand a large octavo of Johnson and Steevens's ' Shakespeare,' which, the time not admitting of my carrying it home, of course went with me to the theatre. Just in the very heat and pressure of the doors opening—the *rush*, as they term

it—I deliberately held the volume over my head, open
at the scene in which the young Roscius had been
most cried up, and quietly read by the lamp-light.
The clamour became universal. ' The affectation of
the fellow,' cried one. ' Look at that gentleman
reading, papa,' squeaked a young lady, who, in her
admiration of the novelty, almost forgot her fears. I
read on. ' He ought to have his book knocked out
of his hand,' exclaimed a pursy cit, whose arms were
too fast pinioned to his side to suffer him to execute
his kind intention. Still I read on—and, till the time
came to pay my money, kept as unmoved as Saint
Anthony at his holy offices, with the satyrs, apes, and
hobgoblins mopping and making mouths at him, in
the picture, while the good man sits as undisturbed
at the sight as if he were the sole tenant of the desert.
—The individual rabble (I recognised more than one
of their ugly faces) had damned a slight piece of mine
a few nights before, and I was determined the culprits
should not a second time put me out of countenance."

" *Martin B————*." Martin Burney.

" *First folio of Shakespeare.*" After these words came the pas
sage :—

" You cannot make a pet book of an author whom everybody reads."

" *I have no sympathy with them.*" Here was added originally :
" Nor with Mr. Gifford'a Ben Jonson."

" *The Chronicle is in hand, sir.*" This was followed originally
by : " As in these little diurnals I generally skip the Foreign News,
the Debates, and the Politics, I find the *Morning Herald* by far the
most entertaining of them. It is an agreeable miscellany rather than
a newspaper."

" *Alone, and reading Candide.*" Originally there was an air
of surprise, and it was thus printed : " Alone, and reading——
Candide !"

" *I saw a boy.*" The name of the poem was originally supplied,
" *The Two Boys.*"

I have tried, with Professor Morley and others, to discover the poetess alluded to, but in vain. Mr. Charles Kent's conjecture, that the author was Mary Lamb, and the piece one of those in the lost "Poetry for Children," seems well founded.

STAGE ILLUSIONS.

[*Lond. Mag.*, August, 1825.]

TO THE SHADE OF ELLISTON.

These two papers on Elliston virtually make one, as in the *Englishman's Magazine*, where they appeared, the second followed the first.

"*Thin ghosts of Figurantes*," &c. Originally the paragraph ran:
"Thin ghosts of Figurantes (never plump on earth) admire, while with uplifted toe retributive you inflict vengeance incorporeal upon the shadowy rear of obnoxious author, just arrived.

> "What *seemed* his tail,
> The likeness of a kingly kick had on.
> *   *   *   *   *   *
> Yet soon he heals: for spirits, that live throughout
> Vital in every part, not as frail man
> In entrails, head, or heart, liver or reins,
> Can in this liquid texture mortal wound
> Receive no more, than can the liquid air.
> All heart they live, all head, all," &c.

Elliston was engaged in many quarrels with authors and actors; notably with Mathews and Poole; and the latter sketched him in "Little Pedlington."

"*The same natural easy creature on the stage that he is off.*" Compare Goldsmith's lines ou Garrick:—

> "On the stage he was natural, simple, affecting;
> 'Twas only that when he was off, he was acting."

"*That sceptre had been wrested from his hand.*" *I.e.*, of Drury Lane. After spending a vast sum on the improvement of the theatre, he was harshly deprived of the management, on the pretext of being a little in arrear with the rent.

[*Englishman's Magazine*, August, 1831.]

This Essay was signed originally :

" PLAUDITO ET VALETO."

" Thy friend upon earth,
Though thou didst connive at his d————n.

Mr. H."

Lamb no doubt felt that this charge was not warranted, and re-tracted the passage ; the truth being that Elliston did his best for the piece, and after having announced it for repetition, only withdrew it at Lamb's expressed desire.

END OF VOL. III.